An Illustrated History of
BRITISH RAILWAYS
REVENUE WAGONS

Volume One

Frontispiece The most common type of BR wagon, albeit with many variations, was the 16T Mineral. No. B88672 was built by Pressed Steel in 1953 to Lot 2255 as an unfitted vehicle. When photographed at Derby on 7th June 1957, it had been fitted with clasp vacuum brake gear (highlighted in grey), change-over lever, screw couplings and extended buffer housings, and repainted in bauxite livery.

BR/OPC

An Illustrated History of
BRITISH RAILWAYS
REVENUE WAGONS

by
Paul W. Bartlett, David Larkin
Trevor Mann, Roger Silsbury
and Andrew T. Ward

Volume One

Oxford Publishing Company

Typesetting by:
Aquarius Typesetting Services, New Milton, Hants.

Printed in Great Britain by:
Biddles Ltd., Guildford, Surrey.

Published by:
Oxford Publishing Co.
Link House
West Street
POOLE, Dorset

DEDICATION

To all of the many railwaymen who have helped us with the research for this book and fellow members of the British Railways Historical Study Group.

Contents

Preface

This is the first of two volumes which present a pictorial history of the freight rolling stock built for use by British Railways. BR has been prolific both in the the acquisition of wagons and in the diversity of design. There has been continual pressure to meet the requirements for modern equipment, both to improve the ways in which goods are handled and also to allow the wagons to speed on their way. Because of this diversity, limitations of space have meant that we have had to restrict ourselves to discussing only the wagons built for the revenue (traffic) fleet. We have omitted all wagons built new for use by the Engineers, and also all conversions of wagons to new types. We have included wagons which have been rebuilt and renumbered. However, our publishers have allowed us generous space to integrate text, photographs and drawings of each series of wagons.

The main part of each volume is a chapter by chapter analysis of wagon types. There is no one logical format for arranging this. The BR diagram books tend to mix very different types freely and the TOPS computer system is too modern to be completely relevant, and also uses too many subdivisions. We have largely adopted the broad divisions used by the BR Accounts Division, Central Stock Registry, as our guide; however they would have included 'Tank' wagons with the 'Open' and given 'Cattle' wagons their own division. The order is, therefore, a compromise which we hope the reader finds acceptable. Additionally, in **Volume One**, there are chapters dealing with the development of the fleet and describing components, brake gear and construction. When known, we have used the official name of these components, otherwise we have used appropriate names, commonly used by enthusiasts, throughout the two volumes. In **Volume Two**, there is a chapter about liveries prepared from official documents and personal observations.

In the preparation of these books we have tried to be as factual as possible, and where assumptions have been made, we have tried to make this clear. Writing about an organisation which still exists has advantages and disadvantages. The advantages have included our ability to draw extensively on our own photographic records, and to prepare most of the drawings from our own measurements. The disadvantages include the problem that none of the information has become a public record, that there has been insufficient time to apply a suitable historical perspective to events, and that there is no obvious date at which to conclude. **Volume One** is accurate up to the end of 1984.

The drawings are all reproduced to the common modelling scale of 4mm. to 1ft., and we hope that these volumes will stimulate the construction of accurate scale models.

Many people have helped and encouraged us during the preparation of these books, and we would like to acknowledge the generous help given by T. Scrivener and his staff at the Rolling Stock Library, Derby, the Research Development Division, Derby, and the many other railwaymen who have also helped us by permitting us to photograph and measure wagons, or allowed us access to written records. We hope that any opinions which we have expressed do not cause offence to them; the opinions are all our own and we accept responsibility for any errors or omissions. We are particularly grateful to A. W. Bartlett, R. J. E. Bayliffe, D. Carman, R. J. Essery, D. Farmborough, A. Foulner, D. Fountain, E. Gent, D. J. Hyde, A. Lambert, D. Monk-Steel, D. P. Rowland, P. Tatlow, and all members of the British Railways Historical Study Group who have given us encouragement with this project. Special thanks go to R. N. Moore of Cosham who has advised and assisted on the selection and printing of photographs. Finally, but most importantly, we must thank our wives, Julie Bartlett, Audrey Mann, Maureen Silsbury and Elizabeth Ward who have supported this project so well and, in the case of Audrey and Julie, have also helped with measuring for some of the drawings.

In the text, some other books which are used to illustrate points are referred to by initials, the key to which is:

FWLGW	Russell, J. H., (1981) *GWR Freight Wagons and Loads in service on the Great Western Railway and British Rail, Western Region*, published by Oxford Publishing Co.
GWR Wagons	Atkins, A. G., Beard, W., Hyde, D. G. & Tourret, R. (1975) *A History of GWR Goods Wagons. Volumes 1 & 2*, published by David and Charles.
LMS Wagons	Essery, R. J., (1981) *An Illustrated History of LMS Wagons. Volumes 1 & 2*, published by Oxford Publishing Co.
LNER Wagons	Tatlow, P., (1976) *A Pictorial Record of LNER Wagons*, published by Oxford Publishing Co.
MRC	*Model Railway Constructor*, published by Ian Allan.
MRC Annual	*Model Railway Constructor Annual*, published by Ian Allan.

Paul W. Bartlett, David Larkin, Trevor Mann,
Roger Silsbury and Andrew T. Ward
February 1985

Taken to illustrate the newly-installed lighting, this view of Bristol Yard, Severn Tunnel Junction, on 25th January 1961, shows a wide variety of freight stock; the preponderance of mineral wagons should be noted.

BR, (WR)

Chapter 1

Introduction to the BR Wagon Fleet; A Brief History

When British Railways was formed in 1948, it inherited an immense fleet of wagons. Including brake vans, but excluding Engineer's wagons, there were 1,197,561 which had a capacity of 14,855,000 tons. These came from the four pre-nationalisation companies, from the nationalisation of many of the previously privately-owned wagons (probably nearly half a million), and from the War Department and Ministry of War Transport. Many of these wagons were very old and, because of the lack of maintenance during World War II, in poor condition.

Post-War Devolopments

The Government gave a high priority to the rebuilding of British Railways and made considerable resources available. Large orders for new wagons had been placed before nationalisation, and these were completed during 1948. The 1949 programme continued largely on a regional basis, with numbering remaining in the regional series with the wagons being given a pre-nationalisation prefix to the number. They are not included in these books.

Diagrams

Each of the pre-nationalisation companies had issued diagrams to identify the wagons available for use. These were collected into loose leaf books and revisions issued as necessary. They had each used differing styles of presentation and format, and the content of each diagram varied.

Initially British Railways appear to have allowed the Western Region to continue the GWR diagram book, which was smaller in format than those used by the other companies, but they were more accurate, having the appearance of miniature general arrangement drawings. This book was arranged by grouping all wagons of the same type together and giving them an alpha prefix. Numbers were then issued in this 'chapter' as necessary **(see GWR Wagons)**. When BR issued a diagram in this series we have referred to it in the text. All of these GWR/BR diagrams were also given numbers in the BR diagram series, but the drawings used were different. One final point was that the GWR was careful to reflect all important design changes by issuing new diagrams, so that vacuum-braked and unfitted wagons were distinguished, as were changes in brake rigging.

From our point of view, it was unfortunate that the LMS ideas in the design of diagram books became the BR standard. A series of books was issued and we have consistently used the system of giving each book a numeric prefix; BR does not seem to have distinguished them in this way until the late 1960s. Book 1 was for 'Revenue and Departmental' wagons, Book 2 for 'Specially Constructed' wagons, Book 3 for 'Containers' and Book 6 for 'Private Owner' wagons. Each diagram was given a number, and each book was broadly divided into categories, e.g. all 'Opens' were grouped separately to the 'Vans'. In time, some of the room given to a particular category proved inadequate, and then any other page number could be allocated, apparently arbitrarily.

The diagrams gave all the details needed by the commercial staff who were ordering wagons to load; the internal dimensions, capacity, tonnage and nominal tare, and an outline drawing of the side and end elevation **(see Figure 1)**. A plan was occasion-

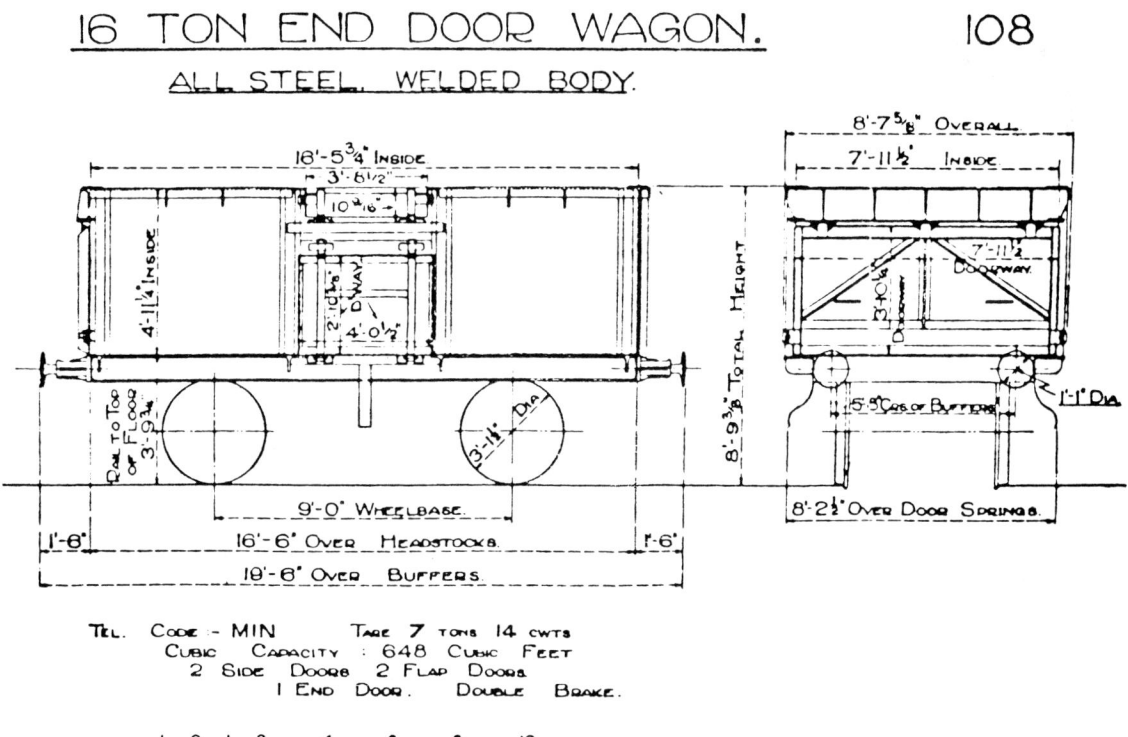

Figure 1 A typical BR diagram — **page 108** depicts the most common type of BR wagon, the 16 ton all steel, welded end door Mineral. The dimensions give full details regarding the body, which satisfied the needs of the Commercial Department, but the lack of information regarding the underframe clearly illustrates the limitations of the drawn diagram when compared with **Table 33** in **Chapter 7**. The brake type, given as 'Double Brake' was only true for about one per-cent of the total built to this diagram, a staggering 197,459 vehicles.

ally included. Sometimes separate diagrams were issued when the same body was mounted on underframes fitted with or without continuous brake, and sometimes new diagrams were issued to reflect important changes in running gear, such as the use of roller bearings or hydraulic/pneumatic buffers. However, none of this was done consistently, and extensive rebuilds often went unrecorded. It was also only rarely that lot numbers or running numbers appeared, except on the first issue of the container diagram book when they were given together with the general arrangement drawing number, perhaps because no building details normally appeared on the container. When this diagram book was reissued with all diagrams prefixed '3', most of these details were removed.

At first, newly-constructed air brake wagons were included in these books, but in the mid-1970s new diagram numbers based on the TOPS codes were issued. This system was developed until new 'design codes' were allocated to all extant wagons. Each has the first two letters of the TOPS code, three numbers, and an alpha suffix which subdivides the general design code to reflect the minutiae of detail differences which are important to the Engineers but not normally to the commercial user of the wagon. The drawings on the design code sheets are dimensioned metrically. In many ways this system reflects the GWR organisation of the diagram book!

One complication which should be mentioned is that the TOPS codes are not immutable. At the end of 1983 many were changed, and in particular the K--, J-- and U-- series were abandoned and the wagons recoded (the text records these changes). Thus, it is preferable to use a commonly agreed name for each wagon design instead of simply refering to them by the TOPS code.

In the text we have used the early diagram numbers as the main way of referring to all pre-air brake wagon designs. The design codes for air brake wagons are given, referred to as diagram numbers, but this more recent system is unsuitable as the basis for an historical treatise as many early diagrams did not survive to receive the new design codes.

Orders and Numbering

During 1949 a new standard system of building orders (lots), and numbering was decided upon which was implemented during that autumn. Lots followed the old LMS series, after a gap, and started at No. 2001. It would appear that most of the first one hundred or so lots were superimposed on to the regional orders, but unfortunately these files are missing, having been destroyed in a fire at the Rolling Stock Library at Derby. We have not yet been able to check the regional registers. Container construction was also included in the series of wagon lots. Originally lot numbers were issued only to new construction but, since 1970, have been extended to include the majority of conversions of otherwise redundant stock, including coaches for the Engineers.

Block series of numbers, prefixed 'B', were allocated to wagon types. These blocks have remained substantially intact, and modified as necessary to accommodate new designs or a greater number of wagons than originally envisaged. The first air-braked wagons, the '32 ton Hoppers' and 'Freightliner flats', continued to be numbered in the original 'B' prefix series. In 1969, a new series, without prefix, was devised for all new air-braked stock but, because of the quantities of 'Hoppers' and 'Freightliner Flats' already in existence, those two series were continued, omitting the prefix. Air-braked 'Vans' and 'Covhops' on order, which had been allocated numbers in the original series, were renumbered before delivery. Containers had their own number series with the prefix letter(s) denoting the type, and a 'B' suffix to indicate BR build. Containers ceased to be included after 'Freightliner' became a separate company in 1971.

The development of designs

As time went by, new ways of handling traditional traffics developed and new traffics arose, so designs either changed or completely new ones were introduced. The wagons for these traffics are described as appropriate in the chapters which detail the various wagon types, but some more general policy decisions also influenced the designs.

Initially, many designs were perpetuated from the pre-nationalisation companies, sometimes with slight modification to allow for new methods of construction and continued shortages of materials. In particular, wooden planks were in short supply and plywood was substituted. These early BR vehicles immediately show their parentage.

New standard designs were introduced by 1951 which combined the best features of more than one design; e.g. vans were essentially GWR, but with pressed steel ends as favoured by the LMS and LNER, whilst bogie vehicles used a BR version of the GWR plateback bogie.

The first all-new designs appeared in 1952 and were for '24 ton Hopper Minerals', '24 ton non-Hopper Minerals' and '27 ton Iron Ore Tipplers'. Other new designs were produced in response to new traffics; some of these did not proceed further than a single batch; e.g. 'Bulk Salt wagons', whilst others became standard types; e.g. 'Presflos'.

During the 1960s, there were many experiments in both body and running gear design, but few types were built in large numbers, the main effort going into production of 'Freightliner Flats' and 'Merry-go-round Hoppers'. The 1970s and 1980s saw a greater diversity of designs introduced, with various covered and open merchandise wagons, and many wagons for semi-finished and finished steel; this was in spite of the encouragement of private ownership of wagons for most traffics. Another important development in this period was reusing underframes, either by rebuilding with new bodies or conversion to another type. This policy was introduced in about 1965 with the introduction of the air-braked fleet. These had underframes with a design life of 40 years, and bodies with a design life of 20 years. The policy was extended to include many wagons built earlier, and was a result of the acceptance that predicting traffic requirements over long periods was no longer possible.

Generally, BR designs have been successful, but ones which had mixed fortunes were the 'Palbrick' and 'Palvan' which are discussed in more detail in **Chapters 4 and 9**. 'Road-railer' vehicles, based on an American design, were experimented with during the early 1960s, and although they proved technically successful, the idea did not catch on with industry.

Continuous Brakes and Improved Underframes

An important policy change concerned the fitting of the continuous brake. At nationalisation there were only 122,500 continuously-braked wagons, nearly all using vacuum. By 1952, this had risen to 154,000, when a series of trials was carried out to compare vacuum and air (Westinghouse) brakes. One hundred '16 ton Mineral' wagons were equipped with vacuum brake, another hundred with air, and trials were run on the Midland main line between Toton and Brent. By 1956, although the air brake had proved to be technically superior, the additional cost of £30 million required to equip the fleet weighed against it, and the vacuum brake was chosen as standard.

The 'Modernisation and Re-equipment Plan' of 1955 envisaged the fitting of the vacuum brake to all wagons within ten years. Additionally, all wagons which had a capacity of 20 tons or greater would also have roller bearings. Lists of pre-nationalisation merchandise wagons and brake vans to be vacuum-fitted were issued, but similar lists were not issued for BR-built wagons, or for any of the more specialised wagons. This meant that, although a high proportion of the merchandise wagons were dealt with, fewer of the specialised wagons changed. In fact, except for some easily definable fleets, neither aim was achieved.

Until 1960, the basic features of the underframes of merchandise wagons remained similar to final pre-nationalisation practice — an RCH approved 17ft. 6in. length underframe with a 10ft. wheelbase. Similar designs were used for other wagons including 16ft. 6in. with 9ft. wheelbase, 21ft. 6in. with 12ft. wheelbase, and 27ft. 1½in. with 15ft. wheelbase. They all developed similarly with roller bearings, vacuum brake and self-adjusting brake.

The first radical departures from this were manifest as various experiments. During 1960/1, Ashford Works produced six wagons to Lot 3362 which, although differing in the bodies fitted, utilised a vacuum-braked underframe which was 35ft. over headstocks with a wheelbase of 20ft. 9in. None of the experimental bodies were put into production, but one was quickly rebuilt as a 'Palvan'. The design was put into production in 1963 with a similar underframe, and continued through 1964 when it was decided that all newly-constructed wagons, which would operate in block trains, (in reality all wagons), would have air brakes, so two batches of these 'Palvans' were so equipped.

Concurrently, new air brake designs were introduced; the 'Merry-go-round Coal Hopper' was successful immediately and production continued until 1983, substantially to the design of the prototype, apart from an upgrading in the permitted maximum speed when loaded, from 45 to 60m.p.h. with the later-built ones.

However, further experiments were needed before a standard underframe for merchandise wagons was developed. Six experimental wagons were built at Ashford to Lots 3566-3569, each lot having a different body on a common underframe of 33ft. 6in. over headstocks, with a wheelbase of 20ft. 9in. They were low, with 2ft. 8in. wheels, to allow for a more convenient loading height, and the conveyance of containers of 8ft. by 8ft. profile. A production batch of low height 'Conflats' soon followed, capable of carrying 35 tons and running at 75m.p.h.

A similar conventional height underframe with 3ft. 1½in. wheels was used for vans, opens and steel carriers from 1969; we have referred to it as 'Type 1'. Later, the 2-axle air brake underframe evolved, the length and wheelbase increased, and the suspension improved, but the important design features had been crystallised, and BR became world leaders in the design of 2-axle underframes. The technology was successfully employed for passenger vehicles in the late 1970s.

In 1970, BR considered retrospectively fitting air brakes to existing wagons, and a series of trials was carried out. For this, 40 wagons (12 'Opens', 12 'Vans', 7 'Palvans', 5 'Plates' and 4 'Tubes') received two pipe air brakes and UIC double-link suspension, of a type originally used to improve the running of some 10ft. wheelbase 'Palvans' in 1966. Test trains ran between Oxford and Worcester from 1970 to 1972. Nothing directly came of this experiment but, from the mid-1970s, various older wagons were rebuilt with air brakes. These included 'Vanwides' and 'Pipes', which had the most similarities with the earlier experiments, and 'Bogie Bolsters', 'Borails', 'Trestles', etc. These are discussed in the relevant chapters.

The fitting of the continuous brake was still progressing slowly so, in the mid-1970s, BR again planned for the final elimination of the unfitted wagon, this time by the mid-1980s. The northern part of Scotland and the Southern Region became the first to be 'fully fitted', although piped wagons were still permitted. By the end of 1983, most important traffic fleets were air or vacuum-braked, with the exception of coal, as some unfitted 'Mineral' fleets remained in South Wales and South Yorkshire. The remaining unfitted wagons were due for withdrawal by May 1984 and, similarly, the Engineers were losing all unfitted wagons,

except the ballast-carrying 'Grampus'. The vacuum brake was scheduled for elimination by 1985 and was well on target at the beginning of 1984.

Disc Brakes
Whichever system of braking is used, the traditional method of actually stopping a wagon has been the application of a brake shoe to the wheel tread. From 1955, BR experimented with disc brakes, initially on passenger stock. From 1961, BR and Girling Co. Ltd., conducted a series of trials and a total of 212 wagons was involved; 62 '21 ton Hoppers' in regular service between Mansfield and Wood Green, London, 100 new '24½ ton Hoppers' running between the Kent coalfields and Richborough Power-Station, and 50 '16 ton Minerals' in general service. The trials were successful and disc brakes were more generally adopted from 1965; by the beginning of 1966 some 1,800 wagons were using disc brakes. Initially, the brake discs were fixed to the wheels, and later axle-mounted discs were also used.

Bogie Wagons
For a variety of economic reasons, BR has always considered the 2-axle wagon to be preferable to bogied wagons when the commodity to be carried allowed. At all times, bogie wagons developed in similar ways to 2-axle types but the design of bogies was largely influenced by private companies at home and abroad. From the early 1960s to the late 1970s, BR bought in proprietary bogies, but in the late 1970s Derby Locomotive Works was set up to build the French-designed Y25C bogies, and BR developed its own design for export in 1982.

Containerisation
The development of containers paralleled the changes in the wagon fleet. In the early years, BR continued to build containers to RCH designs, but many new designs and unsuccessful experiments were introduced as new traffics were offered. During the late 1950s, experiments were made using fibreglass, as this material had proved particularly successful for some coach components, but were not successful, and light alloy replaced the traditional timber bodies. The final developments were influenced greatly by the international container revolution.

The fleet of containers has increased, then decreased. In 1938, there were 15,000, and by the beginning of the 1960s there was about 44,000, which had decreased to 32,000 by the end of 1966. In 1977, BR ceased carrying the conventional small containers except for the 'L' type, a few of which remained in use until 1983.

Container services
Originally, most containers were transported as part of the overall freight pattern. The London Midland Region first realised the potential of dedicated container train services, and in March 1959 started the 'Condor' overnight service between London and Glasgow, running at an average speed of 40m.p.h. This service carried conventional 'A' and 'B' size containers. The next development was 'Speedfreight' between London and Manchester, for which a new series of designs of alloy containers were built, and it was from these that the 'Freightliner' concept was born. This required a new generation of containers, the design and construction of which was governed by the ISO regulations. Initially converted 'Lowmacs' were used to carry these containers to the docks, and then BR pioneered the concept of using the same type of containers for internal block trains, running to a strict timetable, between custom-built depots. The inaugural 'Freightliner' service ran between Glasgow and London in November 1965 using different terminals to the 'Condor' service, which it later replaced. Many more services were developed and 'Freightliner' became a separate company in 1971.

Although the conveyance of international (maritime) containers was profitable, one problem was that the largest operator, 'Sealand', used containers which were 8ft. 6in. high, and therefore out of gauge. BR experimented with extra-low container wagons but decided that increasing the loading gauge on key routes was preferable. This was done in the late 1970s, being brought to public attention in 1979 by the fatal collapse of Penmanshiel Tunnel during conversion.

Post-1955 Developments in the Fleet

The 1955 'Modernisation and Re-equipment Plan' also foresaw a reduction in the fleet from 1,141,500 to 720,000 wagons as train speeds would be increased and turn-round times improved. Once again extensive lists of wagons for early retirement were prepared, starting in particular with wooden-underframed wagons. These plans took two to three years to get underway so, by 1958, the fleet had only been reduced to 1,020,197 while capacity had increased to 14,982,000 tons, this being due to new construction. The later tables in these books show that BR had replaced a considerable proportion of the fleet by this time.

The reduction in the fleet continued to be slow until 1961, when the fleet was down to 956,284. After that, the year on year reduction was between 5 and 10 per cent; thus by 1966 there were 551,422 wagons (including fish vans now reclassified as freight) and by 1976, a total of 187,000. At the end of 1983, the fleet was reduced to 55,568.

Traffic Statistics

These fleet size statistics could give a false impression of an excessive fall in freight traffic on British Rail. Although there are various ways that the actual traffic in freight can be expressed, none of them show such a dramatic fall. Between 1948 and 1976 the total tonnage carried was reduced from 273 million tons to 176 million tonnes; net ton-miles reduced from 21,662 million to 12,706 million; loaded freight train miles operated fell from 118 million to 43.3 million, and loaded wagons forwarded fell from 36.3 million to 7.84 million. However, the average wagon load increased from 7.96 tons to 22.98 tonnes. The average length of haul varied little, as it was 74.5 miles in 1948 and 75.2 miles in 1976. An interesting but irrelevant statistic, due to inflation, is that the average receipt per ton forwarded increased from 66p to £1.73. Taken altogether, although these statistics show a considerable reduction in traffic, there is also a very creditable improvement in productivity.

Components of Improved Productivity

Many factors affected this productivity. In 1963, the Beeching Report on 'The Reshaping of British Railways' proposed the closure of some 800 freight depots, with the development of 'Liner' train services concentrated at 55 terminals, and the consequent reduction of the wagon fleet by 350,000. Later the Transport Act of 1968 released BR from its 'Common Carrier' obligations.

At the time of nationalisation, private ownership of wagons almost ceased. Only wagons designated as non-pool and either specially-constructed or set apart for the conveyance of particular traffics such as cement, night soil, salt and fuel oil, remained. This policy was reversed from 1965 onwards, and since 1974 substantial Government grants, usually called 'Section 8 Grants', have been available for both improving privately-owned terminals and for building accompanying wagons.

As a result of these changes, BR now had to provide only a small fleet of vans and open wagons for general merchandise, and also the specialist wagons needed by other nationalised industries, in particular the National Coal Board and British Steel.

In addition, during the mid-1960s, policy changed towards running all trains as 'blocks' of similar wagons carrying similar commodities. This entailed phasing out all 'wagonload' traffic, but this proved to be misguided. In its place a network of air-braked trains was introduced between major centres which had feeder services from smaller yards. This was marketed as 'Speedlink' and, from May 1984, replaced all the conventional 'wagonload' traffic. This network was also important for carrying the increasing traffic worked from Europe on train ferries.

Wagon Control

These improvements relied on better means of monitoring where a particular wagon or load was at any given time, so that loaded wagons would not be delayed unnecessarily, and empty wagons could be provided to the location where a traffic was on offer, as efficiently as possible, whilst minimising the time a wagon was idle. A simple means was to allocate a fleet of wagons to a particular traffic or station. Originally, this was usually indicated by a 'Return to . . .' branding on the wagon side. In the 1970s, yellow circles lettered 'Circuit' were applied as transfers to the wagon side, and the details of the circuit were inscribed on a plate fixed behind the label clip. Later, all wagons in a circuit were grouped into a 'Pool' and the four figure number which identified this was painted on the wagon side. These numbers were used for computer retrieval.

Irrespective of whether wagons were in a circuit or not, details of where they were and what they were doing had to be reported. Procedures varied according to the type of wagon but, in general in 1950, every station had to report the wagons on hand at 10.00 every day, and which empty wagons it required. The report form was despatched to the District Commercial Office and the District Operating Office. Later similar returns were sent to Headquarters at Marylebone using the GPO telex network. The telegraph and telex abbreviations gave rise to many of the code names used on the wagons.

By the early 1960s, many more specialised wagons were having to be reported upon twice per day and, at some large yards, staff read train consists directly into the, then, newly available portable tape recorders which were transcribed direct to the telex. The Eastern Region and other marshalling yards in the London area used this system to transmit information between themselves about trains.

The labour involved in recording train consists led BR to seek automation of the process and, in 1962, it undertook an imaginative experiment in automatic recording and computerisation. Wagons were fitted with a metal code plate over the left-hand wheel, with each figure represented by a binary code in a similar fashion to that used in supermarket bar codes. Yards on the Blackburn to Hellifield line had automatic readers capable of working at up to 60m.p.h., which transmitted the numbers to a central control. Nothing more came of this bold experiment and automatic train recording was not tried again.

The TOPS System

The benefits of computer recording were obvious so, in the mid-1970s, BR invested in a complex real-time computer program which had been developed in the USA for train control. Always known by its acronym, TOPS, the system was most obvious as all wagons received a three letter code which described them. This replaced the normal code names, except that the Engineer's fleet continued to use their water animal names. In the later chapters, the TOPS code of each wagon type is given.

Briefly, the first letter divides the fleet into broad categories, e.g. 'V' is for 'Van', 'M' for 'Mineral', 'Y' for bogied Engineer's wagons and 'Z' for 2-axle Engineer's wagons. The second letter subdivides each category and usually allows an accurate description of the wagon; e.g. MC — '16 ton Mineral with clasp brake', MD — '21 ton Mineral', ME — '24½ ton Mineral' and MX — '16 ton Mineral with RCH brake'. The final letter describes the brake type, the full list is:

'A' — Air; 'B' — Air brake and vacuum pipe; 'F' — AFI vacuum; 'G' — AFI vacuum brake and air pipe; 'H' — Dual brake (AFI and air); 'O' — Unfitted; 'P' — Vacuum-piped; 'Q' — Air-piped; 'R' — Dual air and vacuum-piped; 'V' — Vacuum; 'W' — Vacuum brake and air pipe; 'X' — Dual brake (vacuum and air) and 'Z' — Automatic brake of unknown working order.

For TOPS, every Area Freight Centre has computer terminals for inputting and printing information. Each time a wagon arrives, it is placed in position, its loading status changes, it is released, or forwarded, then this has to be reported. Every location at which a wagon could be found is identified by a five figure code. The computer also holds many other details about the status of each wagon such as when it is due for routine maintenance, if it is condemned, crippled, etc.

Handling Methods

Various aspects of the way commodities were handled are described as necessary in the chapters on wagon types. There were some general trends which are worthy of mention here. Different forms of mechanisation were increasingly used. Gravity discharge had long been used for coal, chemicals, iron ore, etc., and its use was extended by the provision of many more facilities for these commodities, and by its use for new ones. An important related development was the use of air, pumped into an enclosed wagon to fluidise powders; this was first used in 'Pres-flos'. Tippling was also used, the entire wagon being inverted for gravity discharge.

Pallets were another post-war development which revolutionised the handling of merchandise. A pallet is a type of double skinned false floor on to which goods are loaded. A fork-lift truck inserts metal tines between the upper and lower part of the pallet and raises it to transfer it from place to place, such as factory to wagon, etc. As discussed later, pallets proved difficult to cope with as the entire loading area of the wagon had to be easily accessible, and the diversity of sizes was also a problem, but they were commonly used from the late 1950s.

There were many other specialised handling methods and techniques. 'Banana Vans' were steam-heated to ripen the fruit in transit, some containers and vans were highly insulated so that frozen meat and other food could be carried, whilst other vans were well ventilated for the carriage of fresh meat, fruit and vegetables. Cars were an increasingly important traffic and many wagons were introduced for them.

Fleet Composition

In **Table 1**, we have used BR information to give a more detailed breakdown of the fleet at three periods. It uses the same categories as the Central Stock Registry used for the 1966 accounts. By 1977, some of the separate categories were no longer used, and this is shown. Air braking had been introduced by 1966 but these wagons were not separately identified. Ferry vehicles were included in the general totals in 1966, but are separately identifiable in 1977. Wagons with only through pipes are included in the unfitted categories.

In later tables the totals of each type of wagon built are given; it is reasonable to assume that by 1966 very few BR built wagons had been withdrawn (some notable exceptions are discussed in the text) so, by comparison with **Table 1**, the proportion of each wagon type replaced, can be calculated.

TABLE 1
CENSUS OF FREIGHT ROLLING STOCK ON B.R.
(Includes wagons built before 1948 but excludes all Engineers wagons)

Book Stock on Brake type	10/9/66 fitted	unfit	21/03/77 air	vacuum	unfit	05/84 air	vacuum	unfit
WAGON TYPE								
OPEN								
Low	1676	2	0	396	0	0	0	0
Medium	1859	27	0	0	0	0	0	0
Medium shock	30	0	0	0	0	0	0	0
High goods	58493	1381	111	9601	0	625	0	0
High goods sheet support	8565	6	-	-	-	-	-	-
High goods shock	2978	26	0	698	0	0	0	0
High goods shock sheet supp.	3630	8	-	-	-	0	0	0
High goods shock roof	102	0	0	40	0	0	0	0
High goods shock hood B	327	0	0	396	0	0	100	0
Anhydrite hopper	150	0	0	150	0	0	0	0
Brick	8	2	0	0	0	0	0	0
Carriage truck & carflat	1050	0	51	1122	0	47	386	0
China clay	875	2	0	871	0	0	483	0
Concrete slab/beam	12	28	0	0	0	0	0	0
Match & deal	26	16	0	0	0	0	0	0
Timber	115	0	0	127	0	0	0	0
Palbricks	1191	0	0	0	0	0	0	0
Pig iron	6	597	0	1	223	0	0	0
Roadstone	61	0	0	0	0	0	0	0
Salt	9	6	-	-	-	-	-	-
Sand	547	7	0	31	0	0	0	0

TABLE 1 continued

Book Stock on Brake type	10/9/66		21/03/77			05/84		
	fitted	unfit	air	vacuum	unfit	air	vacuum	unfit
WAGON TYPE continued								
Sleeper	0	5	0	0	0	0	0	0
Soda ash	0	11	0	0	0	0	0	0
Sulphate	0	38	0	0	0	0	0	0
Tank (fixed or demountable)	87	61	0	10	4	0	0	0
Tank underframe	72	1	0	0	0	0	0	0
Road rail goods flat	2	0	0	0	0	0	0	0
Road rail adaptor truck	7	0	0	0	0	0	0	0
Freightflat	0	0	6	0	0	14	0	0
Cartic	0	0	36	0	0	36	0	0
Ale pallet	0	0	0	4	0	0	0	0
CONTAINER CARRYING								
Container chassis	8	0	0	0	0	0	0	0
Conflat L	1940	0	0	299	0	0	0	0
Conflat LD	0	55	0	0	0	0	0	0
Conflat other types (A,B,D,)	14696	0	28	1288	0	29	48	0
Freightliner flat	127	0	2104	0	0	2081	0	0
COVERED								
Goods van	197	62	1080	0	0	1404	0	0
Goods van - insulated	250	0	0	0	0	0	0	0
Goods van - ventilated	66865	224	35	14894 @	0	550	75	0
Goods van - vent. UIC type 3	398	0	0	0	0	0	0	0
Goods van - shock	5135	0	0	329	0	0	0	0
Goods van - palvan	2173	0	90	359	0	51	0	0
WAGON TYPE continued								
Goods van - fruit	3463	1	0	0	0	0	0	0
Goods van - banana	2522	0	0	220	0	0	0	0
Goods van - meat	92	0	0	0	0	0	0	0
Goods van - ale	164	0	0	0	0	0	0	0
Goods van - fish	1373	0	0	2	0	0	0	0
Bulk material - alumina	0	40	0	0	35	0	0	0
Bulk material - ash	212	0	208	85	0	208	85	0
Bulk material - carbide	40	0	0	0	0	0	0	0
Bulk material - covhop	120	1246	47	119	1050	52	44	87
Bulk material - grain	100	779	0	99	586	0	61	0
Bulk material - presflo	1918	10	0	1921	0	0	709	0
Bulk material - prestwin	131	0	0	123	0	0	0	0
Bulk material - clinker etc	0	0	0	67	26	0	0	0
Fish offal - ex cattle	1	0	0	0	0	0	0	0
Gunpowder	207	38	0	185	5	0	0	0
Motor car van	175	0	0	0	0	0	0	0
Scenery van	4	0	0	0	0	0	0	0
Road rail van	51	0	0	0	0	0	0	0
Cattle	906	5	0	0	0	0	0	0
MINERAL - NOT HOPPERED								
Coal 16 tons	11104	247266	0	18863	37100	0	4865	0
Coal 20/21 tons	4948	5700	0	4922	4460	0	4571	1934
Coal 24½ tons	0	3391	0	0	2838	0	0	0
Coal other capacities	0	584	0	0	0	0	0	0
Coal side door ex SNCF	0	116	0	0	0	0	0	0
Coal 20 tons thru top plank	0	2162	-	-	-	0	0	0
Coal other cap. thru top pl.	0	35	-	-	-	0	0	0
Ironstone	1002	8960	0	1822	2864	2	1179	0
Stone	0	0	0	150	0	0	149	0
Coke	0	6	0	0	0	0	0	0
Ferrous scrap	0	0	2	0	0	0	0	0
MINERAL - HOPPERED								
Coal 13 tons	0	1990	0	0	49	0	0	0
Coal 20/21 tons	1050	36411	0	8552	17456	0	8061	358
Coal 24/24½ tons	250	5007	0	0	5134	0	0	865
Coal 26/32 tons	1824	0	10153	0	0	13006	0	0
Coal other capacity	24	30	0	0	0	0	0	0
Ironstone	1015	5479	0	1049	1460	0	693	0
Coke	0	2175	0	1	1128	0	0	0

TABLE 1 continued

Book Stock on Brake type	10/9/66 fitted	unfit	21/03/77 air	vacuum	unfit	05/84 air	vacuum	unfit
STEEL CARRYING								
Single bolster	5	313	0	0	0	0	0	0
Double bolster	0	244	282	0	0	0	0	0
Twin bolster	1238	7	0	104	0	0	0	0
Twin case	0	2	0	0	0	0	0	0
Bogie bolster A	0	16	0	0	0	0	0	0
Bogie bolster B	22	43	0	237	0	1	0	0
Bogie bolster C	1399	4944	2	1068	2057	0	327	0
Bogie bolster D	799	2936	1	734	1947	1011	302	0
Bogie bolster E	1200	0	0	1083	0	0	115	0
Bogie bolster Q, H, T, special	165	244	0	72	0	0	287	0
BAA, BBA & BLA	0	0	712	0	0	854	0	0
Plate	4247	5272	7	3627	161	654	168	0
Bogie plate	550	1023	0	469	645	50	52	0
Tube	3051	2099	5	2879	6	0	428	0
Pipe	2053	12	0	1556	0	50	469	0
Coil	189	406	2	1356	494	85	503	176
Bogie coil	254	0	20	483	28	19	73	0
Slab	88	0	–	–	–	–	–	–
Borails	–	–	44	160	21	0	0	0
SPECIALS								
Armour plate	0	64	–	–	–	0	0	0
Boiler	1	4	–	–	–	0	0	0
Flat	44	51	–	–	–	0	0	0
Girder – twin	0	10	–	–	–	0	0	0
Glass	15	77	–	–	–	0	0	0
Lowmac	289	376	–	–	–	0	0	0
Hymac	5	22	–	–	–	0	0	0
Motor car – 2 tier	10	0	–	–	–	0	0	0
Rectank	0	72	–	–	–	0	0	0
Roll	0	19	–	–	–	0	0	0
Transformer	0	4	–	–	–	0	0	2
Flatrol	45	145	–	–	–	0	0	0
Protrol	0	8	–	–	–	0	0	0
Trestrol	0	165	–	–	–	0	0	0
Weltrol	6	114	–	–	–	0	0	2
Trestle – plate	81	180	1	–	–	50	0	0
Wheel	1	4	–	–	–	0	0	0
Nuclear flask	0	0	–	–	–	41	0	0
Specials – all	–	–	12	273	406	–	–	4
GOODS BRAKE & OPERATING VEHICLES								
Brake van liner	14	0	0	0	0	0	0	0
Brake van	4457	5752	0	12	3389	0	0	867
Brake tender	120	0	0	45	0	0	0	0
Barrier	0	0	11	128	0	211	0	0
Runner	0	0	0	9	170	362	37	0
Freightliner & tippler adaptor	0	0	0	0	78	0	2	89
INTERNATIONAL								
Carfits and bogie steel	(22)	0	30	0	0	0	0	0
Ferry & ex ferry open	(110)	0	59	0	0	27	0	0
Ferry van	(440)	0	427	0	0	87	0	0
Ferry specials	(49)	0	3	0	0	0	0	0

Key   –   total included in other figures in Table
         @   known to include 1,962 vanwides

Chapter 2
Construction and Components

Plate 1 This view of No. B932849, a Plate wagon converted to a Conflat, shows the principal construction of a steel underframe, and is fitted with self-contained drawgear and clasp vacuum brakes. When photographed at Sheffield on 16th September 1983, it was in use as a runner.

R. A. Silsbury

Underframe construction has followed established practice with steel being used almost exclusively **(see Plate 1)**. The only exceptions were both to pre-nationalisation orders; a batch of LNER '13 ton Coal Hoppers' were all wood, with steel-flitched solebars **(see Chapter 8)**, and the 'Lowmac MR' had reversed channel headstocks, infilled with wood **(see Chapter 12)**. Welding has tended to replace riveting. The depth of underframe members is from 9in. to 12in. depending on the type of vehicle, with bogie wagons having trussing to help maintain rigidity. Some '50 ton Borails' and '60 ton Coils' had fish-belly members instead of trussing. The longer wheelbases of 2-axle air-braked stock has resulted in underframes combining deep longitudinals and shaped solebars to accommodate the suspension. The greater loads of new construction 'Bogie Steel Carriers' has also seen very deep fabricated frames.

Bodywork has depended on the role of the vehicle. General merchandise wagons have traditionally been built of wooden planks, latterly with steel framing, and BR continued this practice, usually in combination with wood-lined pressed-steel ends. All-steel bodies were used for some 'Low', 'Medium' and 'High' open wagons. Plywood was used on some early 'Vans', because of post-war shortages, and reappeared on later standard 'Vans'. Although offering a saving in weight, it was not so easily repaired when damaged. BR continued the practice of constructing 'Specials', 'Minerals', 'Hoppers' and 'Steel Carriers' mainly of steel and, like the LNER, developed this for open merchandise wagons. Early experiments using aluminium instead of steel were not successful, but lightweight alloys were successful when used in the construction of 'Merry-go-round Coal Hoppers' and air-braked 'Vans'.

Suspensions

Many 2-axle wagons of traditional design had shoe suspension, where the ends of the springs fitted in shoes fixed to the solebars **(Plate 2)**, whilst others employed an auxiliary suspension, popularly known as 'J-hanger' **(Plate 3)**. Exceptions were vehicles built to RIV specifications, which employed the UIC link suspension **(Plate 4)**, and some 'Special' wagons with bar frames and eye-bolt suspension **(Plate 5)**. The requirement for long wheelbase air-braked stock to run at much higher speeds than hitherto, has required extensive research into suspensions, and several different types have developed. These designs usually combine links and auxiliary hangers, sometimes with traction rods or damping mechanisms. Each design is identified by a code in the 'FAT' series **(Plates 6 to 11)**.

Plate 2 The common shoe suspension, fitted to 16T Mineral No. B277700, supports a six leaf spring. Note the stop fixed to the solebar above the spring buckle, and the plain, or plate-front, axlebox. The hole in the 'W' iron could be used for the hook when shunting by capstan or horse. It is photographed at Barry on 2nd April 1982.

R. A. Silsbury

Plate 3 Auxiliary rubber suspension and 'J' hangers fitted to 10T Tank wagon No. B749101, pictured at Wimbledon on 7th April 1983.

R. A. Silsbury

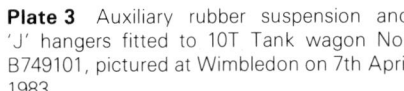

Plate 4 RIV link suspension on Ferry Open No. B715018, pictured at Luton on 13th February 1982. The angled one piece axlebox is of the design peculiar to ferry stock.

P. W. Bartlett

Plate 5 With the bar frames used in some specially-constructed wagons, the springs are suspended on eyebolts bracketed from the frame, as on Lowmac WE, No. B905097, seen at Eastleigh on 17th November 1983. An end view appears in **Plate 43**. The split pattern axleboxes evidence the GWR origin of the design.

R. A. Silsbury

Plate 6 The single-link, two-stage auxiliary suspension is employed on air-braked merry-go-round coal hoppers, seen here on No. 359296 at Wellingborough on 11th June 1978.

R. A. Silsbury

Plate 7 OBA No. 110769 employs the FAT 7 type suspension, combined with a 4-leaf Bruninghaus spring, and recorded at Fratton on 26th September 1980. The metre rule gives a good indication of scale.

R. A. Silsbury

Plate 8 The air-braked series of covered vans were the subject of many different types of suspension; many experimental. No. 200235 has the FAT 6 type, known also as DOD Mk. 1, utilising large brackets to support the vertical single links, and with lateral and longitudinal damping. Note also the brake pads and calipers in this view of the left-hand wheel, taken at Fratton on 7th July 1980.

R. A. Silsbury

Plate 9 With the FAT 8, or DOD Mk. II suspension, the links are inclined inwards at the top. The generally similar layout to the FAT 6 type is evident in this photograph of the right-hand wheel of No. 200211 at Fratton on 4th May 1978.

R. A. Silsbury

Plate 10 The FAT 5 Taperlite suspension was introduced experimentally on the vans built to Lot 3686. Hydraulic damping is evident, but the 'flimsy' appearance of the springs is most noticeable. This is the right-hand wheel of No. 200225, pictured at Wednesbury Steel Terminal on 19th August 1983.

P. W. Bartlett

Plate 11 Production Taperlite, FAT 13, was used under some of the VD type vans, as here on No. 201076, seen at Fratton on 21st June 1978, where the differences to the experimental type can be compared. Also clearly visible are the disc brake pads bolted to the wheel web, and the caliper actuated brake shoes.

R. A. Silsbury

Bogies (Plates 12 to 21)

Bogie design has similarly evolved. The diamond-frame bogies, popular with the LNER and LMS, which appeared on some early designs, was abandoned in favour of an improved GWR 5ft. 6in. wheelbase plateback type. This also appeared in an 8ft. wheelbase version. Six-wheeled bogies were of varied design often of LNER/LMS origin.

Later, the diamond-frame type reappeared in different forms, as the cast three-piece, secondary suspension bogies being manufactured by English Steel Co. (Davis and Lloyd) and Gloucester RC&W, including one with 2ft. 8in. diameter wheels for 'Freightliner' flats. In 1970, BR decided that rigid-frame primary suspension bogies were better suited to the heavier loads and faster speeds of the new generation air-braked stock, and several types have developed. BR has used the French Y25C and developed its own designs which are identified by an 'FBT' series code.

These modern 2-axle and bogie designs are too complex for study in depth in these volumes and the illustrations have been chosen to portray the principle types.

Plate 12 The LNER design diamond-frame bogie was a simple rugged type with a single large coil spring each side. This example belongs to Bogie Bolster D, No. B941316, and also illustrates well the 3-hole disc wheel. It had been withdrawn for maintenance when seen at Carlisle, Kingmoor, on 6th August 1980.

R. A. Silsbury

Plate 13 The LMS diamond-frame bogie employed a similar frame to the LNER type, but can be distinguished by having a pair of smaller coil springs on each side. This example, recorded under Boplate E, No. B947017, at Doncaster on 2nd July 1983, is fitted with 2ft. 8½in. diameter wheels.
P. W. Bartlett

Plate 14 The plate-back bogie derives from the GWR design. That fitted to Bogie Bolster C, No. B940425 is the pure GWR design, with a pair of coil springs on each side, and two holes cut in the side frame. The continuing use of spoked wheels, when seen at Wellingborough on 17th February 1984, is noteworthy.
P. W. Bartlett

Plate 15 The BR version of the plate-back bogie differed by having radiused ends, a single coil spring, and no holes. The journal size has been increased to 9in. x 4½in., as on this example fitted to Bogie Bolster C, No. B943679, seen at Wellingborough on 17th February 1984.
P. W. Bartlett

Plate 16 Later BR plate-back bogies reverted to having two holes in the frame, and many were fitted with roller bearings as in this example under Bogie Bolster C, No. B922584, pictured at Fratton on 19th June 1980.

R. A. Silsbury

Plate 17 The English Steel Co. 'Ridemaster' cast three-piece bogie, built under licence by Davis & Lloyd, is seen here fitted to Boflat, (ex-Boplate E), No. B947909, and is also seen at Fratton on 19th June 1980.

R. A. Silsbury

Plate 18 Gloucester RC&W Co. produced a similar type, with slightly deeper side frames, seen fitted to Bogie Bolster D, No. B928172, and pictured at Northampton on 8th January 1983.

P. W. Bartlett

Plate 19 Six-wheeled bogies are comparatively rare. This example, under Weltrol EJC, No. B901205 employs deep bar frames and eyebolt suspension to the springs. Note also the secondary suspension between the outer and centre axles, and the wheel handbrake. It is photographed at Eastleigh on 15th November 1982.

R. A. Silsbury

Plate 20 (Above) Recorded at Grimsby on 17th September 1983, air-braked Bogie Bolster D, No. 950575 is fitted with the French Y25C bogie, and employs clasp brakes. An end view of this bogie appears in **Plate 45**.

R. A. Silsbury

Plate 21 The similar BR-designed air-braked bogie, coded FBT6, here fitted to nuclear flask wagon No. 550014 has disc brakes and a wheel handbrake photographed at Warrington (Bank Quay) on 11th April 1980.

P. W. Bartlett

Axleboxes and 'W' Irons (Plates 22 to 26)

The axlebox contains the bearing surface of the axle journal, and fits in a vertical assembly known as a 'W' iron on most 2-axle wagons, or the side frame of a bogie. In the early years of BR, plain bearings were universal, and the different types of axle-boxes are referred to by their appearance as split (i.e. in two halves) one piece or plate-fronted. Hyde, Athermos and Isothermos, etc., are developments of the plain bearing. Following the recommendations of the 1955 'Modernisation Plan', roller bearing axleboxes have been increasingly fitted, and these are known by their trade name, e.g. Timken, SKF. Plain bearing journal sizes depend on the type of vehicle and its capacity, but range from 9in. x 4¼in. for 13 ton wagons to 12in. x 6in. for 30 ton 2-axle types and 10in. x 5in. on bogie vehicles. The equivalent roller bearings range from 4⅜in. to 6in. diameters. RIV vehicles use metric 250mm. x 130mm. journals.

Wheels

Three-hole disc wheels have been standard throughout BR history, but steel shortages during the early 1950s meant that repro-filed spoke and split-spoke wheels appeared under some new wagons. During repairs, like was not always replaced with like, and vehicles have appeared with a mixture of wheels. The normal wagon wheel diameter is 3ft. 1½in., although 2ft. 8in. and 2ft. 10in. diameter types appear under vehicles whose construction would preclude the larger size. RIV wagons usually have 1 metre diameter wheels.

Plate 23 (Below) The plate-front axlebox fitted to Orehop No. B438736 contains a 10in. x 5in. journal. It is carried in a heavy duty 'W' iron and restrained by a nine leaf spring — all necessary to permit the carriage of 25½ tons of ore. The hand-wheel operates the hopper mechanism. It is pictured on 12th October 1975 at Wellingborough.

P. W. Bartlett

Plate 22 A cast two-piece 9in. x 4¼in. axlebox, commonly referred to as the 'split' type, fitted to Vanwide No. B783896. During repairs, a new 'W' iron has been fitted with the hook-hole towards the centre of the wagon, and fixed with hucksbolts instead of common rivets. The clasp brakes have composition brakeshoes. It is seen at Salisbury on 22nd March 1982.

R. A. Silsbury

Plate 24 'Hybox' and 'Athermos' are the commercial names of developments of the oil axlebox. Here, one of the former is fitted to Engineering Dept. 'Grampus' wagon No. DB991516, seen at Salisbury on 22nd March 1982.

R. A. Silsbury

Plate 25 The 1955 modernisation plan envisaged the fitting of roller bearings to all wagons with a capacity of 20 tons and over. Iron Ore Tippler No. B380088 had a 4⅞in. diameter BR RIV type when photographed at Luton on 26th August 1980.

P. W. Bartlett

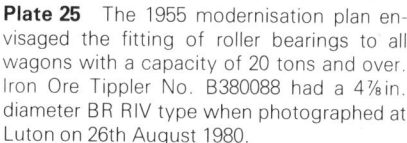

Plate 26 An inverted-U housing protects the 4⅞in. diameter Timken roller bearing fitted to Anhydrite Hopper No. B747124, recorded at Wellingborough in October 1975. Note also the independent clasp brakes. Other pattern roller bearings are illustrated with individual wagon types.

P. W. Bartlett

Buffers

Buffers fall into three main categories; spindle, self-contained and pneumatic/hydraulic. The spindle type consists of a separate cast or fabricated guide bolted to the headstock, with a spring between the headstock and trimmer. The buffer ram passes through these, and is secured behind the trimmer by a cotter pin, the buffing forces being transmitted to the spring by washers. The guides usually have stiffening webs, and we have used this feature in our description (e.g. half-rib). Normally, spindle buffers project 1ft. 6in. from the headstock, but 1ft. 8½in. and 2ft. 0½in. long types are found on some fitted stock. When unfitted wagons were subsequently vacuum-braked, a 2½in. collar was sometimes welded to the outer end of the guide. A selection of spindle buffers is illustrated in **Plates 27 to 30**. A special spindle buffer, known as the Duplex, was fitted to many shock-absorbing wagons **(Plate 31)**.

Plate 27 (Below) A 1ft. 6in. spindle buffer, with four ribs cast as part of the guide. The top one is shorter, and extended upwards against the body. This example is fitted to steel-bodied 'High' No. B490042, as seen in February 1981.

R. A. Silsbury

Plate 28 Whilst essentially similar to that shown in **Plate 27**, this type of 1ft. 6in. spindle buffer has no upward extension to the top rib, and is additionally fitted with a fabricated step. It appears on Grain Hopper B885008 at Wellingborough on 11th June 1978.

R. A. Silsbury

Plate 29 The BR standard 'F4' 1ft. 6in. spindle buffer has two short ribs welded to the sides of the guide, as here on Iron Ore Tippler No. B384705, seen at Warrington on 7th August 1980.

R. A. Silsbury

Plate 30 When unfitted vehicles received vacuum brakes, the spindle buffers often had collars welded to the guides to extend their reach, as depicted in the **frontispiece**; for vehicles vacuum braked from new, a 1ft. 8½ in. version was produced. This type has step grips cast on the upper side of the guide, and is fitted to Pipe wagon No. B741691, pictured at Willesden on 2nd February 1984.

R. A. Silsbury

Plate 31 A distinctive 1ft. 6in. Duplex spindle buffer was fitted to many shock-absorbing wagons, in this case Shocvan No. B851249, seen at Barry on 2nd April 1982.

R. A. Silsbury

A self-contained buffer, as its name implies, consists of a complete unit which is bolted to the headstock. A coil, volute or rubber spring is contained within the housing, and a hole in the headstock is provided for the travel of the buffer ram when under compression. 1ft. 6in. length units were usual on unfitted stock, a 2½ in. thick wooden packing piece being inserted next to the headstock for wagons subsequently fitted, whilst 1ft. 8½ in. or 2ft. 0½ in. long units were provided on stock built vacuum-fitted. RIV wagons had 2ft. 0½ in. long rubber-sprung, self-contained buffers with an aperture in the side of the housing **(Plates 32 to 35)**.

Plate 32 (Above) China clay open No. B743626 features a 1ft. 6in. self-contained buffer, with fabricated step, also seen at Barry on 2nd April 1982.

R. A. Silsbury

Plate 33 Recorded here at Fratton on 19th June 1980, No. B947909 was built as a Bo-plate E. When converted to a Boflat, its 1ft. 8½ in. oval-headed self-contained buffers were extended to accommodate the end drop flaps by inserting a wooden packing piece.

R. A. Silsbury

Plate 34 At Fratton on 11th September 1980, 2ft. 0½ in. and 1ft. 8½ in. self-contained buffers fitted to Lowmacs, Nos. E230965 and E230966 offer a comparison. Identical types of buffer were fitted to BR vehicles.

R. A. Silsbury

Plate 35 The distinctive 2ft. 0½in. self-contained buffer fitted to RIV stock had an aperture on the side through which the volute spring was visible. This example, pictured on 13th February 1982 at Luton, is fitted to Ferry Open No. B715018.

P. W. Bartlett

Plate 36 The unique square housing, hydraulic buffer, manufactured by Dowty, only appeared on 10ft. wheelbase Single Bolster wagons. One is depicted here, under full compression, on No. B916099 at Newport Docks on 9th September 1980.

P. W. Bartlett

Plate 37 (Below) This Dowty hydraulic buffer features parallel round housing, and a step cast on top. It is 1ft. 8½in. long, and fitted to Vanwide No. B784755, seen at Salisbury on 22nd March 1982.

R. A. Silsbury

The third buffer type is also a self-contained unit, but relies upon either the compression of oil alone (hydraulic) or air by oil (pneumatic) to absorb the buffing shocks. The two principle manufacturers were Oleo and Dowty, the latter ceasing to build buffers in the mid-1960s. 1ft. 6in., 1ft. 8½in. and 2ft. 0½in. long units were used; this type of buffer is characterised by the bright steel rams **(Plates 36 to 39)**.

Buffer head size and shape varied. The commonest were of 1ft. 1in. diameter, but round heads could be up to 1ft. 6in. in diameter and oval heads between 1ft. 1in. x 1ft. 7in. and 1ft. 2in. x 2ft. 0in. on some long wheelbase 2-axle and bogie wagons. RIV wagons had 1ft. 3¾in. round heads on normal wagons and 1ft. 2in. x 2ft. 0in. oval heads on long wheelbase and bogie stock.

Buffers are fitted at horizontal centres between 5ft. 7½in. and 5ft. 8½in., and between 3ft. 4in. and 3ft. 6in. above rail level, the most usual being 3ft. 5¼in.

Plate 38 Oleo pneumatic buffers combine a cast section which is bolted to the head-stock, usually with some form of footgrip to its upper surface, and a long narrower guide. This 2ft. 0½in. example appears on demountable tank chassis No. B749046, pictured at Eastleigh on 8th April 1983.

R. A. Silsbury

Plate 39 Much stock has been fitted with replacement Oleo pneumatic buffers, and the 1ft. 8½in. type, fitted to vacuum braked 16 ton Mineral No. B552506, and seen at Fratton on 19th June 1980, is one such. Note also the fabrication to extend the reach of the drawhook, and the screw coupling on the adjacent vehicle.

R. A. Silsbury

Drawgear

The function of the drawgear is to transmit the motive force of the locomotive to the vehicle. This may be achieved by 'pushing' or 'pulling'. Drawgear may be continuous, where the drawbars from each end of the wagon are joined by a cradle, within which is a volute spring. A pull from either direction compresses the spring, giving an element of cushioning, whilst also causing the drawbar at the opposite end to be pulled in until the shoulder of the drawhook is against the drawbar hole stiffening plate. The wagon will move because of a compression force on the rearward headstocks (i.e. a 'pushing' force).

Because of their construction, some wagons (e.g. 'Hoppers' and 'Specials') are unable to be fitted with continuous drawgear and employ self-contained drawgear at each end. In this system, a short drawbar with a volute spring bears on a drawbar plate behind the headstock and, when a pull is exerted, the vehicle is pulled along. The underframe members impart the motive force to the rear drawbar.

Couplings (Plates 39 to 42)

The links by which one vehicle may be coupled to the next are of one of the following forms:

(a) 3-link, found on unfitted stock.

(b) Screw, found on fitted stock.

(c) Instanter, fitted to both types of stock. This is a form of 3-link coupling with a cast triangular-shaped centre link. When used in the long position it acts as an ordinary 3-link coupling; in the short position it keeps vehicles closer coupled, more akin to a screw coupling, but does not require the shunter to go between wagons to couple or uncouple them. The two tags assist in turning the coupling from short to long mode, using a shunters pole.

(d) RIV screw, used mainly on vehicles for international working, although it also appeared on some brake vans. The innermost shackle is longer, and of flattened section.

It was policy to recover all screw and instanter couplings from condemned wagons to use them to replace 3-link couplings until all stock was provided with them.

Plate 40 The standard 3-link coupling is here featured on 16 ton Mineral No. B192292, which was in NCB ownership by 15th September 1981 at Bargoed.

R. A. Silsbury

Plate 41 (Below) At Fareham on 11th October 1984. An Instanter coupling in the short position between two Iron Ore Tipplers. The two tags enable the centre link to be turned from short to long position using a shunter's pole. Note that the buffer faces are not in contact when the coupling is tight.

R. A. Silsbury

Plate 42 (Above) No. B904534, a Lowmac SC, features the RIV screw coupling, with elongated, flat section inner link pictured at Fratton on 14th November 1982.

R. A. Silsbury

Brakes

All wagons must have brakes which can be applied by hand from either side of the wagon. The usual method of application is by means of a side brake lever fitted towards the right-hand end. When downward pressure is applied to the lever, a system of shafts and rods cause the brake shoes to come into contact with the wheel tread. The lever is contained by a guide, and may be kept in the 'on' position by a pin through holes in the guide, or by a sawtooth **(see Plates 24, 43 & 50)**. The alternative method of application is by the use of a handwheel, fixed to a shaft which partially has a square or coarse section thread. When rotated, this causes a die connected to the brake rodding to apply the brakes **(see Plate 44)**. The screw handbrake is used exclusively on 'Brake Vans' where it is mounted vertically within the 'Van' body, and on many vehicles designed for heavier loads because of its greater efficiency.

Following trials started in 1961, the disc brake became standard on most new vehicles. Here the brake application is made by the linkage actuating calipers, which force the brake pads against machined plates on both sides of the wheel web **(see Plates 8 & 11)**. Some problems were experienced with the bolts that held the disc brake pads, shearing off in use. An alternative method was developed, which has been used quite extensively on bogie vehicles, in particular on the 'Mark 2 Freightliners'; this consists of honeycombed webs fitted to the axles, upon which the brake pads act. The honeycombing allows rapid dispersal of the heat caused by brake application **(Plate 45)**. In the late 1970s, BR experimented with fitting composition brake blocks to newly-constructed air-braked vans. At the time of writing, future policy is unclear but there may be reversion to using brake blocks.

Some vehicles built to pre-nationalisation orders and designs have the company-favoured system; e.g. Dean-Churchward brakes on GWR 'Flatrol WX' and Simplex brake on LMS 'Boplates' **(see Plates 46 & 47)**, and are referred to in the text, as appropriate.

All vehicles where the only method of application of the brakes is by hand are known as 'unfitted'. The main disadvantage of unfitted wagons is that the brake can only be applied individually when the wagon is stopped or only moving slowly. To enable the braking to be under the control of the train crew, a system of continuous braking is required, which is superimposed on the handbrake. Two systems have been used, vacuum and air. Both utilise a cylinder with a moving piston connected to the brake rigging. The cylinder is fed by a brake pipe running along each vehicle, with flexible hose connections between wagons. The train pipe is connected to the brake pump on the locomotive, and sealed at the other end. The vacuum brake relies on the creation of a vacuum in the cylinder to keep the brakes off, whilst the air brake requires air pressure to release the brakes. In both systems a return to atmospheric pressure will cause 'fail-safe' brake application.

Wagons with either of these automatic brakes are known as 'fitted', and 'dual fitted' if both systems are employed on the same wagon. To enable the continuity of the brake pipe to be maintained throughout the length of the train, an unfitted wagon may be provided with a through brake pipe only, and is known as a 'piped' vehicle ('dual piped' if both brake pipes are provided). Some fitted wagons also carry a brake pipe for the other system.

To enable the brake force to be adjusted to compensate for empty or loaded condition, either a manual lever or automatic changeover system may be employed, and in the case of the vacuum brake requires the provision of a second brake cylinder.

With the air brake, another lever may switch between 'Goods' and 'Passenger'. This simply differentiates between brakes with a slow and a fast application and release time. The setting 'Goods' takes 18-30 secs. to apply and 30-35 secs. to release, whilst the 'Passenger' setting takes 3-5 secs. to apply and 15-20 secs. to release. If a train has greater than 100 axles, then 'Goods' should be selected.

Initially, BR chose to have the two-pipe air brake, which is more efficient. However, European railways use only single pipe and the inclusion of one single-piped Continental ferry wagon in a train meant that the advantages of the second pipe and auxiliary reservoirs were lost. Because of this, BR adopted the single pipe air brake from 1983.

Plate 43 A sawtooth brake lever guide fitted to Lowmac WE, No. B905097. This view, taken at Eastleigh on 17th November 1983, also depicts the end of the eyebolt and bracket suspension shown in side elevation in **Plate 5**. The brake lever guide with holes and pin appears in detail in **Plates 24 & 52**.

R. A. Silsbury

Plate 44 Where a wheel handbrake is used, a die on a thread actuates the brakes, and is seen here in close-up on Flatrol EZ, No. B900507 at Connington on 15th September 1983.

R. A. Silsbury

Plate 45 Recorded at Fratton on 29th June 1983, BDA, No. 950832 features axle-mounted honeycomb disc brake webs. Also noteworthy is the distinctive shape of the end of the Y25C bogie, and the screw coupling.

R. A. Silsbury

Plate 46 Pure GWR, at Basingstoke on 9th March 1982, except that Flatrol WX No. B901000 was built by BR; The Dean-Churchward brake is in the 'on' position. The GWR design of self-contained buffer also appeared on early builds of Bogie Bolster C.

R. A. Silsbury

Plate 47 Pure LMS is this Simplex-braked diamond frame bogie, fitted with 2ft. 8½in. wheels, and found under Boplate E, No. B947017 at Doncaster on 2nd July 1983.

P. W. Bartlett

The main configurations of brakes are best described with the help of the figures in the text and the photographs. Exceptions are discussed in the body of the text.

Unfitted Brake Types

Double Brake (Figures 12, 47 & 48 and Plate 48). This employs an independent set of brakes on either side of the vehicle and is characterised by the double 'V' hangers. Although obsolescent on merchandise wagons, this type was often applied to vehicles designed for 'Hopper' or 'Tippler' discharge where cross-shafting would have fouled the doors or unloading installation.

Morton Brake (Figure 50 and Plate 49). The simplest form of handbrake, with two brake shoes on one side only and either-side levers connected by a cross-shaft. A dog-clutch arrangement reverses the action of one lever.

RCH (or 4-shoe Morton) Brake (Figure 33). An improved Morton brake utilising four brake shoes, one on each wheel. We have used the name RCH to differentiate from the simple Morton brake. This brake was rarely used on BR-built wagons.

Long-link or Standard 20 ton Brake (Figure 34 and Plate 50). Essentially an elongated version of the Morton 4-shoe type, but utilising reversing linkage instead of a dog-clutch.

Clasp Brake (Figure 46 and Plate 51). Eight brake shoes, two per wheel; often this type of unfitted wagon has all the parts for vacuum braking but the brake cylinder was never provided. Some 'Hoppers' have an unusual clasp system working on one side only, whilst others have the independent double clasp brake.

Plate 50 (Above) The Long-link, or Standard 20 ton brake, fitted to ex-Plate wagon B932504, seen at Toton on 17th September 1978, illustrates the linkage used to reverse action of the nearside brake lever.
R. A. Sils

Plate 48 (Left) Detail of the double 'V' hangers, characteristic of the independent brakes, and fitted to dropside 'High' No. B483700, and seen on the Isle of Wight on July 1983.
R. A. Sils

Plate 49 (Below) The Morton brake only had brake shoes on one side; this view of underframe of 16 ton Mineral No. B561490, taken at Avonmouth on 9th June 1980, showing the non-brake shoe side. Note the doorstop, to prevent damage to the 'V' hanger, and stiffening on the brake lever.
R. A. Sils

Fitted Brake Types

Morton 4-shoe (RCH) Vacuum Brake (Figure 4 and Plate 52). Adopted by the GWR, this is a fitted version of the Morton brake, and usually employs a tiebar between the lower ends of the 'W' irons to compensate for the greater brake force applied by the automatic brake.

SR Vacuum Brake (for Figure, see SR van in Volume 2 and Plate 53). Characterised by the 'V' hanger being offset to the right on the vacuum cylinder side, and using linkages on both brake levers; it appears only under one lot of SR design 'Vans' and one lot of 'Shock Opens'.

LMS 8-shoe Clasp Brake (Figures 2 & 5 and Plate 54). Usually combined with 'J' hanger auxiliary suspension, the dog-clutch is usually on the same side as the vacuum cylinder, and the short brake lever lies entirely within the wheelbase. The modified LMS clasp brake uses a normal length brake lever.

LNER 8-shoe Clasp Brake (Figure 9 and Plate 55). In this system the 'V' hangers are offset, with one to the right on the vacuum cylinder side and two symmetrically disposed on the opposite side.

BR 8-shoe Clasp Brake (Figures 3 & 20 and Plate 56). The BR clasp brake uses reverse linkage on one brake lever and has the 'V' hangers offset. This is to the right on the vacuum cylinder side. The air-braked version is illustrated by the VEA in **Volume 2 and Plate 57.**

Plate 51 The linkages associated with the independent, one side clasp brake can be seen clearly in this view. The vehicle is 21 ton Mineral No. B316850, which had been rebuilt on a hopper wagon underframe. It is photographed at Oxford on 17th June 1980.

R. A. Silsbury

Plate 52 Morton 4-shoe (RCH) vacuum brake, showing the dog-clutch arrangement to reverse the action of the brake lever. Details to note include the tie-bar between the bottoms of the 'W' irons, and the brake lever guide. All are seen on demountable tank chassis No. B749045 at Eastleigh on 8th April 1983.

R. A. Silsbury

Plate 53 The SR vacuum brake, with offset 'V' hanger, as fitted to Shock Open No. B720797, seen Carlisle on 14th August 1981.

R. A. Silsbury

Plate 54 The arrangement of the LMS 8-shoe clasp vacuum brake can be seen in detail under 'High' No. B494006 at Fratton on 20th August 1979. The brake cylinder can be seen behind the 'V' hanger.

R. A. Silsbury

Plate 55 Illustrated is the non-cylinder side of the LNER 8-shoe clasp vacuum brake, with the two 'V' hangers. A clear view of the opposite side, which features only one offset 'V' hanger, appears in **Plate 127**. This photograph is of 'High' No. B488826 at Fratton on 26th September 1980.

R. A. Silsbury

Plate 56 The BR 8-shoe clasp vacuum brake appears in two forms. In one, the 'V' hangers are on the centre line, and this appears in **Plate 91**. The most common form has the 'V' hangers offset, to the right on the brake cylinder side, as in this view of Iron Ore Tippler, No. B385827, seen at Fratton on 5th January 1979. Although the lever has a linkage, the action is not reversed; the opposite side of this type is shown in **Plate 62**.

R. A. Silsbury

Disc Brake. The experimental discs fitted in the 1961 trials are shown in **Plates 58 & 59**, and were combined with conventional shoe brakes at the other end of the wagon. This system was adopted on the 'Merry-go-round Hopper'. The air disc brakes are shown in **Plate 6** which is a close-up of one wheel only. Standard air-braked wagons built from the late 1960s usually have only disc brakes. The early 'Open Merchandise' (OAA), 'Vans' (VAA etc.) and 'Bolster' wagons (SAA) shared a common underframe arrangement **(see Figure 11)** which we have called Type 1, but more recently the detail of the brake rigging and solebar has varied between designs.

Bogie Wagons

Bogie wagons usually employed a separate set of brakegear for each bogie; 4-shoe, clasp or disc brake may be used. Basically they are a compact version of the normal 2-axle type, with the handbrake cross-shaft outside the bogie wheelbase. Other bogie designs incorporate the brake lever or wheel on the bogie frame.

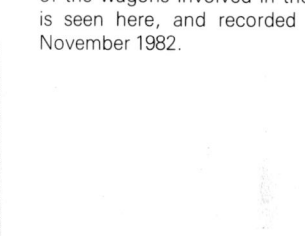

Plate 57 (Above) The modified suspension and brake linkage fitted to Vanfit No. ADB778246, one of the wagons involved in the 1970 air-brake trials, is seen here, and recorded at Eastleigh on 15th November 1982.

R. A. Silsbury

Plate 58 Some 24½ ton Hoppers were fitted with a combination of shoe and disc brakes. No. B335638, recorded at Toton on 17th September 1978, illustrates this, also the two 'V' hangers necessary for the cross shafts to clear the hopper outlets, and the very long brake lever.

R. A. Silsbury

Plate 59 Details of the disc brake calipers on Hopper No. B335687.

R. A. Silsbury

Chapter 3

Open Merchandise Wagons

This chapter deals only with open merchandise wagons, the specialist designs being dealt with in **Chapter 4**. Together with vans they are the main component of the fleet which is used to carry general merchandise. At first, BR tended to give equal importance to the construction of 'Opens' and 'Vans', but, during the 1960s and early 1970s, fewer open merchandise wagons than vans were constructed. More recently, relatively large batches of 'Opens' have once again been built.

Traditional open wagons were broadly grouped by the telegraph code names which they carried, into 'lows', which were one plank high; 'mediums', which were two or three planks and 'highs', which were over three planks high (in reality, five or six).

There were all steel equivalents of each of these.

During the first decade, BR standardised by only using the RCH-approved underframes which measured 17ft. 6in. over headstocks, with a 10ft. wheelbase, although a range of brake riggings were employed. These will be referred to by the names used in **Chapter 2**.

Lows

The first type of wagon to be considered is the 13 ton 'Low', **(see Table 2)**. These were designed for the carriage of road vehicles and had drop sides and ends.

TABLE 2

LOWFITS

Diag No.	Lot No.	Qnty	Builder	Year	Running numbers	Underframe type	Body type
1/001	2107	400	Wolverton	1950	B450000 − 450399	LMS clasp	Wood
1/002	2194	1000	Shildon	1951	B450400 − 451399	LNER clasp	Steel
1/002	2340	200	Shildon	1952	B451700 − 451899	RCH vacuum	Steel
1/002	2420	300	Shildon	1953	B451900 − 452199	RCH vacuum	Steel
1/002	2461	200	Shildon	1957	B452200 − 452399	RCH vacuum	Steel
1/002	2467	200	Shildon	1955	B452400 − 452599	RCH vacuum	Steel
1/002	2729	300	Shildon	1957	B452600 − 452899	RCH vacuum	Steel
1/002	2998	550	Shildon	1959	B452900 − 453449	BR clasp	Steel
Total		3150					

The first variant, allocated Diagram No. 1/001, was the only one built with wooden-plank sides and ends. This body style was of LNER design but, as the wagons were built at the ex-LMS Wolverton Works, they all received LMS clasp-brake underframes **(see Figure 2 and Plate 60)**.

Diagram No. 1/002 followed. These were all-steel wagons which had a variety of underframes **(see Table 2)** and minor body differences. The early part of Lot 2194 had only four vertical webs on the side **(Plate 61)**, the remainder, and all later lots, had nine vertical webs **(Plate 62)**. **Figure 3** illustrates the final lot.

All the 'Lows' were vacuum-braked from new and thus carried the code name 'LOWFIT' until replaced by the TOPS code OLV. Lettering varied, but all wagons carried 'NOT TO BE LOADED WITH CONTAINERS', usually in 2in. high lettering. In use, trains of 50 vehicles could often be seen, usually with each wagon carrying an identical load, such as military road vehicles, three-wheeled invalid cars or agricultural implements. They also worked singly. For example, muck spreaders and ambulances were a common load into the 1970s. Few LOWFITS survived after the mid-1970s, although some were transferred to the Engineer's Department; 216 had been converted to 'Twin Bolster' sets in 1961.

Plate 60 No. B450394 (Wolverton 1950, 2107) to Diagram 1/001 displays the full range of lettering normally found on the Lowfit; the script 'Not to be loaded with Containers' being noteworthy. This low angle view, taken at Hoo Junction in April 1970, also shows the LMS clasp vacuum brake underframe to advantage.

D. Larkin

Figure 2

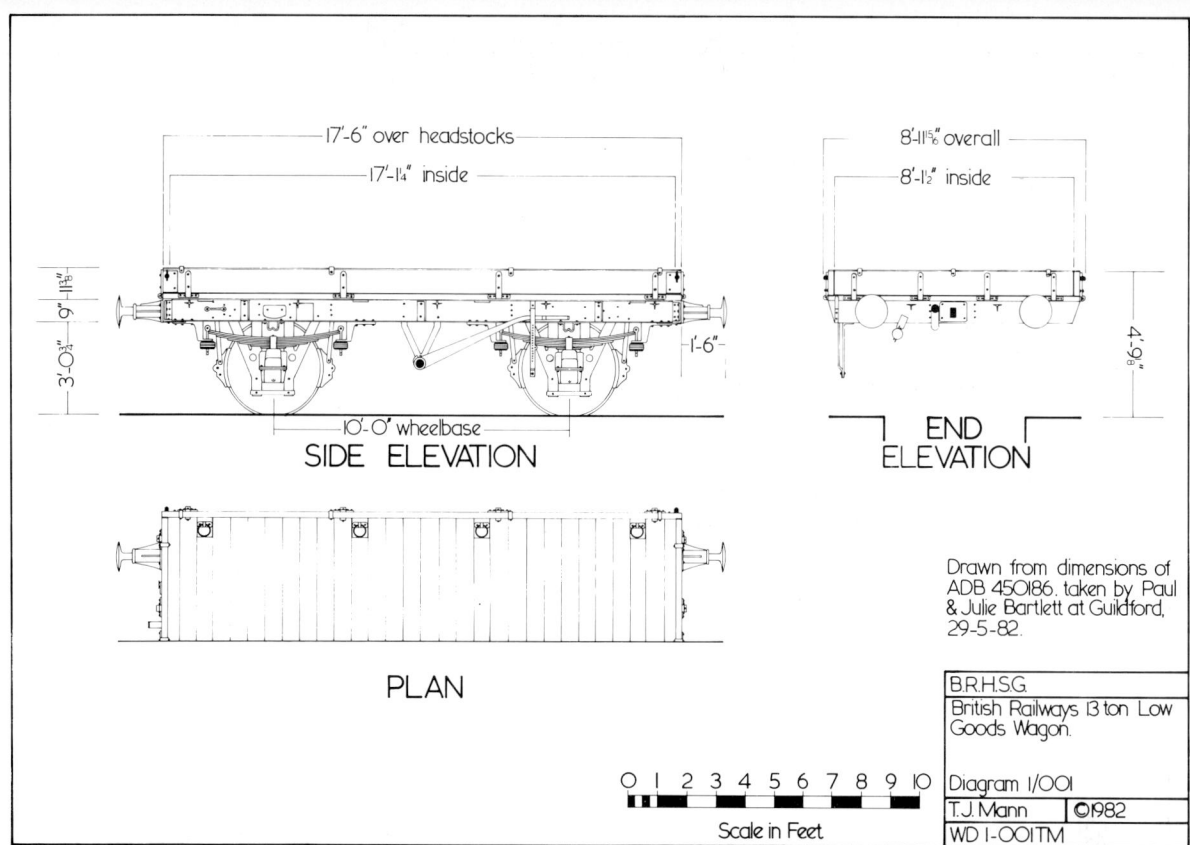

17'-6" over headstocks
17'-1¼" inside

8'-11⅝" overall
8'-1½" inside

3'-0¼" 9" 11⅝"

1'-6"

10'-0" wheelbase

SIDE ELEVATION

4'-9⅜"

END ELEVATION

PLAN

Drawn from dimensions of ADB 450186. taken by Paul & Julie Bartlett at Guildford, 29-5-82.

B.R.H.S.G.
British Railways 13 ton Low Goods Wagon.

Diagram 1/001

T.J. Mann   ©1982

WD 1-001TM

0 1 2 3 4 5 6 7 8 9 10
Scale in Feet

Plates 61 & 62 These two views illustrate the differences of body and underframe found on Diagram 1/002 vehicles. No. B451962 (Shildon 1953, 2420) — **Plate 61** — photographed at Eastleigh on 4th March 1976, has a RCH (Morton) vacuum brake underframe, and a body with only four webs, and is carrying a typical load for a Lowfit. No. B453058, (Shildon 1959, 2998) — **Plate 62** — seen at Park Royal on 18th November 1980, has a BR clasp vacuum brake underframe and a later body with nine webs, and replacement Oleo pneumatic buffers. The rusty bodywork, obliterating most of the lettering, is typical of the period.

R. A. Silsbury

Figure 3

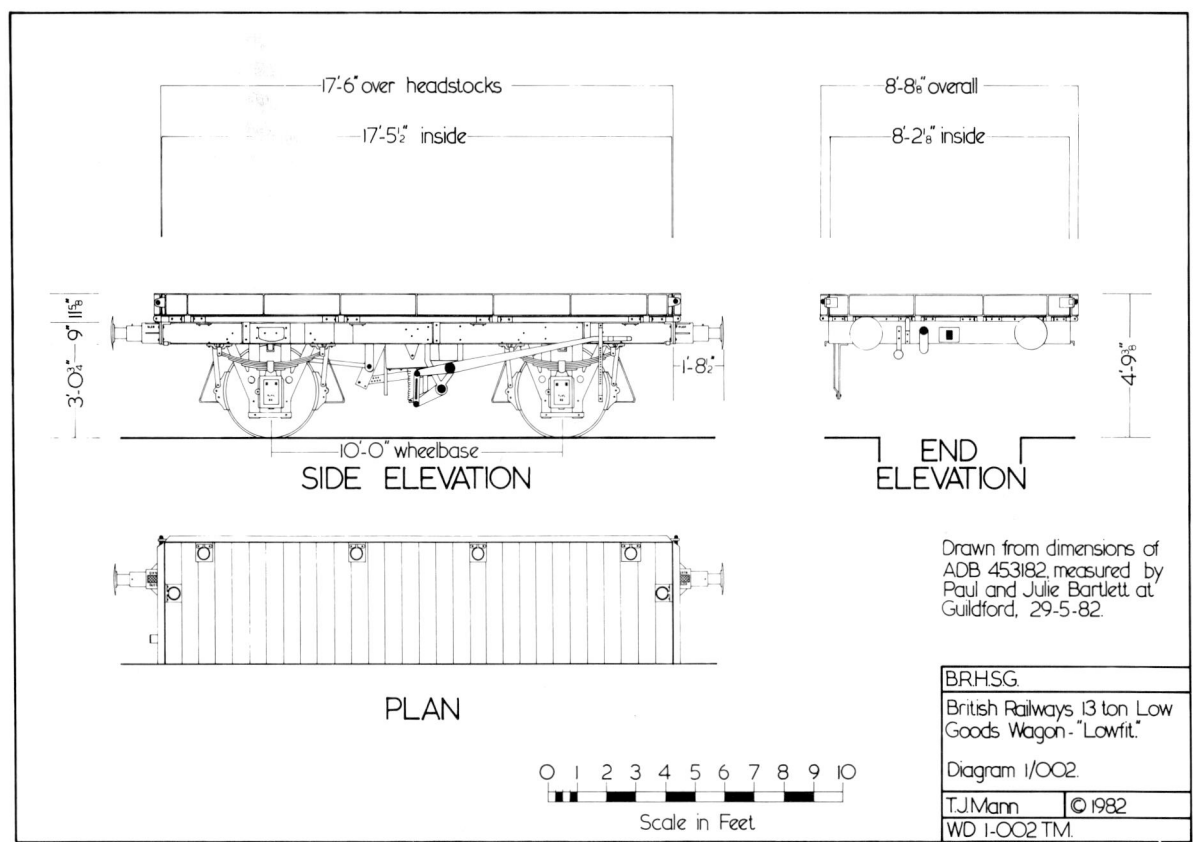

17'-6" over headstocks
17'-5½" inside
8'-8⅛" overall
8'-2⅛" inside
3'-0¼" · 9' 11⅝"
1'-8½"
10'-0" wheelbase
4'-9⅛"

SIDE ELEVATION

END ELEVATION

PLAN

0 1 2 3 4 5 6 7 8 9 10
Scale in Feet

Drawn from dimensions of
ADB 453182, measured by
Paul and Julie Bartlett at
Guildford, 29-5-82.

B.R.H.S.G.
British Railways 13 ton Low
Goods Wagon - "Lowfit."
Diagram 1/002.
T.J.Mann   © 1982
WD 1-002 TM.

TABLE 3

MEDIUMS

Diag No.	Lot No.	Qnty	Builder	Year	Running numbers	Underframe type	Design & body type
1/016	pt2061	100	Ashford	1949	B457100 – 457199	Double	SR wood
1/017	2108	397	Wolverton	1950	B457200 – 457596	Morton	LMS wood
1/019	2235	1000	Ashford	1950/1	B457597 – 458596	LMS clasp	BR steel
1/019	2236	1000	Ashford	1950/1	B458597 – 459596	LMS clasp	BR steel
1/019	2351	400	Ashford	1952	B459597 – 460396	LMS clasp	BR steel
1/019	2430	200	Ashford	1955	B460397 – 460596	RCH vacuum	BR steel
1/019	2352	400	Ashford	1953	B460597 – 460996	LMS clasp	BR steel
1/019	2488	600	Ashford	1955	B460997 – 461596	RCH vacuum	BR steel
Total		4097					

Mediums (see Table 3)

The 13 ton 'Mediums' had several interesting features. Of the pre-nationalisation companies only the LMS built them in quantity. However, the first BR wagons which were built to a part of Lot 2061 (see High Open Merchandise wagons for remainder) were of an SR design, Diagram No. 1/016. The ends had high 'U' channel stanchions and flush 'L' angle corner posts. The dropside was more typical of the LMS wagons. They were originally unfitted wagons equipped with the double handbrake, but were converted to RCH vacuum brake later **(Plate 63)**.

Lot 2108, Diagram No. 1/017 was typically LMS in design with wood dropsides and fixed ends, supported by four 'L' angle stanchions. Originally these had Morton brake underframes most of which were converted to RCH vacuum brake in the late 1950s. A few survived into the 1980s unfitted **(see Figure 4 and Plate 64)**.

The remainder of the 'Mediums' were of a new design, Diagram No. 1/019, which although largely following the earlier designs, were all-steel **(see Figure 5 and Plates 65 & 66)**. It is possible that these were either of SR or LNER design which was not produced before nationalisation. All were vacuum-braked from new **(see Table 3)**.

No special lettering was applied to the 'Mediums' but they have had various code names including 'MEDIUM', 'MEDFIT' and 'MED GOODS'. The use of these wagons for merchandise such as agricultural implements and containers was short-lived. Soon after introduction many of these vehicles were passed to the Engineer's Department and all had been transferred by the mid-1960s. The 'Mediums' were useful departmental wagons and many survived into the 1980s, some having had their vacuum brakes removed; the TOPS codes were normally ZAV or ZAO. The conversion of some of these wagons to 'Palbricks' during the mid-1950s shows that the design was soon surplus to requirements.

Some 'Lows' and 'Mediums' were fitted with second-hand split-spoke wheels from new, an expedient made necessary by post-war steel shortages, and some kept these wheels into the early 1980s. No more modern designs of either 'Lows' or 'Mediums' were introduced, although, some more specialist designs such as 'Carfit C' and air-braked 'Plates' (SPA) had some features in common with them.

Plate 63 No. DB457158 is one of the SR-designed vehicles built at Ashford in 1949 as part of Lot 2061. When recorded at Hoo Tip on 12th March 1978, it had been vacuum-braked, with tiebar and collared extensions to the spindle buffers. The livery was bare wood, with white lettering on black patches, and the remains of the green triangle on the top plank, denoting an Engineer's vehicle.

R. A. Silsbury

Plate 64 No. DB457203 (Wolverton 1950, 2108) is one of the Diagram 1/017 LMS-designed Mediums that had been vacuum-braked at some stage in its career, as witnessed by the tiebar, collared buffers and 'Medfit' code, but by 17th September 1978, when noted at Toton, the vacuum cylinder had been removed and the Engineer's TOPS code 'ZAO' applied.

R. A. Silsbury

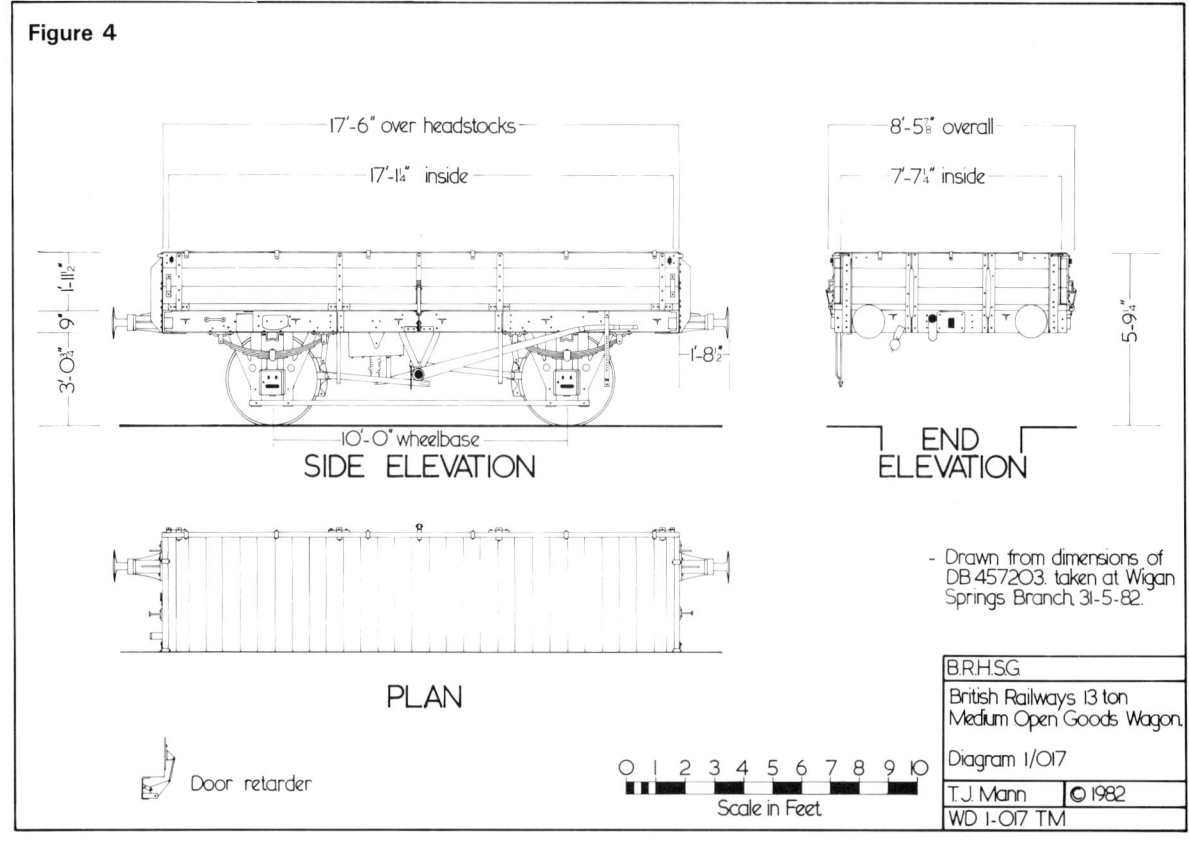

Figure 4

17'-6" over headstocks
17'-1¼" inside
8'-5⅞" overall
7'-7¼" inside

3'-0¼" 9" 1-11½"
1-8½"
5-9¼"

10'-0" wheelbase

SIDE ELEVATION

END ELEVATION

PLAN

- Drawn from dimensions of DB 457203. taken at Wigan Springs Branch. 31-5-82.

Door retarder

Scale in Feet
0 1 2 3 4 5 6 7 8 9 10

B.R.H.S.G
British Railways 13 ton Medium Open Goods Wagon.
Diagram 1/017
T. J. Mann   © 1982
WD 1-017 TM

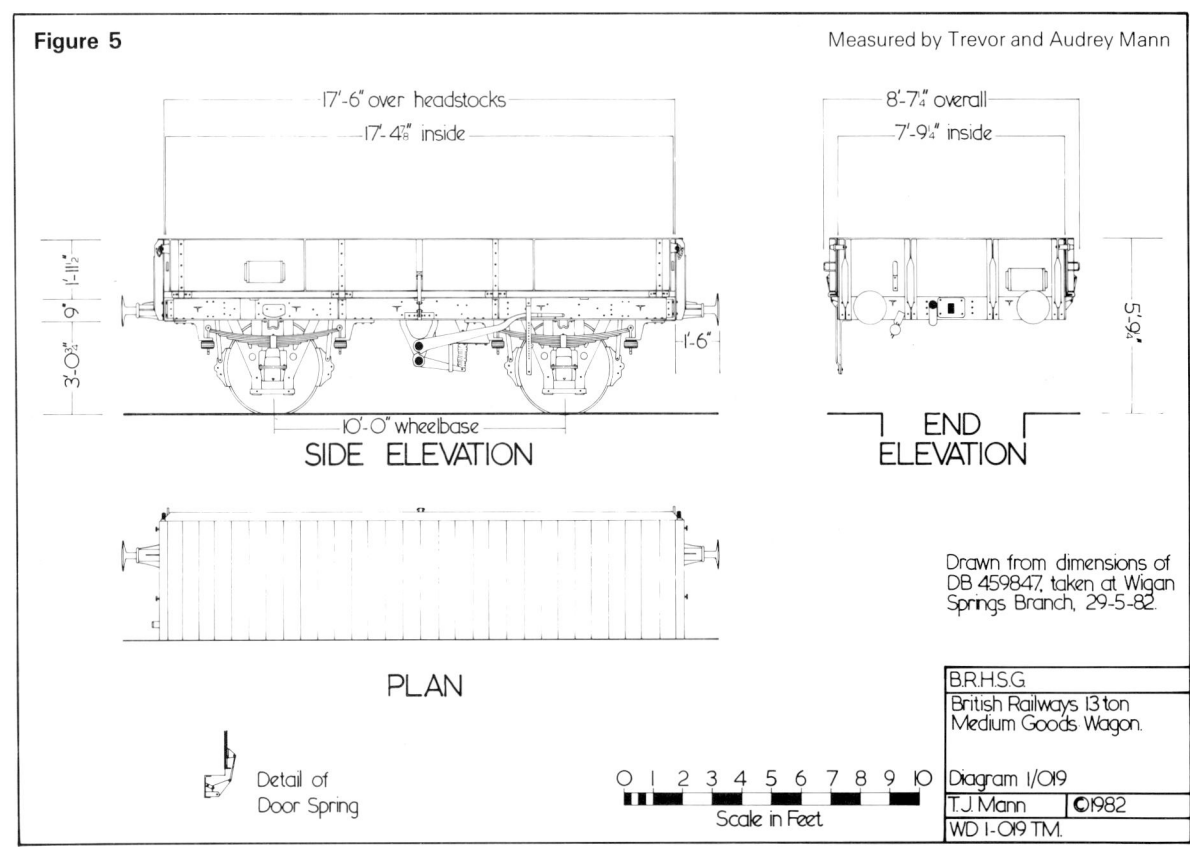

Figure 5   Measured by Trevor and Audrey Mann

17'-6" over headstocks
17'-4⅞" inside

8'-7¼" overall
7'-9¼" inside

3'-0¾"   9"   1'-11½"

1'-6"

10'-0" wheelbase

SIDE ELEVATION

5'-9¼"

END ELEVATION

PLAN

Drawn from dimensions of DB 459847, taken at Wigan Springs Branch, 29-5-82.

Detail of Door Spring

0 1 2 3 4 5 6 7 8 9 10
Scale in Feet

| B.R.H.S.G. |
| British Railways 13 ton Medium Goods Wagon. |
| Diagram 1/019 |
| T.J.Mann   ©1982 |
| WD 1-019 TM. |

Highs

The 'Highs' were much more numerous, of varied design, and have continued to be built into the 1980s. **Table 4** gives details of the earlier 13 ton examples.

Numerically, the first vehicles were built to Diagram No. 1/032. These were all-planked vacuum-fitted wagons of GWR design (GWR Diagram No. O42); typically they had 5½ plank sides and 'T' end stanchions **(see Plate 67 and Figure 6)**.

The next five plank design was to Diagram No. 1/034. Built to Lot 2153, they were a standard SR design (Diagram No. 1375) with 'T' end stanchions. These were built with a double brake and later vacuum-braked **(see Plate 68)**.

Other all-plank bodied 'Highs' were built. One batch was part of Lot 2314 and allocated Diagram No. 1/042. These were unusual in having steel channel for the two lower planks and inverted 'U' stanchion supports on the ends. Thus they were unlike any company design although they were reminiscent of both LMS and SR practice **(see Plate 69)**. The final all-plank bodied wagons were part of Lot 2409. These were given Diagram No. 1/045 and were very similar to LMS Diagram No. 2094. It is likely that these were built without corrugated ends because of post-war steel shortages, which were at their most severe for BR during 1952; indeed fixing holes for the corrugated ends were drilled in the curbrail. Like all of the other 'Highs' most of these were vacuum-fitted later.

Many of the wooden-ended 'Highs' were used for china clay from Cornwall and, during the 1970s, some were fitted with roller bearing axleboxes.

The next diagram was No. 1/039 **(see Figure 7 and Plates 70 & 71)**. These were the standard LMS 'Open Merchandise' with five plank sides and corrugated steel ends. They became a standard BR design. They were provided with a tarpaulin bar, and the underframe was either LMS clasp brake, RCH vacuum brake or Morton unfitted, which was converted to vacuum brake later. Diagram No. 1/044 was identical except for the omission of the tarpaulin bar **(see Figure 8 and Plate 72)** although many were so fitted later. Most wagons had their tarpaulin bars removed during the 1970s. Up to the end of production in 1957, the LMS design remained unaltered. All the surviving five plank open wagons were given the code OWV on TOPS; earlier they had been branded HIGH, HIGH FIT, HYBAR, HYBAR FIT or HIGH BAR FIT.

TABLE 4

HIGHS

Diag No.	Lot No.	Qnty	Builder	Year	Running numbers	Underframe type	Body type
1/032	2082	50	Swindon	1949	B475000 – 475049	RCH vacuum	GWR wood side & end
1/033	pt2061	100	Ashford	1949	B457000 – 457099 (B483650 – 483749)	Double	SR dropside wood side & end
1/034	2153	600	Ashford	1949/50	B477050 – 477649	RCH unfit	SR highbar wood side & end
1/037	2128	2000	Shildon	1950	B475050 – 477049	LNER clasp	LNER steel
1/039	2179	1500	Derby	1950-2	B477650 – 479149	LMS clasp	LMS hybar wood side corr. end
1/039	2315	500	Derby	1952	B484750 – 485249	RCH vacuum	LMS hybar wood side corr. end
1/039	2415	750	Derby	1953	B485250 – 485999	RCH vacuum	LMS hybar wood side corr. end
1/039	2462	750	Derby	1953/4	B486000 – 486749	Morton	LMS hybar wood side corr. end
1/039	2551	1000	Ashford	1954	B498020 – 499019	RCH vacuum	LMS hybar wood side corr. end
1/039	2723	500	Ashford	1955	B491700 – 492199	RCH vacuum	LMS hybar wood side corr. end
1/039	2834	500	Ashford	1957	B492200 – 492699	RCH vacuum	LMS hybar wood side corr. end
1/039	3026	150	Ashford	1957	B484000 – 484149	RCH vacuum	LMS hybar wood side corr. end
1/041	2195	1500	Shildon	1950/1	B479150 – 480649	LNER clasp	LNER steel
1/041	2196	1500	Shildon	1951	B480650 – 482149	LNER clasp	LNER steel
1/041	2197	1500	Shildon	1951/2	B482150 – 483649	LNER clasp	LNER steel
1/041	2341	970	Shildon	1952	B486750 – 487719	Morton	LNER steel
1/041	2366	499	Shildon	1952	B490251 – 490749	Morton	LNER steel
1/041	2361	1500	Birmingham	1953/4	B488750 – 490249	LNER clasp	LNER steel
1/042	pt2314	249	Derby	1952	B483750 – 483999	Morton	LMS wood side & end
1/043	pt2314	1	Derby	1952	B483793	Morton	BR steel
1/044	pt2409	350	Ashford	1952/3	B494770 – 495119	Morton	LMS wood side corrugated end
1/044	2397	870	Pickering	1953	B493900 – 494769	LMS clasp	LMS wood side corrugated end
1/044	2484	400	Ashford	1954	B497620 – 498019	Morton	LMS wood side corrugated end
1/044	2396	1200	Gloucester	1955/6	B492700 – 493899	LMS clasp	LMS wood side corrugated end
1/045	pt2409	150	Ashford	1952	B495120 – 495269	Morton	SR wood side & end
1/047	2342	1030	Shildon	1952/3	B487720 – 488749	RCH unfit	BR steel
1/047	2366	1	Shildon	1952	B490250	? unfit?	BR steel
1/047	2468	250	Shildon	1954	B495270 – 495519	RCH vacuum	BR steel
1/047	2479	650	Shildon	1955/6	B495970 – 496619	RCH vacuum	BR steel
1/049	2469	550	Shildon	1954	B496620 – 497169	RCH vacuum	BR steel highbar
1/049	2704	450	Shildon	1955	B495520 – 495969	RCH vacuum	BR steel highbar
	Total	22020					

Plate 67 No. KDB475017 (Swindon 1949, 2082) to Diagram 1/032 retains its 5½ plank construction in parts, and is photographed at Exeter in April 1984, still without a TOPS code.

P. W. Bartlett

Figure 6

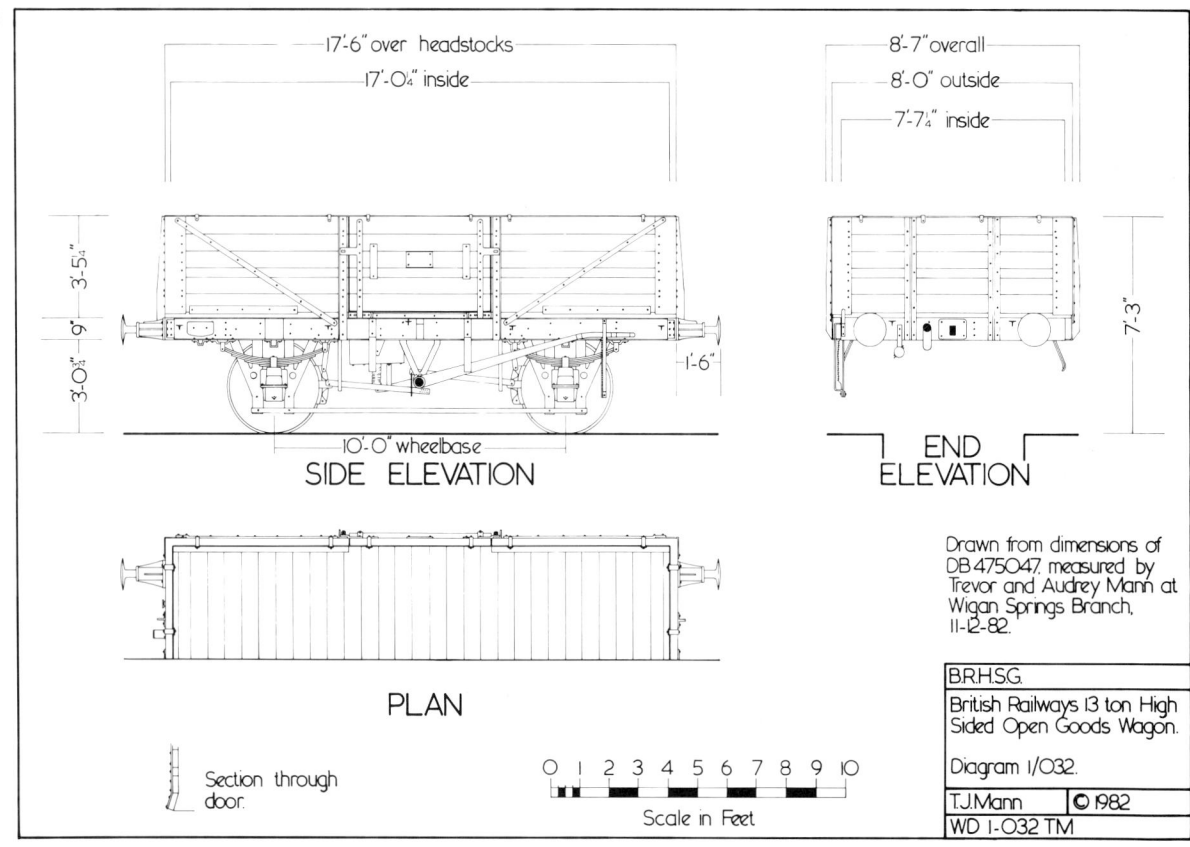

17'-6" over headstocks
17'-0¼" inside

8'-7" overall
8'-0" outside
7'-7¼" inside

3'-5¼"
9"
3'-0¼"

1'-6"

10'-0" wheelbase

SIDE ELEVATION

7'-3"

END ELEVATION

Section through door.

Drawn from dimensions of DB 475047, measured by Trevor and Audrey Mann at Wigan Springs Branch, 11-12-82.

PLAN

0 1 2 3 4 5 6 7 8 9 10
Scale in Feet

B.R.H.S.G.
British Railways 13 ton High Sided Open Goods Wagon.
Diagram 1/032.
T.J. Mann © 1982
WD 1-032 TM

Plate 68 No. B477615 (Ashford 1950, 2153) is a Diagram 1/034 vehicle which had been fitted with vacuum brake and associated fittings, and was recorded at Fareham in March 1974.

R. A. Silsbury

Plate 69 Another all-wood bodied type is Diagram 1/042, represented by No. B483866 (Derby 1952, 2314) and photographed at Eastleigh on 4th September 1975.

R. A. Silsbury

Plate 70 An official picture of No. B486144 when new. The lift date painted on the solebar is 13-11-53, although the photograph is dated 1954 at Derby. Built under Lot 2462 to Diagram 1/039, this batch was officially unfitted with the Morton brake, but as can be seen it has the RCH vacuum brake, and is in bauxite livery.

BR/OPC

HYBAR
13 T tare 7-000 kg
B478315
XP
W.B.10'0"

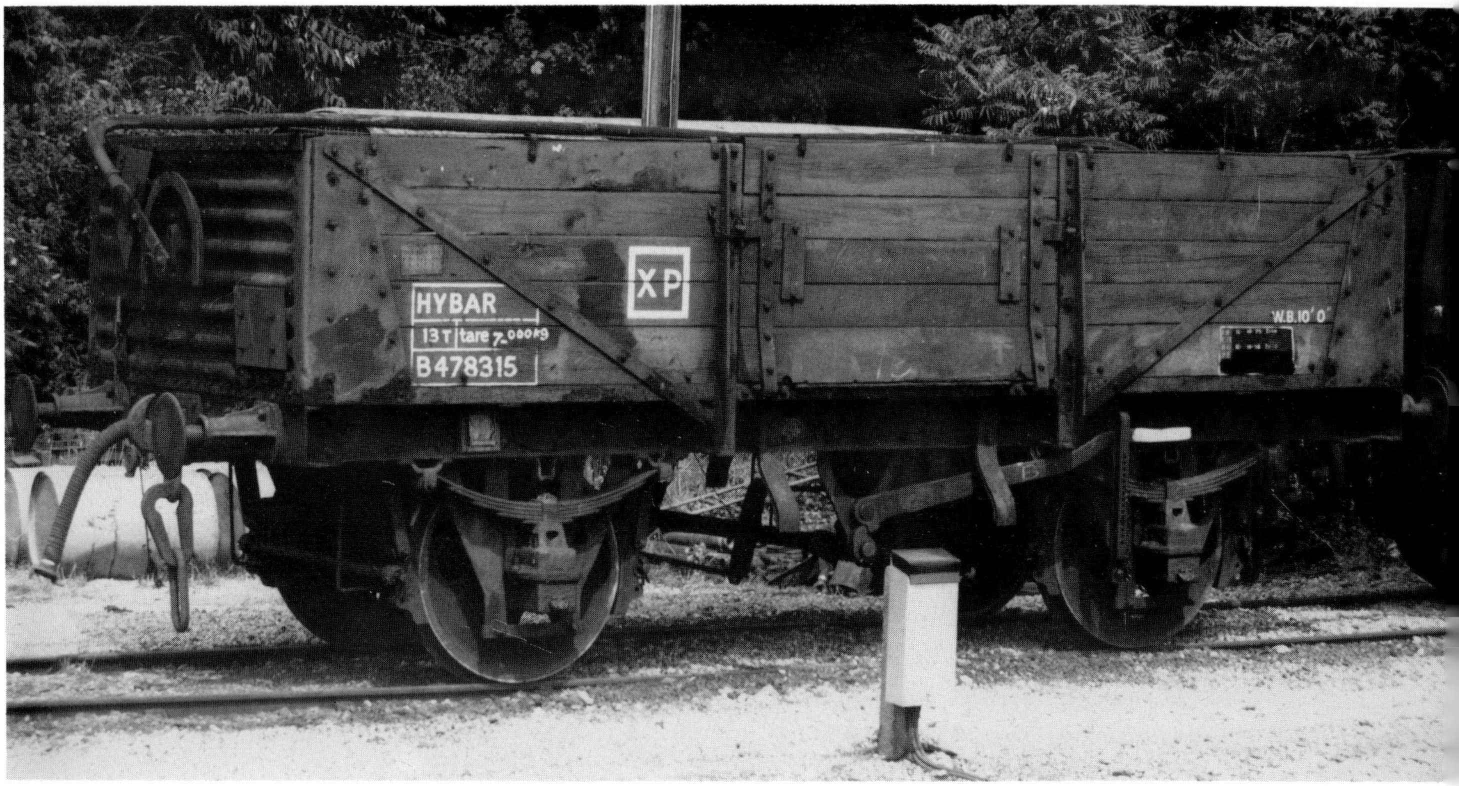

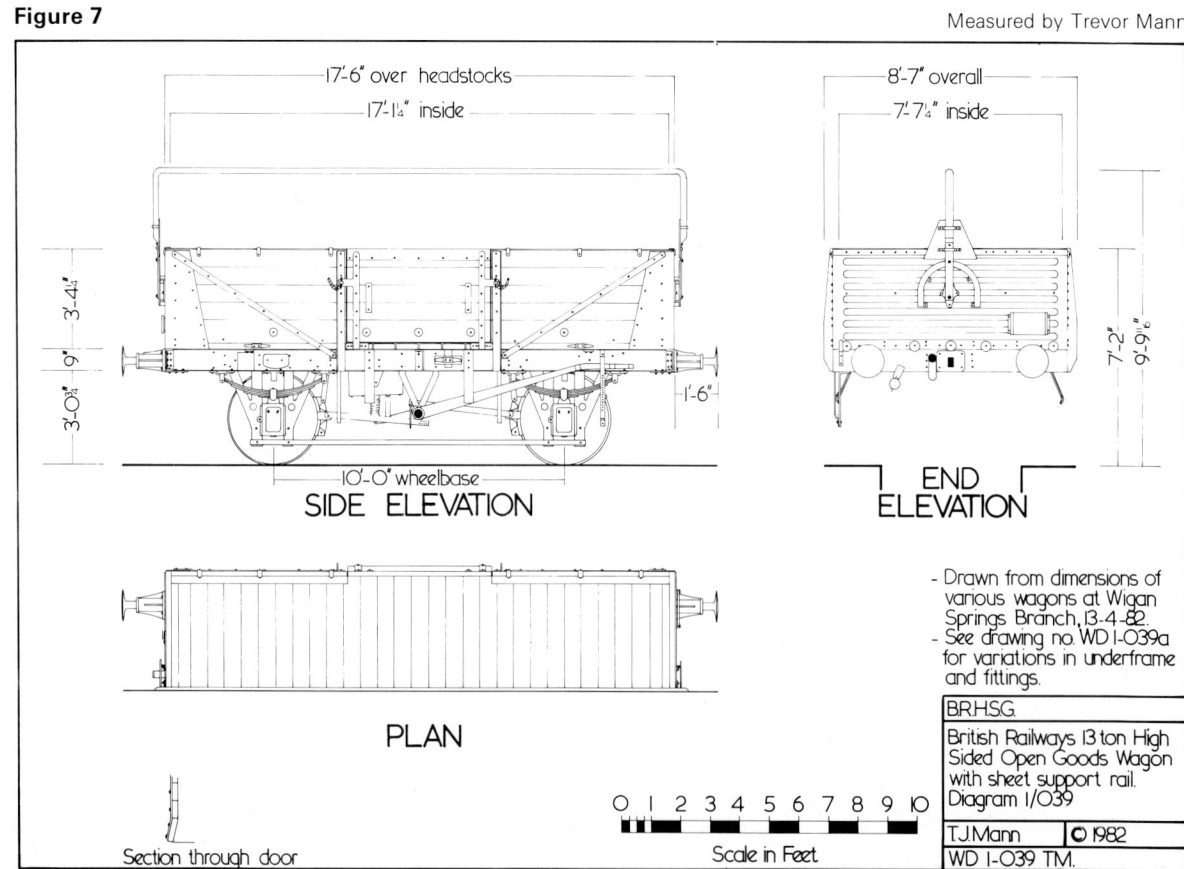

Plate 71 The standard LMS open High adopted by BR as Diagram 1/039 is depicted by No. B478315 (Derby 1951, 2179) at Fishguard on 11th August 1977. It had LMS clasp vacuum brake from new, with 1ft. 6in. spindle buffers and instanter couplings. The 1964 style blocked lettering has been ammended to show the tare weight in metric.

R. A. Silsbury

Figure 7

Measured by Trevor Mann

17'-6" over headstocks
17'-1¼" inside
8'-7" overall
7'-7¼" inside
3'-4½"
9"
3'-0¾"
1'-6"
7'-2"
9'-9 11/16"
10'-0" wheelbase
SIDE ELEVATION
END ELEVATION
PLAN
- Drawn from dimensions of various wagons at Wigan Springs Branch, 13-4-82.
- See drawing no. WD 1-039a for variations in underframe and fittings.
BRHSG
British Railways 13 ton High Sided Open Goods Wagon with sheet support rail. Diagram 1/039
T.J.Mann
© 1982
WD 1-039 TM.
0 1 2 3 4 5 6 7 8 9 10
Scale in Feet
Section through door

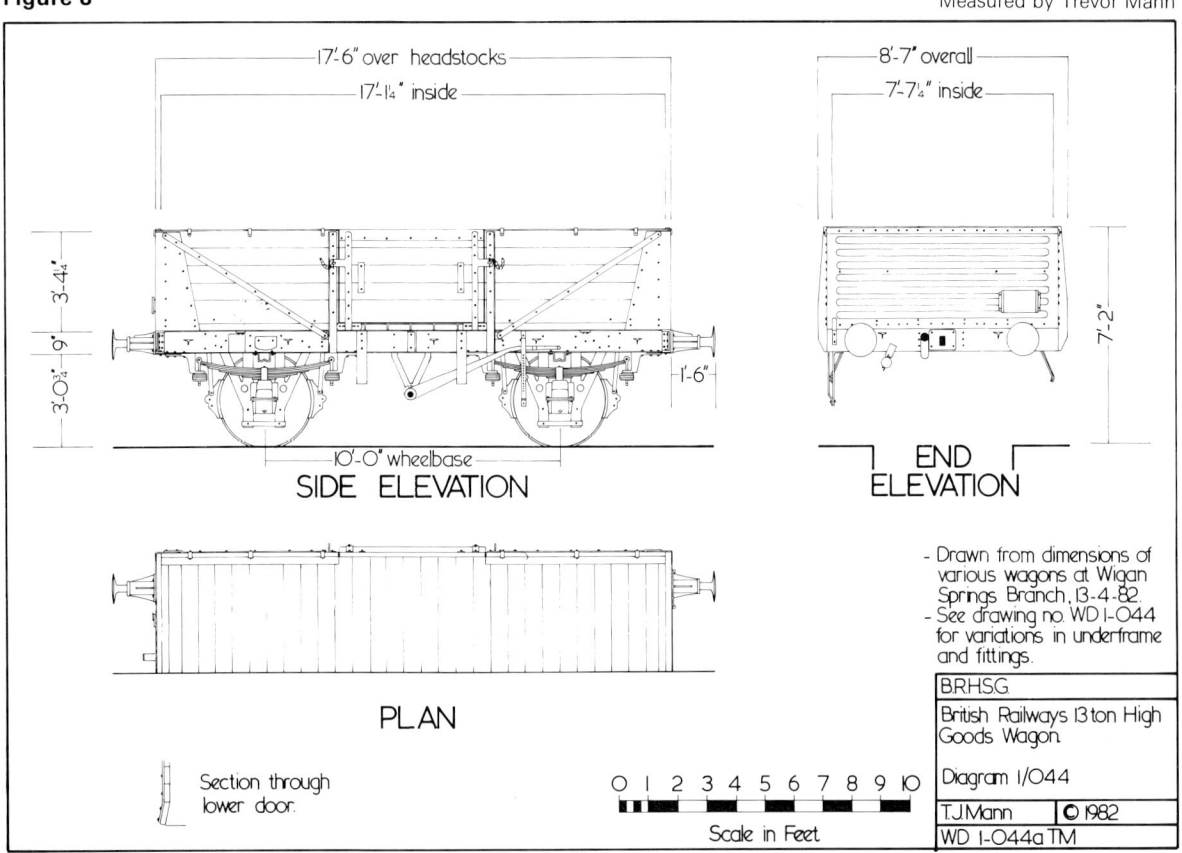

Plate 72 No. B494990, to Diagram 1/044, was built at Ashford in July 1952 as part of Lot 2409, and complies with official records, being unfitted. The LMS pattern body is painted light grey, with black patches for the lettering. The use of split spoke wheels should be noted.

D. Larkin Collection

Figure 8

Measured by Trevor Mann

17'-6" over headstocks
17'-1¼" inside

8'-7" overall
7'-7¼" inside

3'-4¼"
9"
3'-0¾"
1'-6"
7'-2"

10'-0" wheelbase

SIDE ELEVATION

END ELEVATION

PLAN

Section through lower door.

- Drawn from dimensions of various wagons at Wigan Springs Branch, 13-4-82.
- See drawing no. WD 1-044 for variations in underframe and fittings.

BRHSG

British Railways 13 ton High Goods Wagon.

Diagram 1/044

T.J.Mann   © 1982

WD 1-044a TM

0 1 2 3 4 5 6 7 8 9 10
Scale in Feet

The stability of design found in the LMS type 'High' was not mirrored by the other major type of 'High', the LNER design, which had all-steel bodies with wooden floors. This design was post-war in origin and its evolution continued during the BR period, up to 1955. The first variant were the wagons of the single Lot 2128 of Diagram No. 1/037 which had the LNER clasp brake, **(Plate 73 and Figure 9)**. Diagram No. 1/041 followed and it was identical to Diagram No. 1/037 except that it provided for the inclusion of unfitted wagons, and a variety of fitted brake riggings were used. All had the same body appearance except Lot 2341 which had a pair of vertical welded straps on the door.

Diagrams Nos. 1/047 and 1/049 **(see Figure 10 and Plates 74 & 75)** were for the remaining lots, which all had the new type of door, the ends of the floor planks showing beneath the sides and ends, and a corrugation low down on the side. Diagram No. 1/049 differs from Diagram 1/047 in having tarpaulin bars. Nos. B488505 and B488506, and perhaps others as a small batch, were galvanised and left unpainted with black number panels. The single wagon of Diagram No. 1/043 has the features of Diagram No. 1/047 except that the diagram does not show the extra strapping on the door. On the inside of these all-steel wagons there were rings for chaining down loads, their location being shown by the raised pockets on the sides. These wagons had the same brandings as the wood 'Highs', but were later distinguished by the TOPS code OHV.

Plate 73 The LNER parentage of the Diagram 1/037 steel-bodied High is obvious from this view of No. B475728 (Shildon 1950, 2128) pictured at Llandeilo Junction on 13th July 1978.

R. A. Silsbury

Figure 9

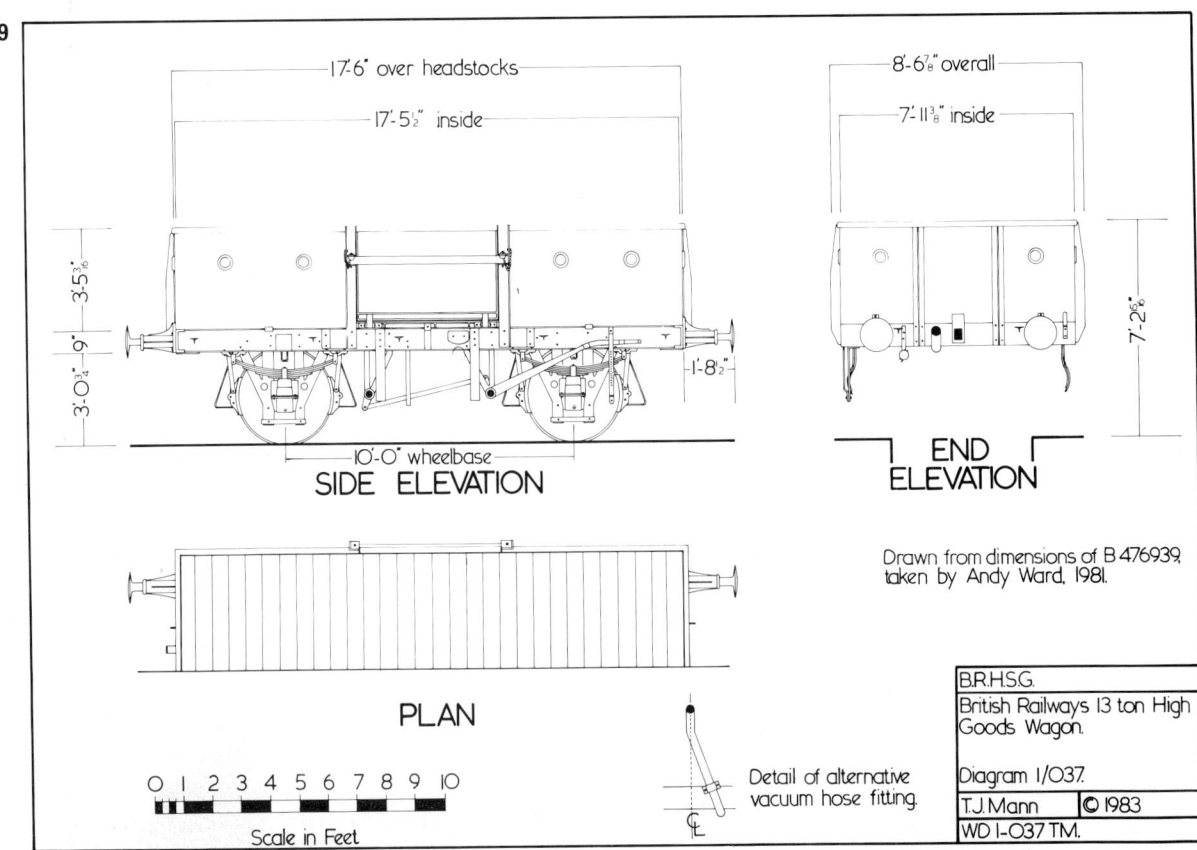

17'-6" over headstocks
17'-5½" inside
3'-5 3/16"
3'-0¼" 9"
10'-0" wheelbase
1'-8½"

SIDE ELEVATION

8'-6 7/8" overall
7'-11 3/8" inside
7'-2 5/8"

END ELEVATION

Drawn from dimensions of B.476939, taken by Andy Ward, 1981.

PLAN

0 1 2 3 4 5 6 7 8 9 10
Scale in Feet

Detail of alternative vacuum hose fitting.

B.R.H.S.G.
British Railways 13 ton High Goods Wagon.
Diagram 1/037.
T.J.Mann   © 1983
WD 1-037 TM.

Plates 74 & 75 Compared with the original LNER design, Diagrams 1/047 & 1/049 vehicles present an untidy appearance around the bottom of the body, which is fixed to the underframe by the side and end stanchions. Three end and two side brackets help to keep the body in position, whilst the half-round stiffener provided rigidity to the lower side. No. B496405 (Shildon 1955, 2479) is to Diagram 1/047 and was recorded at Cowley, Oxford, on 17th June 1980 **(Plate 74)**, whilst No. B495568 (Shildon 1955, 2704) is the Diagram 1/049 type with sheet support rail, seen at Fratton on 11th October 1979 **(Plate 75)**. Note the ends of lashing that had been used to tie down the wagon sheet. Both vehicles are in bauxite livery.

R. A. Silsbury

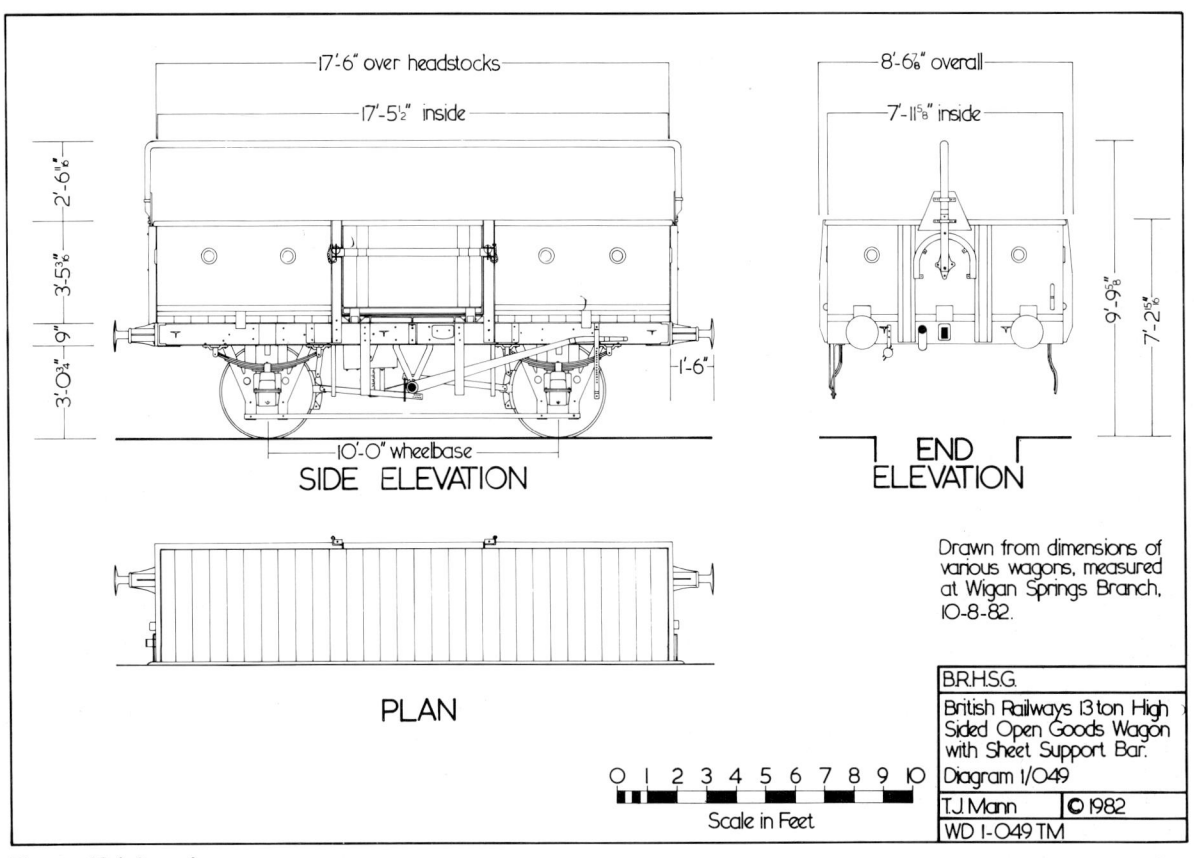

17'-6" over headstocks
17'-5½" inside
2'-6⅝"
3'-5⅜"
9"
3'-0¼"
10'-0" wheelbase
1'-6"

SIDE ELEVATION

8'-6⅞" overall
7'-11⅝" inside
9'-9⅝"
7'-2⅝"

END ELEVATION

Drawn from dimensions of various wagons, measured at Wigan Springs Branch, 10-8-82.

B.R.H.S.G.
British Railways 13 ton High Sided Open Goods Wagon with Sheet Support Bar.
Diagram 1/049
T.J. Mann   © 1982
WD 1-049 TM.

PLAN

0 1 2 3 4 5 6 7 8 9 10
Scale in Feet

Figure 10 (above)

Measured by Trevor Mann

Figure 11 (below)

17'-6" over headstocks
17'-5½" inside
3'-5⅜"
9"
3'-0¼"
10'-0" wheelbase
1'-8½"

SIDE ELEVATION

8'-6⅞" overall
7'-11⅝" inside
9'-8⅝"
7'-2⅝"

END ELEVATION

Drawn from dimensions of B 745577, taken at Wigan Springs Branch, 29-5-82, by Trevor & Audrey Mann.

B.R.H.S.G.
British Railways 13 ton Soda Ash Wagon.
Diagram 1/046
T.J. Mann   © 1983
WD 1-046 TM.

PLAN

0 1 2 3 4 5 6 7 8 9 10
Scale in Feet

Plate 76 Soda Ash 'High' No. B745543 to Lot 2369, recorded new at Shildon in October 1952. The wagon is in unfitted grey livery, only the number having a black patch. The brand, 3-link coupling and split-spoke wheels should be noted.

D. Larkin Collection

Soda Ash

The LNER design 'High' was also modified to carry soda ash. Initially unfitted and fitted wagons of Diagram No. 1/041 were converted, and later two lots were built new to Diagram No. 1/046 which were unfitted and similar to Diagram No. 1/041 **(see Table 5, Figure 11 and Plate 76)**. Later some BR-built vacuum-braked 'Highs' were similarly converted. They had a new door design with two horizontal straps on the door and four large wing nuts to close the door firmly. They also had a tarpaulin bar. They were lettered SODA ASH and DOORS TO BE LOWERED WITH CARE. Later, these wagons became part of the general merchandise fleet and the tarpaulin bars were removed.

TABLE 5

SODA ASH

Diag No.	Lot No.	Qnty	Builder	Year	Running numbers	Under-frame	Body type
1/046	2369	50	Shildon	1951	B745500 – 745549	Morton	LNER steel
1/046	2466	30	Shildon	1952	B745550 – 745579	Morton	LNER steel
	Total	80					

Dropsided High

An interesting 'High' drop-sided open merchandise wagon was built to part of Lot 2061. Originally ordered as three plank wagons to be numbered B457000 to B457099, this part of the order was altered to Diagram No. 1/033 **(see Table 4)** and they carried the earlier numbers until recalled for renumbering during 1954. They were built to an SR design, although that company never built any, and were delivered with double brakes **(see Figure 12 and Plate 77)**. Some were transferred to Engineer's use very early in their lives. Others were used into the early 1970s, at least, for 'Pipe' and 'Glass' traffic and were so lettered. Many were never vacuum-braked but persisted in Engineer's use into the 1980s, whilst others were converted to RCH vacuum brake. A few of these continued in revenue stock into the 1980s with the TOPS code OWV.

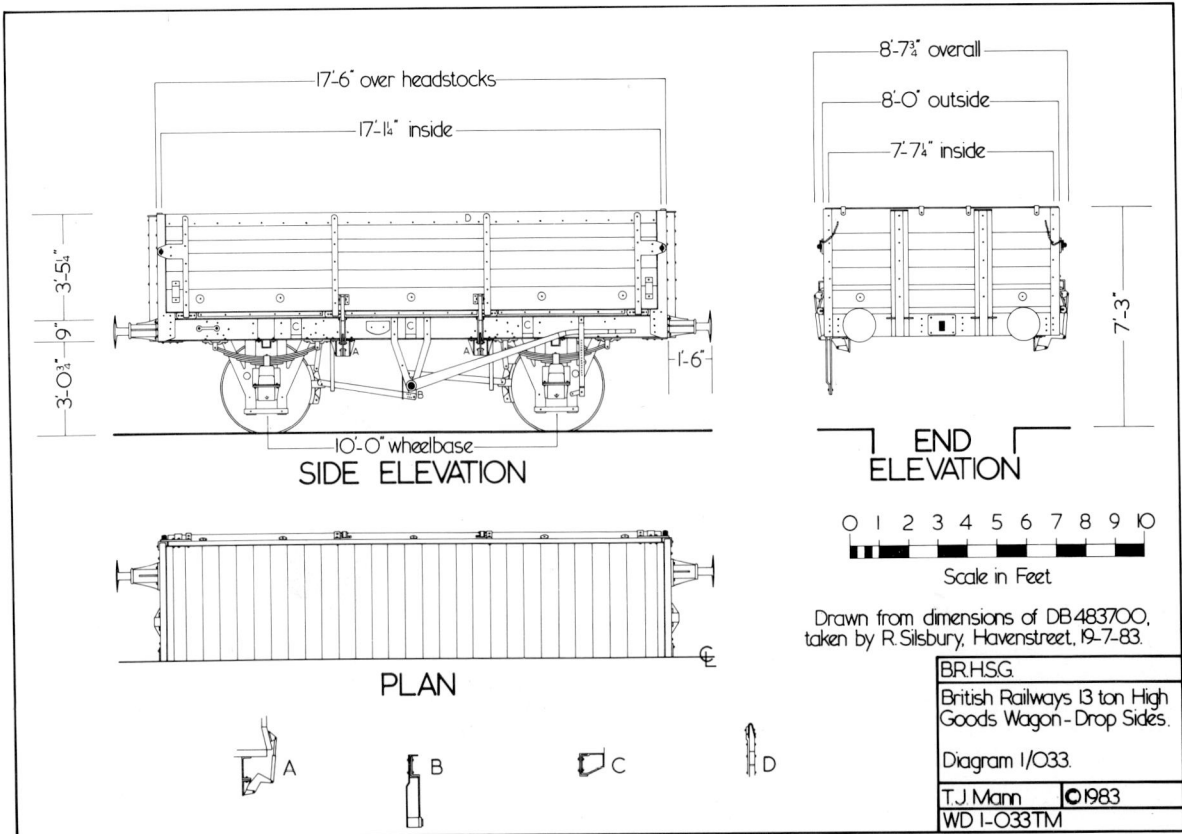

Plate 77 Some Diagram 1/033 vehicles were vacuum-braked during their lives, but No. DB483686 (Ashford 1949, 2061) survived unfitted in original condition apart from some body repairs and bauxite livery when caught by the camera at Barnetby Tip on 2nd May 1981. Compared with the 'Medium' version of Lot 2061 in **Plate 63**, it should be noted that the bottom side plank kicks outwards, necessitating different hinge straps; also two door springs are needed to take the extra weight of the five plank door.

R. A. Silsbury

Figure 12

17'-6" over headstocks

17'-1¼" inside

3'-0¼" 9" 3'-5¼"

10'-0" wheelbase

1'-6"

SIDE ELEVATION

8'-7¾" overall

8'-0" outside

7'-7¼" inside

7'-3"

END ELEVATION

0 1 2 3 4 5 6 7 8 9 10

Scale in Feet

Drawn from dimensions of DB483700, taken by R. Silsbury, Havenstreet, 19-7-83.

PLAN

A   B   C   D

B.R.H.S.G.

British Railways 13 ton High Goods Wagon - Drop Sides.

Diagram 1/033.

T.J. Mann   © 1983

WD 1-033TM

TABLE 6

AIR BRAKED OPENS

Design Code	Lot No.	Qnty	Builder	Year	Running numbers	Type of side & end
OA001A	3727	100	Ashford	1971	100000 - 100099	3 door pl. side, sheet steel end
OB001B	3861	(1)	Shildon	1974	450000 (110000)	4 door pl. side, high sheet st. end
OB001A	3909	500	Ashford	1977/8	110001 - 110500	4 door pl. side, high pl. end
OB001C	3930	300	Shildon	1979/80	110501 - 110800	4 door pl. side, high pl. end
OC001A	4014	400	Shildon	1981/2	112000 - 112399	4 door st. side, fixed st. end
Total		1300				

Air-Braked 'Opens'

The building of general purpose open merchandise wagons ceased in 1957 and was not resumed until 1971. A series of air-braked opens followed (see Table 6).

The first, Lot 3727, carried 31 tonnes and had the Type 1 underframe (see Chapter 2), which was 33ft. 6in. over headstocks with a wheelbase of 20ft. 9in. They had no vacuum brake fittings and were lettered 'OPEN AB'. The sides were six planks high and dropped as three doors with removable stanchions between. The ends were sheet steel, lined with wood, (see Figure 13 and Plate 78). These became TOPS code OAA and, from 1979, some were repainted with the upper two planks and all the end in 'Railfreight' red and the lower planks in 'Railfreight' grey.

The year 1974 saw the introduction of a prototype which had a new body built on the underframe from No. 100043. Originally numbered 450000, it soon became 110000. It had four drop doors and the original ends which had the addition of a drop down extension which was higher than the sides. Between each door were removable stanchions, which had a telescopic inner part, and which could be pulled upwards until it was the same height as the steel panelled ends (see Plate 79).

In 1977, production started of the similar 31 tonne OBAs, although dimensions differed. Each door was five plank, the end was permanently higher than the sides, and the underframe was of new design which had the same 20ft. 9in. wheelbase, but was extended to 34ft. 3½in. over headstocks. Internally they had six turnover bolsters.

In many respects these wagons would better be regarded as a modern 'Tube' wagon and the prototype was thus described on the diagram and was still identified as such in the 1977 part of Table 1.

The production batch was introduced in maroon and, by 1982, some had been repainted in the red and grey livery as described for the OAA. A seperate modification was respringing with Bruninghaus springs to allow 75m.p.h. running, and these springs were fitted new to some of Lot 3930, (see Plates 80 & 81). In 1982, many were transferred to the Engineer's fleet for the rapid carriage of spare parts, these being code-named 'BASS'. Repainting with 'Railfreight' yellow upper and 'Railfreight' grey lower sides and ends had also begun. This was the newly introduced livery for Engineer's wagons.

Another new design followed in 1981, the 31½ tonne OCAs (see Figure 14 and Plate 82). These were all-steel wagons on a newly designed underframe which had the same dimensions as the OBAs and all had Bruninghaus springs. The side had three drop doors with removable stanchions between. The fixed ends were of the same height as the sides and there were no extending stanchions. However, this design may also be considered as a steel carrier as the floor has six turnover bolsters. The wagon bodies were all in 'Railfreight' red. In early 1984 many were transferred to the Engineer's fleet and were code-named 'BASS'.

Plate 78 Originally Diagram 1/191, and now design code OA 001A, 100003 (Ashford 1971, 3727) retains original bauxite livery. Also visible are the BR double arrow symbol (partly obscured) and, to the right of the lettering box, a yellow disc with 'ABN' in black, indicating 'Air Brake Network', which was added early in the vehicle's life. When seen at Methil Docks on 18th August 1981, its load of paper required the use of a grey wagon sheet. *R. A. Silsbury*

Figure 13

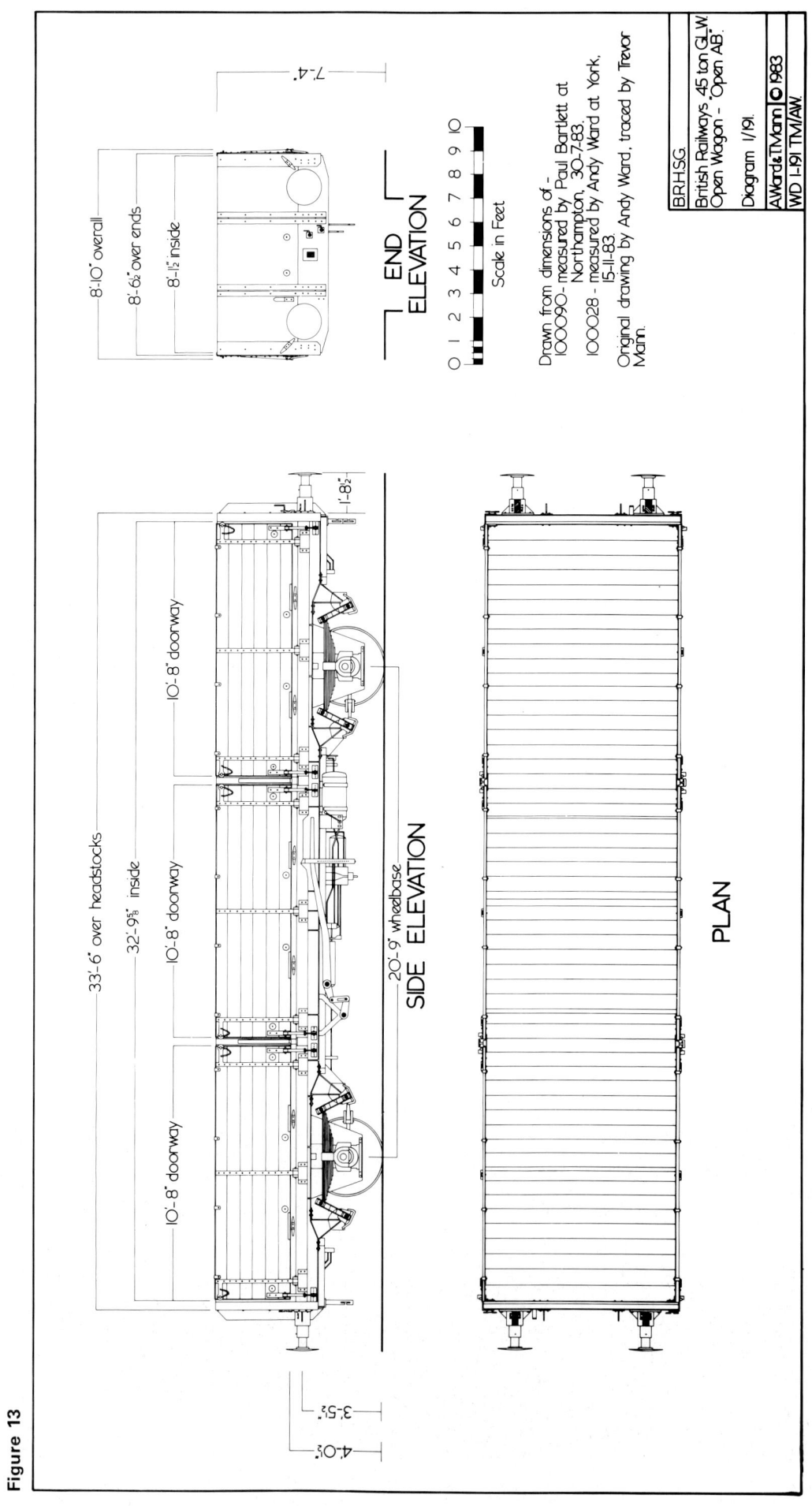

7'-4"

8'-10" overall

8'-6½" over ends

8'-1½" inside

END ELEVATION

Scale in Feet

0 1 2 3 4 5 6 7 8 9 10

Drawn from dimensions of –
100090 – measured by Paul Bartlett at
Northampton, 30-7-83.
100028 – measured by Andy Ward at York,
15-11-83.

Original drawing by Andy Ward, traced by Trevor Mann.

BRHSG

British Railways 45 ton G.L.W.
Open Wagon – "Open AB".

Diagram 1/191.

A.Ward & T.Mann © 1983
WD 1-91 TM/AW.

1'-8½"

10'-8" doorway

10'-8" doorway

10'-8" doorway

33'-6" over headstocks

32'-9⅝" inside

10'-8" doorway

20'-9" wheelbase

SIDE ELEVATION

PLAN

3'-5½"

4'-0½"

52

Plate 79 No. DC110000 was rebuilt from Open-AB No. 100043 at Shildon in 1974 to Lot 3861, as the prototype OBA. When seen at Millerhill in July 1984, it had entered the Engineer's fleet, and had been repainted in the new yellow and grey livery, with code name 'Bass', and was being used with production OBAs carrying new sleepers from Ditton. The drop-down arrangement of the upper part of the end is clearly visible.

P. W. Bartlett

Plate 80 This view of No. 110041 shows the original form of OBA, and is painted in maroon livery, as seen at Southampton on 2nd April 1979. Note the handles at the top of the telescopic stanchions between the doors.

R. A. Silsbury

Plate 81 The second batch of OBAs, to Lot 3930, featured Bruninghaus springs. This photograph of No. 110613 at Cowley, Oxford, on 17th June 1980, shows the opposite side of the underframe from that in **Plate 80**. Compare the different type of door stops fitted to Nos. 110613 and 110041; a further variation is a more solid round type.

R. A. Silsbury

Plate 82 The simple rugged lines of OCA No. 112260 (Shildon 1982, 4014) are shown to advantage in this view taken at Goole Docks in April 1982, when the wagon was nearly new. Livery is Railfreight red, and the similarity with the air-braked SPA Plate wagon **(Plate 164)** from which it derived, is noticeable.

P. W. Bartlett

Figure 14

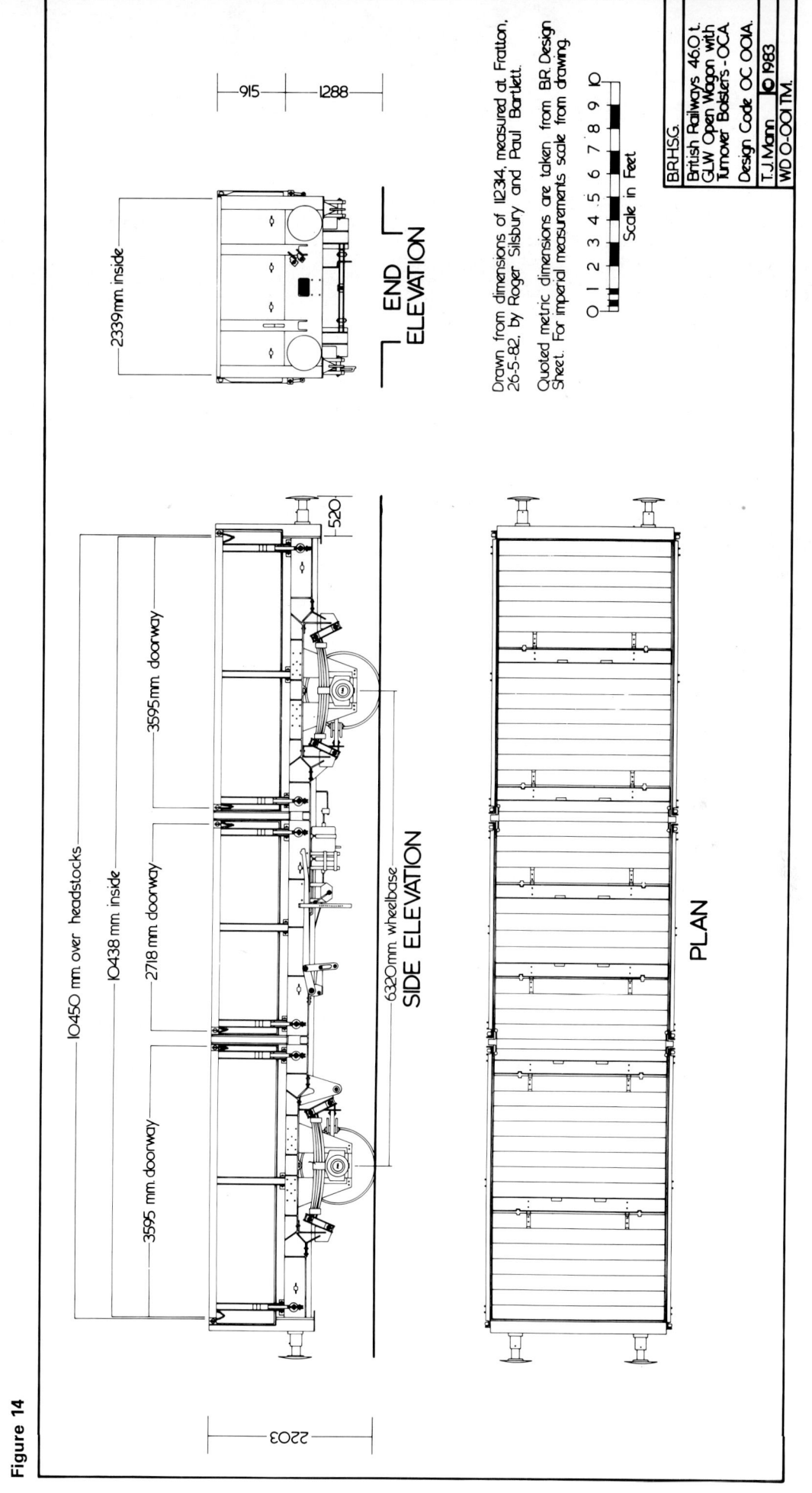

END ELEVATION

2339mm inside

915 | 1288

SIDE ELEVATION

10450 mm over headstocks

10438 mm inside

2718 mm doorway

3595mm doorway

3595 mm. doorway

6320mm wheelbase

520

2203

PLAN

Drawn from dimensions of 11234, measured at Fratton, 26-5-82, by Roger Silsbury and Paul Bartlett.

Quoted metric dimensions are taken from BR Design Sheet. For imperial measurements scale from drawing.

Scale in Feet

0 1 2 3 4 5 6 7 8 9 10

B.R.H.S.G.

British Railways 46.0 t. GLW Open Wagon with Turnover Bolsters - OCA.

Design Code OC OOIA.

T.J.Mann © 1983

WD O-OOITM.

Chapter 4
Specialist Open Merchandise Wagons

In addition to the general purpose open merchandise wagons **(see Chapter 3)** there was a variety of more specialised 'Opens'. Some were also reasonably general in the traffic which they carried, whilst others were very specialised. It would have been possible to have also included many of the steel carriers and 'specials' in this chapter, but BR deliberately put them into their separate categories.

Shock Opens

Shock-absorbing wagons were so called because they were designed to protect the goods from the buffeting that they normally receive during loose shunting. They do this by allowing the shortened body to move on the underframe. The backward and forward oscillations of the body are dampened by springs. **Table 7** gives the details of the 'Shock Opens'. Until the 'Shochood Bs' all the 'Shock Opens' were 17ft. 6in. over headstocks with a 10ft. wheelbase.

TABLE 7

SHOCK OPEN MERCHANDISE

Diag No.	Lot No.	Qnty	Builder	Year	Running numbers	Brake type	Body design
1/018	2152	25	Darlington	1950	B474800 – 474824	LNER clasp,	LMS Medium dropside
1/031	2031	50	Shildon	1949	B720000 – 720049	LNER clasp,	LNER all steel design
1/031	2032	200	Shildon	1949	B720050 – 720249	LNER clasp,	LNER all steel design
1/031	2033	175	Shildon	1949	B720250 – 720424	LNER clasp,	LNER all steel design
1/035	2154	500	Ashford	1950	B720425 – 720924	SR vacuum,	SR design
1/035	2155	300	Ashford	1950	B720925 – 721224	Double,	SR design
1/036	2156	100	Ashford	1950	B721225 – 721324	Double,	SR design highbar
1/040	2180	500	Derby	1951	B721325 – 721824	LMS clasp,	LMS highbar, corr. end
1/040	2317	600	Derby	1952	B721825 – 722424	RCH vacuum,	LMS highbar, wood & corr. ends
1/040	2416	850	Derby	1953/4	B722425 – 723274	RCH vacuum,	LMS highbar, corr. end
1/040	2546	250	Derby	1954	B723775 – 724024	RCH vacuum,	LMS highbar, corr. end
1/048	2445	250	Derby	1954	B723525 – 723774	RCH vacuum,	LMS highbar, corr. end
1/050	2650	250	Derby	1955/6	B723275 – 723524	RCH vacuum,	LMS corr. end
1/050	2776	400	Derby	1955/6	B724275 – 724674	RCH vacuum,	LMS highbar, corr. end
1/050	2839	299	Derby	1956	B724675 – 724973	RCH vacuum,	LMS corr. end
1/050	2983	300	Derby	1958	B724975 – 725274	RCH vacuum,	LMS corr. end
1/052	2705	250	Derby	1955	B724025 – 724274	RCH vacuum,	LMS highbar corr. end
1/056	3082	400	Derby	1958/9	B725275 – 725674	LMS clasp,	LMS highbar corr. end
1/056	3232	200	Derby	1958/9	B725675 – 725874	LM/BR clasp,	LMS highbar corr. end
1/056	3275	250	Derby	1958/9	B725875 – 726124	BR clasp,	LMS highbar corr. end
1/057	3383	100	Derby	1962	B726125 – 726224	LMS clasp,	Shocroof A
1/058	3429	300	Derby	1962/3	B726225 – 726524	BR clasp,	Shocroof B
	Total	6549					

Medium Shocks

No shock equivalent of the 'Lows' was built and there was only a single batch of 'Medium Shocks'. These 13 ton-rated wagons of Diagram No. 1/018 were to an LMS body design with a dropside and fixed end. The 25 built to Lot 2152 joined the 6 built in 1949 to an LMS order for carrying glass traffic from St. Helens. All were originally fitted with cradles in which the sheet glass was loaded. The BR batch was clearly distinguishable from the earlier LMS wagons as it was built at Darlington with the LNER design of clasp vacuum brake **(see Plate 83)**.

Plate 83 In contrast to the Diagram 1/001 Lowfits **(Plate 60)** which combined an LNER body with an LMS underframe, the Diagram 1/108 Medium Shock wagons reversed the order. No. B474806 (Darlington 1950, 2152) photographed at St. Helens in August 1970, displays these features, as well as an abundance of lettering. The yellow circuit disc points to the route instructions behind the label clip, although the earlier 'Empty to St. Helens, LMR' brand still remains. Note also that tare weights with and without glass cradles are given.

D. Larkin

High Shocks

Three companies, the GWR, LMS and SR had produced shock-absorbing versions of their five plank open merchandise wagons. The first BR designs were all rated to carry 13 tons.

The first which BR introduced were based upon LNER practice and may have been ordered by that company. They had all-steel bodies with LNER clasp brake underframes and were allocated Diagram No. 1/031 **(see Figure 15 and Plate 84)**. The all-steel body allowed them to be longer than the later builds, being of 16ft. 5½ in. inside length. They were branded in a similar way to the wooden-bodied 'Shock Opens' except that no TOPS codes were carried as these wagons were withdrawn from revenue use during the early 1970s, when many were passed to the Engineer's Department. After these no more all-steel shock opens were built.

The next Diagram, No. 1/035, was an SR design with five planked sides and ends. Two lots were built, the first being vacuum-braked, using the SR brake arrangement **(Plate 85)**, and the second was originally unfitted. Later these were vacuum-fitted with the RCH brake arrangement. The ends had 'U' shaped vertical stanchions. Diagram No. 1/036 was identical to No. 1/035 except that a tarpaulin bar was fitted, and the end stanchions were 'T' shaped **(see FWLGW, Figure 36)**. Originally unfitted, these were also vacuum-braked later. All were of 16ft. 1¼ in. inside length. Neither of the SR designs were fitted with Duplex buffers.

The next Diagram, No. 1/040, was an LMS design with an inside length of only 15ft. 8in. Four batches were built and the first had an LMS clasp brake underframe but the brake lever was of full length to avoid fouling the external shock absorber **(see Plates 86 & 87)**; the others had RCH underframes. Although

corrugated-steel ends were standard, part of Lot 2317 (Nos. B721825 to 722102, at least, but not higher than No. B722124) had planked ends. These were similar to wartime-built LMS plank-ended open merchandise wagons. Steel shortages made their building necessary. Diagram No. 1/040 had a tarpaulin bar and Diagram No. 1/048 was identical except that no tarpaulin bar was fitted. Diagram No. 1/050 appears to be identical to No. 1/048 except that the nominal tare of No. 1/050 was 7 tons 18cwt. **(Plate 88)** in comparison with 8 tons 1cwt. of No. 1/048 and rated to carry 12 tons. All had RCH underframes and many later received tarpaulin bars. Diagram No. 1/052 was identical to No. 1/050, except for the fitting of tarpaulin bars from new.

The same body design was continued with Diagram No. 1/056, also rated for 12 tons, except for a nominal change in floor height which meant ⅜in. was lost in internal height; externally the height remained the same. The underframe, however, did have some new features. Lot 3082 had the most differences as the external solebar-mounted shock-absorbing springs were removed to the centre line of the wagon **(see Plate 89)**. This may have been because accidents had been caused to staff by the external springs. This lot had an LMS clasp brake underframe without rubber auxiliary suspension but with a short hand lever. Lots 3232 and 3275 had the usual solebar-mounted shock-absorbing springs; Lot 3232 had LMS clasp brake without auxiliary rubber suspension and with a full length brake lever, and the final lot had a BR clasp underframe. All of Diagram No. 1/056 had tarpaulin bars **(Figure 16)**.

The 'Shock Opens' were taken out of general use by 1978 and few carried the TOPS code OSV. Other lettering varied, and SHOCK, SHOCHIGH and SHOCBAR were common. After the mid-1970s, the Engineers used many of them for carrying spoil.

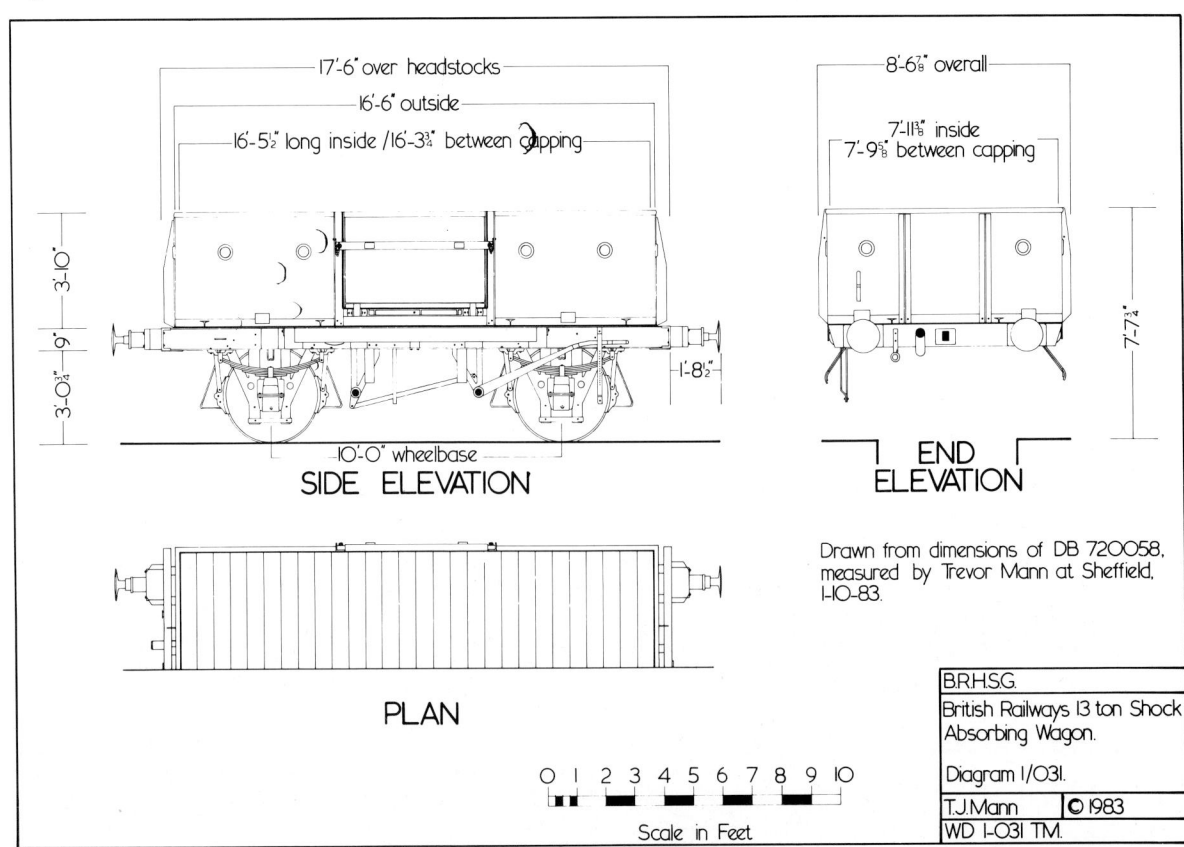

Plate 84 The LNER origin of Diagram 1/031, here represented by No. DB720202 (Shildon 1949, 2032) is clearly illustrated in this view taken at Barnetby Tip on 2nd May 1981. Some repairs have been carried out to the body, which retains most of its bauxite traffic livery, including post-1964 style short wide shock stripes.

R. A. Silsbury

Figure 15

17'-6" over headstocks
16'-6" outside
16'-5½" long inside /16'-3¾" between capping

8'-6⅞" overall
7'-11⅜" inside
7'-9⅝" between capping

3'-10"
3'-0¾"
9"

7'-7½"

10'-0" wheelbase

1'-8½"

SIDE ELEVATION

END ELEVATION

Drawn from dimensions of DB 720058, measured by Trevor Mann at Sheffield, 1-10-83.

PLAN

0 1 2 3 4 5 6 7 8 9 10
Scale in Feet

B.R.H.S.G.	
British Railways 13 ton Shock Absorbing Wagon.	
Diagram 1/031.	
T.J.Mann	© 1983
WD 1-031 TM.	

Plate 85 No. ADB720856 (Ashford 1950, 2154) had passed to the CM&EE Power Supply Section, and had been repainted in Olive livery when recorded at Fratton on 26th February 1979. The all wooden body, exposed floor plank ends, and distinctive stiffeners below the door, as well as the SR pattern vacuum brakegear, are all highlighted by the low winter sun. *R. A. Silsbury*

Plate 86 No. B721326 is a Diagram 1/040 vehicle with an LMS clasp vacuum brake, built at Derby in 1951 to Lot 2180, and photographed when new. The shock absorbing springs are unprotected; later all shock wagons had a fashion plate covering the springs. The livery style should be noted; the brand reads 'Empty to East Usk Branch, Newport, W.R.' Many shock opens had brandings, when new. *D. Larkin Collection*

Plate 87 No. B721385 is also a Diagram 1/040 vehicle built to Lot 2180 at Derby, but differs in having LMS clasp vacuum brakegear without auxiliary suspension. The difference in length between the body and underframe is very evident. Note the legend 'Battens' below the number to indicate that transverse battens have been fitted to the floor to assist handling loads. It is pictured at Fareham in March 1974.

R. A. Silsbury

Plate 88 The RCH vacuum brake underframe features under No. B723326 (Derby 1955, 2650) to Diagram 1/050. When seen at Fratton on 11th December 1975, it was carrying a large crate destined for the Royal Navy.

R. A. Silsbury

SHOC-BAR
12T
D B725342
XP
10'0"

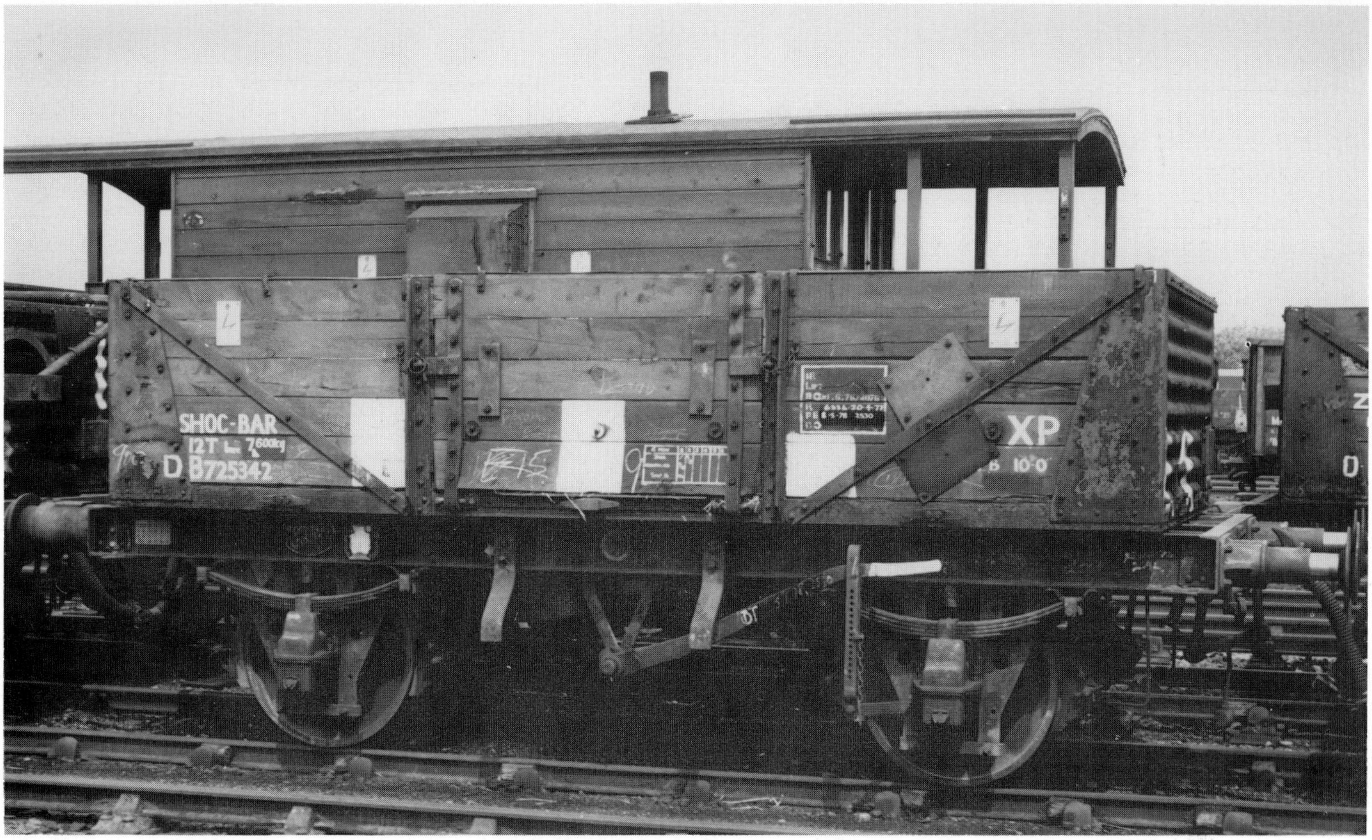

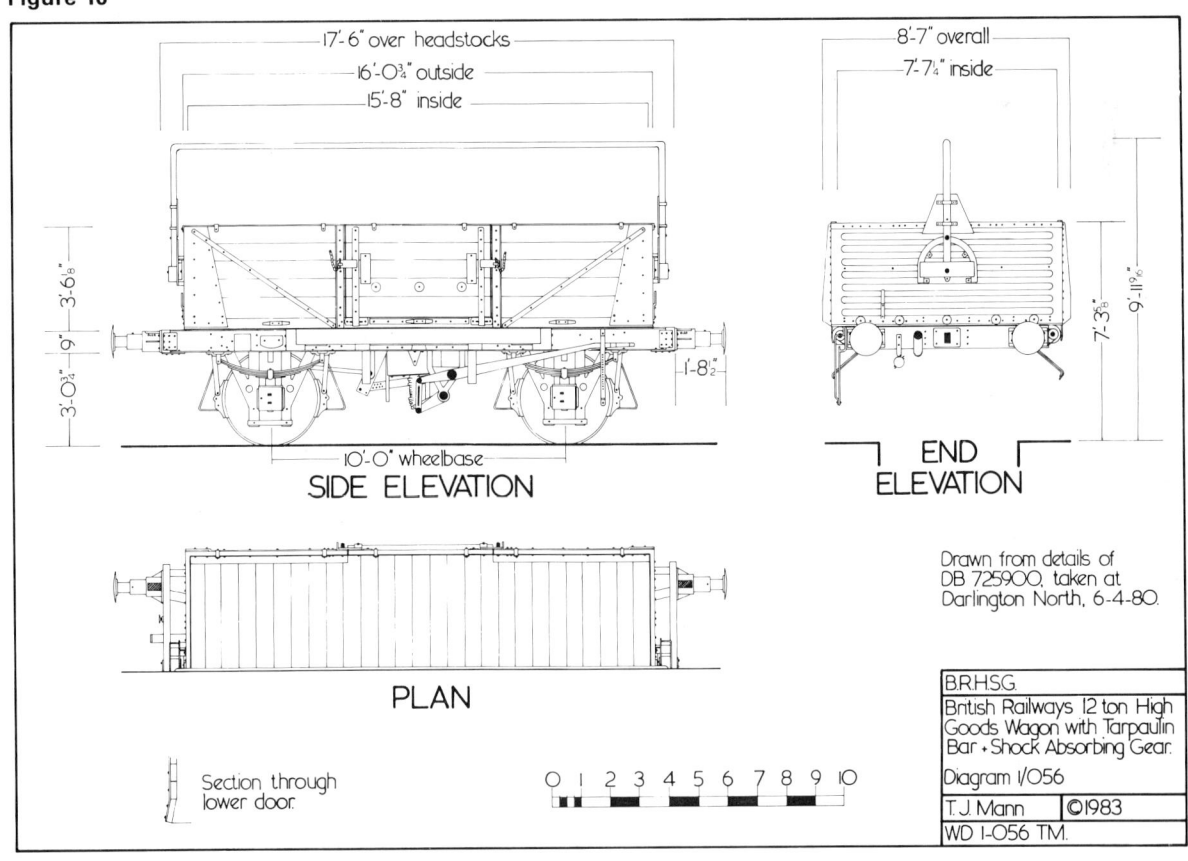

Plate 89 Recently transferred to the Engineers, No. DB725342 is a Diagram 1/056 vehicle, built at Derby in 1958, to Lot 3082. The shock-absorbing springs are mounted near the centre line of the underframe, permitting use of a short brake lever, and LMS clasp vacuum brakegear without the auxiliary suspension. The original pneumatic buffers at the right-hand end have been replaced by later pattern Oleo type, and the tarpaulin bar had been removed when recorded at Wellingborough on 11th June 1978. **Figure 16** shows a Diagram 1/056 vehicle with externally-mounted shock springs, and the BR clasp vacuum brake, measured by Trevor Mann.

R. A. Silsbury

Figure 16

17'-6" over headstocks
16'-0¾" outside
15'-8" inside
3'-6⅛"
9"
3'-0¼"
1'-8½"
10'-0" wheelbase
SIDE ELEVATION
8'-7" overall
7'-7¼" inside
7'-3⅝"
9'-11⁹⁄₁₆"
END ELEVATION
PLAN
Drawn from details of DB 725900, taken at Darlington North, 6-4-80.
Section through lower door.
0 1 2 3 4 5 6 7 8 9 10
B.R.H.S.G.
British Railways 12 ton High Goods Wagon with Tarpaulin Bar + Shock Absorbing Gear.
Diagram 1/056
T.J. Mann
©1983
WD 1-056 TM.

Shocroof A and Shochood B

The next Diagram, No. 1/057, retained an underframe of 17ft. 6in. over headstocks and a 10ft. wheelbase **(see Plate 90)**. It had a LMS clasp brake, without rubber auxiliary suspension, and had a short brake lever and roller bearings. The body was of a new design which was developed from prototypes fitted to No. B494175, which did not have shock fittings or partitions, and No. B722090 which had both and was branded 'Shocroof A'. The sides were steel panels without doors and the ends were the conventional corrugated-steel type. At one end there was a large open-ended box into which a flat roof was wound, using a hand-wheel on the side. This was a MacGregor folding panel roof. Internally, the floor had five battens and the sides had 39 guides down each for timber partitions. These modifications increased the tare to 9 tons 10cwt. and decreased the capacity to 12 tons. One use of these wagons was between Gartcosh and Birmingham for Colcrest. They were branded 'Shocroof A' and later the TOPS code was OVV. All were condemned by 1979 and no further wagons of this design were built.

The last of the 'Shock Opens', the 'Shochood B' of Diagram No. 1/058, also broke new design ground. Originally rated as 20 tons, they were uprated to carry 22 tons. They had some similarities to the 'Shocroof As', as the sides were steel-panelled without doors and internally there were floor battens and 49 guides down the sides. However, they were 21ft. 6in. over headstocks, had a 12ft. wheelbase, and an internal length of 18ft. 4½in. **(see Figure 17)**. Instead of the folding roof they had a nylon hood supported by three tarpaulin bars; some of the earlier LMS style 'Shock Opens' had a similar hood conversion. All of these wagons were allocated to the Western Region for metals traffic, from South Wales **(see Plate 91)**. Forty five were converted to 'Coil L' in 1971, for use in Scotland. In 1981 many were converted for Engineer's use by losing their shock absorbers and hood. These were code-named DACE. Unconverted 'Shochood Bs' continued in use and are TOPS code OUV. From March 1985 air pipes were fitted to these wagons at New Cross Gate; they received the new TOPS code SUW.

Shock Liveries

All of the 'Shock Opens' had a distinguishing livery of three stripes on both the sides and ends. Early on, the end stripes were arranged with one on the centre line and two to the left-hand side. By about 1950, this had altered to being equally spaced across the end. In more recent years the stripes were sometimes broader, and only on the lower half of the end. These stripes were repeated on the door. On the early unpainted livery for unfitted wagons there was an application problem with these stripes. LMS series BR-built wagons lacked end stripes and the side stripes were outlined in black **(see LMS Wagons 1, Plate 320)**. Later, unfitted wagons were painted grey **(see FWLGW, Figure 36)**.

Plate 90 It is unfortunate that a container, which might be confused as part of the wagon, is visible over Shocroof A, No. B726172 (Derby 1962, 3383). Because of the comprehensive instructions for operating the roof, the number, code and brand are unusally placed at the right-hand end of the body. The photograph was taken at Derby in January 1962.

D. Larkin Collection

Figure 17

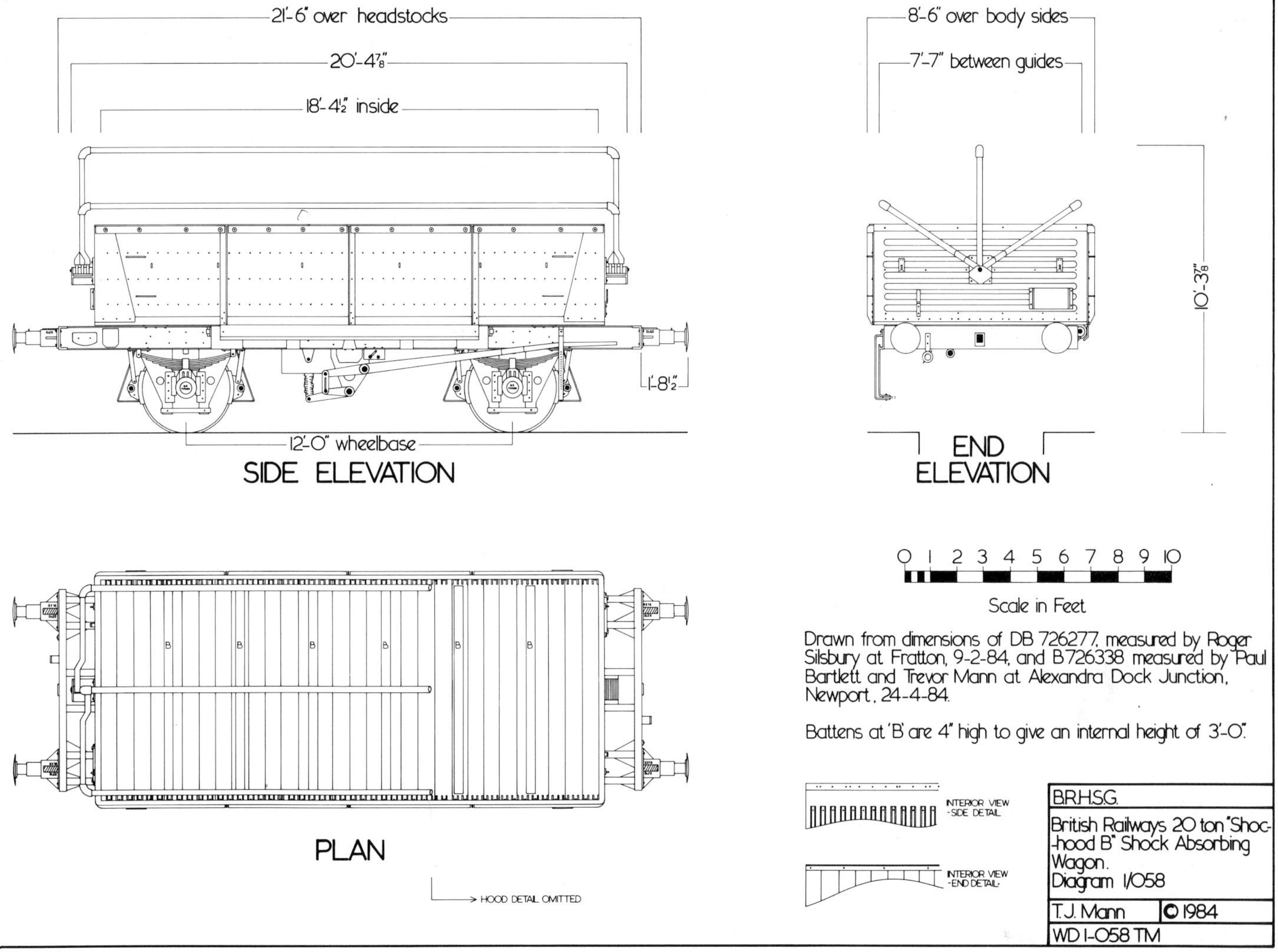

21'-6" over headstocks
20'-4⅞"
18'-4½" inside
1'-8½"
12'-0" wheelbase
SIDE ELEVATION
8'-6" over body sides
7'-7" between guides
10'-3⅜"
END ELEVATION
0 1 2 3 4 5 6 7 8 9 10
Scale in Feet
Drawn from dimensions of DB 726277, measured by Roger Silsbury at Fratton, 9-2-84, and B726338 measured by Paul Bartlett and Trevor Mann at Alexandra Dock Junction, Newport, 24-4-84.
Battens at 'B' are 4" high to give an internal height of 3'-0".
PLAN
HOOD DETAIL OMITTED
INTERIOR VIEW -SIDE DETAIL
INTERIOR VIEW -END DETAIL-
B.R.H.S.G.
British Railways 20 ton "Shoc-hood B" Shock Absorbing Wagon.
Diagram 1/058
T.J. Mann
© 1984
WD 1-058 TM

Plate 91 Compared to the adjacent vehicles, and photographed at Margam on 13th October 1981, Shochood B, No. B726272 (Derby 1962, 3429) retains its original Dowty hydraulic buffers. Because the nylon hood is a permanent part of the wagon, it is held in place by snap-clips fitting on eyes on the wagon side. The first 40 and last 60 Shochood Bs were branded 'Empty to Newport (Mon) W.R.', the other 200 'Empty to Port Talbot W.R.', and all originally had 'Western Region' below the number. *R. A. Silsbury*

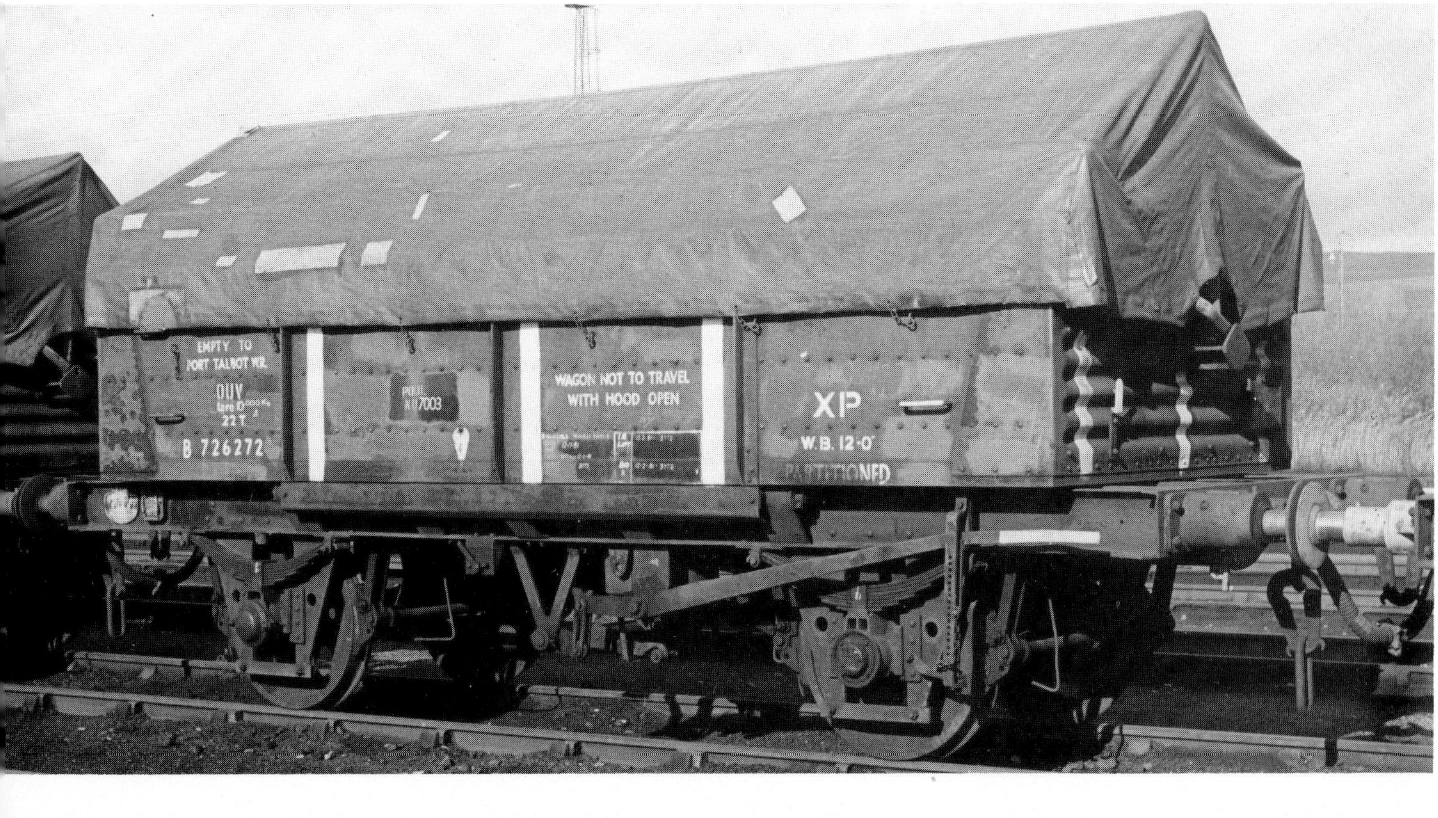

EMPTY TO
PORT TALBOT W.R.
B 726272
WAGON NOT TO TRAVEL
WITH HOOD OPEN
XP
W.B. 12-0

China Clay

Of the pre-nationalisation companies, only the GWR had had specialised 'China Clay' wagons. Together with the similar ex-privately-owned, wagons, BR had sufficient of these wagons until 1954, when Diagram No. 1/051 was introduced. They were built up to 1960, carried 13 tons, and were unusually short being only 16ft. over headstocks with a 9ft. wheelbase. The body was five planks high with a drop door in the side and a top-hinged door in one end. The floor was unusual in that it was longitudinally-planked to assist the clay to slide to the end during unloading **(see Figure 18, Plate 92 and Table 8)**. Lot 2590 was built unfitted with the double brake, and vacuum-braked later. The other lots were all vacuum-braked from new. GWR self-contained buffers were standard.

Later, 700 of these wagons were converted to CLAY HOODS. These had blue nylon covers which had the English China Clay Company symbol on them. This hood was supported on a fixed tarpaulin bar and Diagram No. 1/013 was allocated to these. These wagons were lettered 'FOR BALL CLAY ONLY' and worked to Fowey Docks.

The unmodified wagons worked in block train workings for long distances, in particular to Stoke, Aberdeen and Rochester. The TOPS code for all 'China Clays' was UCV, which was altered to OOV from late 1983. Very few of these wagons were withdrawn before 1982 but, from then, specialist privately-owned wagons began to replace them. The livery was the standard grey or bauxite, and the diagonal strapping at the door end was painted white.

TABLE 8

CHINA CLAY

Diag No.	Lot No.	Qnty	Builder	Year	Running numbers	Brake type
1/051	2590	100	Swindon	1954	B743000 - 743099	Double
1/051	2697	100	Swindon	1955	B743100 - 743199	RCH vacuum
1/051	2871	100	Swindon	1956	B743200 - 743299	RCH vacuum
1/051	2974	100	Swindon	1957	B743300 - 743399	RCH vacuum
1/051	3098	175	Swindon	1958/9	B743400 - 743574	RCH vacuum
1/051	3195	100	Swindon	1959	B743575 - 743674	RCH vacuum
1/051	3296	200	Swindon	1960	B743675 - 743874	RCH vacuum
	Total	875				

Figure 18

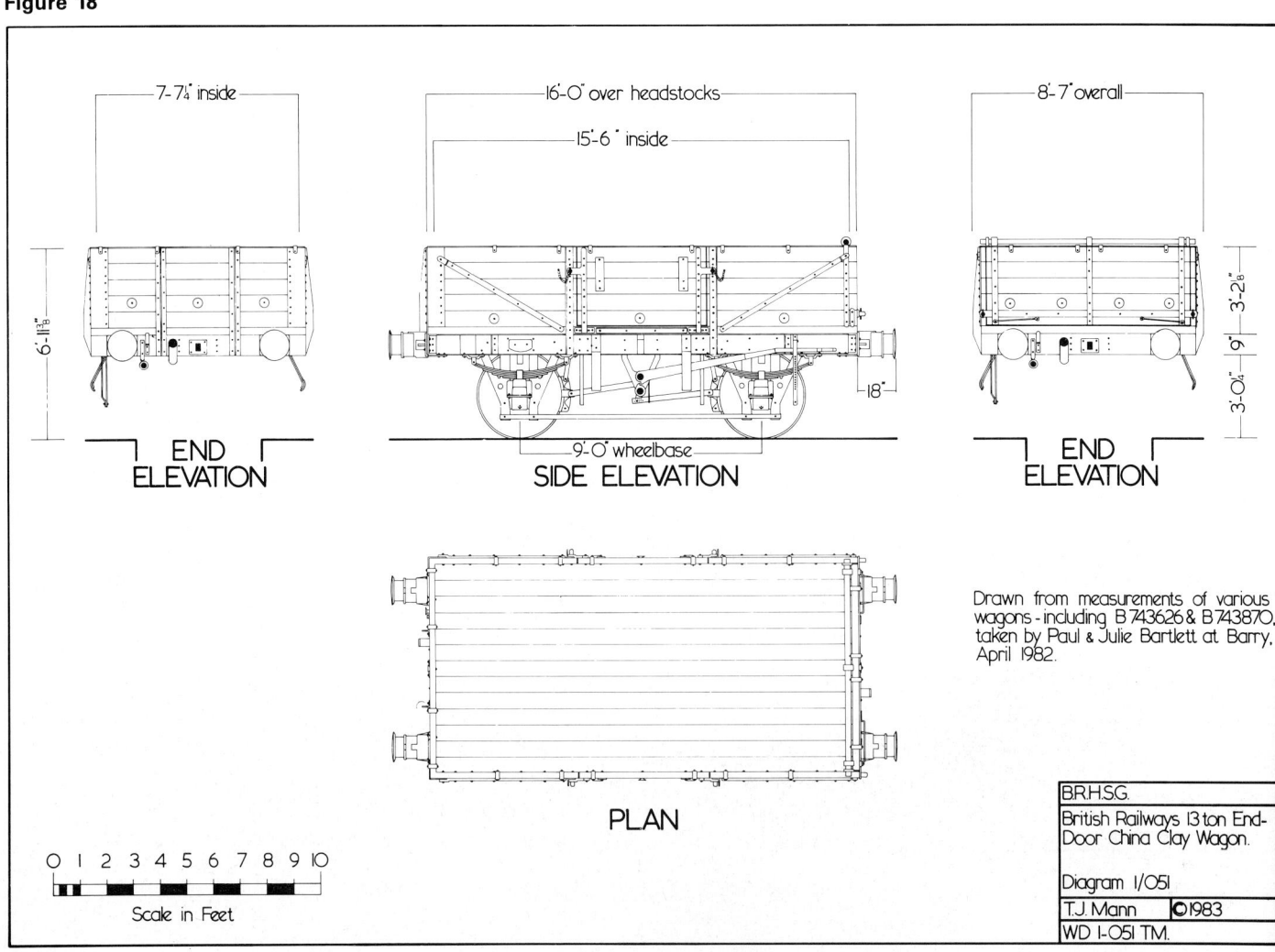

END ELEVATION   SIDE ELEVATION   END ELEVATION

PLAN

7-7¼" inside — 16-0" over headstocks — 15-6" inside — 8-7" overall — 6-11⅜" — 9-0" wheelbase — 18" — 3-0¼" — 9" — 3-2⅞"

0 1 2 3 4 5 6 7 8 9 10
Scale in Feet

Drawn from measurements of various wagons - including B743626 & B743870, taken by Paul & Julie Bartlett at Barry, April 1982.

B.R.H.S.G.
British Railways 13 ton End-Door China Clay Wagon.
Diagram 1/051
T.J. Mann   ©1983
WD 1-051 TM.

Plate 92 Liberally dusted with remains of its load, this view of China Clay Open No. B743285 (Swindon 1956, 2871) at Plymouth Friary on 5th March 1977, shows the end door arrangement. Just visible on the top plank to the left of the side door is the brand 'For China Clay Only'. Many of these vehicles also often carried a 'Return to . . .' brand.

R. A. Silsbury

Sand Wagons

This was a new design introduced in 1951. These wagons had low all-steel bodies and floors, which meant they were well sealed to carry 13 tons of sand **(see Table 9)**. Diagram Nos. 1/071 and 1/072 varied solely in having a ½ in. difference in the buffer centres. They had Morton unfitted underframes with a 9ft. wheelbase, and later, many, but not all, were converted to vacuum brake **(see Figure 19 and Plate 93)**. The later Diagram No. 1/073 had the same body but had a BR clasp brake fitted underframe with a 10ft. wheelbase.

These wagons were normally branded SAND, but only a few remained to receive the TOPS code USV, as most were transferred to the Engineer's fleet, who had had some of them from the mid-1960s. 'Empty to' brandings were common, Congleton and Leighton Buzzard being usual.

In 1974, a total of 150 of a new design of 'Sand' wagon was built at Standard Wagon, Reddish. They had a new welded body built on second-hand 15ft. wheelbase underframes from Esso tank wagons which were built originally about 1959 **(see Plate 94)**. These wagons were TOPS-coded MTV from new and, although they did not have a code name, some were branded MTV-SAND and others had a STONE symbol. As well as sand they carry aggregates and limestone. Later privately-owned wagons of a similar design were introduced.

TABLE 9

SAND OPENS

Diag No.	Lot No.	Qnty	Builder	Year	Running numbers	Brake type
1/071	2157	500	Ashford	1950	B746000 - 746499	Morton
1/072	2267	250	Swindon	1951	B746500 - 746749	Morton
1/073	2986	100	Derby	1957/8	B746750 - 746849	BR clasp
1/193	3859	150	Standard	1974/5	B390000 - 390149	secondhand clasp
Total		1000				

SAND
KDB 746479
CHOLSEY
SHRIVENHAM

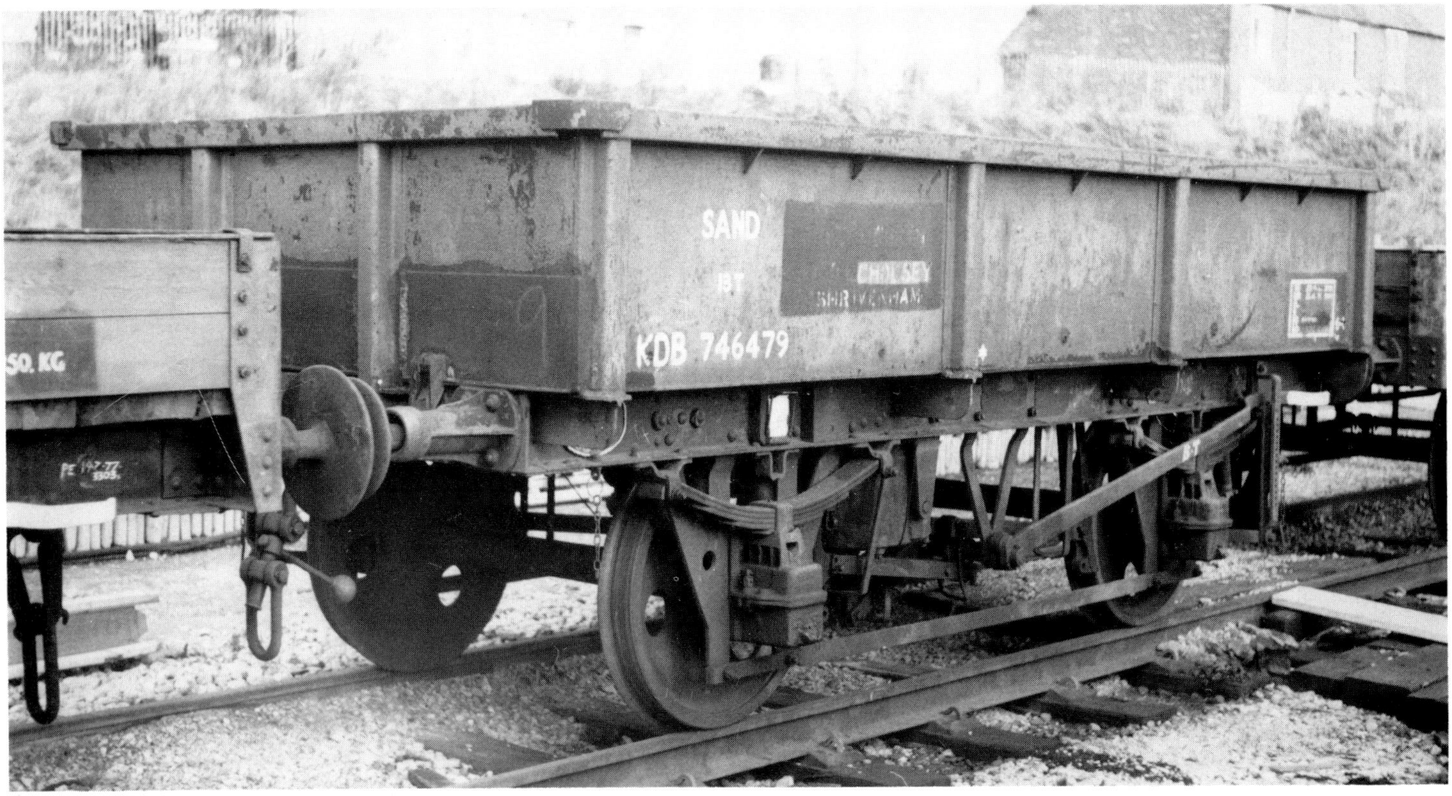

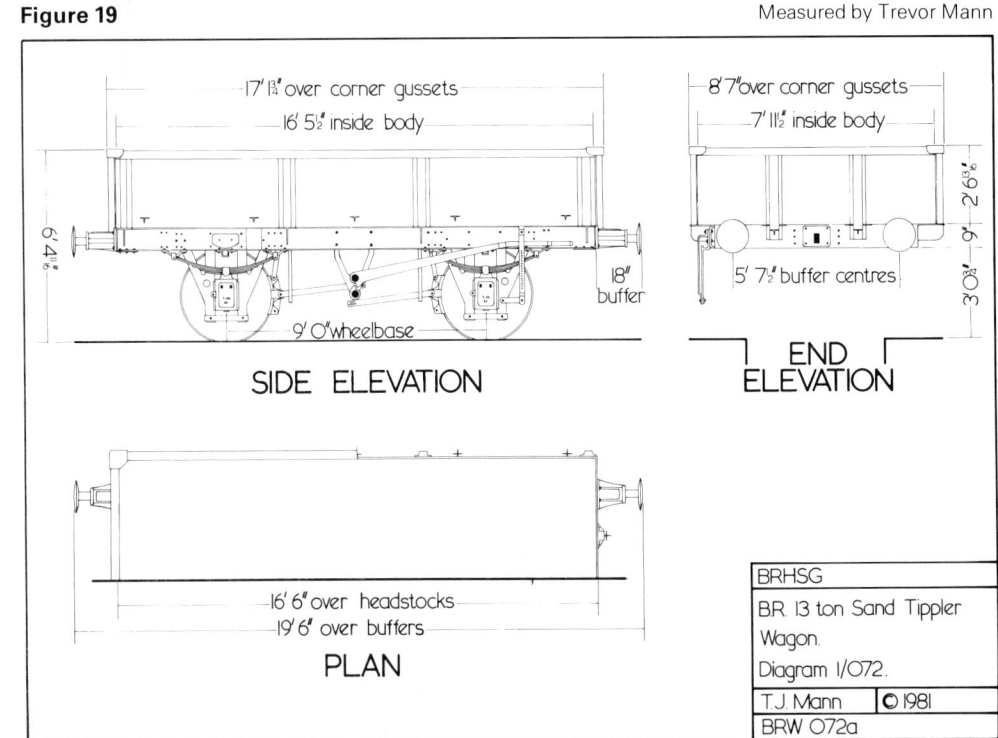

Plate 93 Having carried the brand 'Empty to Leighton Buzzard; LMR' when new, No. KDB746479 (Ashford 1950, 2157) to Diagram 1/071, has also been directed to Cholsey, and Shrivenham at different stages in its career. Here it rests at Newbury on 24th November 1977 between duties for the S&T Engineer.

R. A. Silsbury

Figure 19 Measured by Trevor Mann

17' 1¾" over corner gussets
16' 5½" inside body
6' 4⅞"
18" buffer
9' 0" wheelbase
SIDE ELEVATION
8' 7" over corner gussets
7' 11½" inside body
2' 6¹³⁄₁₆"
9"
3' 0¾"
5' 7½" buffer centres
END ELEVATION
16' 6" over headstocks
19' 6" over buffers
PLAN
BRHSG
BR 13 ton Sand Tippler Wagon.
Diagram 1/072.
T.J. Mann
© 1981
BRW 072a

Plate 94 No. B390098, rebuilt by Standard Wagon in 1975, under Lot 3859, utilises a second-hand tank wagon underframe and new body, and its simple rugged lines can be clearly seen when recorded at South Lambeth on 19th April 1980. The livery is bauxite, and the TOPS pool number, 7613, is prominently displayed as these wagons normally worked in block formations on regular circuits.
R. A. Silsbury

Plate 95 The three experimental brick wagons built to Diagram 1/038 were rarely photographed. Luckily No. B748502 was recorded at Bordesley Junction during August 1963. The brand reads 'Experimental Brick/Wagon/Return to/Millbrook, LMR.'; Millbrook being in the heart of the brick industry on the ex-LNWR line between Bedford and Bletchley.
E. Gent

Brick and Palbrick Wagons

Apart from the LNER 'Bogie Brick' wagons and 'H' containers, BR did not inherit any specialist brick-carrying wagons; they were simply packed in straw in 'Open Merchandise' wagons. The building of 'H' containers continued, and later 'Shock Opens' were commonly used for brick traffic.

In 1950, three experimental wagons were introduced for bricks **(see Table 10)**. These were allocated Diagram No. 1/038 and were 17ft. 6in. over headstocks with a 10ft. wheelbase. Initially they had Morton unfitted underframes, which were later converted to vacuum brake. The bodies had an internal length of 17ft. 10in. so they overhung the ends. The ends were fixed-steel and the sides were a pair of drop doors which allowed easy access. The design was not a success and the wagons were passed to the Engineer's Department, who condemned the last towards the end of 1981 **(see Plate 95)**.

Palbricks

In the mid-1950s, redundant 'Medfits' were converted to a new design, the 'Palbricks' and very similar newly-built 'Palbricks' followed. The sides were a pair of plywood panels which slid downwards into grooves in the ends and into a removable central stanchion. Each panel had a pair of strengthened rectangular cut-outs so that they could be lifted out by using a fork-lift truck. One end was planked and supported by four steel buttresses, and the other end had a top rail and a pair of cross-wise steel channels through which some large screws passed. These pushed another pair of cross-wise steel channels on to the palletised bricks to hold them firmly in place. This end was also supported by four buttresses and was partly open.

Seven diagrams were issued for 'Palbricks'. All had wheelbases of 10ft. and vacuum-braked underframes. **Table 10** gives the minimum interior length and width; 'As', 'Bs' and 'Cs' varied in these, each being designed as suitable for a popular pallet size used by the manufacturers. 'As' carried 13 tons and 'Bs' and 'Cs', 16 tons. 'As' and 'Bs' had four pallet-tensioning screws, 'Cs' had six screws and the central stanchion was wider and stronger. All of the wagons built with clasp brake also had hydraulic buffers and roller bearings **(see Figure 20 and Plates 96 and 97)**.

Unfortunately, at that time, common house bricks were usually made locally to their place of use, and BR was unable to retain its brick traffic in the face of road competition, even by using these modern handling methods, and Lots 3432 and 3433 for 150 wagons were cancelled.

By the late 1960s, most 'Palbricks' were out of use and many were converted to 'Coil P', 'Shellcase' and 'Freightliner Match' wagons; the latter remain in use but the former were redundant by 1975 and the chassis were used for 396 16 ton mineral wagons **(see Chapter 7)**.

TABLE 10

BRICK AND PALBRICKS

Diag No.	Lot No.	Qnty	Builder	Year	Running numbers	Type	Under-frame	length inside	width inside
1/038	2233	3	Wolverton	1950	B748500 - 748502	Expt Brick, Morton		17' 10" :	7' 8"
1/020	2668	8	Ashford	1957	B461609 - 461616	Palbrick A, RCH UF		12' 8 1/16" :	7' 4 7/8"
1/021	3138	12	Ashford	1957	B461597 - 461608	Palbrick B, RCH UF		12' 10 1/4" :	8' 3"
1/022	pt2724	330	Ashford	1957/8	B462117 - 462446	Palbrick B, RCH UF		13' 0 13/16" :	8' 2½"
1/023	3140	380	Ashford	1957	B461617 - 461996	Palbrick A, RCH UF		12' 7" :	7' 4½"
1/024	pt2724	120	Ashford	1957/8	B461997 - 462116	Palbrick B, RCH UF		13' 0" :	8' 2½"
1/024	3141	80	Ashford	1958	B462447 - 462526	Palbrick B, RCH UF		13' 0" :	8' 2½"
1/025	3242	160	Ashford	1959	B462527 - 462686	Palbrick C, BR clasp		12' 10" :	6' 6¾"
1/025	3322	50	Ashford	1960	B462797 - 462846	Palbrick C, BR clasp		12' 10" :	6' 6¾"
1/025	3365	190	Ashford	1961	B462847 - 463036	Palbrick C, BR clasp		12' 10" :	6' 6¾"
1/026	3243	90	Ashford	1959	B462707 - 462796	Palbrick B, BR clasp		13' 0" :	8' 2½"
	Total	1423							

Plate 96 The screw tensioners and metal-edged plywood lift-out panels, which formed the sides of the Palbrick family, are featured in this view of Palbrick A, No. B461829 (Ashford 1957, 3140) a Diagram 1/023 type, and pictured at Wrexham in August 1968.

D. Larkin

Plate 97 Pictured at Ashford when new in November 1959, No. B462527 (Lot 3242) is to Diagram 1/025 Palbrick C configuration, with six end tensioning screws, BR clasp vacuum brake, roller bearing axleboxes and Oleo pneumatic buffers. The brand 'Return to Manuel, ScR (NB)' was carried by many of Lot 3242. Manuel is about five miles east of Falkirk.

BR/SR

Figure 20

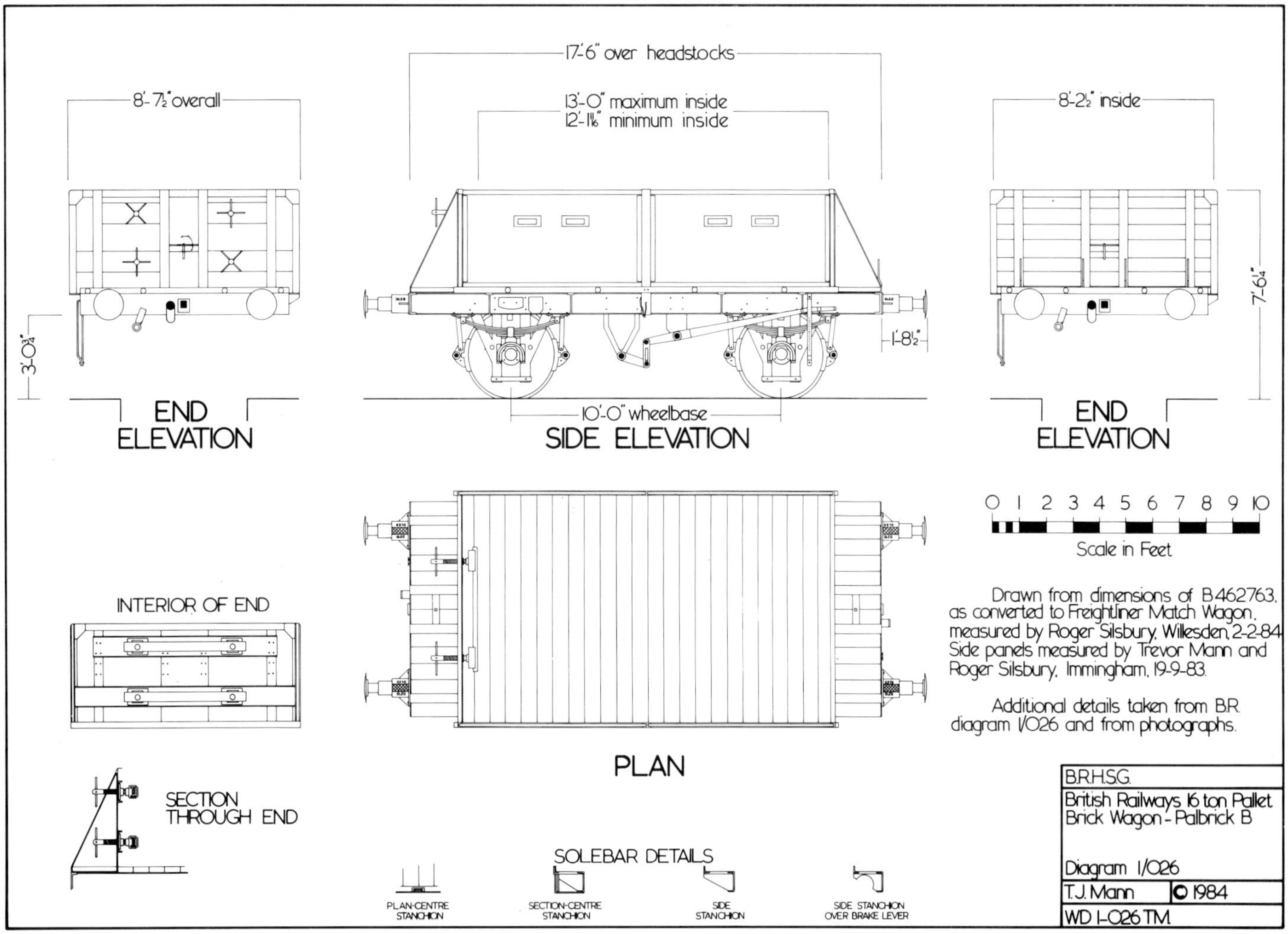

END ELEVATION

SIDE ELEVATION

END ELEVATION

17'-6" over headstocks
13'-0" maximum inside
12'-11⅛" minimum inside
8'-7½" overall
8'-2½" inside
10'-0" wheelbase
3'-0¼"
7'-6¼"
1'-8½"

0 1 2 3 4 5 6 7 8 9 10
Scale in Feet

INTERIOR OF END

PLAN

SECTION THROUGH END

SOLEBAR DETAILS

PLAN-CENTRE STANCHION

SECTION-CENTRE STANCHION

SIDE STANCHION

SIDE STANCHION OVER BRAKE LEVER

Drawn from dimensions of B.462763, as converted to Freightliner Match Wagon, measured by Roger Silsbury, Willesden, 2-2-84. Side panels measured by Trevor Mann and Roger Silsbury, Immingham, 19-9-83.

Additional details taken from B.R. diagram 1/026 and from photographs.

B.R.H.S.G.
British Railways 16 ton Pallet
Brick Wagon - Palbrick B

Diagram 1/026

T.J. Mann   © 1984

WD 1-026 TM.

69

TABLE 11

MATCH,FERRY HIGH, TIMBER, SALT, EXPERIMENTAL LOW GOODS AND SCRAP WAGONS

Diag No.	Lot No.	Qnty	Builder	Year	Running numbers	Wagon type
1/099	2858	200	Shildon	1956	B456000 - 456199	Match
1/098	2999	150	Shildon	1957	B456200 - 456349	Match
1/055	2579	20	Lancing	1957/8	B715000 - 715019	Ferry High
1/055	2851	20	Lancing	1957	B715020 - 715039	Ferry High
1/420	3465	80	Ashford	1962/3	B455500 - 455579	Timber
1/085	3134	15	Derby	1957	B884500 - 884514	Bulk Salt
-	3473	2	Pressed Steel	1962	B540001 - 540002	Expt. Low Goods
MF001A	3903	2	Shildon	1976	390000 - 390001	Scrap
	Total	489				

Match Wagons (see Table 11)

'Match' wagons were part of the 'operating' stock, but carried no load. Instead, they were used as under runners where a long load overhung the end of the wagon which was carrying the load. Only two batches were built, and both were similar to the contemporary 'Single Bolsters' **(see Chapter 6)** except they had no bodywork. The plank floor was bound with angle-iron and they were 15ft. 6in. over headstocks. Diagram No. 1/099 had the Morton unfitted brake on an 8ft. wheelbase **(see Plate 98)**, whilst Diagram No. 1/098 had a wheelbase of 10ft. and, although given screw couplings and hydraulic buffers, was also unfitted. Later, Lot 3115 was issued for 250 similar wagons with vacuum brake but, like the contemporary 'Single Bolsters', the order was cancelled.

No more 'Match' wagons were built new. 'Single' and 'Double Bolsters' performed this duty and, once these went out of use, 'Conflat As' were commonly used during the 1970s along with 'Steel ABs'. In 1978, the withdrawn Diagram No. 1/420 'Timber' wagons had their ends cut down and side stanchions removed, and they became under runners, TOPS code RRV, a role they shared with many ex-'Plate' wagons which had their sides removed. By 1984, these vacuum-braked under runners were largely redundant, so air-braked runners were made by removing the bodies from both redundant 'Ford Palvans' and damaged air-braked vans of later build (TOPS code RRA).

Plate 98 Although unable to carry any load, Match wagons were part of the revenue (operating) fleet. After a life of only 13 years, Diagram 1/099 Match wagon No. B456011 (Shildon 1956, 2858) lies condemned at Alnmouth during the summer of 1969.

D. Larkin

High Goods for Continental Traffic

Table 11 gives details of the two batches of 21 ton 'Open Merchandise Ferry Wagons' of Diagram No. 1/055 (Continental Diagram No. SFV6125), built in 1957. They were similar to some European designs, being eight planks high with a 5ft. drop door in the side, which had a pair of cupboard doors over it. They were 23ft. over headstocks with a 14ft. 10in. wheelbase. They had a vacuum brake and a through air pipe, Continental buffers, bearings and chaining-down eyes **(see Figure 21 and Plate 99)**.

Although they were allocated UIC numbers 21 70 619 000-039 we have no evidence that they were carried. The TOPS code was OJX.

By the late 1970s, some were in chalk traffic from Beverley and others were used by the Engineer's Department. Some were reduced in height and used as barrier wagons. Seven were rebuilt to form an overhead wiring train during the electrification of the Midland suburban line to Moorgate.

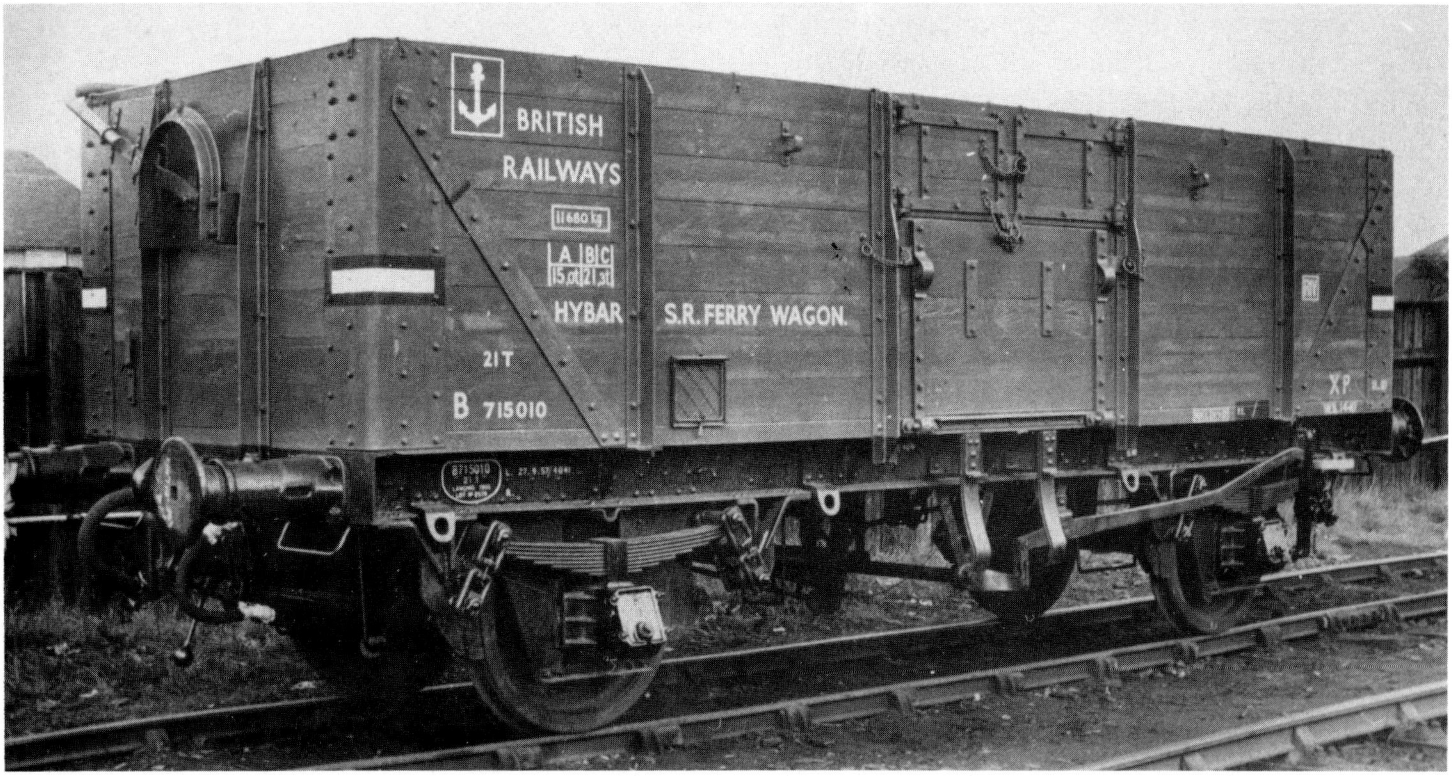
BRITISH
RAILWAYS
HYBAR
S.R. FERRY WAGON.
21T
B 715010
XP

Plate 99 Resplendent in bauxite livery when new at Lancing in September 1957, Diagram 1/055 Ferry High, No. B715010 displays all the features and markings to enable it to work to the Continent. The lugs along the lower edge of the solebar are to permit chaining down on the train ferry. Nearly all the specialist ferry vehicles were allocated to the Southern Region, as evidenced by the brand.

D. Larkin Collection

Figure 21

Measured by Trevor and Audrey Mann

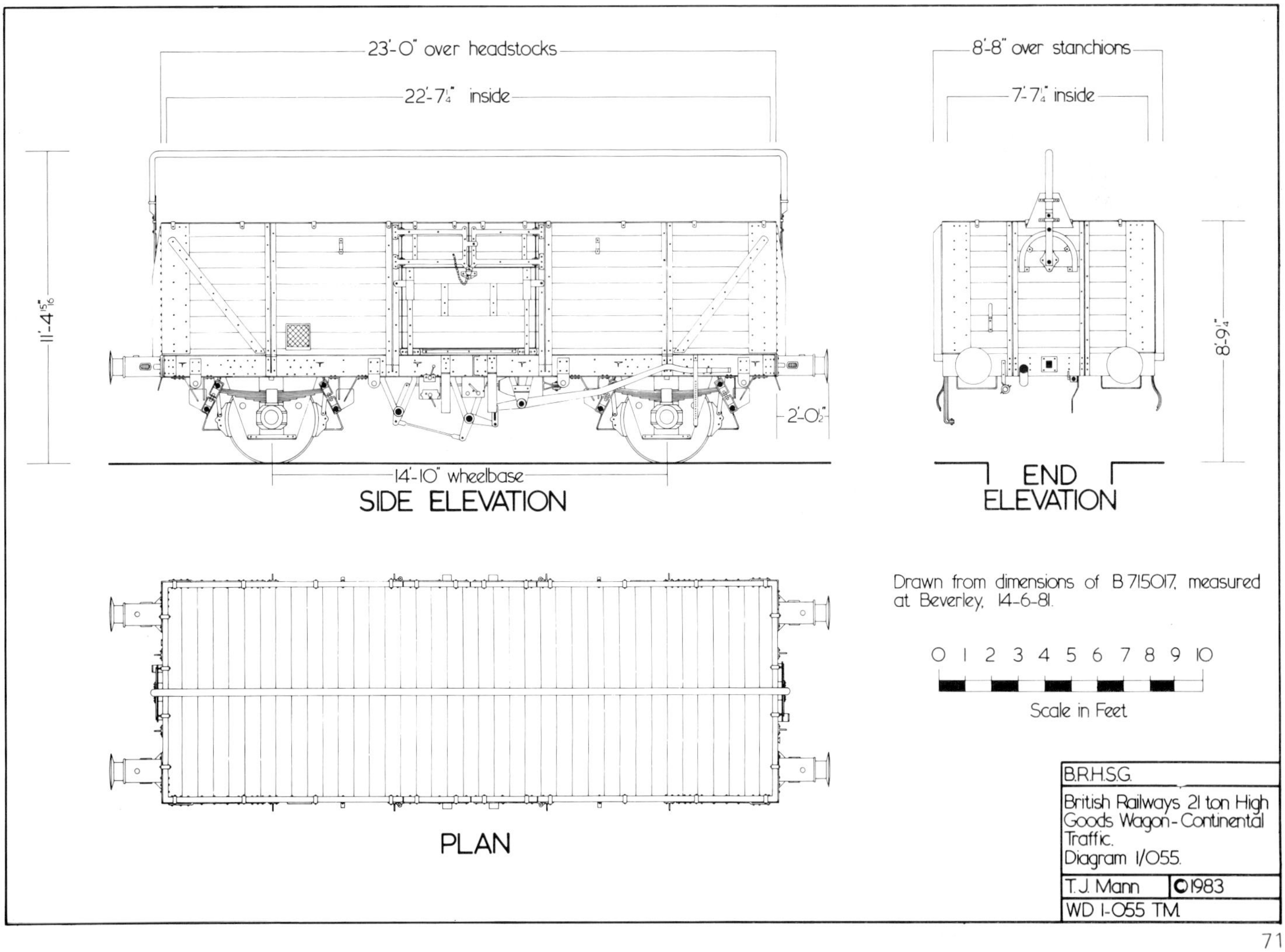
23'-0" over headstocks
22'-7¼" inside
11'-4 15/16"
2'-0½"
14'-10" wheelbase
SIDE ELEVATION
8'-8" over stanchions
7'-7¼" inside
8'-9¼"
END ELEVATION
PLAN
Drawn from dimensions of B 715017, measured at Beverley, 14-6-81.
0 1 2 3 4 5 6 7 8 9 10
Scale in Feet
B.R.H.S.G.
British Railways 21 ton High Goods Wagon - Continental Traffic.
Diagram 1/055.
T.J. Mann
©1983
WD 1-055 TM

Plate 100 The high ends are a dominant feature of the Diagram 1/420 Timber Wagons. The tall, removable side stanchions could be supplemented with others along the centre line, and the reducing height of the transverse baulks should be noted (see also **Figure 22**). No. B455555 was recorded at Lowestoft in August 1969.

D. Larkin

Figure 22

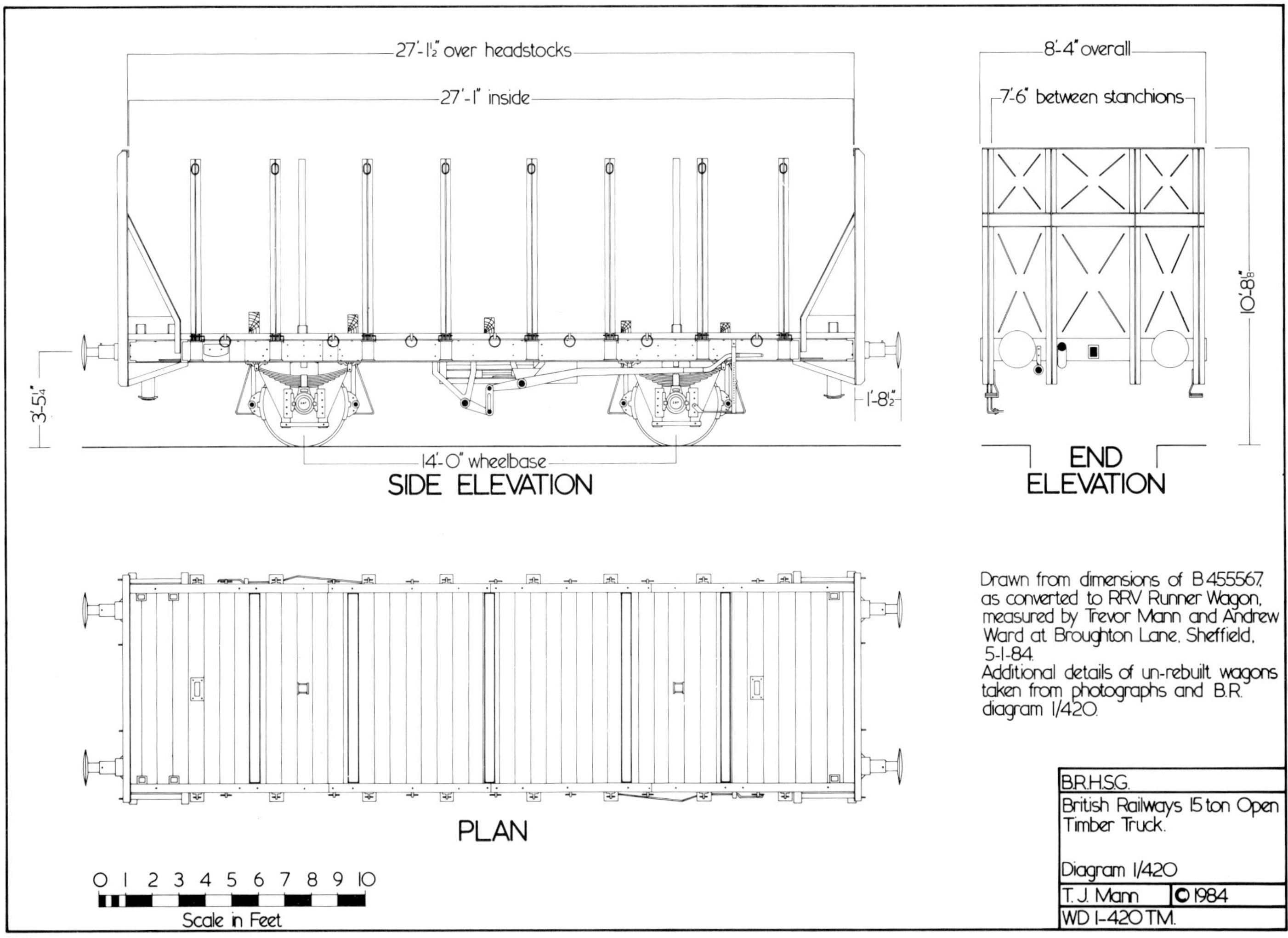

27'-1½" over headstocks

27'-1" inside

8'-4" overall

7'-6" between stanchions

10'-8⅛"

3'-5¼"

1'-8½"

14'-0" wheelbase

SIDE ELEVATION

END ELEVATION

PLAN

Drawn from dimensions of B.455567, as converted to RRV Runner Wagon, measured by Trevor Mann and Andrew Ward at Broughton Lane, Sheffield, 5-1-84.
Additional details of un-rebuilt wagons taken from photographs and B.R. diagram 1/420.

B.R.H.S.G.
British Railways 15 ton Open Timber Truck.

Diagram 1/420

T. J. Mann   © 1984

WD 1-420 TM.

O 1 2 3 4 5 6 7 8 9 10
Scale in Feet

Timber Wagons

As shown in **Table 11**, only one batch of specialist wagons were built for the carriage of timber by BR. Allocated Diagram No. 1/420 to carry 15 tons, the underframe was vacuum clasp-braked with a 14ft. wheelbase and 27ft. 1½ in. over headstocks. The ends were high steel plates with welded strengthening struts, and the sides had a series of removable stanchions **(see Figure 22 and Plate 100)**.

Most of these were branded: TO WORK BETWEEN MARSH POND & PORTISHEAD ONLY at the right-hand end. Others worked from East Anglian ports. The entire class was withdrawn during 1978 and converted to under runner wagons. Other timber wagons were made by converting 'Plate' wagons in 1965 **(see MRC Annual 1983, page 103)**.

Bulk Salt

Designing suitable wagons to carry salt is very difficult because it is so corrosive and dampness may spoil the load. BR built only 15 of these specialist wagons for this commodity, as shown in **Table 11**, but they also built some 'Presflos' for this traffic **(see Chapter 10)**.

This 20 ton design was originally allocated Diagram No. 1/274 but this was later altered to No. 1/085. This may have been connected with the original classification of this wagon as a covered hopper, which was corrected in 1961 when they were grouped with the 'Opens' and described as for wet salt. It was a complex design **(see Plate 101)** and the underframe had a vacuum clasp brake with a 15ft. 4in. wheelbase and was 24ft. 3in. over headstocks. Unusually the buffers and couplings were of the Continental type, but there were no other ferry features. The twin compartment body was steel-panelled. The sides were hinged from the top as a pair of doors which covered most of the solebar. The opening of these doors was controlled by a hand wheel and complex linkages at both ends which pushed them out sideways. Above these was a fixed upper part which sloped in towards the open top.

These wagons were specially painted, receiving an extra undercoat which would have meant that the bauxite finish appeared richer. They were branded 'Empty to Winsford & Over CLC' and, in later years, BULK SALT. These wagons were withdrawn in 1972, due to corrosion. After a period when salt was carried in converted ex-Iron Ore Hoppers, privately-owned hoppers were introduced.

Experimental Low Goods

Some details of these experimental 'Low Goods' are included in **Table 11**, but we have no further details of their appearance.

Plate 101 The complex nature of the Bulk Salt hopper wagons is clearly shown in this official view of No. B884505, taken at Derby in September 1957, when new. The brand shown has only been observed on this vehicle, others being lettered as given in the text. The legend at the top of the end reads 'Locking handles at bottom of side doors to be securely fastened before loading'.

BR/OPC

Prototype Scrap Carrier (see Table 11)

Scrap steel has been an important traffic for many years, carried in ordinary mineral wagons. Unfortunately many different sites provide the traffic but usually only a few wagon loads are available at the same time. Thus, when the abandonment of wagon load traffic was forseen, to be replaced by a completely air-braked 'Speedlink' service, BR produced two prototype wagons for this commodity.

Two underframes from the HBA Hopper building programme were diverted for these wagons and rugged all-steel bodies were built on them **(see Figure 23 and Plate 102)**. Given Diagram No. MF001A, these 32½ tonne wagons were designed to be loaded from above, and for unloading by using either electro-magnets or tippling. Because the wagons are high, they have an access ladder on one end and a small access door in each side. The TOPS code was MFA.

We understand that BR never intended to own a fleet of similar wagons, but they were built to show the trade what was needed and in this, they succeeded. Privately-owned bogie and 2-axle scrap carriers were introduced which had bodies similar to the BR design. After a period as runner wagons, these wagons returned to carrying scrap steel during 1984.

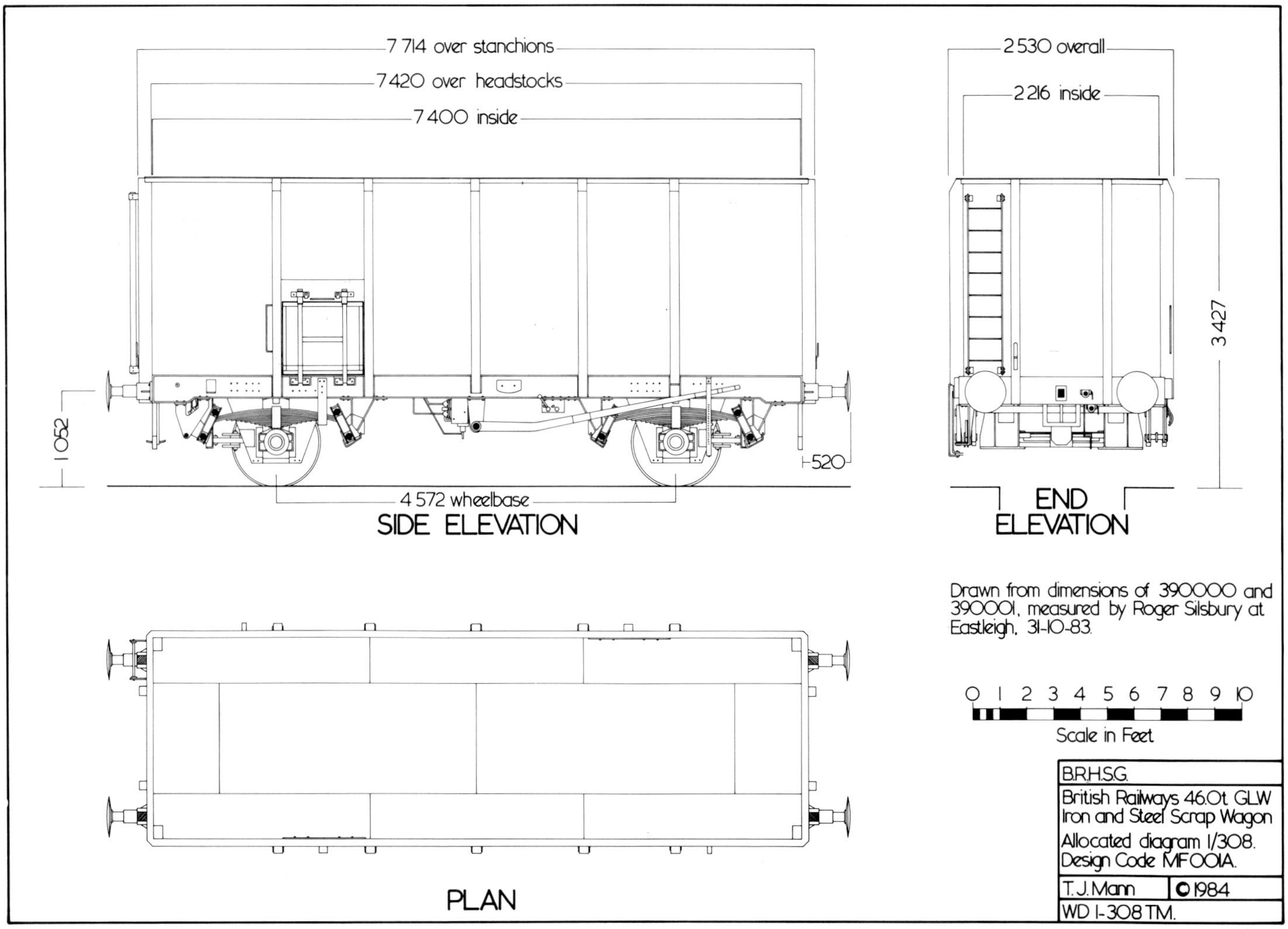

7 714 over stanchions
7 420 over headstocks
7 400 inside
1 052
4 572 wheelbase
520
SIDE ELEVATION

2 530 overall
2 216 inside
3 427
END ELEVATION

Drawn from dimensions of 390000 and 390001, measured by Roger Silsbury at Eastleigh, 31-10-83.

0 1 2 3 4 5 6 7 8 9 10
Scale in Feet

B.R.H.S.G.
British Railways 46.0t. GLW
Iron and Steel Scrap Wagon
Allocated diagram 1/308.
Design Code MF00IA.
T.J.Mann © 1984
WD I-308 TM.

PLAN

Figure 23

Plate 102 The two prototype scrap carriers languished at Eastleigh for a period during 1983, when No. 390000 was photographed and measured on 31st October of that year. Although retaining bauxite livery, it has been recoded ZRA, and prefixed ADC for use by the Southern Region's Rolling Stock Engineer. As depicted in **Figure 23**, the ladder features at one end only.

R. A. Silsbury

Car Carriers

The carriage of road vehicles by BR has become increasingly important throughout its history. Early on they were called CAR . . . because larger vehicles were carried on specially-constructed 'Lowmacs'. Later, a wider variety of road vehicles were carried on the wagons considered here.

Cartrucks (see Table 12)
The first design was a simple 12 ton 'Cartruck'. It was given GWR Diagram No. G49, as well as BR Diagram No. 1/090. It had an unfitted Morton underframe, 18ft. over headstocks with a 10ft. 6in. wheelbase. The body had low steel sides with adjustable roll bars across the wagon to hold the road vehicle wheels in place. The buffers were covered by a plate which allowed the road vehicle to be driven on. **Plate 103 and Figure 168 in FWLGW** show these, but the caption of the latter is inaccurate. These wagons were probably withdrawn by the early 1970s.

'Carfit A' (see Table 12)
Another wagon design of GWR origin followed, the 12 ton 'Carfit A'. Originally GWR Diagram No. G52, they became BR Diagram No. 1/091. Similar to the 'Cartruck', they were longer, being 21ft. over headstocks with a 13ft. 6in. wheelbase. All three batches had an elongated RCH vacuum-braked underframe. The body had open sides with adjustable chains and straps on metal strips on the outer panels **(see Plate 104 and Figure 170 in FWLGW)**.

Although built as recently as 1958, they had an early demise, probably by the early 1970s. Both the 'Cartruck' and 'Carfit A' were designed for traffic from Morris Cowley, Oxford, and 'Carfit As' were also used to ferry private cars through the Severn Tunnel before the motorway bridge opened.

'Carfit C' (see Table 12)
The year 1958 also saw the introduction of two batches of the ferry-fitted 20 ton 'Carfit C'. Diagram No. 1/092 (Continental Diagram No. SFV6212) was issued for these, and this brands them as 'Carfit B', but we have not seen them so lettered. As is appropriate for ferry vehicles, these had a more advanced appearance and a 22ft. 6in. wheelbase and a length over headstocks of 33ft. They had the clasp vacuum brake with long link suspension, and through air and steam pipes. In 1961, the diagram was amended so that 'Carfit B' was used for wagons with steel floors, and 'Carfit C' for the more common ones with wood floors. Perhaps, at the same time, or later, they gained air brakes. The low ends dropped down and the similarly low sides dropped as six panels. The stanchions between had hoops for chains.

Sometime after 1967, they acquired UIC numbers in the 21 70 414 000 to 039 series. They were always branded as SR FERRY WAGON, and later they were often simply branded CAR C and the TOPS code was FIX, **(see Plate 105)**. Although most were extensively refurbished during 1978, by 1980 most were out of ferry use and were used as under runners, barriers or by the Engineer's Department. The October 1983 Continental Diagram No. E212 shows Nos. 003/011/013/015/017/024 and 025.

Experimental Prototype Car Carrier
In 1960, BR built a series of prototype wagons which all shared a common design of underframe and all were built to Lot 3362. Two of these, Nos. B710250 and 710254, were 22 ton long low car-carrying wagons with a two plank end and a simple low rail side **(see Table 12)**. The underframe had a wheelbase of 20ft. 9in., was 35ft. over headstocks, and had auxiliary rubber suspension. No. B710250 was quickly converted to the prototype of the 'Ford Palvans' **(see Chapter 9)**. No. B710254 was transferred to Engineer's use on the Eastern Region **(see Plate 106 and Figure 24)**.

Plates 103 & 104 Although both these views have appeared before, they are used again for completeness of the record. No. B748011 (Swindon 1950, 2088) to Diagram 1/090, **(Plate 103)** displays the unfitted livery of light grey, with white lettering on black patches, when photographed on 30th May 1951 at Swindon; note the spoked wheels, Morton brake and three-link couplings. In contrast, No. B748050 (Swindon 1954, 2587) to Diagram 1/091 **(Plate 104)** is in bauxite livery as befits its RCH vacuum braking, on 22nd April 1954.

TABLE 12

CARTRUCK & CARFIT

Diag No.	Lot No.	Qnty	Builder	Year	Running number	Brake type	Branding
1/090	2088	20	Swindon	1950/1	B748000 - 748019	Morton	CARTRUCK
1/091	2265	30	Swindon	1952	B748020 - 748049	RCH vacuum	CARFIT A
1/091	2587	10	Swindon	1954	B748050 - 748059	RCH vacuum	CARFIT A
1/091	2989	50	Wolverton	1958	B748060 - 748109	RCH vacuum	CARFIT A
1/092	2770	20	Ashford	1958	B748110 - 748129	Vac & air	CARFIT C
1/092	2850	20	Ashford	1958	B748130 - 748149	Vac & air	CARFIT C
-	3362	2	Ashford	1960	B710250, B710254	BR clasp vac	Experimental
1/127	3713	2	Ashford	1970	150000 - 150001	Air	LOWLINER outer
1/128	3714	3	Ashford	1970	150002 - 150004	Air	LOWLINER inner
		Total 157					

Plate 104

Plate 105 Diagram 1/092 Carfit C, 21 70 414-0 004-5 (BR number No. B748114; Ashford 1958, 2770) displays a full range of lettering when recorded at March on 27th June 1980. Continental pattern roller bearing axleboxes are fitted, although the buffers have been replaced by large headed Oleo pneumatic types. The back of the head of the original type is just visible on the vehicle to the right.

R. A. Silsbury

Figure 24

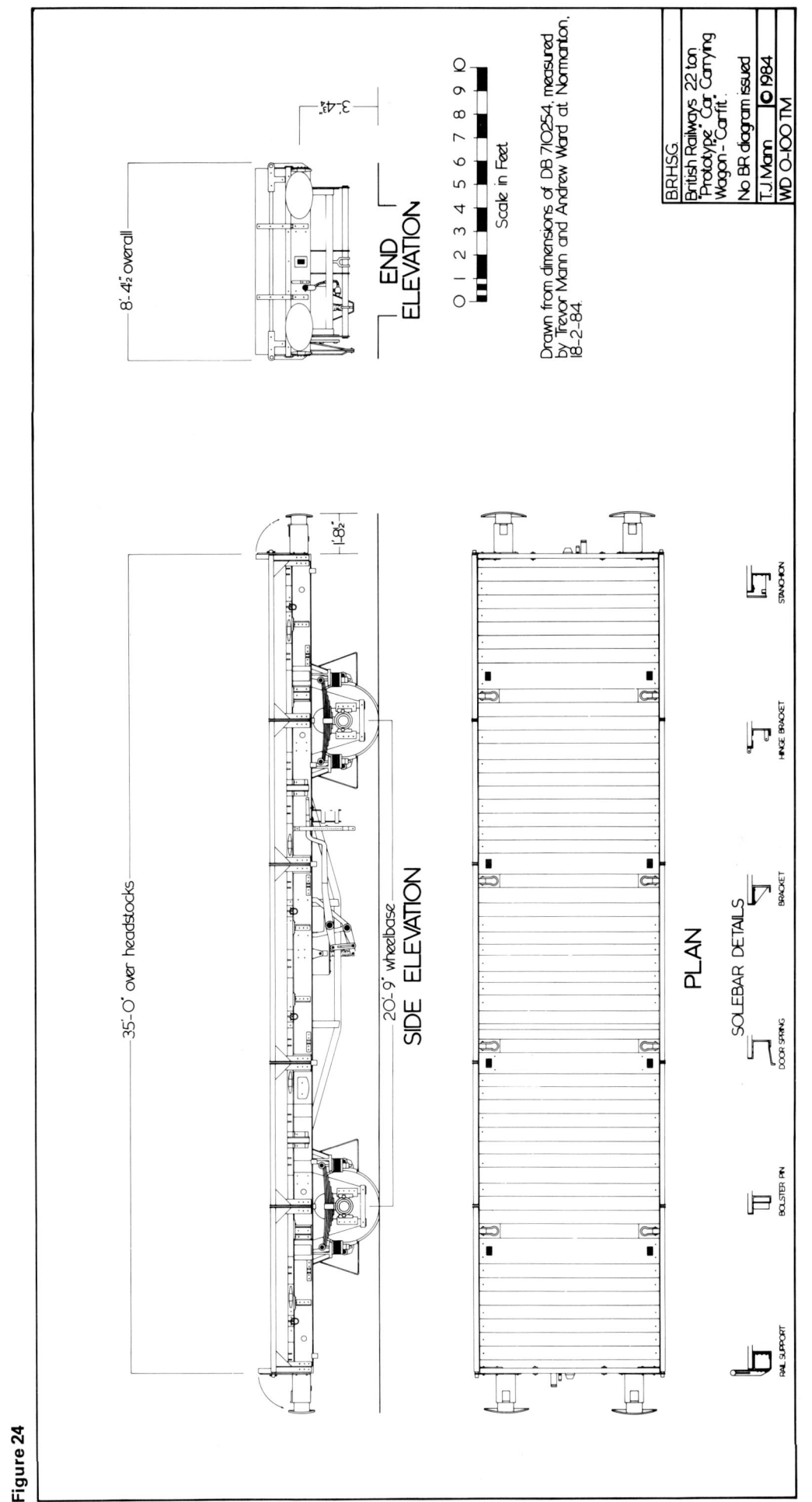

8' 4½" overall

3' 4½"

END ELEVATION

0 1 2 3 4 5 6 7 8 9 10

Scale in Feet

Drawn from dimensions of DB 710254, measured by Trevor Mann and Andrew Ward at Normanton. 18-2-84.

1' 8½"

35'-0" over headstocks

20'-9" wheelbase

SIDE ELEVATION

PLAN

SOLEBAR DETAILS

RAIL SUPPORT

BOLSTER PIN

DOOR SPRING

BRACKET

HINGE BRACKET

STANCHION

B.R.H.S.G.
British Railways 22 ton 'Prototype' Car Carrying Wagon — Carflat.
No BR diagram issued
T.J.Mann   © 1984
WD O-IOO TM

Plate 106 No. DB710254, one of the 1960-built experimental wagons, has been relegated to use by the Engineers when seen at Normanton on 6th September 1982, carrying concrete troughing. It is, however, unaltered and retains somewhat rusty bauxite livery.

R. A. Silsbury

TABLE 13

BOCARS, TIERWAG, CARTIC 4 AND CARFLATS

Diag No.	Lot No.	Qnty	Builder	Year	Running numbers	bogie wb	length of	& underframe	type	Wagon type
1/290	3090	36	Wolv'ton	1957/8	B889100 - 889135	9'-0"	57' 0"		LMS	BOCAR P
-	3327	4		1960	(B889030 - 889033)	8'-6"	60' 0"		LNER	CCT
1/293	3547	8	Derby	1965	B889136 - 889143	9'-0"	60' 0"		LMS	BOCAR P
1/096	3370	40	Cowlairs	1962	B748428 - 748467	8'-6"	60' 0"		LNER	CARFLAT P
2/293	3260	6	Newton Ch.	1959	B909200 - 909205	6'-7"	56' 0"		-	TIERWAG
2/294	3518	2	Ashford	1964	B909300 - 909301	6'-6¾"	45' 4½"			CARTIC 4 (inner)
2/295	3519	2	Ashford	1964	B909400 - 909401	6'-6¾"	54' 0 1/4"			CARTIC 4 (outer)
1/093	pt3283	112	Swindon	1959	B748150 - 748287*	7'-0"	59' 2 - 60' 9¾"		GWR	CARFLAT
1/093	3326	12	Doncaster	1960	B748577 - 748588	8'-6"	60' 0"		LNER	CARFLAT
1/094	3305	6	Gorton	1959	B748182 - 748187	9'-0"	57' 0'		LMS	CARFLAT A
1/094	3312	44	Gorton	1959/60	B748503 - 748546	9'-0"	57' 0"		LMS	CARFLAT A
1/094	pt3320	60	Central	1959/60	B748288 - 748347	9'-0"	57' 0"		LMS	CARFLAT A
1/094	pt3320	30	Central	1960	B748547 - 748576	9'-0"	57' 0"		LMS	CARFLAT A
1/094	3321	80	Rigley	1959	B748348 - 748427	9'-0"	57' 0" (1 @ 54')		LMS	CARFLAT A
1/095	3358	68	Swindon	1960	B748589 - 748656	7'-0"	59' 2" - 60' 0"		GWR	CARFLAT A
1/097	pt3283	20	Swindon	1959	B748159 - 748276*	7'-0"	60' 9¾"		GWR	CARFLAT
1/089	3479	24	Cowlairs	1963	B748468 - 748491	8'-6"	60' 0'		LNER	CARFLAT A
1/089	3485	16	Cowlairs	1963	B748657 - 748672	8'-6"	60' 0"		LNER	CARFLAT A
1/088	3532	25	Cowlairs	1964	B748673 - 748697	8'-6"	60' 0" & 61' 6"	LMS & LNER	CARFLAT A
1/088	3533	25	Ashford	1964	B748698 - 748722	8'-6"	63' 5" (2 @ 60')	BR & LMS	CARFLAT A
1/088	3534	25	Horwich	1964	B748723 - 748747	9'-0"	60' 0"		LMS	CARFLAT A
1/088	3535	21	Derby	1964	B748748 - 748768	9'-0"	60' 0"	8 LMS + 13 LNER		CARFLAT A
1/088	3541	15	Ashford	1965	B745650 - 745664	9'-0"	62' 0"		LMS	CARFLAT A
1/088	3542	15	Cowlairs	1965	B745665 - 745679	9'-0"	60' 0"		LMS	CARFLAT A
1/088	3543	20	Horwich	1965	B745680 - 745699	9'-0"	60' 0" (1 @ 62')		LMS	CARFLAT A
1/088	3544	20	Derby	1965	B745700 - 745719	9'-0"	60' 0"		LMS	CARFLAT A
1/088	3548	2	Horwich	1965	B745648 - 745649	9'-0"	60' 0" & 62' 0"		LMS	CARFLAT A
1/088	3550	1	St Rollox	1965	B748492	9'-0"	?		LMS	CARFLAT A
1/088	3552	12	Derby	1965	B745720 - 745731	9'-0"	60' 0"		LMS	CARFLAT A
1/088	3553	14	Cowlairs	1965	B745732 - 745745	9'-0"	60' 0"		LMS	CARFLAT A
1/088	3554	14	Horwich	1965	B745746 - 745759	9'-0"	60' 0"		LMS	CARFLAT A
1/088	3562	30	Derby	1965	B745760 - 745789	9'-0"	60' 0" (1 @ 62')		LMS	CARFLAT A
1/088	3563	14	Cowlairs	1964/5	B745790 - 745803	9'-0"	60' 0" (4 @ 62')		LMS	CARFLAT A

TABLE 13 continued

Diag No.	Lot No.	Qnty	Builder	Year	Running numbers	bogie wb	length of	& type underframe	Wagon type
1/088	3564	12	Barassie	1966	B745804 – 745815	9'-0"	60' 0"	(4 @ 62") LMS	CARFLAT A
1/088	3592	20	Derby	1966	B745872 – 745891	9'-0"	60' 0"	LMS	CARFLAT A
1/088	3599	20	Barassie	1966	B745892 – 745911	9'-0"	60' 0"	(1 @ 62") LMS	CARFLAT A
1/088	3637^	40	Barassie	1967	B745912 – 745951	9'-0"	60' 0"	LMS	CARFLAT A
1/088	3640	15	Derby	1967	B745952 – 745966	9'-0"	60' 0"	(2 types) LMS	CARFLAT A
1/088	3641	20	Swindon	1967	B745967 – 745986	9'-0"	60' 0"	(+ 2 odd) LMS	CARFLAT A
1/088	3642	25	Horwich	1967	B748769 – 748793	9'-0"	60' 0"	(2 types) LMS	CARFLAT A
1/088	3679	57	St Rollox	1968	B745000 – 745056	8'-6"	63' 5"	BR	CARFLAT A
1/130	pt3536	8	Swindon	1964	[B745639 – 745640] [B745642 – 745647]	8'-6"	63' 5"	BR	CARFLAT A
1/131	pt3536	40	Swindon	1964	[B745600 – 745638] [B745641]	8'-6"	63' 5"	BR	CARFLAT A
1/132	3588	20	Derby	1966	B745846 – 745865	9'-0"	60' 0"	LMS	CARFLAT AB
1/132	3589	6	Derby	1966	B745866 – 745871	9'-0"	60' 0"	LMS	CARFLAT AB
1/133	3587	30	Barassie	1966	B745816 – 745845	9'-0"	63' 0"	GWR	CARFLAT A
1/134	3715	5	Barassie	1970	B745057 – 745061	8'-6"	63' 5"	BR	CARFLAT AB
1/134	3758	14	Barassie	1971	B745074 – 745087	8'-6"	63' 5"	BR	CARFLAT AB
1/137	3757	12	Barassie	1971	B745062 – 745073	8'-6"	63' 5"	BR	CARFLAT AB
1/177	3831#	140	[Swindon/ 1973/4 [Doncaster 1973		B745088 – 745227] B745168 – 745187]	8'-6"	63' 5"	BR	CARFLAT A
1/177	3867	70	Swindon	1974/5	B745228 – 745297	8'-6"	63' 5"	BR	CARFLAT A
1/177	3868	5	Swindon	1975	B745298 – 745302	8'-6"	63' 5"	BR	CARFLAT A
Total		1382							

```
* - Range of the number series
^ - Official lot 3637 are plated 3647
# - Official lot 3831 are plated 3821
```

Bogie Car Carrying Wagons

The next wagons were varied bogie vehicles usually built on redundant coach underframes. In **Table 13** we have tried to be as accurate as we are able to be, but there may be mistakes and omissions. It is important to realise that a diagram number means little; coach underframes from very different sources may be allocated to the same diagram.

'Bocar'

The first design of this type, introduced in 1957, allocated Diagram No. 1/290, was the 5 ton 'Bocar A' **(see Plate 107)**. Initially, 36 vehicles were converted from redundant Fowler LMS 57ft. carriage underframes to carry motor car bodies, probably on pallets. These were similar to LMS 'Bocars' having a full height planked wooden end, framework sides which supported a roof, and curtain sides. In 1965, eight similar wagons were built, which utilised Stanier 60ft. carriage underframes. These were allocated Diagram No. 1/293 which was not issued. Later, the ends, sides and roof were removed and they continued to carry palletised car bodies from Morris Cowley at Oxford. In this form they were 'Bocar P'. Finally they were converted to the appearance of the 'Carflats' and were withdrawn towards the end of the 1970s.

Another vehicle for carrying palletised car bodies was introduced in 1962 and branded 'Carflat P'. Allocated Diagram No. 1/096, to carry 10 tons, they were a skeletal Gresley LNER carriage underframe which was loaded with pairs of PP containers (Diagram No. 3/170). These carried Rover cars.

Table 13 also shows a 'Bocar B' allocated Lot 3327. These were built on redundant Gresley LNER carriage underframes as 'Covered Carriage Trucks' for use on the initial 'Motorail' service from King's Cross to Edinburgh. They were transferred to coaching stock and became Nos. E96200-E96203. Other freight CCT and GUV were built, and these are discussed in **Chapter 10**, with 'Special' covereds.

Tierwag

Six wagons of unusual appearance were introduced in 1959 which were branded 'Tierwag' **(see Table 13)**. They appear to be identical to a design introduced by the car transporting firm MAT during 1957 and, like them, they carried up to seven cars of 12½ tons. BR put them in the 'Special' diagram book as No. 2/293. They were 56ft. over headstocks with plate back bogies of 6ft. 7in. wheelbase at 44ft. centres. The loading deck was 6ft. 4¾in. above rail height and had guides running along its length located at the inside of the cars wheelbase. These were used for fixing wheel chocks.

The most interesting feature of the design was that the body had a well between the bogies. The first two cars loaded were lowered into the well, and the other cars were then loaded over the top of them. The body was complex with 'L' angle extensively used to form the sides of the lifting section and the sides and ends of the upper deck. Vacuum brake, 2ft. 10½in. diameter wheels and oval-head hydro-pneumatic buffers were fitted **(see Plate 108)**.

They worked with the MAT-owned versions from Morris Cowley (WR), and possibly other Midlands car factories to the Continent, and had partial ferry fittings. The diagram was cancelled during 1971 and the wagons were withdrawn prior to that date.

'Cartic 4'

A much more successful two-tier car-carrying design was introduced in 1964 **(see Table 13)**. This was to become known as the 'Cartic 4' set. Four wagons were articulated together, and carried on five Ridemaster cast bogies of similar design to those used on 'Freightliner' chassis, which had a wheelbase of 6ft. 6¾in. at 46ft. 6in. centres. This articulation was sensible as cars are light, each set had a capacity of 4 by 8 tons, and carried 120 standard cars or 150 'Mini' cars. The outer wagons were 54ft.

0¼ in. long and the inner wagons were 45ft. 4½ in. Each wagon dipped between the bogies, but a minimum 5ft. clearance was maintained. The low central part of the upper deck allowed higher cars to be loaded in this position. The wagons were air-braked with screw handbrake on the outer bogies, wheels were 2ft. 8in. in diameter, and the buffers self-contained, oval-headed and covered by a hinged flap which allowed for driving over **(see Plate 109)**.

The most important part of the design was that the cars could be driven on to each deck of the wagon at the same time, and rakes were simply loaded from one end with the cars driving the length of the train. The lower and upper decks were 3ft. 10½ in. and 7ft. 0^{11}/$_{16}$in. above rail height respectively. Elaborate dual height loading facilities were provided at some places, especially at the car manufacturers. At others, the lower deck was loaded from a conventional end-loading bay, and the rake was shunted to another siding which had the high loader, often built on an old coach underframe.

Only the first set of wagons was built to a wagon lot and allocated to the 'Special' diagram book as Nos. 2/294 and 2/295. In quick succession, it was lettered and painted for British Railways, then for 'Ford', and by 1966 for 'Motorail' services. 'Ford' initially had sets for their use which were owned by Silcock and Collings. It is not clear if the 8 sets of coach Diagram No. 822 and Lot 30770 included the original freight set or not, but all wagons appear to have had a wagon-type building plate which has been removed. They were numbered M95001-M95016 for the outers, and M95051-M95066 for the inners, and were used on 'Motorail' services. During 1978/9, the wagons were numbered back into the freight fleet by the replacement of the 'M' suffix by a '9', and were used with the many similar privately-owned wagons to transport new cars.

Their introduction was coincident with the introduction of blue for coaches and locomotives, and they were painted to match, which was also in keeping with 'Ford's' style, as they matched the 'Palvans' introduced at the same time **(see Chapter 9)**. When they were transferred to 'Motorail' they continued in blue, and they were not repainted when they returned to the freight fleet.

Plate 107 No. B889107 is a Diagram 1/290 Bocar A, built on the underframe of non-corridor lavatory first No. M18018M at Wolverton under Lot 3090, where it was photographed on 10th October 1957. The canvas side screens are of unequal size, to correspond with the bays between the roof stanchions.

BR/OPC

Plate 108 Although BR included the Tierwag in the Specially Constructed Wagon book, it is more logically included here with the car carriers. The complicated construction, and lifting mechanism can be seen in this view of No. B909201, taken on 21st September 1959, possibly at the builders, Newton Chambers of Sheffield. Although not intended for Continental working, it features chaining down lugs and RIV screw couplings, probably because the MAT-owned vehicles built concurrently had them.

BR/OPC

Plate 109 The solitary Cartic-4, built to a freight lot on a demonstration run for Ford, with a load of Anglia cars, has No. B909401 nearest. Note the 'British Railways — Cartic-4' lettering and the 'Ford' plate. The location is not known, but may be Dagenham; the date is 1965.

Authors' Collection

'Carflats'

By 1960, both the 'Motorail' services and freight carriage of cars demanded many more wagons. Mark I coaches were by now numerous and the underframes from redundant pre-nationalisation carriages were available for conversion to 'Carflats'; later, BR Mark I underframes were used in a similar way. For the new wagons a minimum length over headstocks of 57ft. was specified to enable four cars to be carried. Two types of 'body' were built and all wagons were rated to carry 10 tons, except Lot 3640 of Diagram No. 1/088, which was rated at 20 tons.

Type 1 was designated 'Carflat'. It had a wooden deck with metal wheel channels running the full length, and adjustable chocks. No sides were required; each end had one fixed and one hinged flap which permitted access between wagons.

Type 2 was designated 'Carflat A' and had a wooden deck and low fixed framework sides. These used loose spiked chocks to secure the cars. Full width wooden drop ends provided the access between wagons.

Both types had screw couplings and were vacuum-braked, with a handbrake on one bogie only. Later, air brakes were fitted to some wagons, sometimes from new and also as a conversion. Buckeye couplings were retained on ex-LNER stock and the later ex-BR conversions, as noted below. The variations within a given diagram illustrate the limitations of these drawings, as they relate principally to the commercial aspect of the wagon, rather than its construction.

Three number ranges were used. The first conversions followed logically after the 'Carfit C', from No. B748150. When the series was almost exhausted a second series following the 'Soda Ash Opens' was started at No. B745600, in 1964. By 1967, this series was also exhausted and a small batch infilled the numbers at the end of the first series. A third series, commencing at No. B745000 was started in 1968 and this proved sufficient.

Dealing chronologically with the various diagrams:

Diagram No. 1/093 initially was a 'Carflat' with ex-GWR underframes, later some ex-LNER underframes were added **(see Plate 110)**.

Diagram No. 1/094 covered the more numerous 'Carflat A' with ex-LMS 57ft. Fowler underframes.

Diagram No. 1/095 was coded 'Carflat' but was in fact 'Carflat A'; these had ex-GWR underframes.

Diagram No. 1/097 was issued to cover 20 Diagram No. 1/093 wagons which were fitted with wider 'L' section channels in about 1962; they continued to be 'Carflat'.

Hereafter, all conversions were to 'Carflat A' configuration, although some batches were designated 'Carflat' only, for reasons not known to us.

Diagram No. 1/089 had ex-LNER underframes which retained buckeye couplings.

Diagram No. 1/088 was very extensively used. Most had ex-Stanier LMS 60ft. and 62ft. underframes, but this diagram also included one batch of ex-LNER and two ex-BR underframes **(see Plate 111 & Plate 112)**. Later, 20 of the LMS 60ft. versions, Lots 3534 and 3535, were dual air and vacuum-braked and allocated Diagram No. 1/129, which was not issued.

Diagrams Nos. 1/130 and 1/131 covered the single Lot 3536, a batch of ex-BR long suburban carriage underframes converted to 'Motorail' use. Most had the standard fixed sides (1/131) — **Plate 113** — but 8 were fitted with two removable sections at each end to allow side loading (1/130).

Diagram No. 1/132 had ex-Stanier LMS 60ft. underframes which were dual air and vacuum-braked from new; there does not appear to be any difference to Diagram No. 1/129.

Diagram No. 1/133 had ex-Hawksworth 63ft. underframes; this made them the longest of the pre-nationalisation derived types **(see Plate 114)**.

From this point onwards all the conversions were based upon the BR 63ft. 5in. carriage underframe.

Diagram No. 1/134 had three lots which were dual air and vacuum-braked; this made them different to the single ex-BR batch of Diagram No. 1/088.

Diagram No. 1/137 was not issued but was allocated to a single lot which was similar to No. 1/134 but had buckeye couplings.

Diagram No. 1/177 was not issued but was allocated to three lots which had two removable sections at each end in the style of Diagram No. 1/130. Some had buckeye couplings **(see Figure 25 and Plate 115)**.

Two anomalies in lot numbers occur on 'Carflat As'. All official Lot 3637 vehicles are plated Lot 3647, and all official Lot 3831 are plated Lot 3821.

The 'Bocars' and 'Carflats' were usually bauxite for the curb-rail and bodies, although some all black vehicles have been recorded. Those allocated to 'Motorail' traffic have been painted rail blue with a large white plate placed centrally on the body side. This has 'Motorail' in red. These wagons are often used for ordinary freight duty during the winter. TOPS codes are FVV and FVX.

In 1985 the 16 remaining FVV wagons were transferred to the coaching stock fleet as NGV, and renumbered as M96250-96265.

Plate 110

Plate 111   The first Diagram 1/088 vehicle illustrated is No. B748686 (Cowlairs 1964, 3532) and is seen at Eastleigh on 15th May 1980. It is based on the underframe of LNER 63ft. Corridor Third No. E1084E, and retains its buck-eye coupling and Gresley bogies; the drop-end door is fabricated steel, and the sides have stanchions reaching the full depth of the solebar.

R. A. Silsbury

Plate 110   Unfortunately no better illustration of a Diagram 1/093 Carflat is available, but the principle features of longitudinal channels, adjustable chocks, and hinged end flaps are visible in this official view of No. B748587, built under Lot 3326 at Doncaster during 1960, on the underframe of Corridor Third No. E12614E. It is branded 'Empty to Dagenham Dock'.

BR/OPC

Plate 112   The second Diagram 1/088 vehicle represented is one of the numerous ex-LMS types. No. B745974 (Swindon 1967, 3641) started life as a 60ft. Corridor Composite, latterly No. M4445M. It has the same style fixed sides as No. B748686, but the end door is of the more common plank construction. Compared with the LNER and GWR based conversions, those of LMS origin retained full buffer heads. When recorded at Cowley, Oxford, on 17th June 1980, it was carrying a selection of BL cars.

R. A. Silsbury

Figure 25

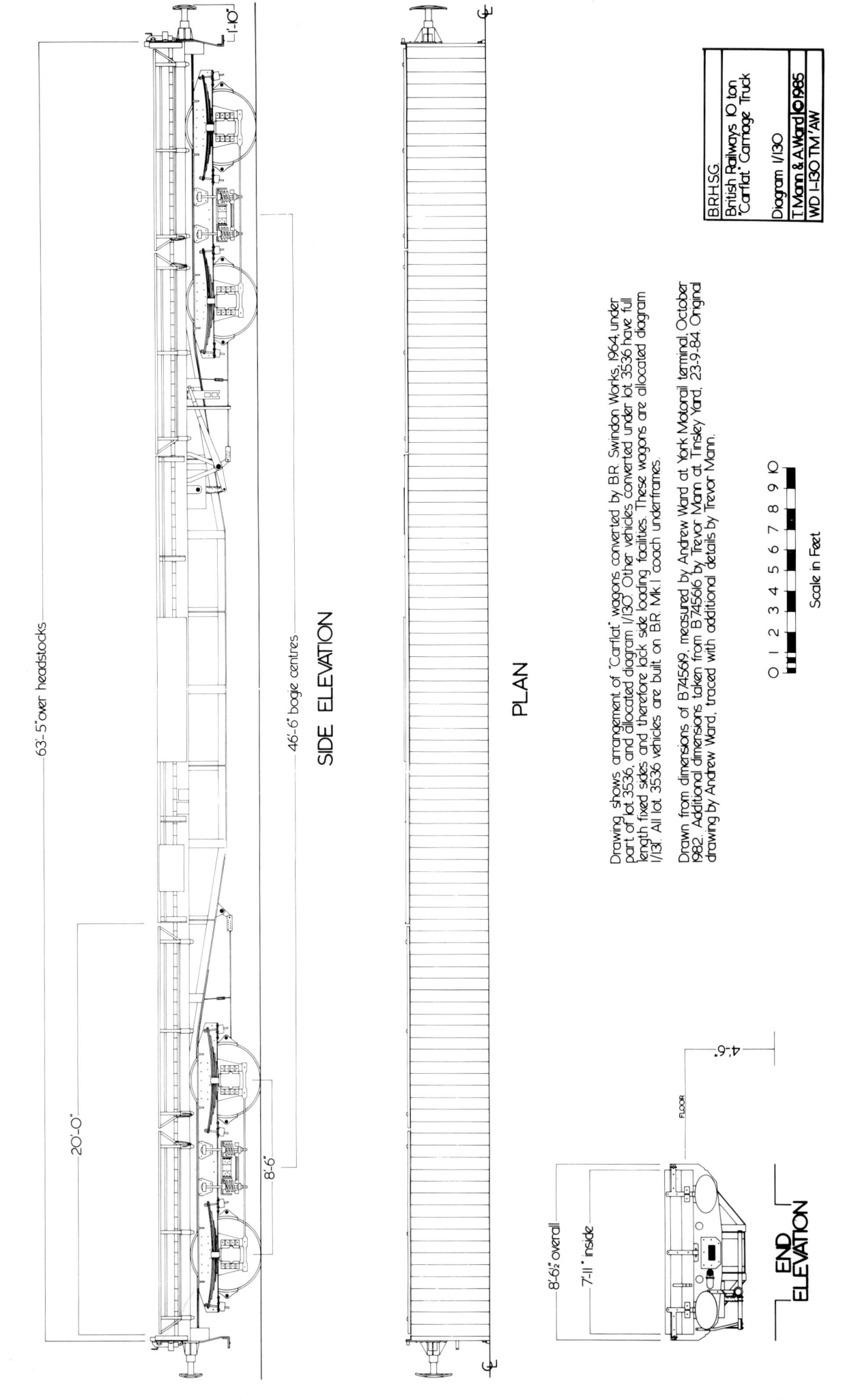

63'-5" over headstocks

1'-0"

20'-0"

8'-6"

46'-6" bogie centres

SIDE ELEVATION

PLAN

4'-6"

FLOOR

8'-6½" overall

7'-11" inside

END ELEVATION

Drawing shows arrangement of 'Carflat' wagons converted by BR Swindon Works, 1964, under part of lot 3536, and allocated diagram 1/130. Other vehicles converted under lot 3536 have full length fixed sides and therefore lack side loading facilities. These wagons are allocated diagram 1/131. All lot 3536 vehicles are built on BR Mk.1 coach underframes.

Drawn from dimensions of B745619, measured by Andrew Ward at York Motorail terminal, October 1982. Additional dimensions taken from B745616 by Trevor Mann at Tinsley Yard, 23-9-84. Original drawing by Andrew Ward, traced with additional details by Trevor Mann.

0 1 2 3 4 5 6 7 8 9 10

Scale in Feet

B.R.H.S.G.
British Railways 10 ton
'Carflat' Carriage Truck

Diagram 1/130

T Mann & A Ward 1985
WD 1-130 TM/AW

84

Plate 113 Withdrawal of a large number of BR long underframe suburban carriages in the early 1960s made available modern underframes for Carflat conversion. Lot 3533 covered those to Diagram 1/088, whilst Lot 3536, illustrated here by No. B745631, ex-Second No. W46287, was to Diagram 1/131, where the side stanchions come only part way down the flush solebars. Although originally used on 'Motorail' services, and painted in blue livery, No. B745631 was in freight bauxite when seen at Fratton on 10th November 1980.

R. A. Silsbury

Plate 114 Diagram 1/133 used ex-GWR underframes, Corridor Third No. W2129W becoming No. B745825 (Barassie 1966, 3587). The basic configuration is similar to Diagram 1/088. Note the spiked wheel chocks to restrain the load, here four Honda cars, at Hoo Junction on 12th March 1978.

R. A. Silsbury

Plate 115 No. B745290 (Swindon 1975, 3867) seen here at Fratton on 4th June 1980, represents one of the final batches of conversion to Carflat, to Diagram 1/177. Based on the underframe of BSK No. M34279, it features a central portion of fixed side rail, with two removable sections at each end to permit side loading. The spiked wheel chocks are stored centrally, tied to the siderail.

R. A. Silsbury

'Lowliner'

During 1970, BR experimented in an effort to overcome the problems caused by the limited height of the loading gauge. Two of the experiments were for container carriers **(see Volume Two)**, but the other was to enable the easier carriage of high, but lightweight, road vehicles such as lorry tractors. Of course, these could be carried on 'Lowmacs' but this was at the cost of very high tares and extended train lengths for a low payload.

The 'Lowliner' consisted of a single unit made up of five 4-wheel flat wagons, semi-permanently coupled together **(see Table 12)**. Each wagon had a floor height of only 2ft. 10½ in., with 2ft. 6in. disc wheels; the wheelbase was 26ft. 3in. which was longer than that conventionally used for air-braked wagons. Each wagon had a wooden floor and low steel side rails **(see Plate 116)**. The inner wagons were 40ft. over headstocks and the outer wagons were 41ft. 6in. These had a 1ft. 3in. long built up area which sloped from the headstocks to the removable ramps which led down on to the deck, thus each wagon had the same usable length. The Oleo-pneumatic buffers were clip-topped and there were ramps which folded down over the buffers between each wagon. The nominal tare of the unit was 51 tons 17cwt. and the payload was 50 tons. The TOPS code was FZA. Although at least partially successful, no more were built and the set was withdrawn by the end of 1983. Instead, some 'Freight-liner' wagons were converted to vehicle carrying 'Freightflats'. Road vehicles were also carried on 'Boflats', a conversion from 'Boplates'. The problem of the carriage of lorry tractors was only resolved with the introduction of privately-owned articulated lowmacs.

Plate 116 As implied by its code name, the Lowliner was fitted with the unusually small wheels, of only 2ft. 6in. diameter, to provide a deck height of 2ft. 10½ in., thus enabling the carriage of commercial vehicle chassis. This low profile is evident in this view of the set at Luton on 12th July 1980, with wagon No. 150000 nearest.

P. W. Bartlett

Chapter 5
Fixed and Demountable Tank Wagons

For accounting purposes, BR included all tank wagons with the open wagons but, because they are so distinct, we have placed them in their own chapter. Freight tank wagons are used to carry many different liquids, such as petroleum products, other chemicals and food commodities. Although at nationalisation most privately-owned wagons became BR property, an exception was made for specialist wagons which included all of the tank wagons. This meant that private companies usually continued to provide for their own requirements and, as there was little common user need for carrying liquids, the BR fleet was small. This continued the policy of the pre-nationalisation railway com-panies, as none of them had ever owned many tank wagons. Even so, during the first decade, BR acquired a varied fleet of tank wagons. Some of these were from private builders who built similar designs for private companies. In most instances, the wagons were hired by BR to private companies and their livery was carried. Several of the designs were suitable for ferry use and the ferry diagram book numbers are given in parentheses. The ferry tanks were also issued with duplicate numbers in the B50XXXX series, after blocks of these numbers were allocated to each of the firms with BR-registered wagons in the mid-1950s.

TABLE 14

TANK WAGONS

Diag No.	Lot No.	Qnty	Builder	Date	Running numbers	Use and	first hirer,	Underframe & brake type
1/300	2076	6	Derby	1949	B749300 - 749305	Rubber latex,	H. Diaper,	Bogie vacuum
1/300	2621	3	Derby	1953	B749306 - 749308	Rubber latex,	H. Diaper,	Bogie vacuum
1/300	3404	6	Earlestown	1961	B749309 - 749314	Rubber latex,	H. Diaper,	Bogie vacuum
1/301	2170	10	Grazebrook	1950/1	B749600 - 749609	Ethylene oxide,	Petrochemicals Ltd,	RCH long-link air-pipe, Ferry
1/302	2074	2	Derby	1950	B749100 - 749101	Beer,	McEwans,	LMS clasp vacuum, Steam pipe
1/303	2306	1	Derby	1952	B749350	Cable compound,	Scottish Cables Ltd,	LMS 6-wh clasp vacuum, Steam pipe
1/304	2240	10	Hurst Nelson	1951	B749650 - 749659	Benzene,	Petrochemicals Ltd,	RCH long-link air-piped Ferry
1/305	2429	20	Ashford	1953	B749660 - 749679	Class A,	Traffic Services Ltd,	RCH long-link dual-piped, Ferry
1/306	2412	10	Lancing	1954	B749900 - 749909	Liquid Petroleum gas	Calor,	RCH long-link, unfitted
1/307	2410	2	Chas Roberts	1954	B749750 - 749751	Class B,	--	RCH long-link, unfitted
--	3644	1	Darlington/ Whessoe	1967	B749910	Corrosive liquids,	--	--
	Total	71						

Fixed Tank Wagons (see Table 14)

The first diagram, No. 1/300, was for a bogie tank which carried 40 tons of rubber latex for H. Diaper of Liverpool **(Plate 117)**. It is probable that the LMS had built four similar tanks earlier. BR only owned the running gear and underframe, as the tanks were owned by Diaper. The plate bogies had a 6ft. wheelbase with 2-piece GWR style axleboxes, except that the last 1961-built batch was fitted with roller bearings. Lot 2621 (Diagram No. C5203) had RIV ferry fittings with air pipe. They had duplicate numbers B502100-02. The tanks were painted blue with white lettering 'HENRY DIAPER (BULK LIQUIDS) LTD, LIVERPOOL', and the underframes were black. These tanks were withdrawn during the early 1970s.

The second diagram, No. 1/301 (C5142) was for ten 9 ton tank wagons built by Grazebrook in 1950 for carrying Ethylene oxide. They had an RCH long-link 12ft. wheelbase underframe with through air pipe and ferry chaining-down eyes. Buffers and axleboxes were to British standards. Originally they were lettered for use by Petrochemicals Ltd. at Irlam, and the BR number ended in a boxed-in P, perhaps to indicate private use **(Plate 118)**. By August 1952, several, if not all, were being used by the same company for liquid chlorine and they had been fitted with sun shields over the upper half of the tank; the diagram shows them in this condition. They also had LMR registration plates although they were on hire.

In May 1956, eight were in the Traffic Services Ltd. fleet and were being used for Butadiene. Two continued in Petrochemi-cals use from Partington to Zeebrugge. By 1958, five, Nos. B749603/04/05/07/09, respectively numbered B500103/04/05/ 07/09 were used by Petrochemicals Ltd. and Nos. B749601/02/ 06/08/00, respectively numbered B500820/21/22/23/26, were used by Traffic Services Ltd. The diagram describes them for use for Ethylene oxide, but it is likely that the diagram had not been updated. At some later date, after 1960, some reverted to liquid chlorine and others are reported as being in liquified ammonia traffic, but in 1977 some had reverted to carrying Ethylene oxide. The tanks were always white with black lettering and red stripes encircling them towards the end. They were out of TSL use by 1980, and most went to Beighton Engineer's Depot where they were used to carry water and had the TOPS code ZRP.

Diagram No. 1/302 was allocated to a pair of 10 ton tanks

which carried Beer for McEwans of Edinburgh — later they were lettered for Scottish and Newcastle Ltd., in brown. The design was identical to LMS Diagram No. 2037 with an LMS clasp brake and a 10ft. wheelbase; a through steam pipe was fitted for use in passenger trains. They probably worked between Edinburgh and Glasgow. Both went to the Engineer's Department at Wimbledon after this use ended **(Figure 26 and Plate 119 illustrate these tanks)**.

Diagram No. 1/303 was a single tank wagon for the carriage of 12 tons of Cable Compound for Scottish Cables Ltd. of Renfrew. This was also an LMS diagram, No. 2030. It had a 6-wheel, 13ft. wheelbase underframe with clasp brakes, auxiliary springs, and a steam pipe for use on passenger trains **(see Plate 120)**. The tank was black with white lettering. At a later date this wagon was transferred to the internal user fleet and stored lubricating oil at York TMD into 1985.

Diagram No. 1/304 (C5143) was for a batch of ten 20 ton anchor-mounted tanks for Class 'A' liquids introduced in 1951. These had a long-link 12ft. wheelbase underframe which had ferry chaining-down eyes, air through pipe, and British style buffers and axleboxes. A drawing and photograph was published in **MRC Annual 1985, page 24**. Initially the tanks were painted silver with PETROCHEMICALS LIMITED lettering and motif; they were used for Benzene **(Plate 121)**. They were given duplicate numbers B500110-19, and operated between Partington and Zeebrugge. In 1964 they were registered by BR using their original numbers. In 1966 the diagram was revised for Shell Chemical Co. Ltd; it was cancelled in 1972. At some stage the wagons reverted to Traffic Services Ltd. livery (if they had been painted for Shell, which is doubtful) and in this condition some of them went into Engineer's use in the late 1970s, especially being used at motive power depots. In the meantime, No. B749654 was sold off to Kilfrost Ltd. and became their No. 1 (KILF48128) in 1969. It was registered by BRB as No. 824 (Diagram No. 6/35) and was used for transporting de-icing liquid from Haltwhistle to the SR.

Diagram No. 1/305 (SFV6210) was for twenty 20 ton anchor-mounted tanks for Class 'A' liquids, introduced in 1953. The wagons were very similar to Diagram No. 1/304 except that they had an additional Continental-style brake platform at one end, giving the wagon an unusual asymmetrical appearance. This was a unique feature for a BR wagon, although it was more common on privately-owned ferry tank wagons. Diagram No. 1/305 wagons were dual air and vacuum through piped **(see Figure 27 and Plate 122)**.

These were delivered directly into the TSL fleet having a silver tank with black lettering. The Continental diagram shows that the first ten became Nos. B500700-09 and were owned by Traffic Services Ltd. Nos. B500700 and 01, at least, were used by British Celanese for Propylene oxide. They had an additional securing bar across the filler. Nos. B749670-79 became Nos. B500810-19, remaining on hire to TSL. No. B749672 was sold off to Kilfrost Ltd. and became No. 2 (KILF48129) in 1971, registered by the BRB as No. 1382 (Diagram No. 6/36). Nos. B749671/75/76/78/79 went into the DCE fleet at Newport, being used for the Severn Tunnel fire train. No. B749674 was painted dark blue for use by the Norwich DCE for water, and No. B749671 went into the LMR Molex drain-cleaning train which was formed during 1983. These twenty wagons were allocated the UIC numbers 21 70 078 0050 to 0069, but we have no evidence that they were carried; the Continental diagram was cancelled in 1972.

Diagram No. 1/306 was for ten 20 ton tanks for Butane and Propane **(see Plate 123)**. These had a 12ft. wheelbase, a long-link underframe, and were unfitted. Initially they were on hire to, and lettered for, Calor Gas use between Fawley and Ince and Saxham, and also Risby, Suffolk; later they were lettered for Esso use. The entire batch was sold to Liquified Pressure Gases Ancillary Services Ltd. of Rushden, Northants., in 1967, but nothing is known regarding their subsequent use. They were numbered RT1-10.

Diagram No. 1/307 was for a pair of 20 ton Class 'B' tanks. Because Class 'B' liquids are viscous they were fitted with four heating coils. A wide pipe at the other end was bifurcated with an opening on both sides of the wagon, and the pipes came together on the centre line, went to the top of the wagon and then right down inside. They had a 12ft. wheelbase and a long-link unfitted underframe. The user of these wagons was Townson Tankers, Oldham, and they were lettered TTR1 and 2, on hire from British Railways. Both tanks became internal user stores at Eastern Region motive power depots **(see Plate 124)**.

The final tank, No. B749910, did not have a diagram allocated. It appeared ten years later than any other BR-owned tank and, apart from being for ICI corrosive liquids, we know no details about it.

Plate 117 This Diagram 1/300 wagon carries two numbers. The underframe is No. B749302 (Derby 1949, 2076) and is railway-owned and the tank belongs to Henry Diaper Ltd., and is their No. 7. Originally a darker shade of blue, the livery carried a middle line of lettering reading 'Kirkby Trading Estate'. It is not known when the change to a lighter blue and the style of lettering depicted here, and photographed at Warrington in April 1972, was made. Note the unusual type of bogie.

D. Larkin

Plate 118 No. B749600 (Cravens 1951, 2170) is the first of the Diagram 1/301 9 ton Ethylene Oxide tanks, and is seen here in original livery. Attention is drawn to the ferry fittings and markings, the anchor symbol, black and yellow flashes at each end, the metric tare and wheelbase, and the legend 'Westinghouse Conduite' on the solebar. The date and location are not known, but is thought to be 1951.

P. W. Bartlett Collection

Plate 119 We have no photograph of a Diagram 1/302 10 ton Beer tank in original livery. When No. DB749101 (Derby 1951, 2074) was photographed at Wimbledon on 7th April 1983, it was in use by the Soil Mechanics Division of the BRB, and carried bright yellow livery on the tank, with white frame and black running gear.

R. A. Silsbury

Figure 26

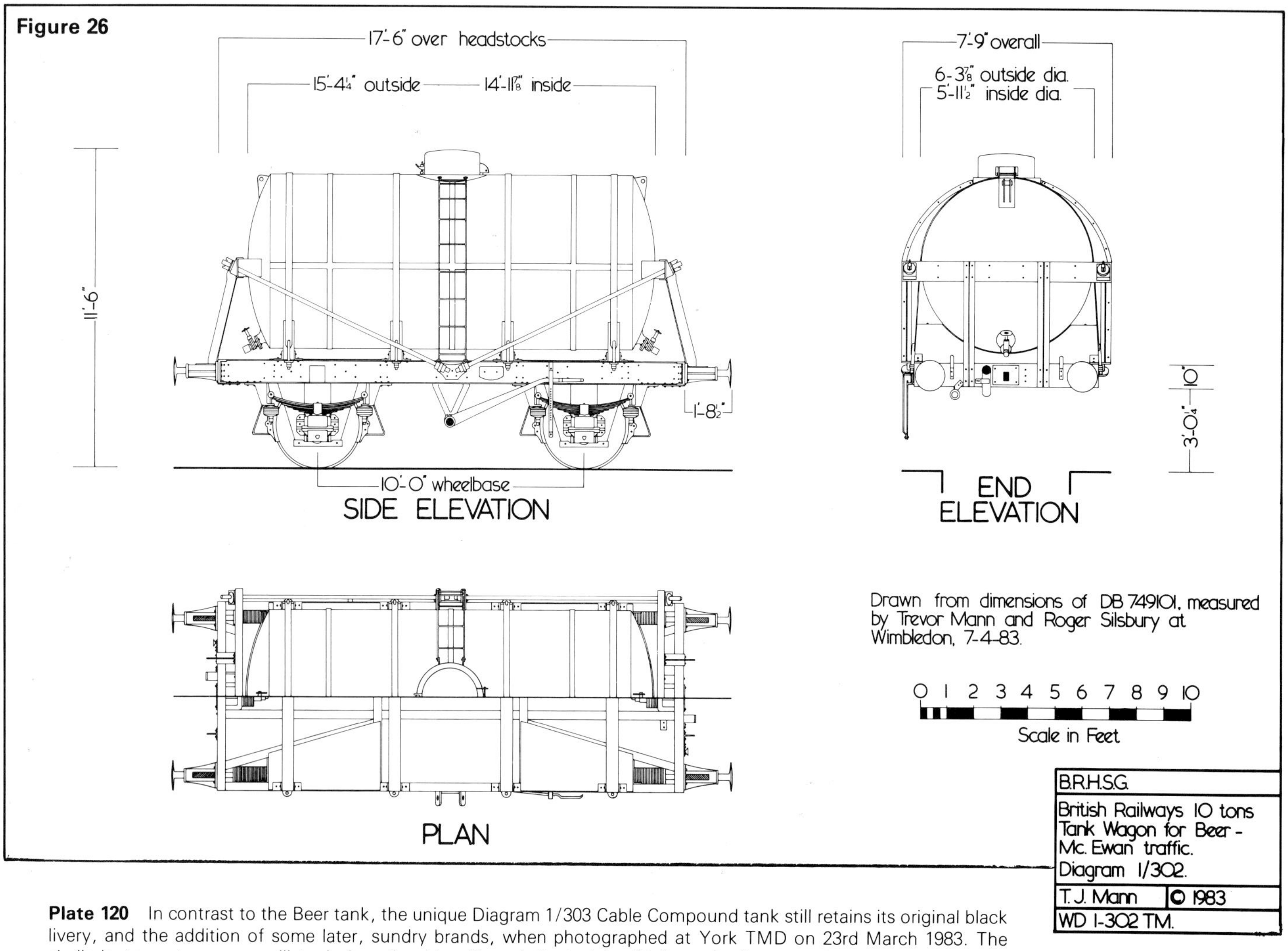

17'-6" over headstocks

15'-4¼" outside — 14'-11⅛" inside

11'-6"

10'-0" wheelbase

SIDE ELEVATION

1'-8½"

7'-9" overall

6'-3⅜" outside dia.

5'-11½" inside dia.

10'-0"

3'-0¼"

END ELEVATION

PLAN

Drawn from dimensions of DB 749101, measured by Trevor Mann and Roger Silsbury at Wimbledon, 7-4-83.

0 1 2 3 4 5 6 7 8 9 10

Scale in Feet

B.R.H.S.G.

British Railways 10 tons Tank Wagon for Beer — Mc. Ewan traffic.

Diagram 1/302.

T. J. Mann   © 1983

WD 1-302 TM.

Plate 120   In contrast to the Beer tank, the unique Diagram 1/303 Cable Compound tank still retains its original black livery, and the addition of some later, sundry brands, when photographed at York TMD on 23rd March 1983. The similarity to contemporary milk tanks is noticeable, although the tank itself is larger in diameter.

P. W. Bartlett

Plate 121 The great similarity between the underframes of the Diagram 1/301 tank **(Plate 118)**, and the 1/304 type, illustrated here by No. B749651 (Hurst Nelson 1951, 2240) which reflected the current private builders' practice, should be noted. However, the tanks of the latter were much larger, to suit the load carried. The location is believed to be Partington, in 1951.
P. W. Bartlett Collection

Plate 122 This view of No. DB749676M (Ashford 1953, 2429) was taken on 12th July 1978 at Monmouthshire Bank, Newport, when in service with the local DCE. It shows the details of the end brake platform of this unique, as far as BR vehicles are concerned, feature (see also **Figure 27**). The grey tank has had a large patch applied to the side to cover the Private Owner markings, and the number board is red, although the significance of the 'M' suffix is not known.
R. A. Silsbury

Figure 27

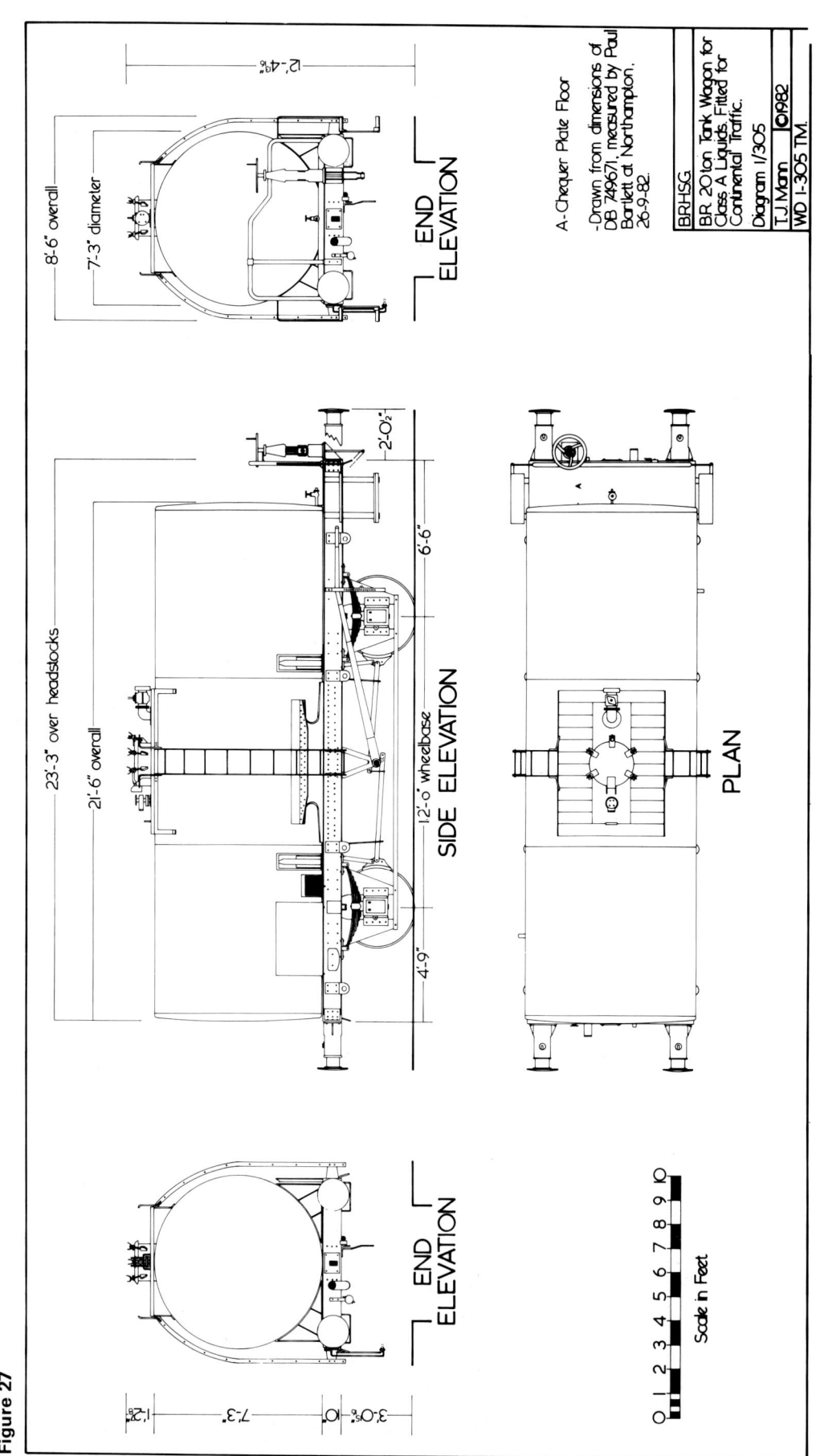

END ELEVATION

12'-4⅞"

8'-6" overall

7'-3" diameter

A – Chequer Plate Floor

– Drawn from dimensions of DB 749671, measured by Paul Bartlett at Northampton. 26-9-82.

BRHSG
BR 20 ton Tank Wagon for Class A Liquids. Fitted for Continental Traffic.

Diagram 1/305

T.J. Mann   10982

WD 1-305 T.M.

23'-3" over headstocks

21'-6" overall

12'-0" wheelbase

2'-0½"

6'-6"

4'-9"

SIDE ELEVATION

PLAN

END ELEVATION

12⅝"

7'-3"

3'-0½"

0 1 2 3 4 5 6 7 8 9 10

Scale in Feet

92

Plate 123 Considering the hazardous nature of the load, it is interesting to note that the Diagram 1/306 LPG tanks were built unfitted, and with three-link couplings. This photograph of No. B749901 was taken at Lancing in the spring of 1954, when new.

D. Larkin Collection

Plate 124 By contrast, at the end of its career, No. B749751, one of only two Diagram 1/307 Class B tanks, and now numbered in the internal user series as 041406, does not even warrant its own piece of track whilst doing duty as a dirty oil storage vehicle at Immingham TMD on 17th September 1983. The unusual pipework at the one end of this type can be seen.

R. A. Silsbury

Demountable Tanks

'Demountable Tanks' is the generic name given to a group of wagons which have a tank which is removable from the chassis. Although similar in many ways to containers, they differ because they are in no way interchangeable. One design of tank had to work with its own design of chassis, whereas containers were usually more flexible in the way they could be loaded. Some of the tanks included in this group had road wheels so that they could be used as road trailers when not loaded on the wagon.

Table 15 gives the details we know about these wagons. There are several gaps, especially in describing the type of underframe.

Tanks for carrying beer were the main component of the fleet. The first diagram, No. 1/325, was for 12 beer tanks, five were for Aitcheson's, three for Youngers, and four for Whiteway's Cider. At some time at least one was used for Gaymer's Cider of Norfolk; this is shown in **Plate 125**. All were vacuum-braked

being 17ft. 6in. over headstocks with a 10ft. wheelbase. We know that Lots 2043 and 2044 had the LNER clasp type brake, **(see Diagram No. 1/329 below)**. A single small tank of 1,080 gallons capacity was carried, which was mounted sloping down at one end.

There were only two Diagram No. 1/326 wagons. These each carried a pair of small 720 gallon tanks for Truman's Beer. They had an LMS clasp brake, and a 10ft. wheelbase underframe which had steam pipes for use in passenger trains. The tanks were mounted so that they sloped away from one another **(see Plate 126)**.

The ten wagons of Diagram No. 1/327 carried a single 'Bass' tank of 1,080 gallons. The framing of the tank was distinctive from those of Diagram No. 1/325. The chassis was an LMS clasp brake type of 10ft. wheelbase and had a steam through pipe.

TABLE 15

DEMOUNTABLE TANKS

Diag No.	Lot No.	Qnty	Builder	Date	Running numbers	Use and	first hirer,	Underframe type
1/325	2041	2	Shildon	1949	B749000 - 749001	Beer,	Aitchesons,	Vacuum
1/325	2042	3	Shildon	1949/51	B749007 - 749009	Beer,	Aitchesons,	Vacuum
1/325	2043	3	Shildon	1949/50	B749014/021/022	Beer,	Youngers,	Vacuum
1/325	2044	4	Shildon	1949/50	B749200 - 749203	Cider,	Whiteways,	LNER clasp
1/326	2075	2	Derby	1950	B749033 - 749034	Beer,	Trumans,	LMS clasp Steam pipe
1/327	2073	10	Derby	1950	B749023 - 749032	Beer,	Bass,	LMS clasp Steam pipe
1/328	2112	1	Swindon	1949	B749500	Paint & Varnish,	ICI,	ex GWR siphon 6-wh Vacuum
1/329	2077	8	Derby	1950	B749400 - 749407	Sodium silicate,	Crosfields,	RCH vacuum
1/329	2277	4	Derby	1950	B749408 - 749411	Sodium silicate,	Crosfields,	LNER clasp
1/330	2278	1	Shildon	1951	B749017	Beer,	Trumans,	Vacuum Steam pipe
1/330	2281	1	Shildon	1950	B749035	Beer,	Trumans,	Vacuum Steam pipe
1/331	2280	3	Shildon	1950	B749038 - 749040	Beer,	Bass,	LNER clasp
1/332	2370	18	Swindon	1951	B748800 - 748817	RoRail,	Guinness,	6-wh vacuum
1/333	2239	1	Derby	1951	B749250	Rum,	Lemon Hart,	Vacuum
1/334	2393	7	Earlestown	1952	B749041 - 749047	Beer,	Bass,	RCH Vacuum
1/334	2394	2	Derby	1952	B749036 - 749037	Beer,	Watneys,	LNER clasp
1/334	2395	2	Derby	1952	B749010 - 749011	Beer,	Aitchesons,	Vacuum
1/334	2566	4	Earlestown	1954	B749050 - 749053	Beer,	Bass,	RCH Vacuum
1/334	2649	5	Earlestown	1954	B749054 - 749058	Beer,	Bass,	RCH Vacuum
1/334	2774	7	Earlestown	1955	B749059 - 749065	Beer,	Bass,	Vacuum
1/334	2946	5	Earlestown	1955	B749066 - 749070	Beer,	Bass,	Vacuum
1/335	2537	10	Darlington	1953	B748818 - 748827	RoRail,	Guinness,	6-wh Vacuum
1/335	2763	3	Swindon	1954	B748828 - 748830	RoRail,	Guinness,	6-wh Vacuum
1/336	2423	1	Shildon	1953	B749048	Beer,	Aitchesons,	Vacuum
1/337	2427	6	Earlestown	1952	B749412 - 749417	Sodium silicate,	Crosfields,	RCH vacuum
1/338	2424	1	Shildon	1953	B749049	Beer,	Trumans,	RCH vacuum
	Total	114						

Diagram No. 1/330 was for two wagons for Truman's Beer which carried only a single small tank of 720 gallons. They were mounted on 10ft. wheelbase underframes which had a vacuum brake with a through steam pipe for use on passenger trains. We do not know what type of brake was fitted, but it seems likely that it was the LNER clasp type (nor do we know what livery was carried).

Diagram No. 1/331 was for another batch of beer tanks of 1,080 gallons; these appear to have been very similar to Diagram No. 1/327 but had shock-absorbing equipment bracing the tank. These tanks were for 'Bass' and had an LNER clasp underframe with a 10ft. wheelbase. The early livery of these tanks is not known, but later they would have appeared as other 'Bass' tanks.

Thirty two tanks were produced of the next diagram, No. 1/334. It appears to have been identical to Diagram No. 1/331 except the buffers were only 1ft. 6in. long instead of 1ft. 8½in. Most were for 'Bass' but lots were also built for Aitcheson's and Watney Combe & Reid Ltd. We have not observed examples of all batches, but those seen have all had an RCH vacuum brake underframe of 10ft. wheelbase and were 17ft. 6in. over headstocks. Some of these were long-lived as beer tanks, existing until 1979 in Bass Charrington traffic, painted in their red livery. Two, at least, of these tanks had air pipes and were lettered for ferry use, but the computer type numbers were not carried. **Figure 28 and Plate 127** is of one of the air-piped ferry wagons.

The single wagon of Diagram No. 1/336 was a beer tank for Aitcheson's. It had a larger tank but the capacity is not given. The chassis is 17ft. 6in. over headstocks with a 10ft. wheelbase, but we do not know what type of vacuum brake gear was fitted. The tank was mounted between shock absorbers.

The final diagram, No. 1/338, was able to carry either one or two tanks for Truman's Beer. The RCH vacuum brake underframe was 17ft. 6in. over headstocks with a 10ft. wheelbase **(see Plate 128)**. Several examples of demountable beer tanks have gone into Engineer's use.

Diagram No. 1/332, which was also designated GWR/BR Diagram No. DD9, was not for a demountable tank but for a 6-wheel road/rail tank which was wheeled on to the rail chassis. These tank wagons were owned by Guinness. The rail chassis deck had low sides and a higher pair of runners on the inside, the road wheels were guided between these, and the trailer was chained down on to them. The rail chassis had a 6-wheel vacuum brake underframe 24ft. 6in. over headstocks with a 16ft. wheelbase. The fittings were of the GWR/RCH standard with 2-piece axleboxes, auxiliary rubber suspension, screw couplings and a short brake lever. Although the diagram does not mention it, a steam heating through pipe was fitted **(see Plate 129)**.

Diagram No. 1/335 was, like No. 1/332, for Guinness road trailers, but, as these were only 4-wheeled, the rail chassis was correspondingly shorter. It had a 6-wheel underframe 20ft. 6in. over headstocks with a 13ft. wheelbase. Fittings differed slightly, such as one-piece axleboxes. Both of these designs had a removable pulley on the centre line of the floor at either end, and other pulleys for wire rope which was used to pull the trailer on. Wheel bars located the trailer on the wagon.

With wagons which were built to a passenger vehicle lot in 1949 to BR/GWR Diagram No. DD8, these wagons travelled overnight carrying the loaded tanks from the Park Royal Brewery, in West London, to Plymouth. The traffic ended in the late 1950s. Subsequently, some of the wagons may have been used for glucose traffic, but we have no details.

The remaining diagrams to be described were for a variety of liquids. A single wagon was allocated Diagram No. 1/333. This design carried two 724 gallon tanks of Lemon Hart Rum. The underframe had a 10ft. wheelbase which was 17ft. 6in. over headstocks with a vacuum brake, but we do not know the type. The tanks were painted in Lemon Hart's yellow-orange with large lettering; the fate of the wagon is not known to us.

Two small batches of Diagram No. 1/329 demountable tanks were built for use by J. Crosfields Ltd. at Warrington. These small tanks, which had two loading hatches, carried 803 gallons of sodium silicate for use in soap making **(see Plate 130)**. In 1960, they were available for hire from the London Midland Region. In 1962, these wagons were being used by ICI and were lettered to be returned to South Bank NER, and the tanks were used via the Dunkerque Ferry for a traffic to Spain. Some of the chassis remain in use as runners with Class 03 diesel shunters on the Eastern Region.

However, there is some confusion about the chassis. Lot 2077 had an RCH vacuum type and appears to have been of 10ft. wheelbase. Lot 2277 had an LNER clasp vacuum type of 10ft. wheelbase. At least one of the latter was plated both 'Lot 2044 Shildon 1949' and 'Lot 2277 Derby 1950' and one of Lot 2043 was also Lot 2277. Thus it may well have been that some of the Whiteway's Cider and Younger's wagons of Diagram No. 1/325 were very short-lived, and that the redundant chassis were reused. The diagram further confuses by showing a wheelbase of both 9ft. and 10ft., but we have no evidence that any had the shorter wheelbase.

Diagram No. 1/337 was for another sodium silicate tank for J. Crosfield Ltd. and worked to Scotland. The tank was of 875 gallons and had only a single filler. Although the chassis was 17ft. 6in. over headstocks and had a vacuum brake, it had only a 9ft. wheelbase. The tank was mounted between shock absorbers **(Plate 131)**.

A single wagon was allocated Diagram No. 1/328. It was also given GWR Diagram No. EE3 and Lot 1647. It carried paints and varnishes from ICI at Slough with some similar GWR wagons. Four 500 gallon tanks were carried on a 6-wheel underframe which came from Siphon No. 1579, built in 1904, of Diagram No. O5 **(see GWR Wagons Vol. 2, page 124 for similar wagon)**. The diagram shows coach size wheels of 3ft. 6½in. diameter, and an underframe 27ft. 4½in. over headstocks with a wheelbase of 19ft. The livery of this wagon is not known to us. Built in April 1949, it was condemned in 1959.

The diagram book continues with several tanks which were loaded on to 'Conflats', but these are outside the scope of this book.

Plate 125 (Overleaf Top) Although the Diagram 1/325 vehicles to Lot 2044 are described as for Whiteway's Cyder traffic, this view of No. B749201 (Shildon 1949) was taken only a year later, at Norwich Thorpe, on 12th September 1950, and is clearly carrying Gaymer's Cyder. We are unsure of the colour of the demountable tank. Clearly visible are the LNER vacuum-braked underframe, and split/spoke wheels.

BR/OPC

Plate 126 (Overleaf Bottom) No. B749034 (Derby 1950, 2075) is a Diagram 1/326 vehicle, and has LMS clasp vacuum brakegear and steam heat pipes to enable it to run in passenger trains. The location is unknown, but may well be its home station of Burton-on-Trent, during 1950.

D. Larkin Collection

CAYMER'S
CYDER
ATTLEBOROUGH
&
LONDON
B 749201
SHUNT
WITH CARE

TRUMAN'S
LONDON
&
BURTON
LONDON & BURTON
B 749034
SHUNT WITH CARE
TRUMAN'S
LONDON
&
BURTON

Plate 127 Diagram 1/334 had most examples, and it is appropriate that we can also include a drawing **(Figure 28)**, as well as this photograph of No. B749036 (Derby 1952, 2394) taken at Burton-on-Trent in February 1976. Although the diagram describes the brakegear as 'AVB & Morton', this example clearly has the LNER clasp vacuum type. A possible explanation is that Nos. B749036/7 were originally allocated to Lot 2279, for Watney, Coombe & Reid traffic, to be built at Shildon. This Lot was cancelled, but the numbers were reissued to Lot 2394, to be built at Derby, and we can only speculate whether the chassis had already been constructed. As discussed in the text, there are other irregularities in batches of demountable tanks, which we have been unable to resolve. Note, in this illustration, the large number panel, various metric information, and the air pipe, RIV screw coupling and 2ft. 0½in. Oleo pneumatic buffers. **Plate 52** illustrates the more common RCH vacuum brake underframe of No. B749045, the vehicle depicted in **Figure 28**, and on the rear of the dust jacket, B749055, which combines RCH vacuum brake and the extra fittings which appear on B749036.

D. Larkin

Plate 128 This illustration of No. B749049 also poses some questions. The numberplate gives the building date as Shildon 1952, but official records quote the date as 1953. Unfortunately, the complete dates for lifting and painting at the left-hand end of the solebar are obscured, although it can be discerned that the lifting date, '53 6003' means year 1953, place Shildon (Code 6003). The paint date '53 2001' again shows year 1953, but 2001 is Derby. The brake overhaul date — centre of solebar, below the 7 point star — is 30-10-53 2001, and the date of the photograph is 10th November 1953, at Derby. We do not know whether the vehicle had been in another use prior to a repaint at Derby, or whether it had been sent new from Shildon to Derby for final livery. This Diagram 1/338 wagon could carry either a single tank centrally, as illustrated, or a pair of tanks; the additional holding down chains can be seen stowed across the end. Note also the round section instanter coupling.

BR/OPC

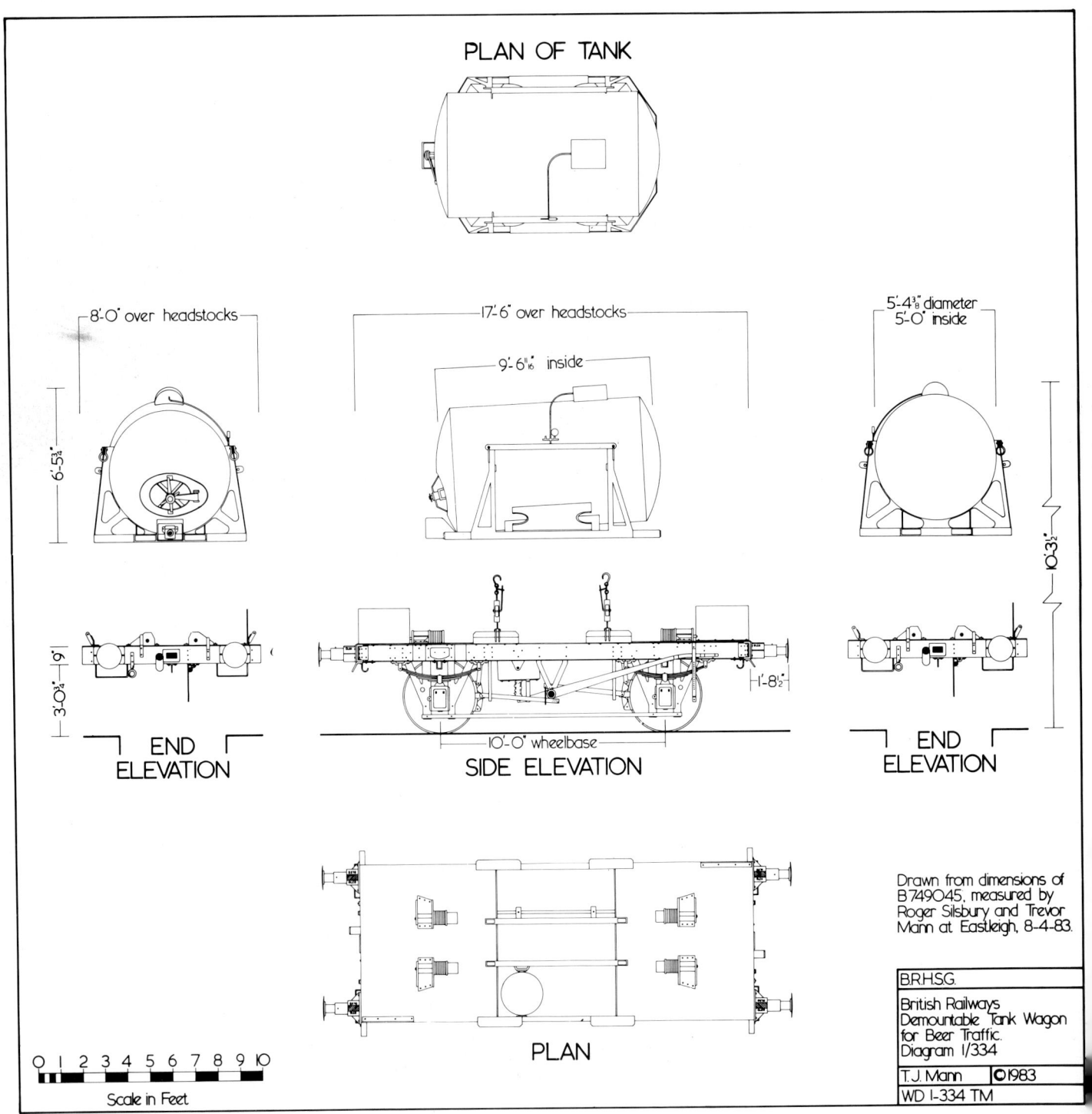

PLAN OF TANK

8'-0" over headstocks

17'-6" over headstocks

5'-4⅜" diameter
5'-0" inside

9'-6¹¹⁄₁₆" inside

6'-5¾"

10'-3½"

END
ELEVATION

SIDE ELEVATION

END
ELEVATION

3'-0¾" / 9"

10'-0" wheelbase

1'-8½"

PLAN

Drawn from dimensions of
B749045, measured by
Roger Silsbury and Trevor
Mann at Eastleigh, 8-4-83.

| B.R.H.S.G. |
| British Railways Demountable Tank Wagon for Beer Traffic. Diagram 1/334 |
| T.J. Mann   © 1983 |
| WD I-334 TM |

0 1 2 3 4 5 6 7 8 9 10
Scale in Feet

Figure 28

Plate 129 (Right Upper) Another official view, dated Swindon, 20th May 1952, depicts No. B748809, one of the six wheel chassis for conveying Guiness road tankers, built under Lot 2370 to Diagram 1/332. Features to note include the axle chocks for the road tanker, the ramped section against the main guides upon which rested the small relieving wheels to take the weight off the road wheels and springs during transit, the rail clamps, and the hinged and fixed corner plates — these appeared later on the early Carflats **(Plate 109)**. Although plated for a load of 14 tons, the difference in tare weights quoted on the diagram indicates a gross weight of road tanker and contents of 15 tons 13cwt.

BR/OPC

Plate 130 (Right Lower) This view of No. B749410 (Derby 1950, 2277) is the only one available to us, although the quality is not as good as we would wish. It depicts a Diagram 1/329 vehicle, probably when new.

D. Larkin Collection

14T B 748809   EMPTY TO PARK ROYAL.

JOSEPH CROSFIELD & SONS LIMITED
WARRINGTON

B 749410

Plate 131 A somewhat better photograph depicts No. B749417, a Diagram 1/337 vehicle built at Earlestown 1952, to Lot 2422. This official view was not taken at Earlestown until 29th October 1954, and shows a wagon very much in traffic. The spillage on the tank should be noted, along with the fact that the 'Empty to Pochins Siding, Warrington, LMR' has been painted out. The form of ladder to gain access to the top of the tank is unusual.

BR/OPC

Chapter 6
Steel-carrying Wagons

The title of this chapter is a slight misnomer. In reality the wagons which were used for carrying the considerable traffic in steel were specialist open wagons but, because there was such a number and variety of them, BR chose to account for them separately. As discussed below, these wagons were not restricted to steel traffic. Some types could also be used for other metals and timber, general merchandise and road vehicles.

Pipes

The LNER introduced a special design of wagon for carrying pipes in 1936, and BR continued to use all of their design features when building their series of 'Pipes'. The bodies were five planks high with fixed ends, and the sides consisted of two drop doors with a removable stanchion between. These were mounted on an underframe 21ft. 6in. long over headstocks with a wheelbase of 12ft.

Table 16 gives details of the 'Pipes'. BR commenced building to both Diagram Nos. 1/460 and 1/461 at the same time. Diagram No. 1/461 was the LNER design, Diagram No. 127, with clasp brake and a central upright strapping on each door. Each of the doors has two door closers mounted on the side strapping **(see Figure 29 and Plate 132)**. Diagram No. 1/460 must have been an LMS design although none were built by them. The doors lacked the central upright strapping, and the door closers were mounted to the outer sides of the upright strappings. Built unfitted with RCH long-link underframes, they were vacuum-braked later **(see Figure 42 FWLGW for unfitted version)**.

Diagram No. 1/462 was issued for wagons that were vacuum-fitted from new, but was otherwise identical to Diagram No. 1/460 **(see Plate 133)**. Wagons built to Lot 3335 were clasp-braked **(see Figure 30 and Plate 134)**. Diagram No. 1/463 additionally specified the fitting of hydraulic buffers. A 12 ton payload remained standard throughout.

In original use, many of these 'Pipe' wagons were branded 'RETURN EMPTY TO STANTON GATE (LMR) OR ILKESTON (GN)'. As this traffic declined, however, these versatile wagons were transferred to other workings, receiving appropriate letterings such as 'EMPTY TO RUNCORN FOR ICI TRAFFIC'. The fifty wagons of Lot 3070, which were numbered in the 'Open Merchandise' series, were introduced for newsprint traffic. Later they were also used as 'Pipe'. Some of all variants remained in capital stock (TOPS code SOV) for general merchandise. Others were transferred to the Engineer's Department, some of these being fully repainted in olive drab.

In 1983, fifty 'Pipes' were converted to air brake for MOD traffic. They were renumbered and allocated Diagram No. OD001A.

TABLE 16

PIPES

Diag No.	Lot No.	Qnty	Builder	Year	Running numbers	Underframe	Brake type
1/460	2004	300	Derby	1949	B740000 - 740299	RCH long-link	Unfit
1/460	2305	50	Cambrian	1951	B740600 - 740649	RCH long-link	Unfit
1/460	2329	50	Swindon	1953	B740650 - 740699	RCH long-link	Unfit
1/460	2458	200	Wolverton	1953	B740700 - 740899	RCH long-link	Unfit
1/460	2545	200	Wolverton	1954	B740900 - 741099	RCH long-link	Unfit
1/461	2046	100	Darlington	1949	B740300 - 740399	LNER clasp	Vacuum
1/461	2047	200	Darlington	1949	B740400 - 740599	LNER clasp	Vacuum
1/462	2712	350	Wolverton	1955/6	B741100 - 741449	RCH long-link	Vacuum
1/462	2845	60	Wolverton	1956	B741500 - 741559	RCH long-link	Vacuum
1/462	2846	170	Wolverton	1957	B741560 - 741729	RCH long-link	Vacuum
1/462	3070	50	Wolverton	1956	B484150 - 484199	RCH long-link	Vacuum
1/462	3335	200	Wolverton	1961	B741750 - 741949	BR clasp	Vacuum
1/463	3167	20	Wolverton	1957	B741730 - 741749	RCH long-link	Vacuum
OD001A	4030	50	Shildon	1983	113000 - 113049	--	Air
Total		2000					

PIPE
RETURN EMPTY TO
STAVELEY WORKS.
12 T.
B74030
XP
W.B.12-0
8-8

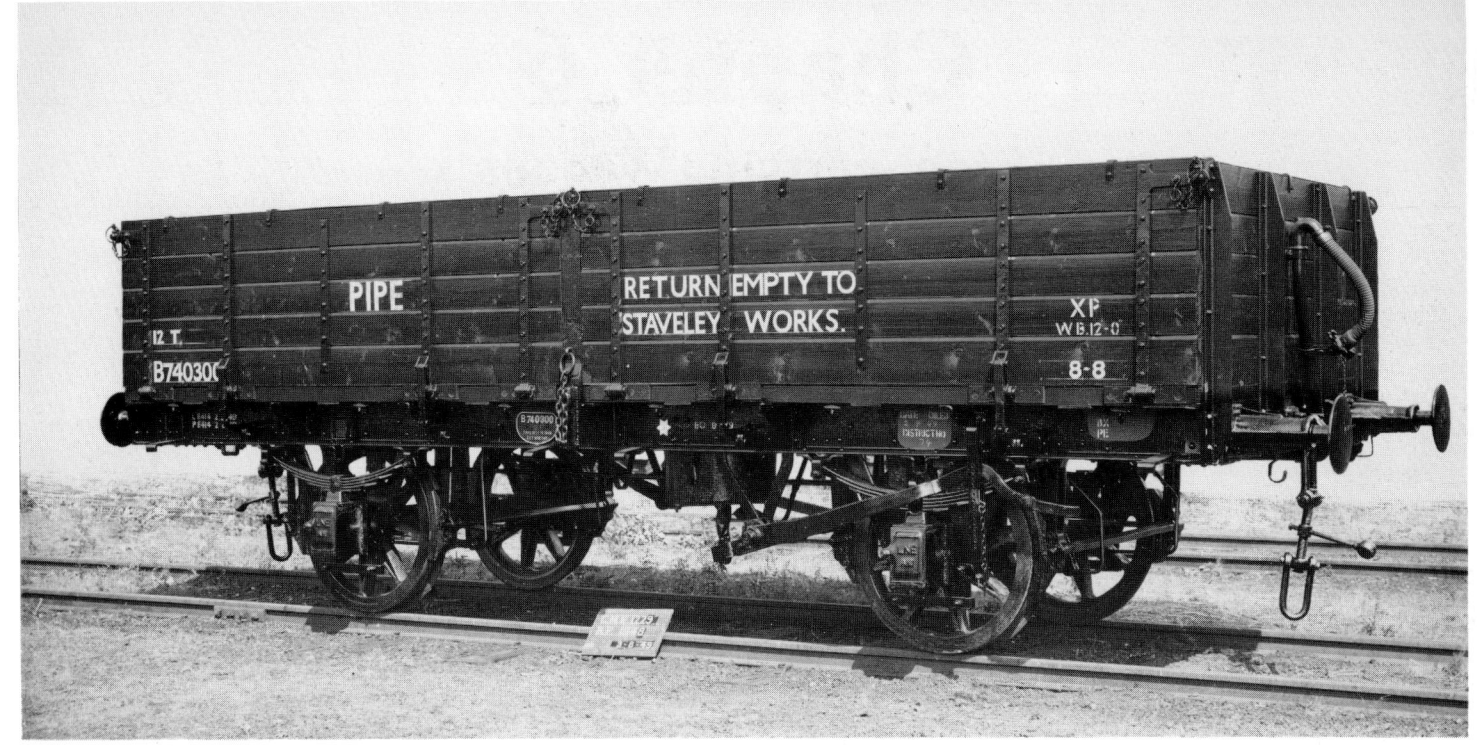

Plate 132 The LNER design, Diagram 1/461, 12 ton 'Pipe' wagon is represented here by the first of the batch, No. B740300, when brand-new on 3rd August 1949 at Darlington. The livery is bauxite, and the brand 'Return empty to Staveley Works' carries no defining initials as appeared later – in this case G. C. Presumably, in 1949, the Darlington painters assumed everyone would know! The works location for the lift and paint dates appear in the LNER Code 414, with an E prefix to differentiate from similar codes on the other pre-nationalisation railways.

P. W. Bartlett Collection

Figure 29

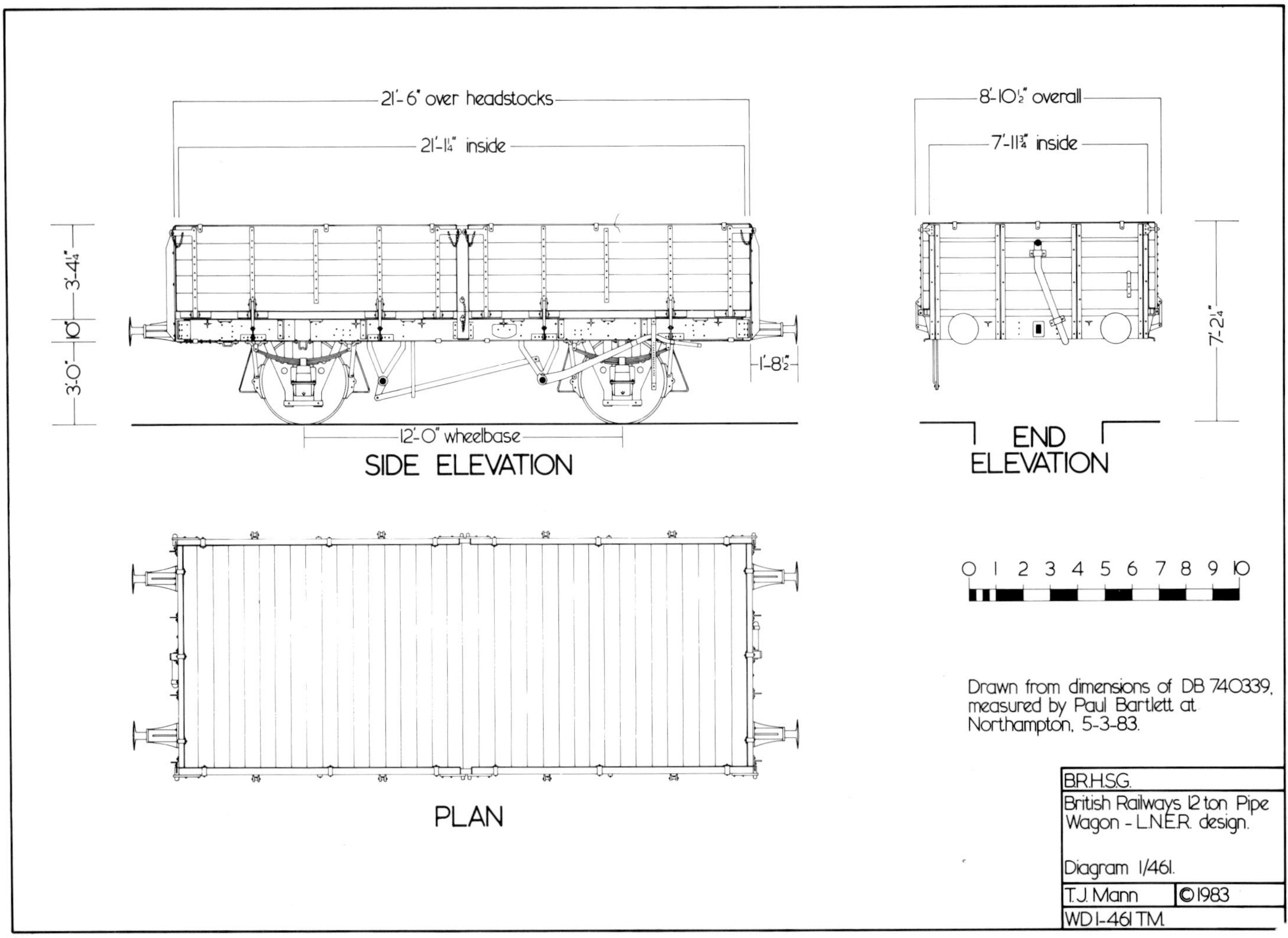
21'-6" over headstocks
21'-1¼" inside
3'-4¼"
10"
3'-0"
1'-8½"
12'-0" wheelbase
SIDE ELEVATION
8'-10½" overall
7'-11¾" inside
7'-2¼"
END ELEVATION
PLAN
0 1 2 3 4 5 6 7 8 9 10
Drawn from dimensions of DB 740339, measured by Paul Bartlett at Northampton, 5-3-83.
B.R.H.S.G.
British Railways 12 ton Pipe Wagon - L.N.E.R. design.
Diagram 1/461.
T.J. Mann
©1983
WD1-461TM

Plate 133 The differences in the bodywork between the two pre-nationalisation designs can be seen by comparing this view of No. B741653 (Wolverton 1957, 2846) photographed at Eastleigh on 18th June 1976, with **Plate 132**. The scalloped edge to the lowest plank was to clear the rope cleats on the curb rail, but as the right-hand door lacks them, they were obviously unnecessary. The livery is bauxite, with the post-1964 boxed lettering and 'Pipe-VB' code.

R. A. Silsbury

Figure 30

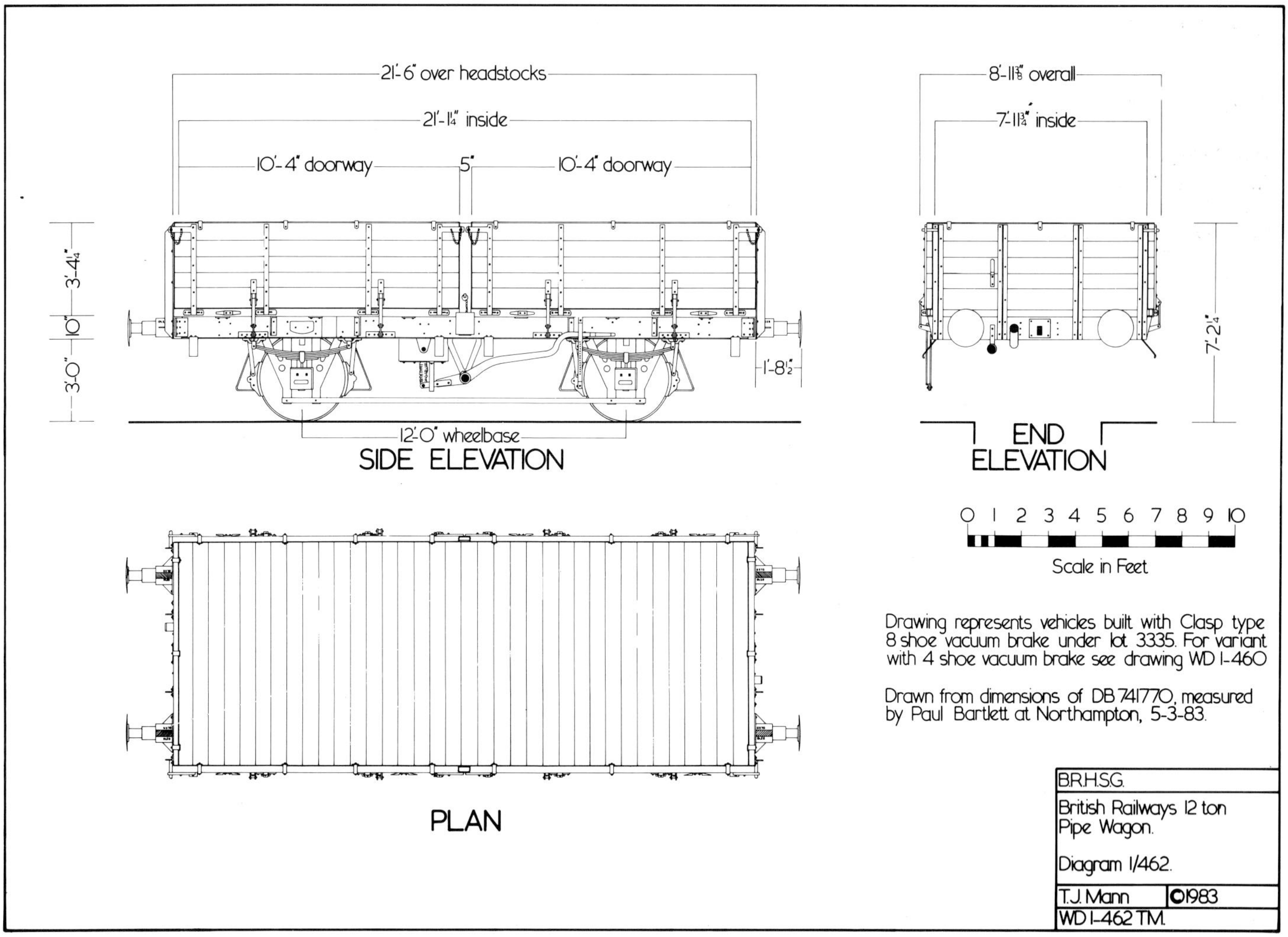

21'-6" over headstocks

21'-1¼" inside

10'-4" doorway   5"   10'-4" doorway

3'-4¼"

3'-0"   10"

1'-8½"

12'-0" wheelbase

SIDE ELEVATION

8'-11⅝" overall

7'-11¾" inside

7'-2¼"

END ELEVATION

0 1 2 3 4 5 6 7 8 9 10

Scale in Feet

Drawing represents vehicles built with Clasp type 8 shoe vacuum brake under lot 3335. For variant with 4 shoe vacuum brake see drawing WD 1-460

Drawn from dimensions of DB 741770, measured by Paul Bartlett at Northampton, 5-3-83.

PLAN

B.R.H.S.G.
British Railways 12 ton Pipe Wagon.
Diagram 1/462.
T. J. Mann   ©1983
WD 1-462 TM.

Plate 134 The LMS pattern bodywork remained standard for all further builds of 'Pipe' wagon, only the underframes being altered. No. B741751 (Wolverton 1961, 3335) is one fitted with BR clasp vacuum brakes and a short unusually-shaped brake lever. When recorded at Fratton on 21st June 1978, it had acquired Oleo pneumatic buffers, and the nearest door restraining spring was missing.

R. A. Silsbury

Tubes

The GWR, LMS and LNER all had their own design of wagons designated 'Tubes' but used for the carriage of lightweight general merchandise as well as steel tubes. At first, BR built examples of all three company designs. **Table 17** gives details of the 'Tubes'.

TABLE 17

TUBE

Diag No.	Lot No.	Qnty	Builder	Year	Running numbers	Underframe	Brake type
1/445	2048	100	Darlington	1949/50	B730000 – 730099	LNER clasp	Vacuum
1/445	2049	400	Darlington	1950	B730100 – 730499	LNER clasp	Vacuum
1/446	2127	100	Swindon	1950	B731000 – 731099	GWR long wb	Unfit
1/447	2204	290	Darlington	1951/2	B731100 – 731389	RCH long-link	Unfit
1/447	2328	100	Swindon	1953	B731390 – 731489	RCH long-link	Unfit
1/447	2457	100	Wolverton	1953	B731490 – 731589	RCH long-link	Unfit
1/448	2554	450	Darlington	1954	B731590 – 732039	RCH long-link	Unfit
1/448	2740	350	Darlington	1955	B732040 – 732389	BR clasp	Vacuum
1/448	2867	650	Darlington	1955/6	B732390 – 733039	BR clasp	Vacuum
1/448	3226	180	Darlington	1959	B733040 – 733219	BR clasp	Vacuum
1/448	3288	420	Derby	1960	B730500 – 730919	BR clasp	Vacuum
1/448	3332	300	Derby	1961	[B730920 – 730999] [B733240 – 733459]	BR clasp	Vacuum
1/449	3258	20	Darlington	1959	B733220 – 733239	Ferry	Air & vac.
Total		3460					

LNER design 'Tube'

Diagram No. 1/445 was LNER Diagram No. 98. It had a payload of 20 tons and was similar to a lengthened 'Pipe' wagon **(see Plate 135)**. All were vacuum-braked using an extended version of the LNER clasp brake arrangement. The underframe was 30ft. 4¾in. over headstocks and had a 19ft. wheelbase. The body was five planks high with a fixed end, and the sides dropping as a pair of doors which had a removable stanchion between. Although not repeated, this design was successful. From the late 1950s onwards some were used for the carriage of palletised canned foods, others, with minor modification, carried palletised car engines and yet others had the ends extended upwards by three planks, presumably for the carriage of three very large tubes. As they were released from the capital stock, the Engineer's Department used them, and few had been scrapped by mid-1984 when some remained in the capital fleet.

GWR design 'Tube'

The least successful 'Tube' design was GWR Diagram No. O/41 which was given BR Diagram No. 1/446. This had a payload of 22 tons. All were unfitted, and the extended Morton underframe with rubber auxiliary suspension was 30ft. over headstocks and had a wheelbase of 19ft. 6in. The body was only four planks high and had a small central drop door in each side. The low sides meant that they were less suitable for bulky, but relatively lightweight, tubes than the other designs. **Figure 40 in FWLGW** shows an example as originally built. Most, if not all, remained in this condition throughout their lives as they were not vacuum-braked, and the last were withdrawn in 1977.

LMS design 'Tube'

In 1951, BR appears to have decided that the simpler and stronger LMS design, Diagram No. 2116, was more suitable, and this became BR Diagram No. 1/447. Three batches of these wagons were built to carry 22 tons. All had an RCH long-link unfitted underframe which was 30ft. 6in. over headstocks and had a 17ft. 6in. wheelbase. The five plank high body had a small drop door located centrally in the side, and a corrugated-steel end **(see Plate 136, and Figure 41 in FWLGW)**. Few, if any, of these wagons were converted to vacuum brake, and they went

out of general use at the end of 1978, except for a small number retained by the Engineer's Department.

BR design 'Tube'

In 1954, the LMS design was altered by simply increasing the length over headstocks to 32ft. and the wheelbase to 18ft. 6in. This became Diagram No. 1/448. The first lot were built unfitted and a few were never vacuum-braked. However, most received the same type of clasp brake that was fitted to all later lots **(see Figure 31 and Plate 137)**. This was a successful design, some continue in capital stock and others are used by the Engineer's Department, often for carrying concrete troughing, signalling components or spoil. During 1983, the code name COD was introduced by the Engineer's Department for some of these wagons.

A common branding on the LNER and LMS/BR design wagons was 'EMPTY TO CORBY AND WELDON'. Many of Diagram No. 1/448 had wood battens fitted across the floor, and these were branded 'TUBE VB BATTEN'. The TOPS codes for all 'Tubes' were STO and STV.

'Ferry Tube'

The final 'Tube' design for the cross-channel ferry services **(see Figure 32 and Plate 138)**. Diagram No. 1/449 (Continental Diagram No. SFV6247) was an interesting adaption of Diagram No. 1/448. The corrugated end and outer portion of each side remained the same, but the central section of the sides and the small drop door were replaced by a pair of large drop doors with a removable central stanchion. They had full vacuum and air braking, together with full ferry fittings, including buffers, axleboxes and cast chaining-down eyes on the solebar. These wagons carried 22 tons, later uprated to 26 tonnes, and had the TOPS code OIX. Their UIC numbers were 21 70 619 0 040 to 059. Many were transferred to the Engineer's Department during 1982 and were painted olive drab. The October 1983 Continental Diagram No. E247 shows Nos. 044/046/048/049 and 053 remaining in international traffic.

The later designs of 'Tubes' were discussed more fully in **MRC Annual 1984**. Later, a prototype air-braked 'Open' was described as a 'Tube' wagon on the diagram, but as these became the OBAs, they are described in **Chapter 3**.

Plate 135 Although designed for the carriage of long tubes, the Tube wagon was equally capable of being used for bulky general merchandise. Here, Diagram 1/445 type, No. B730120 (Darlington 1950, 2049) has five Admiralty container crates at Fratton on 26th February 1979. The large metal plate affixed to the inner end of the left-hand door may have been purely as a repair, but several of these dropside design of Tube wagons had similar plates fitted to both doors when used for carrying palletised car engines, to prevent damage when a fork-lift truck was used to close the doors. As the different designs of Tube wagon varied in length, the legend 'Length Inside' was always applied at the right-hand end; the Diagram 1/445 LNER-inspired type measured 30ft.

R. A. Silsbury

Plate 136 No. B731375 (Darlington 1951, 2204) to Diagram 1/447 remained unfitted throughout its life. When photographed at Luton on 3rd April 1981, it was in use by the S&T Department, although retaining its unfitted livery of light grey, with unpainted replacement planks, and white lettering on black patches. The legend on the bottom plank to the left of the door reads 'Empty to Corby & Weldon'.

R. A. Silsbury

Plate 137 The additional 1ft. 6in. of length of Diagram 1/448, depicted here by No. B733307 (Derby 1961, 3332) is not readily apparent, apart from the 'Length inside 31ft. 7¼ in.' legend. This vehicle would have been fitted with Oleo pneumatic buffers and Hybox axleboxes from new, and is also branded as having 'Battens' fitted, to assist handling its load. It is seen at Wellingborough on 11th June 1978.

R. A. Silsbury

Plate 138 The ferry version of the Tube wagon employed the same basic dimensions as the BR design Diagram 1/448, except that two large doors replaced the single small door, and gave access to half the length of the body. Empty/Loaded and Goods/Passenger changeover gear was provided, and full RIV fittings **(see Figure 32)**. When the 12-digit international numbers were allocated, these were painted on the body, whilst the 'B' prefix number remained on the plate, as seen here with 21 70 619-0 045-2 (No. B733225 — Darlington 1959, 3258) at Ashford in April 1973.

D. Larkin

Figure 31

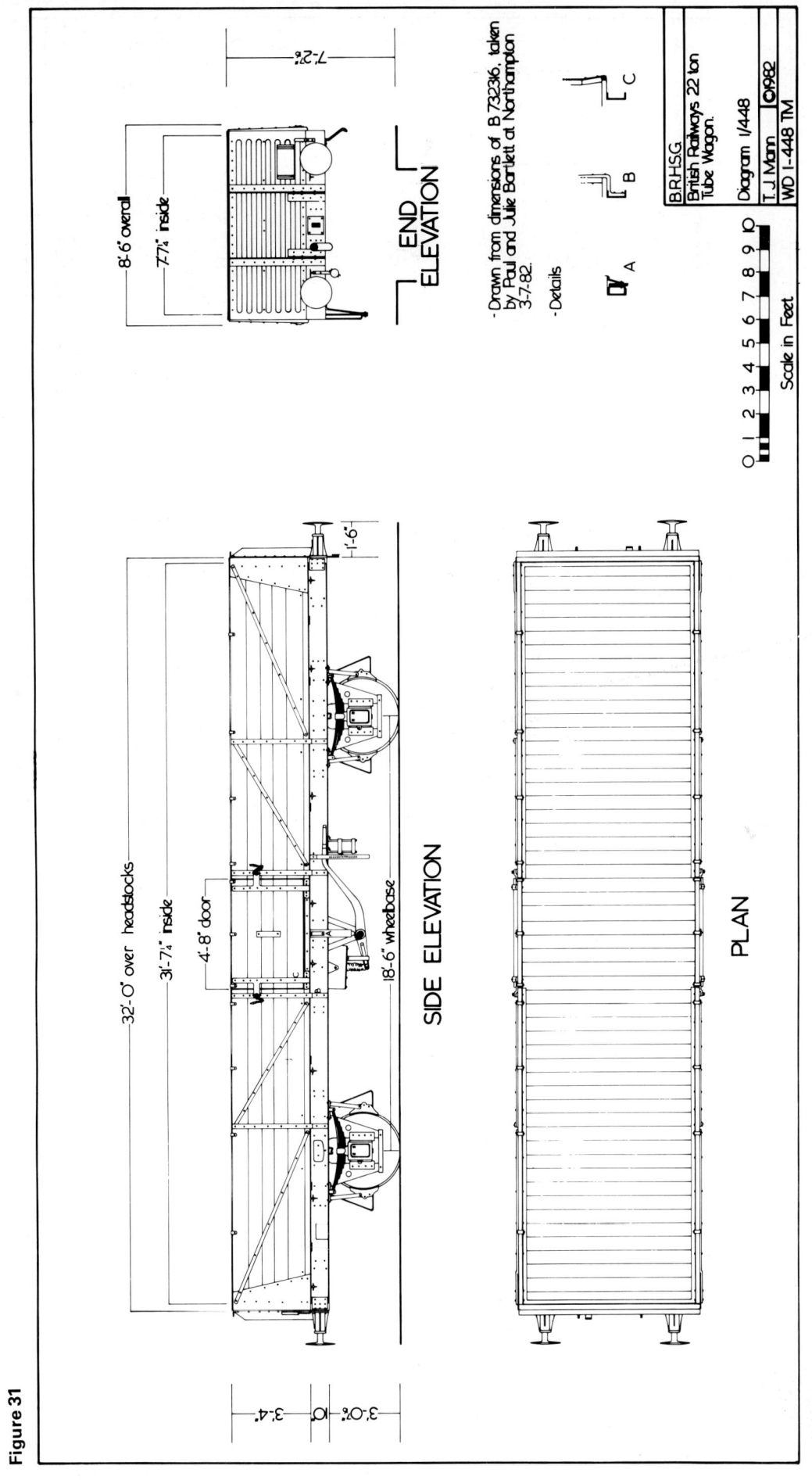

7'-2½"

8'6" overall

7'7½" inside

END ELEVATION

- Drawn from dimensions of B 73236, taken by Paul and Julie Bartlett at Northampton 3-7-82.

- Details

A   B   C

B.R.H.S.G.
British Railways 22 ton Tube Wagon.

Diagram 1/448

T.J.Mann   ©1982
WD 1-448 TM

0 1 2 3 4 5 6 7 8 9 0
Scale in Feet

1'-6"

32'-0" over headstocks

31'-7¼" inside

4'-8" door

18'-6" wheelbase

SIDE ELEVATION

3'-0½"   1'0"   3'-4"

PLAN

Figure 32

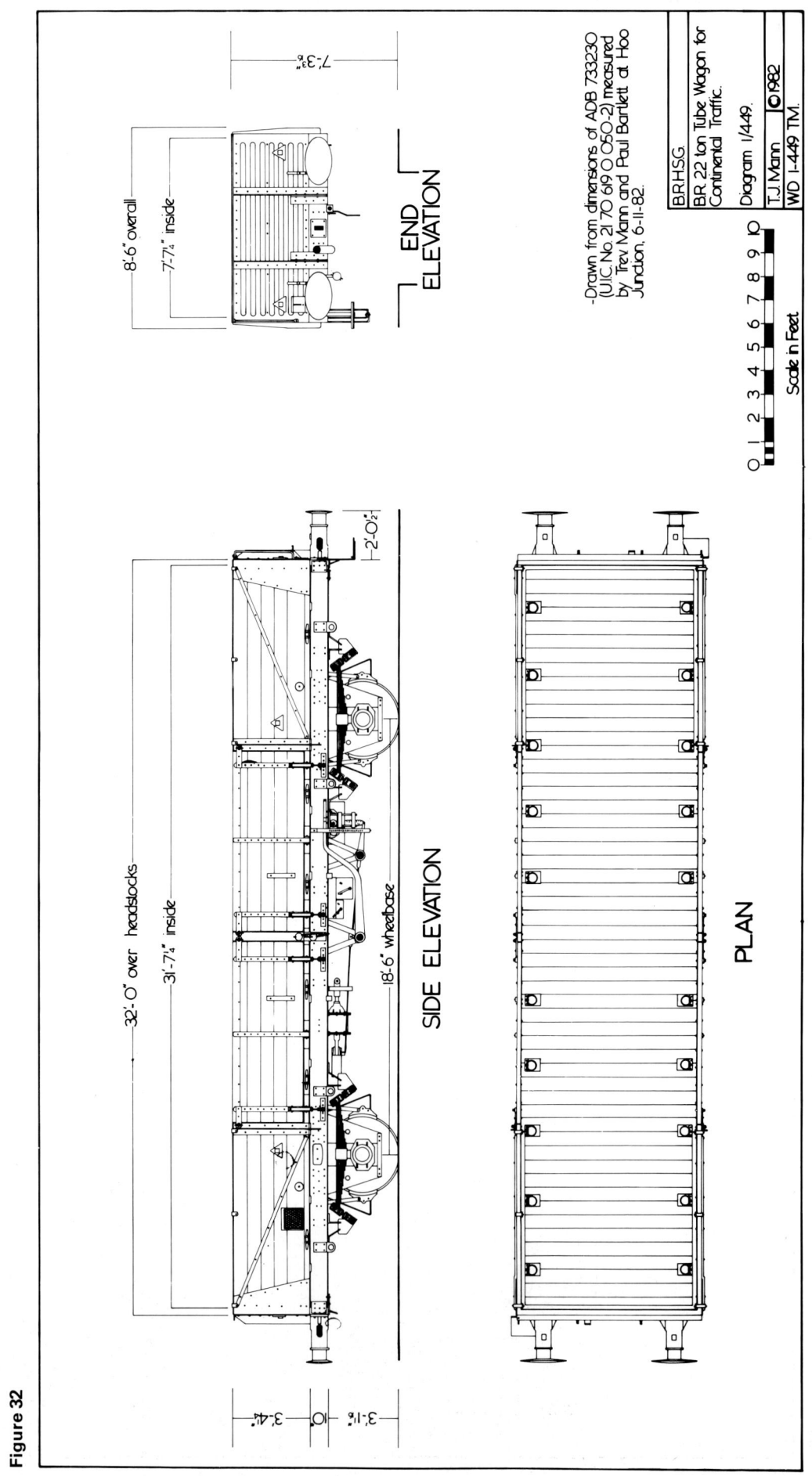

7'-3⅜"

8'-6" overall

7'-7¼" inside

END ELEVATION

-Drawn from dimensions of ADB 733230 (U.I.C. No 21 70 619 0 050-2) measured by Trev Mann and Paul Bartlett at Hoo Junction, 6-11-82.

BRHSG

BR 22 ton Tube Wagon for Continental Traffic.

Diagram 1/449.

T.J Mann   ©1982

WD 1-449 T.M.

0 1 2 3 4 5 6 7 8 9 10

Scale in Feet

32'-0" over headstocks

31'-7¼" inside

18'-6" wheelbase

2'-0½"

3'-4¼"   10   3'-1½"

SIDE ELEVATION

PLAN

Bolsters

'Bolster' wagons were designed to carry long lengths of steel and timber such as channel, pipes, rods, telegraph poles, etc. Each had at least one raised baulk lying across the wagon on which the load rested; this was the bolster. To prevent excessive sideways movement of the load, upright stanchions were pushed into sockets in the baulk(s). Often, the positions of both the baulk(s) and the stanchions were variable. BR had many different designs of 'Bolster' wagons and these will now be described.

'Single Bolsters'

Table 18 details the 'Single Bolsters' which were amongst the smallest wagons built by BR, and amongst the least successful. All had a payload of 13 tons and were 15ft. 6in. long over headstocks. They had low steel sides and a fixed bolster across the centre line of the wagon. BR had inherited many 'Single Bolsters' so, at first, only relatively small numbers were built using LNER Diagram No. 197, which became BR Diagram No. 1/400 **(see Plate 139)**. They had 8ft. wheelbases and the Morton unfitted brake. In the mid-1950s, many more were built which had the RCH unfitted brake, although the need for such wagons must already have been limited.

In 1957, the design was partially modernised by increasing the wheelbase to 10ft., these being Diagram No. 1/402 **(see Figure 33 and Plate 140)**. Lot 3125 was given Diagram No. 1/405 and 1,000 of these vacuum-braked 'Single Bolsters' were ordered but, after 497 had been built, the remainder were cancelled, as was Lot 3126.

All of Diagram No. 1/405 and many of Diagram No. 1/402 were semi-permanently coupled together as 'Twin Bolsters' **(Plate 141)**. Other 'Single Bolsters' often worked in pairs to carry short loads, and they also acted as under runners for loads carried on 'Bogie Bolsters'. The number built was remarkable in view of how soon they went out of use. By mid-1966, there were only five vacuum-fitted and 313 unfitted 'Single Bolsters' remaining, together with 1,242 (multiply by two) 'Twins' in capital stock, although many others had been transferred to the Engineer's Department. Any that remained were withdrawn during 1972. The internal user fleets at some docks, especially Newport and Grangemouth, had many of these wagons into the 1980s, and others were commonly used as runners for small cranes. Interestingly, many of Lots 3005 and 3006 were fitted with the first design of Dowty hydraulic buffer, which had a distinctive square base **(as shown in Figure 33 and Plate 36)**.

TABLE 18

SINGLE BOLSTERS

Diag No.	Lot No.	Qnty	Builder	Year	Running numbers	Underframe type	Brake type
1/400	2034	500	Shildon	1949	B910000 - 910499	Morton	Unfit
1/400	2131	500	Shildon	1950	B910500 - 910999	Morton	Unfit
1/400	2783	1000	Shildon	1955	B911000 - 911999	RCH	Unfit
1/400	2860	1000	Shildon	1956	B912000 - 912999	RCH	Unfit
1/400	2861	1000	Shildon	1956	B913000 - 913999	RCH	Unfit
1/402	3005	2000	Shildon	1957	B914000 - 915999	RCH	Unfit
1/402	3006	2000	Shildon	1957	B916000 - 917999	RCH	Unfit
					Range		
1/405	3125	497	Shildon	1958	B918000 - 918709	BR clasp	Vacuum
Total		8497					

Plate 139 No. B910420 (Shildon 1949, 2034) to Diagram 1/400 is one of the smallest revenue wagons built by BR. It was photographed in Newport Docks on 12th July 1978, and was unique amongst the many Single Bolsters there in retaining its full light grey traffic livery and lettering, and not having its allocated internal user number, 076058, applied.

R. A. Silsbury

PE 24-9-76 3614
X
THE LATCHKEY GANG
COND

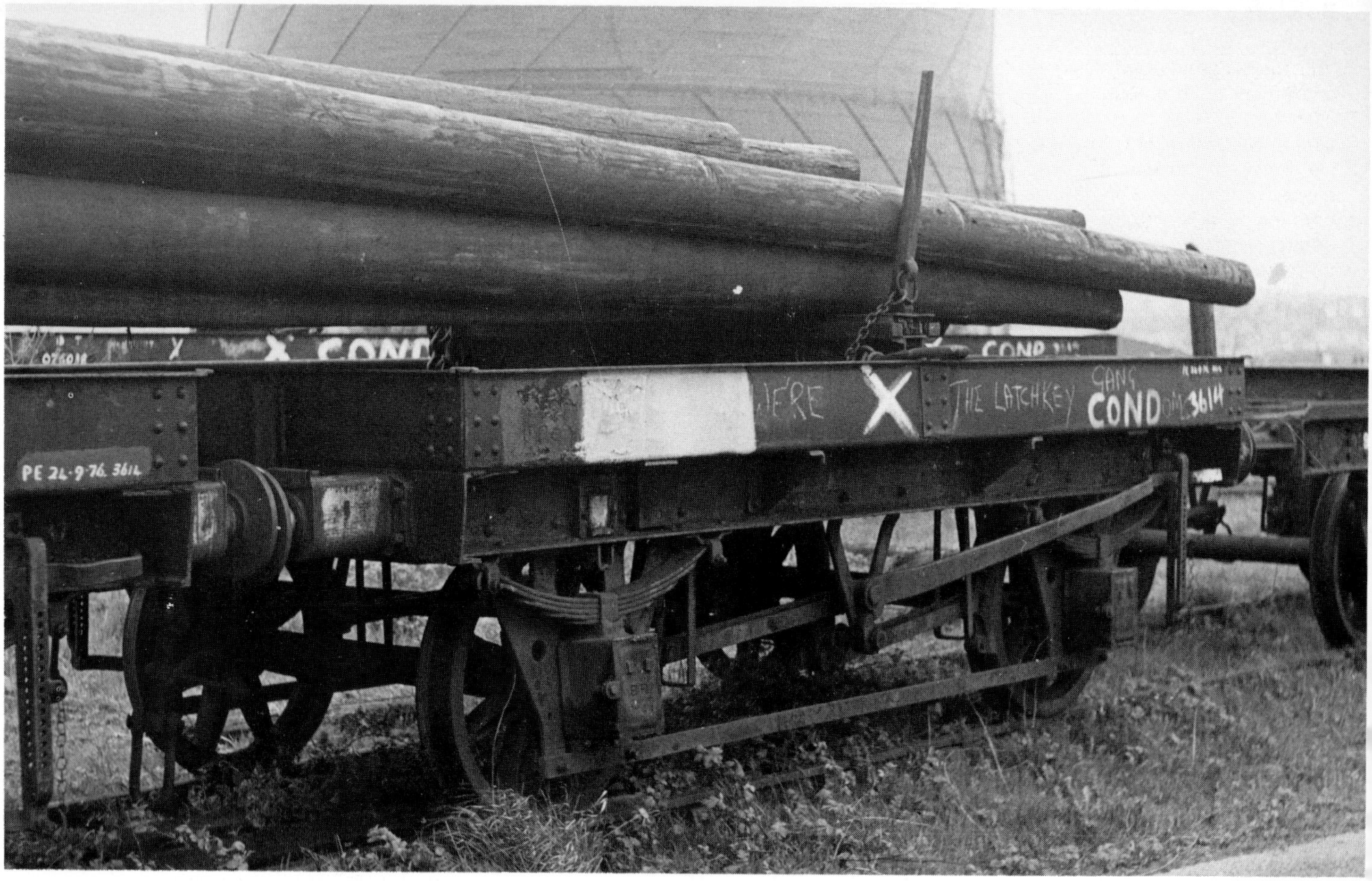

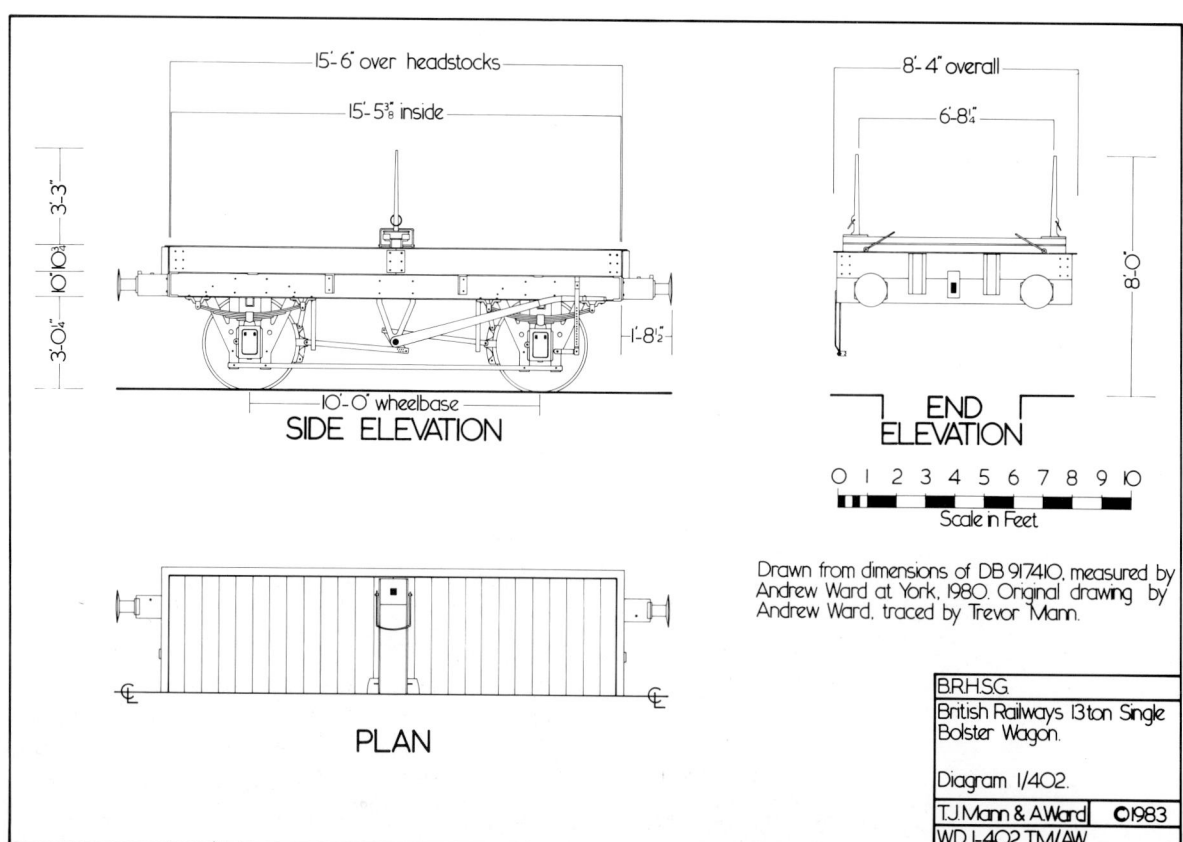

Plate 140 Again in Newport Docks, this time on 15th April 1981, 10ft. wheelbase Diagram 1/402 Single Bolster No. B914974 (Shildon 1957, 3005) — internal user number 076060 — was recorded carrying a suitable load. A fleet of Single Bolsters was kept in the docks for the seasonal trade in telegraph poles, to transport them from ship to treatment works within the docks complex. The livery was almost universally rusty.

R. A. Silsbury

Figure 33

15'-6" over headstocks
15'-5⅜" inside
3'-3"
10¾"
3'-0¼"
1'-8½"
10'-0" wheelbase
SIDE ELEVATION
8'-4" overall
6'-8¼"
8'-0"
END ELEVATION
0 1 2 3 4 5 6 7 8 9 10
Scale in Feet
Drawn from dimensions of DB 917410, measured by Andrew Ward at York, 1980. Original drawing by Andrew Ward, traced by Trevor Mann.
PLAN
B.R.H.S.G.
British Railways 13ton Single Bolster Wagon.
Diagram 1/402.
T.J.Mann & A.Ward
©1983
WD 1-402 TM/AW.

Plate 141 The final diagram of Single Bolsters, 1/405, had BR clasp vacuum brakegear, and were permanently coupled as 26 ton Twin Bolsters. The pairings were not sequential, and the pair illustrated, Nos. B918689 and B918194, built in 1958, were recorded at Doncaster in April 1960, still lettered 'For Test Purpose Only'.

BR/OPC

'Double Bolsters' (see Table 19)

Both the LMS and LNER built 'Double Bolsters' to a similar design, and BR built a single batch of each, probably to complete orders placed by these companies. LNER Diagram No. 209 became Diagram No. 1/415, and LMS Digram No. 2105 became Diagram No. 1/416 **(see Figure 34 and Plate 142)**. These differed by only a marginal ¼ in. in total height. They had an RCH long-link underframe which was 27ft. 1½ in. over headstocks and had a 15ft. wheelbase. The all steel body had fixed ends and drop sides. The pair of bolsters, which were at 15ft. centres, were removable. Once removed, the wagons were almost identical with 'Plates' and many were so converted by the mid-1960s when they were suitably branded. Some others became 'Trestles', whilst others were transferred to the Engineer's Department who rebuilt the body and fitted vacuum brakes for the carriage of long welded rail.

In 1957, Lot 3127 was issued to cover construction of 400 vacuum-braked 'Double Bolsters'. Not surprisingly, in view of the limited use of the earlier wagons, the order was cancelled before building began. Nevertheless, BR continued to experiment with wagons of this basic type. Lot 3362, covering construction of six 'Prototype' long wheelbase vacuum-braked wagons, included a single 'Experimental Long Low (Bolster)' with four bolsters, No. B710251 **(see Plate 143)**. It was quickly coverted to a 'Plate' and no more were built.

In 1966, Ashford Works built another experimental air-braked prototype, No. B920500 of Lot 3569. It was allocated Diagram

No. 1/456. Although it was later converted for coil traffic, and later still for barrier use, many of the design features were incorporated in the 'Steel AB', the 'Double Bolster' included in the group of air-braked designs introduced in 1969.

The single batch of air-braked 'Double Bolsters' built under Lot 3728 included several variants. All had a standard Type 1 underframe, being 33ft. 6in. over headstocks with a 20ft. 9in. wheelbase. Up to No. 400045 (Diagram No. SA001B) had through vacuum pipes and were TOPS-coded SAB; others lacked this and were SAA, these were Diagram No. SA001A **(see Plate 144)**. All the bodies had a drop down end. The floor had eight turnover bolsters across the wagon and various slots for stanchions. Four swivel side stanchions were laid along the curbrail and folded upwards for use. These varied in position resulting in the need to issue a third diagram, No. SB001A.

From their introduction, these wagons were only partially successful. They were rarely loaded with steel, although a number were used to carry agricultural tractors in the mid-1970s. Their most frequent use has always been as barrier or under runner wagons, and by 1983 all surviving examples had been recoded for such use, apart from 35 converted to carry coils which were TOPS-coded KTA (SHA from 1984). It was intended that 100 would be rebuilt as SPA 'Plate' wagons, but this was not carried out. Instead, during 1984, 170 were resprung and converted to 'Conflat P' (TOPS code FPA) wagons to carry 30ft. containers of domestic coal to Scotland.

TABLE 19

DOUBLE BOLSTERS

Diag No.	Lot	Qnty	Builder	Year	Running numbers	Underframe type	Brake type
1/415	2035	200	Shildon	1949	B920200 - 920399	RCH long-link	Unfit
1/416	2020	200	Wolverton	1949	B920000 - 920199	RCH long-link	Unfit
-	3362	1	Ashford	1960	B710251	BR clasp	Vacuum
SA001A/B	pt3728	250	Ashford	1970/1	400000 - 400249	1st type	Air
SB001A	pt3728	50	Ashford	1971	400250 - 400299	1st type	Air
Total		701					

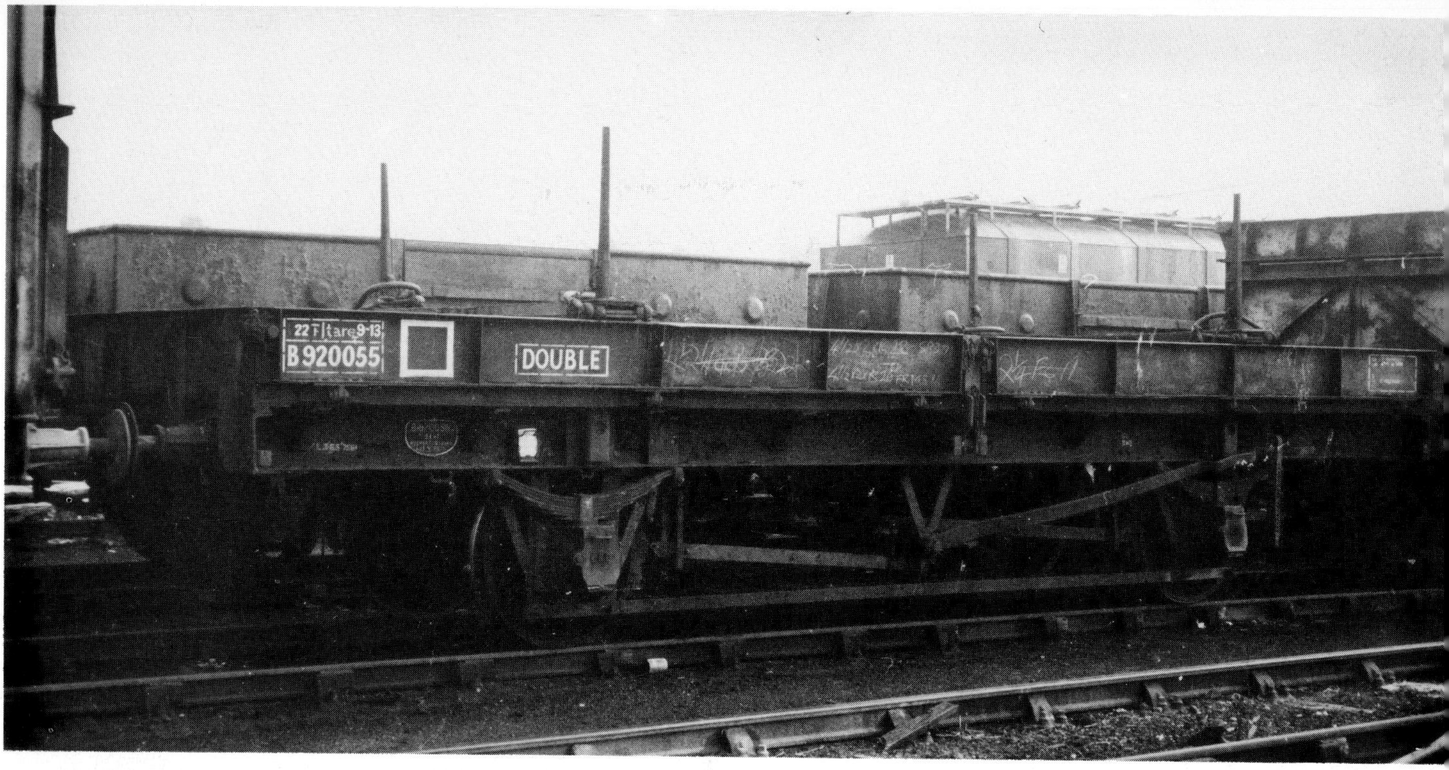
22 T tare 9-13
B920055
DOUBLE

Plate 142 Although fitted with LNER axleboxes, No. B920055 (Wolverton 1949, 2020) is a Diagram 1/416 vehicle to LMS design. Apart from the number series, the pockets on the solebars beneath each bolster was the feature which remained, and identified those Double Bolsters converted to Plate wagons. When recorded at Northwich in August 1968, No. B920055 was painted in the post-1964 'Freight Brown' livery for unfitted vehicles.

D. Larkin

Figure 34

Measured by Trevor Mann

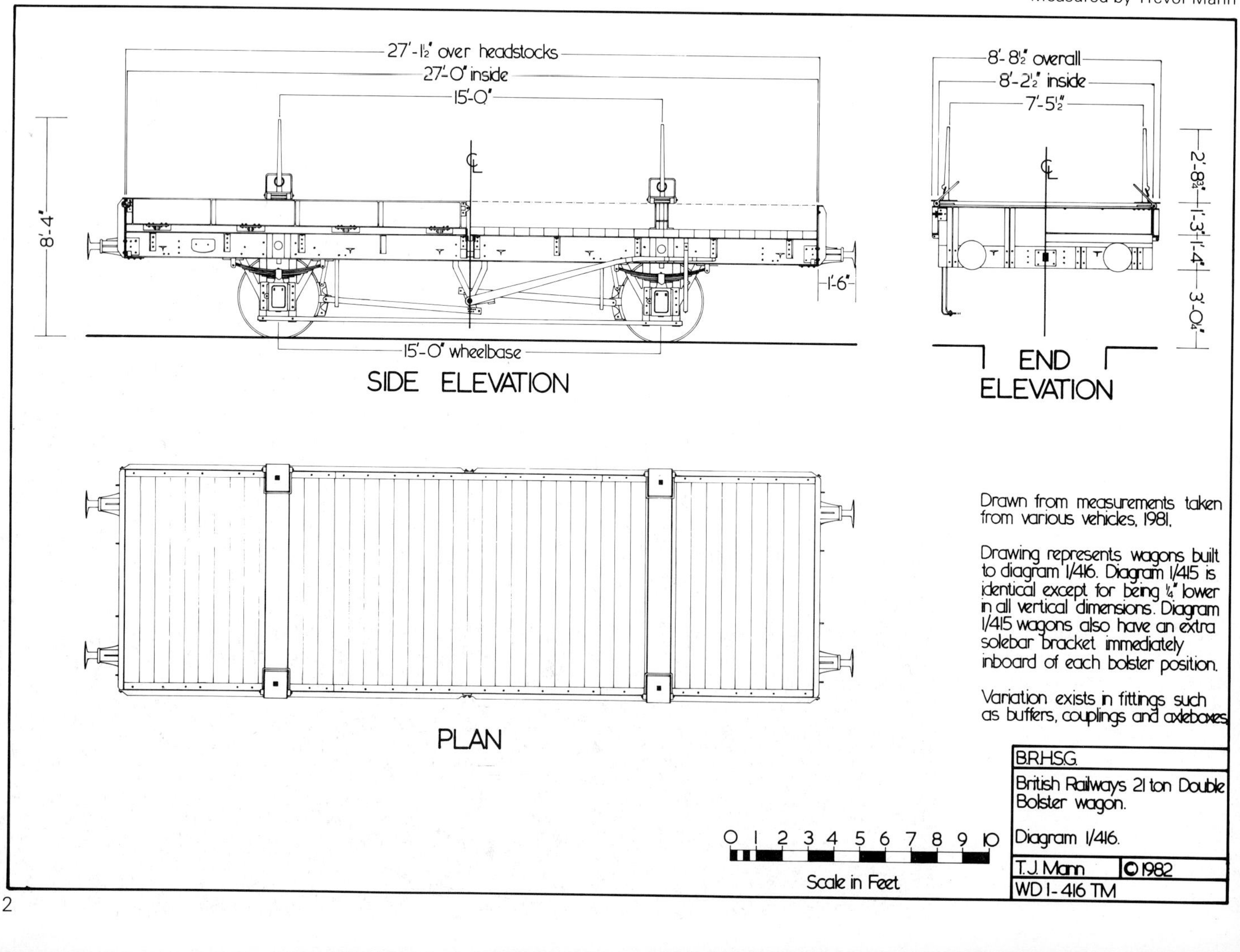
27'-1½" over headstocks
27'-0" inside
15'-0"
8'-4"
1'-6"
15'-0" wheelbase
SIDE ELEVATION
8'-8½" overall
8'-2½" inside
7'-5½"
2'-8¾"
1'-3"
1'-4"
3'-0¼"
END ELEVATION
PLAN
Drawn from measurements taken from various vehicles, 1981.
Drawing represents wagons built to diagram 1/416. Diagram 1/415 is identical except for being ¼" lower in all vertical dimensions. Diagram 1/415 wagons also have an extra solebar bracket immediately inboard of each bolster position.
Variation exists in fittings such as buffers, couplings and axleboxes.
0 1 2 3 4 5 6 7 8 9 10
Scale in Feet
B.R.H.S.G.
British Railways 21 ton Double Bolster wagon.
Diagram 1/416.
T.J. Mann
© 1982
WD 1-416 TM

Plate 143   The vehicles to Lot 3362 shared a common underframe, and No. B710251, seen on exhibition at Euston on 11th December 1961, was the one fitted as a Bolster Wagon. Features common to all included the curb rail cleats, lashing rings and hinge lugs. The drilled solebar brackets were to support body framing, and **Plate 105**, of the prototype car carrier, shows them so used.

BR/OPC

Plate 144   The air-braked 'Steel-AB' design had limited use in its intended traffic. However, No. 400220 (Ashford 1971, 3728) had recently unloaded steel when photographed at Radyr on 11th July 1978. It was painted in bauxite livery, and features to be noted are the turnover bolsters (with additional chocks at each end), the fold-down stanchions, and the drop-down ends which are held upright by removable bars.

R. A. Silsbury

Bogie Bolster

BR used a series of letter codes to designate 'Bogie Bolsters'. No examples of 'Bogie Bolster A' (less than 30 ton capacity) or 'Bogie Bolster B' (50 ton capacity) were actually built by BR; these codes applying only to wagons of pre-nationalisation origin.

Bogie Bolster C

BR chose to build large numbers of 30 ton payload 'Bogie Bolster Cs' which are detailed in **Table 20**. The GWR design had adjustable bolsters and was, therefore, more advanced than the designs of the other companies. BR was unusually single minded in continuing to build this design alone and, although the design was modified in later years, the basic dimensions remained the same. They were 45ft. long over headstocks with bogies at 35ft. 6in. centres and with steel sides of 9in. channel. Although features such as bogie type and the provision of vacuum brake varied, the main variant in the diagrams is in the type, position and adjustability of the bolsters, and in the height and spacing of the stanchions.

Diagram No. 1/471 was also allocated the new GWR Diagram No. J34 by BR. It had four baulks; the central ones were fixed in place and the outers were adjustable. The stanchions either slotted into these baulks or into the eight pairs of bolster guides on the sides of the wagons **(see Plate 145)**. Many wagons to this diagram had plain spoked wheels and GWR self-contained buffers.

Diagram No. 1/473 differed by having 9 x 4½in. journals instead of the 8 x 4½in. of Diagram No. 1/471. This was because the bogie design was modified from the GWR plate type, which is distinguishable by having a pair of holes in the side and a pair of coil springs, to a BR/GW type which does not have holes, and had only a single coil spring. Bolsters and other fittings remained as Diagram No. 1/471 **(see Figure 35)**.

Diagram No. 1/474 had four much larger and heavier bolsters, all of which were adjustable and slotted into eight pairs of guides on the body side. Each bolster had four pairs of slots for locating the stanchions.

The two central bolsters of Diagram No. 1/475 are fixed in place, but they are also high, as the outer bolsters were of the new adjustable type. There were six pairs of guides which these could locate on. The journal size also increased to 10 x 5in. All of the authors' observations place the latter part of Lot 2583 in Diagram No. 1/475, and not in Diagram No. 1/474 as shown on the original diagrams **(Plate 146)**.

Diagram No. 1/477 **(see Plate 147)** differed from No. 1/474 only in detail, the body being mounted ½in. higher on the bogies while the stanchions were reduced in height. Later lots were built to a more modern specification with vacuum brake and self-contained or hydraulic buffers, and more advanced bogie designs incorporating roller bearing axleboxes. The plate-back bogies had holes and single coil springs, while the Davis & Lloyd type were of cast construction. These wagons were branded 'BOGIE BOLSTER-C VB' or 'C-BOLSTER VB', the unfitted examples being similarly lettered but without the VB. Under TOPS, the codes became BCV and BCO respectively.

No more 'Bogie Bolster Cs' were built. Two wagons were converted to air brake as prototypes for a possible rebuilding programme, but no more followed; these were Diagram No. BC008A. They were used by the Engineer's Department until withdrawal in 1983, their withdrawal coinciding with the beginning of fitting air pipes to cast-bogied vacuum-braked wagons; by May 1984 there were 167 BCW wagons. Some other wagons had been given two different types of cradles for carrying large diameter pipes during the 1970s, and some of these were also air-piped during 1984 so that there were 163 BTW, 93 BQV and 1 BQW in May 1984. Vacuum-braked BCV wagons continued in use during 1984.

Unfitted examples were not converted to vacuum brake, and most were withdrawn by about 1980. Several passed into the Engineer's fleet where they joined a small number that had been built specifically for the S&T Department (these purpose-built Engineer's wagons had their own number series and are outside the scope of this book). The Engineer's Department vacuum-piped a few of these wagons.

TABLE 20

BOGIE BOLSTER C

Diag No.	Lot No.	Qnty	Builder	Year	Running numbers	Bogie type	Brake type
1/471	2085	50	Swindon	1949	B940000 – 940049	GWR plate	Unfit
1/471	2308	950	Metro Cammell	1951/2	B940050 – 940999	GWR plate	Unfit
1/471	2326	100	Swindon	1952	B943000 – 943099	GWR plate	Unfit
1/471	2406	250	Metro Cammell	1953	B943100 – 943349	GWR plate	Unfit
1/473	2496	160	Swindon	1953	B943350 – 943509	BR/GW plate	Unfit
1/473	2539	100	Metro Cammell	1954	B943510 – 943609	BR/GW plate	Unfit
1/473	2542	250	Swindon	1954	B943610 – 943859	BR/GW plate	Unfit
1/473	pt2583	200	Metro Cammell	1954	B943860 – 944059	BR/GW plate	Unfit
1/473	pt2616	160	Birmingham	1956	B944310 – 944469	BR/GW plate	Unfit
1/474	pt2616	50	Birmingham	1956	B944470 – 944519	BR/GW plate	Unfit
1/474	2760	300	Birmingham	1956	B944890 – 945189	BR/GW plate	Unfit
1/474	pt2818	401	Metro Cammell	1955/6	B945390 – 945790	BR/GW plate	Unfit
1/475	pt2583	250	Metro Cammell	1954	B944060 – 944309	BR/GW plate	Unfit
1/475	pt2616	120	Birmingham	1956	B944520 – 944639	BR/GW plate	Unfit
1/475	2759	150	Metro Cammell	1955	B944740 – 944889	BR/GW plate	Unfit
1/475	pt2818	200	Metro Cammell	1955	B945190 – 945389	BR/GW plate	Unfit
1/477	3059	100	Teesside	1957/8	B944640 – 944739	BR/GW plate	Unfit
1/477	3060	500	Metro Cammell	1957/8	B922000 – 922499	BR/GW plate	Unfit
1/477	3155	200	Metro Cammell	1958	B945791 – 945990	Plateback	Vacuum
1/477	3162	200	Metro Cammell	1958/9	B922500 – 922699	Plateback	Vacuum
1/477	3200	300	Swindon	1959	B922700 – 922999	Plateback	Vacuum
1/477	3238	100	Swindon	1959	B923000 – 923099	Plateback	Vacuum
1/477	3341	200	Swindon	1961	B923100 – 923299	Davis Lloyd	Vacuum
1/477	3397	400	Metro Cammell	1961/2	B924400 – 924799	Davis Lloyd	Vacuum
BC008A	3889	2	Swindon	1975	960000 – 960001	Y25C	Air

	Total	5693					

Plate 145 (Above) Showing clearly its GWR ancestry, No. B940217 (Met. Cammell 1951, 2308) is a Diagram 1/471 Bogie Bolster C, nearing the end of its life, as internal user No. 081004, on 15th April 1981, when found at Tidal Sidings, Cardiff. The rusty grey livery remains included the 'C-Bolster' code; note also the '⊄' mark on the curb rail to indicate the centre line of the wagon.

R. A. Silsbury

Plate 146 (Below) Photographed at Monmouthshire Bank, Newport, on 12th July 1978, as No. B944500 (Birmingham RC&W 1955, 2616) clearly shows, it is to Diagram 1/475, and not as officially recorded to Diagram 1/474. The centre bolsters are fixed, and have no locating pockets on the curb rail. The livery is somewhat rusty light grey, the lettering being on black patches, and a nice detail is the script legend '30 ton distributed, 25 tons over the two centre bolsters'.

R. A. Silsbury

Plate 147 (Below) Vacuum-braked No. B922745 (Swindon 1959, 3200) is a Diagram 1/477 vehicle on later pattern BR plate-back bogies, with holes in the frames, and fitted with roller bearing axleboxes. It was carrying a load of steel billets when photographed at Llandeilo Junction on 13th July 1978.

R. A. Silsbury

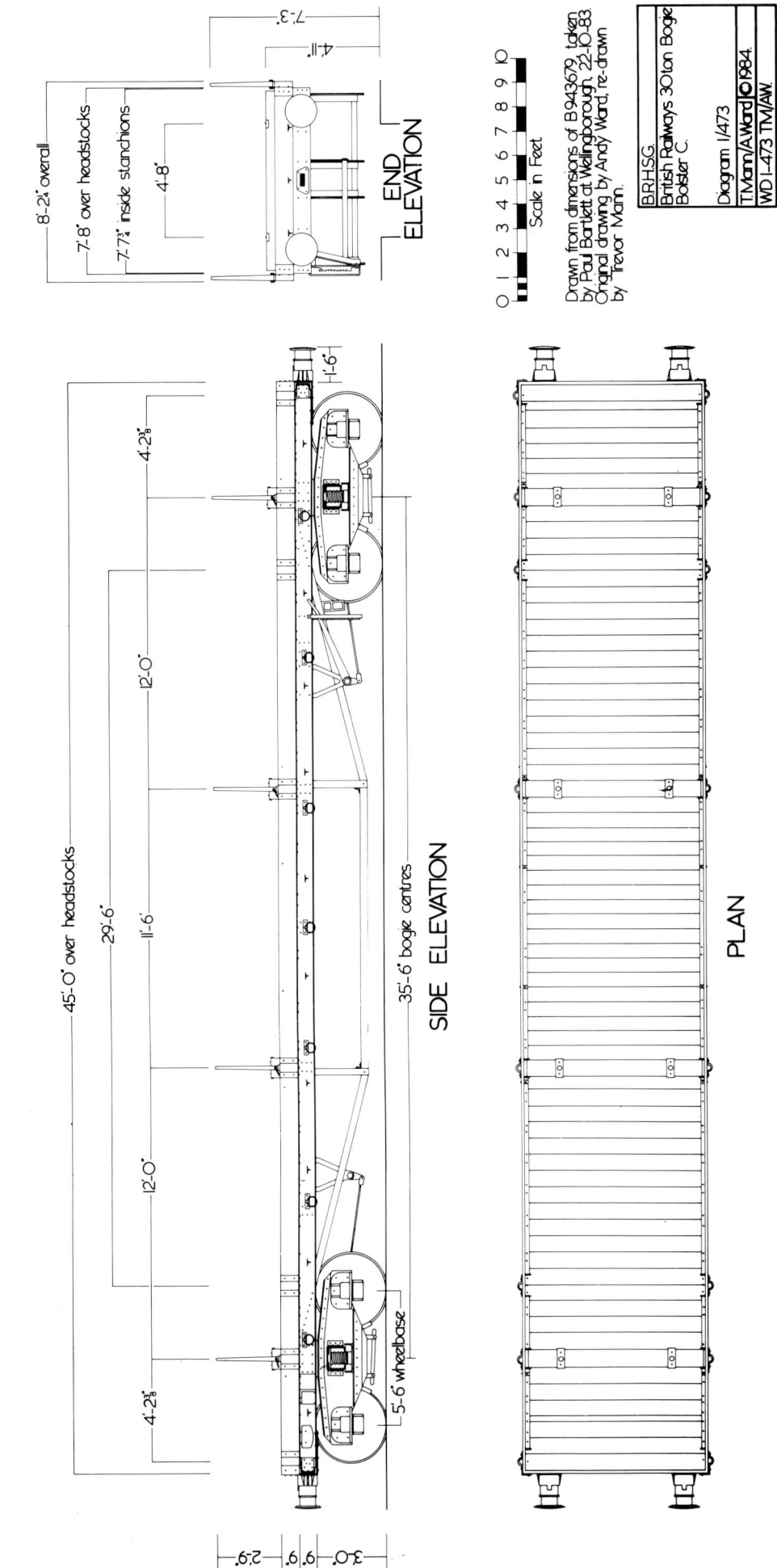

Figure 35

END ELEVATION

7'-3"
4'-11"
8'-2¼" overall
7'-8" over headstocks
7'-7¾" inside stanchions
4'-8"

SIDE ELEVATION

45'-0" over headstocks
29'-6"
12'-0"
11'-6"
12'-0"
4'-2⅛"
4'-2⅛"
11'-6"
35'-6" bogie centres
5'-6" wheelbase

3'-0"
2'-9"
9'-6"

PLAN

Drawn from dimensions of B943679, taken
by Paul Bartlett at Wellingborough 22-10-83.
Original drawing by Andy Ward, re-drawn
by Trevor Mann.

B.R.H.S.G.
British Railways 30ton Bogie
Bolster C.
Diagram 1/473
T.Mann/A.Ward © 1984
WD 1-473 TM/AW

Scale in Feet
0 1 2 3 4 5 6 7 8 9 10

Bogie Bolster D

The 'Bogie Bolster D' had a payload of 42 tons and all of the diagrams had the same basic dimensions of 40ft. between bogie centres and 52ft. over headstocks. They are detailed in **Table 21**.

Only a single batch was built of the first diagram, No. 1/470, which was the same as LMS Diagram No. P18C **(see Plate 150)**. It had LMS diamond frame bogies of 6ft. wheelbase with 2ft. 8½in. diameter wheels. There was only one brake lever on each side and these braked only one bogie. The five bolsters were all fixed in position, and there were lashing down rings on the solebar.

Diagram No. 1/472 was LNER Diagram No. 205 **(see Plates 148 & 149)**. Only the first lot had LNER diamond bogies of 5ft. 6in. wheelbase, some of which had split spoke wheels. All remaining batches of unfitted wagons were given BR/GW plate bogies, although variations occurred in the detail of bogie design. Lot 2979 alone had the GWR type with a pair of holes in the side plate and a single coil spring. All the others had bogies without holes in the backplate, Lots 2237 to 2358 had a pair of coil springs, and all the remainder had only a single spring. Each side had two brake levers which independently braked each bogie. There were five bolsters, only the end ones of which were adjustable. The last two lots were vacuum-braked with Davis & Lloyd cast bogies.

The single lot of Diagram No. 1/476 was identical to Diagram No. 1/472 except that the stanchions were reduced in height. This feature was repeated on Diagram No. 1/478, the first to acknowledge that self-adjusting vacuum brakes were being fitted. Roller bearing axleboxes are not specified by the diagram, but were fitted to the plate-back bogies. This diagram had a screw-hand brake at each end. The body of Diagram No. 1/484 was identical and was issued because cast-steel Gloucester bogies with roller bearings and the self-adjusting vacuum brake were fitted **(see Plate 151)**.

Apart from the initial diagram, this series of wagons was very consistent, with the general design remaining unvaried, but with steady improvements in the running gear.

By 1984, most of the vacuum-braked wagons which continued in use had had an air pipe added so that there were 283 by May. As well as general steel traffic, they are often used for the carriage of new rail from Workington. Brandings were 'BOGIE BOLSTER D' and 'D-BOLSTER' with VB when vacuum brakes were fitted. The TOPS codes are BDO, BDV and BDW respectively.

In the late 1970s, 1,251 of the unfitted 'Bogie Bolster Ds' were rebuilt with air brakes, the remainder being withdrawn. Initially, the prototype BDA, Diagram No. BD006B had five low-height bolsters, but when observed in 1982, it had been replated as 'Lot 3926 Shildon 1979' and rebuilt with six bolsters. All of the production wagons also had six bolsters **(see Figure 36)**. The first of these, Diagram No. BD006A, and up to at least No. 950510 of Diagram No. BD006C, had low height bolsters of timber construction. From No. 950514, or before, the bolster design was modified, being formed from steel sections recovered from the original wagon, topped by a wooden rubbing strip. They were higher than previously. The steel of the four central bolsters is mounted lower than the outer ones but they have deeper wood rubbing strips so that they all attain the same height. 'Railfreight Red' for the body of the wagons was introduced between Nos. 950743 and 950787. A small batch of wagons, Nos. 950564-66, was fitted with 'Outreau APO 22Y' bogies. Diagram No. BD006D **(see Plate 152)** had a wheel handbrake located slightly off centre on each bogie, whereas the earlier wagons had a single hand lever brake on each side. Because they could negotiate tighter curves, from December 1984 the TOPS code BLA was used to distinguish them. Lot 3968 was incomplete as it had originally been for 650. Nos. DC950001-202 and Nos. DC950801-51 were transferred to the Engineer's Department in November 1983 and given the code name BRILL and TOPS code YAA.

TABLE 21
BOGIE BOLSTER D

Diag No.	Lot No.	Qnty	Builder	Year	Running numbers	Bogie type	Brake type
1/470	2021	150	Derby	1949	B941000 – 941149	LMS diamond	Unfit
1/472	2211	200	Tees-side SBE	1950/1	B941150 – 941349	LNER diamond	Unfit
1/472	2237	67	Lancing	1951/2	B941350 – 941416	BR/GW plate	Unfit
1/472	2238	58	Swindon	1952	B941417 – 941474	BR/GW plate	Unfit
1/472	2358	80	Lancing	1952/3	B941475 – 941554	BR/GW plate	Unfit
1/472	2487	75	Lancing	1953/4	B941555 – 941629	BR/GW plate	Unfit
1/472	2623	150	Tees-side SBE	1954	B941630 – 941779	BR/GW plate	Unfit
1/472	2624	150	Cravens	1954/5	B941780 – 941929	BR/GW plate	Unfit
1/472	2625	100	Pickering	1955	B941930 – 942029	BR/GW plate	Unfit
1/472	2690	100	Tees-side SBE	1955	B942230 – 942329	BR/GW plate	Unfit
1/472	2691	100	Swindon	1955	B942030 – 942229	BR/GW plate	Unfit
1/472	2787	200	Tees-side SBE	1955/6	B942330 – 942529	BR/GW plate	Unfit
1/472	2852	150	Lancing	1956/7	B942530 – 942679	BR/GW plate	Unfit
1/472	2882	250	Swindon	1955/6	B942680 – 942929	BR/GW plate	Unfit
1/472	2979	130	Swindon	1958	B927000 – 927129	GWR plate	Unfit
1/472	3021	70	Lancing	1957	B927130 – 927199	BR/GW plate	Unfit
1/472	pt3028	14	Tees-side SBE	1956/7	B927200 – 927213	BR/GW plate	Unfit
1/472	3104	100	Swindon	1958	B927400 – 927499	Davis & Lloyd	Vacuum
1/472	3113	100	Lancing	1958/9	B927500 – 927599	Davis & Lloyd	Vacuum
1/476	pt3028	186	Lancing	1956/7	B927214 – 927399	BR/GW plate	Unfit
1/478	3246	200	Lancing	1959	B927600 – 927799	Plateback	Vacuum
1/484	3407	200	Cambrian	1961	B927800 – 927999	Gloucester	Vacuum
1/484	3408	200	Chas Roberts	1962	B928000 – 928199	Gloucester	Vacuum
BD006B	3888	1	Swindon	1975	950000	Y25C	Air
BD006A	3907	200	Ashford	1978	950001 – 950200	Y25C	Air
BD006C	3925	600	Shildon	1977-9	950201 – 950800	Y25C	Air
BD006D	3965	100	Shildon	1978	950801 – 950900	Y25C	Air
BD006D	3968	350	Shildon	1979	950901 – 951250	Y25C	Air

	Total	4281					

Plate 148 (Above) The LNER design Bogie Bolster D, Diagram 1/472, featured independent handbrakes for each bogie, and open guide buffers. No. B942497 (Tees-side S&E 1956, 2787) has BR plate-back bogies, and is in clean light grey livery with a chocolate brown underframe, and is seen at Radyr on 11th July 1978.

R. A. Silsbury

Plate 149 This deck view of No. B942255 (Tees-side S&E 1955, 2690), pictured at Temple Mills on 22nd September 1977, is included to illustrate the top of the bolsters, with the four positions for each stanchion, and the lashing-down rings set into the decking. The middle three fixed bolsters are bolted through their lower webs, whilst the two end ones, being adjustable, are not.

R. A. Silsbury

Plate 150   In contrast to the LNER design, the LMS type to Diagram 1/470 had only one brake lever at each side, wooden bolsters with only two positions for each stanchion, and lashing-down rings on the solebar. No. B941018 (Derby 1949, 2021) was in rusty light grey livery, and stored out of use at Ebbw Junction on 26th October 1979.

R. A. Silsbury

Plate 151   Whilst retaining the LNER features in its bodywork, and including the two independent handbrake levers each side, No. B927961 (Cambrian 1961, 3407) is to Diagram 1/484 to reflect the more modern running gear, Gloucester cast bogies and vacuum brakes; it also has unusual 'squared' oval-headed buffers, and was photographed at Southampton on 16th August 1979, loaded with steel girders.

R. A. Silsbury

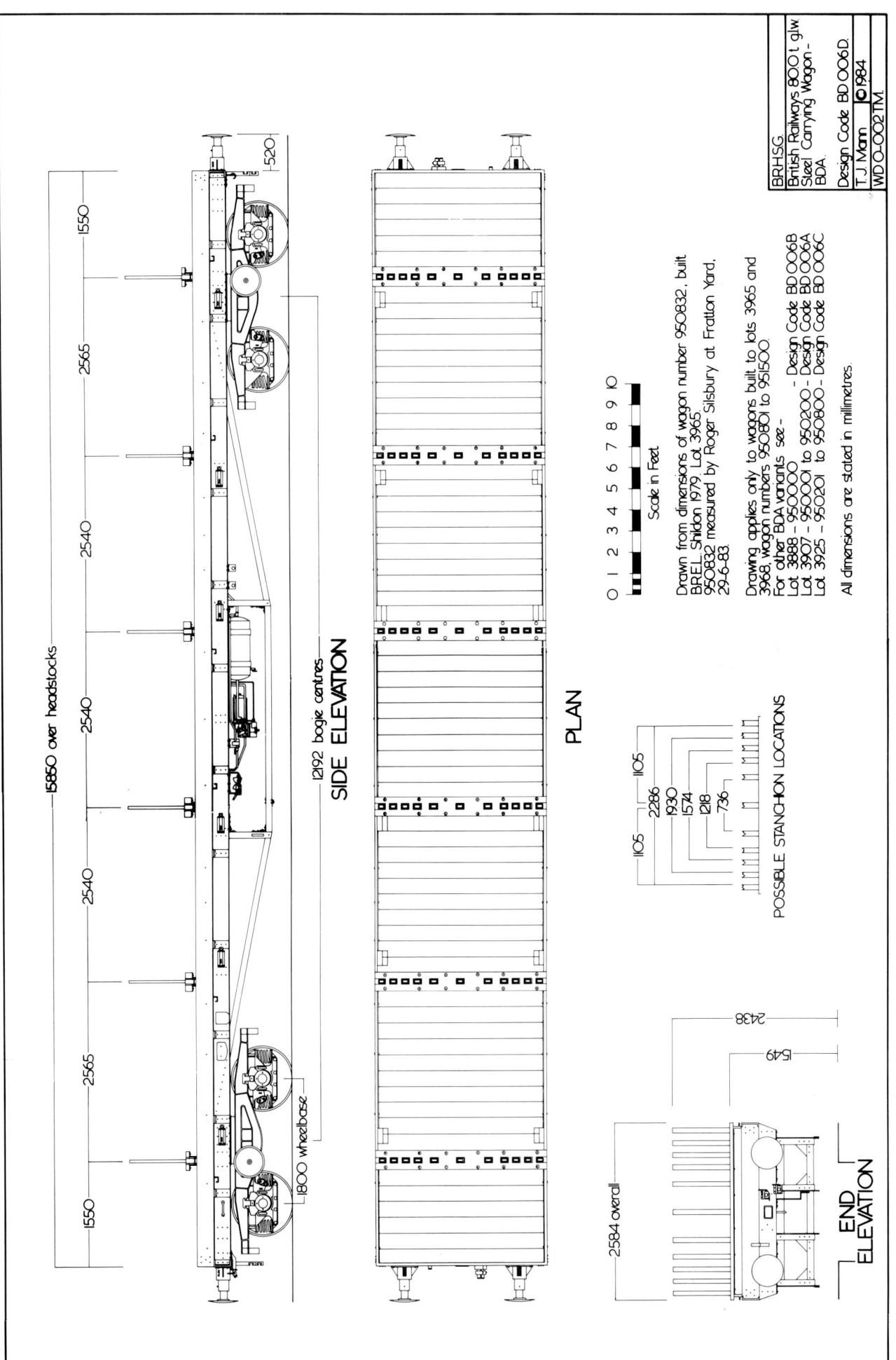

SIDE ELEVATION

1585O over headstocks

1550 2565 2540 2540 2540 2565 1550

1292 bogie centres

1800 wheelbase

520

PLAN

POSSIBLE STANCHION LOCATIONS

1105 1105
2286
1930
1574
1218
736

END ELEVATION

2584 overall

2438

1549

Scale in Feet

0 1 2 3 4 5 6 7 8 9 10

Drawn from dimensions of wagon number 950832, built
BREL Shildon 1979. Lot 3965.
950832 measured by Roger Silsbury at Fratton Yard.
29-6-83

Drawing applies only to wagons built to lots 3965 and
3968, wagon numbers 950801 to 951500.
For other BDA variants see:-
Lot 3888 - 950000   - Design Code BD 006B
Lot 3907 - 950001 to 950200 - Design Code BD 006A
Lot 3925 - 950201 to 950800 - Design Code BD 006C

All dimensions are stated in millimetres.

BRHSG
British Railways 80.0 t. glw
Steel Carrying Wagon-
BDA.

Design Code BD 006D
T.J. Mann   © 1984
WD O-002 TM.

Figure 36

Plate 152 Having been converted from an unfitted Bogie Bolster D in November 1980, BDA, No. 951114 (Shildon 1980, 3968) displays the new flame red livery adopted for air-braked stock. The load of steel slabs are held down by nylon straps on ratchet tensioners, and the end bolsters have a higher steel section, with a correspondingly narrower wooden top. It was recorded at Scunthorpe on 2nd May 1981.

R. A. Silsbury

Bogie Bolster E

BR avoided building any short bogie bolsters until 1961, when a comparatively large fleet of 1,200 vacuum-braked wagons was introduced to an entirely new design and allocated to Diagram No. 1/479 **(see Table 22, Figure 37 and Plate 153)**. With a payload of 30 tons, they were given a new code name which appeared on the wagon as 'BOGIE BOLSTER E VB' or, alternatively, as 'E-BOLSTER VB'; their TOPS code was BEV. They were 32ft. over headstocks, which is the same length as the standard 2-axle 'Tube', but the payload was greater than that normally allowed on 2 axles at the time. The 5ft. 6in. wheelbase Davis & Lloyd bogies were mounted at 22ft. 6in. centres. Four bolsters were provided, the central pair being fixed while the two outer pair were adjustable, having three alternative locations apiece.

By the mid-1970s, many of these wagons were redundant in general steel traffic. Some were converted to a variety of coil wagons **(see MRC 1983 50 No. 587, pages 165-169)**, and many others had a short period in the Engineer's fleet before conversion to TURBOT ballast wagons **(see MRC 1985 52 No. 615 pages 418-422)**.

TABLE 22

BOGIE BOLSTER E

Diag No.	Lot No.	Qnty	Builder	Year	Running numbers	Bogie type	Brake type
1/479	3343	1100	Ashford	1961/2	B923300 - 924399	Davis & Lloyd	Vacuum
1/479	3440	100	Ashford	1962	B924800 - 924899	Davis & Lloyd	Vacuum
	Total	1200					

Figure 37

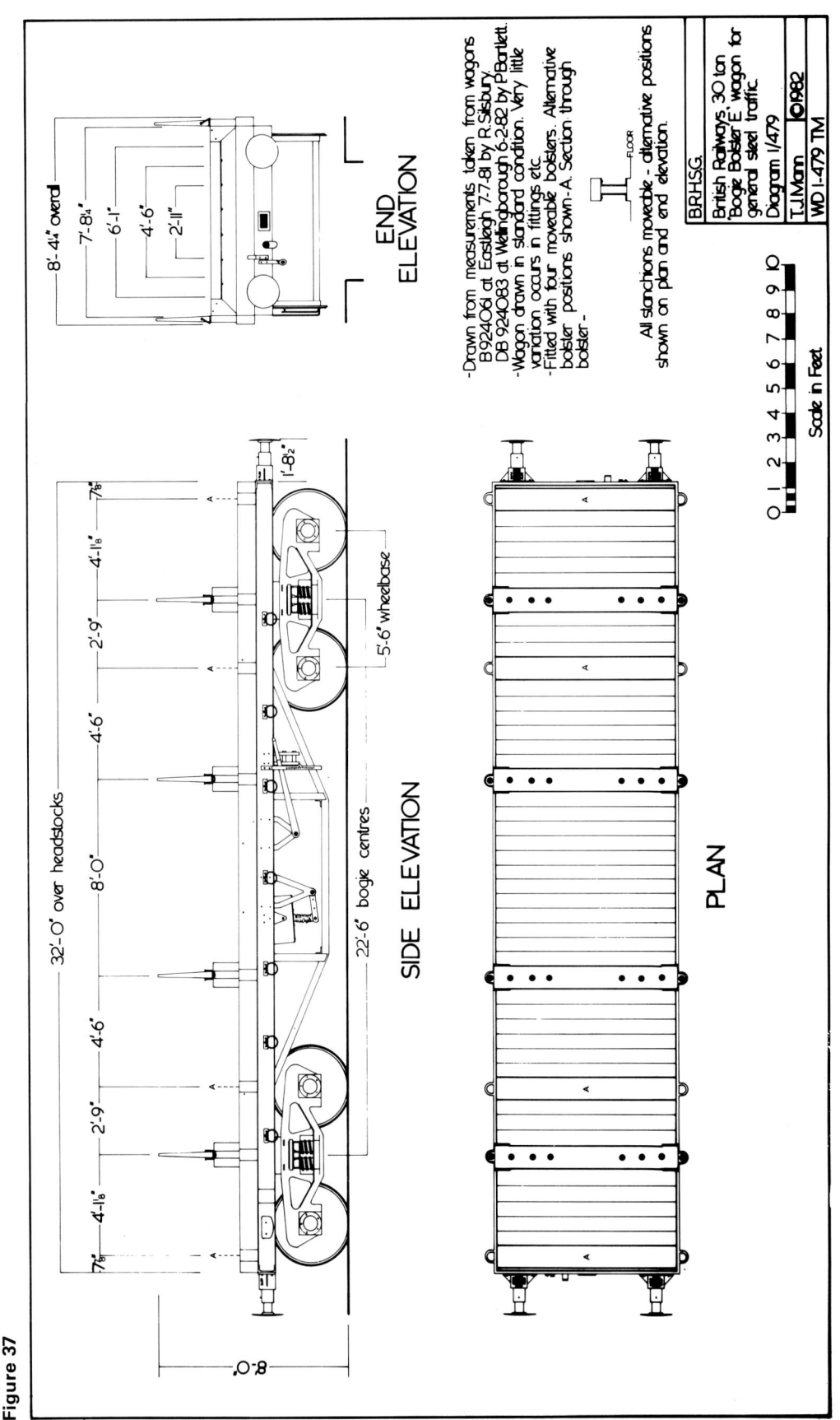

END
ELEVATION

8'-4¼" overall
7'-8¼"
6'-1"
4'-6"
2'-11"

- Drawn from measurements taken from wagons
B924061 at Eastleigh 7-7-81 by R.Silsbury.
DB 924083 at Wellingborough 6-2-82 by P.Bartlett.
- Wagon drawn in standard condition. Very little
variation occurs in fittings etc.
- Fitted with four moveable bolsters. Alternative
bolster positions shown-A. Section through
bolster-.

All stanchions moveable - alternative positions
shown on plan and end elevation.

FLOOR

BRHSG.
British Railways 30 ton
'Bogie Bolster E' wagon for
general steel traffic.
Diagram 1/479
T.J.Mann   1982
WD 1-479 TM

0 1 2 3 4 5 6 7 8 9 10
Scale in Feet

32'-0" over headstocks
7'⅞"
4'-1⅛"
2'-9"
4'-6"
8'-0"
4'-6"
2'-9"
4'-1⅛"
7'⅞"
1'-8½"
5'-6' wheelbase
22'-6' bogie centres

SIDE ELEVATION

8'-0"

PLAN

Plate 153 The only pure BR design was the Bogie Bolster E, to Diagram 1/479. No. B923326 (Ashford 1961, 3343) was still rated at the original 30 tons load when recorded at Llandeilo Junction on 13th July 1978 with a load of steel billets, although most of the class had by then been uprated to 32 tonne.

R. A. Silsbury

Air-Braked Bogie Bolsters

The steel-carrying fleet had to wait until 1972 before the first air-braked 'Bogie Bolsters' were introduced. There then followed a series of successful wagons which was radically different from earlier designs. Details of these are given in **Table 23**. Although they differed in size, they were all rated at 100 tons GLW, were similar in design, and all were mounted on 2 metre (6ft. 6½ in.) wheelbase FBT6 bogies, which had a hand wheel brake at the outer end. They all had high reinforced ends, although the detail of the end varied, while the deck was made up of a series of transverse 'U' channel sections with reinforcing mesh between, thus ensuring rapid heat dissipation when loaded with hot steel products. Rectangular bars could be located in various slots across the wagon or in pockets on the side, and acted as stanchions.

The BAA and BAB were 40ft. over headstock with bogie centres at 26ft. 6in. and a nominal tare of 24½ tonne. Diagram No. BA001A had vacuum pipes which were absent from Diagram No. BA001B **(Plate 154)**; Diagram No. BA001C had a different stronger and lower end. The final BAA diagram, No. BA002A, had a number of differences. The bogies were centred at 8 metres (26ft. 3in.), the headstocks and overall widths were narrower, the web of the sides at 21in. was 4in. deeper than the earlier designs, the stanchions were lower, and the ends were higher and more complex. One BAA, No. 900115, received all the additional fittings necessary for a ferry wagon (Continental Diagram No. E388) was renumbered 31 70 434 3 000-4 **(see Railway Magazine 129 (129), page 355)**. Later it was converted to a 'Nuclear Flask' wagon and Danzas introduced a fleet of bolster wagons which were all passed for Continental running.

The first prototype BBA was branded as 'PROTOTYPE 50FT. STEEL CARRIER'. Allocated Diagram No. BB001A its bogies were at 36ft. 6in. centres and it had a deeper side member than the BAAs. The production batches, Diagram No. BB001C, were very similar, and Diagram No. BB001B differed only slightly in that the end was 0.008 metre higher **(see Figure 38 and Plate 155)**. Part-way into the final batch (between Nos. 910540 and 910542), pairs of lifting lugs (which can also be used for chaining down), were introduced. These protrude from the solebar over each bogie. All this batch, Lot 3959, was introduced in the new livery of black for the bed of the wagon and 'Railfreight' red for the raised portion of the end. Later, this livery became standard for all BAAs and BBAs. The original livery had been all bauxite for the body with black bogies.

In 1976, another prototype was introduced, this time for a longer wagon which was 61ft. over headstocks with bogies at 47ft. 6in. centres. It was TOPS-coded BLA and given Diagram No. BL001A. It had a similar appearance to the BBA. Apparently, the design was unsuccessful, as no more were built, and the wagon was transferred to the Southern Region's Engineer's fleet.

TABLE 23

AIR BRAKE BOGIE BOLSTERS

Diag No.	Lot No.	Qnty	Builder	Year	Running numbers	Bogie type
BA001A	3792	49	Ashford	1972	900000 – 900048	FBT6
BA001B	3803	76	Ashford	1972/3	900049 – 900124	FBT6
BA001B	3805	74	Shildon/ Ashford	1973	900125 – 900198	FBT6
BA001C	3858	74	Ashford	1975	900200 – 900273	FBT6
BA002A	3860	32	Ashford	1976	900274 – 900305	FBT6
BB001A	3845	1	Shildon	1973	910000	FBT6
BB001C	3857	160	Ashford	1974	910001 – 910160	FBT6
BB001B	3872	204	Ashford	1976	910161 – 910365	FBT6
BB001B	3871	125	Ashford	1976	910367 – 910491	FBT6
BB001B	3959	200	Ashford	1979/80	910492 – 910691	FBT6
BL001A	3896	1	Ashford	1976	920000	FBT6(M)
Total		996				

Plate 154 To illustrate the 'BA' series of air-braked Bogie Bolster, we have chosen No. 900187 (Shildon 1973, 3805), seen at Monmouthshire Bank, Newport, on 12th July 1978, which retains the bauxite livery in which it was painted when new. The yellow corner applied to the end was an additional identification to the Pool No. 7135.

R. A. Silsbury

Plate 155 The longer 'BB' series of air-braked Bogie Bolster utilised heavier construction, with deeper side girders. No. 910195 (Ashford 1976, 3872) was loaded with steel coil when photographed at Margam on 13th October 1981, and is also in bauxite livery. Many of these vehicles are now running in the Railfreight red and black. The white edge to the deck was added as a safety measure.

R. A. Silsbury

Figure 38

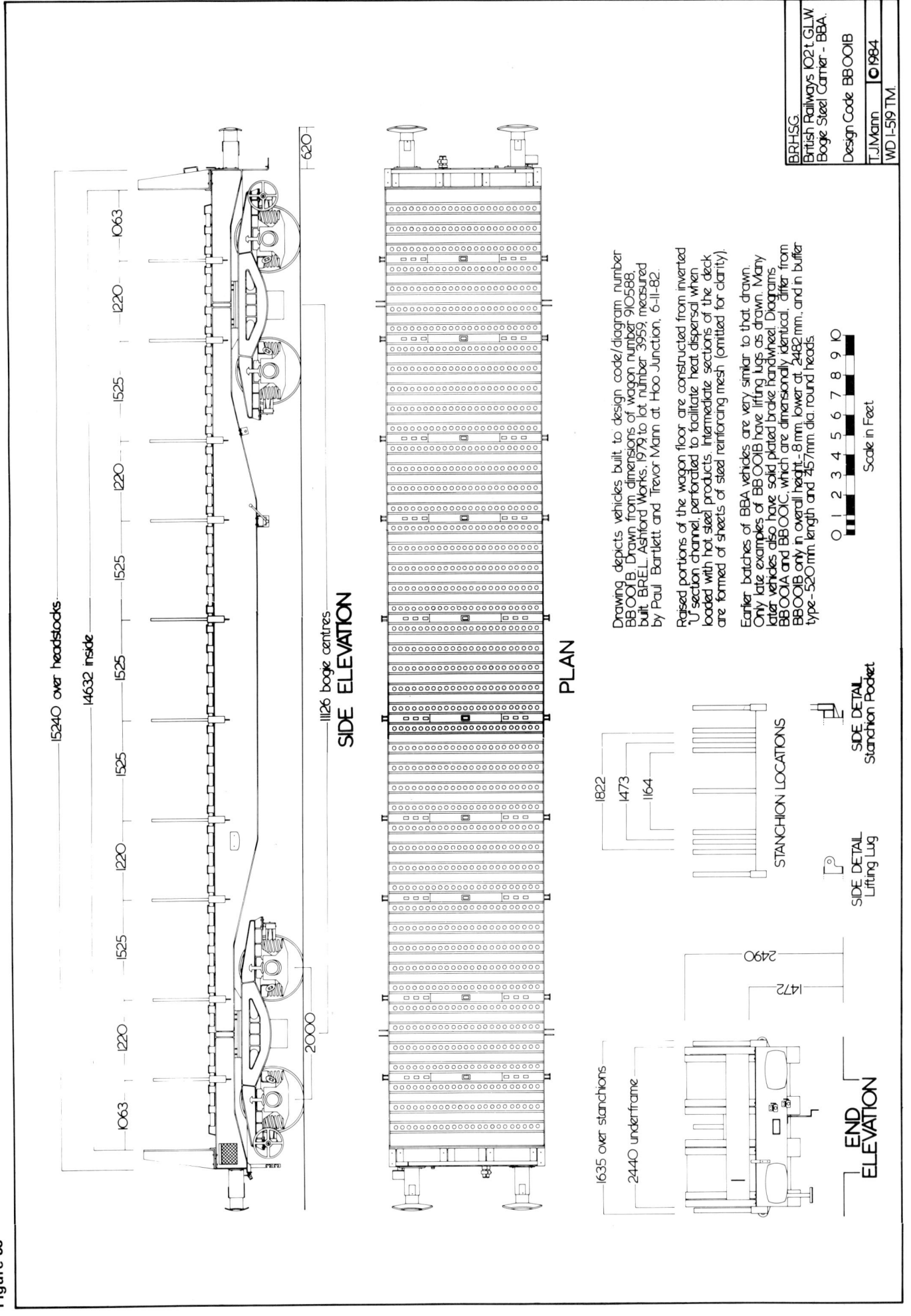

SIDE ELEVATION

PLAN

END ELEVATION

SIDE DETAIL
Lifting Lug

SIDE DETAIL
Stanchion Pocket

STANCHION LOCATIONS

Scale in Feet
0 1 2 3 4 5 6 7 8 9 10

BRHSG.
British Railways 102t GLW.
Bogie Steel Carrier - BBA.

Design Code BB001B

T.J.Mann   © 1984
WD 1-519 T.M.

Drawing depicts vehicles built to design code/diagram number BB001B. Drawn from dimensions of wagon number 910588, built BREL Ashford Works, 1979 to lot number 3959, measured by Paul Bartlett and Trevor Mann at Hoo Junction, 6-11-82.

Raised portions of the wagon floor are constructed from inverted 'U' section channel, perforated to facilitate heat dispersal when loaded with hot steel products. Intermediate sections of the deck are formed of sheets of steel reinforcing mesh (omitted for clarity).

Earlier batches of BBA vehicles are very similar to that drawn. Only late examples of BB001B have lifting lugs as drawn. Many later vehicles also have solid plated brake handwheel. Diagrams BB001A and BB001C, which are dimensionally identical, differ from BB001B only in overall height, -8mm lower at 2482mm, and in buffer type -520mm length and 257mm dia round heads.

Borails

These wagons were similar to 'Bogie Bolsters' but specially designated for the carriage of rail, and of original design. As most rail was carried for the Engineer's Department it would have been more logical to have included them in their fleet. A few rail-carrying wagons were built for their use but, until recently, no wagons were specially reserved for the carriage of new rail by them. The 'Borails' normally carried the new rail from the mills, which in later days were only at Workington, to the track pre-fabrication depots, or to the docks for shipment. The details of these designs are summarised in **Table 24**.

TABLE 24

BORAILS

Diag No.	Lot No.	Qnty	Builder	Date	Running numbers	Bogie type	Brake type	Branding
1/480	2098	50	Swindon	1949	B946000 - 946049	GWR Plate	Unfit	BORAIL WE
1/481	3263	15	L & Y Wagon Co.	1959	B946050 - 946064	Plateback	Vacuum pipe	BORAIL WG
1/482	3267	10	Derby	1959	B946065 - 946074	Plateback	Vacuum brake	BORAIL EC
1/482	3334	20	Derby	1961	B946210 - 946229	Plateback	Vacuum brake	BORAIL EC
1/483	3268	40	Derby	1960	B946075 - 946114	Plateback	Vacuum brake	BORAIL EB
1/483	3333	95	Derby	1961	B946115 - 946209	Plateback	Vacuum brake	BORAIL EB & MB
BR006A	4012	150	Shildon	1981-2	967500 - 967649	Y25C	Air brake	MULLET
Total		380						

Borail WE

The first diagram, No. 1/480, was also given the GWR/BR Diagram No. J35. It was similar to a 'Bogie Bolster C' but able to carry 40 tons (see Plate 156). Although of a GWR design, they had had no identical wagons, as earlier designs had had the Dean-Churchward brake and the bolsters were adjustable in a different way. On the BR wagons, the end bolsters were adjustable but, unlike contemporary 'Bogie Bolsters', there were no pockets for stanchions on the sides. Other dimensions were similar to Diagram No. 1/471 'Bogie Bolster Cs' as they were 45ft. over headstocks with GWR plate bogies at 35ft. 6in. centres. Originally branded BORAIL WE, this was altered very early on to BOGIE BOLSTER C. Twenty four were converted to 'Coil X' during 1975 and most of the others were scrapped by 1980, when unfitted 'Bogie Bolsters' were generally withdrawn. At least one persisted in Engineer's Department use at the end of 1984.

Borail WG

Ten years passed before more 'Borails' were built, and then two very distinctive designs were introduced which both carried 50 tons. The first design, Diagram No. 1/481, was branded BORAIL WG. Appearing to have been largely based on the Engineer's GWR/BR 'Gane A', which had been allocated Diagram No. 1/641 (nine of these had initially been branded BORAIL SA, and given traffic Diagram No. 1/488, but numbered in the Engineer's series) they had conventional 'Bogie Bolster' appearance being 62ft. over headstocks with bogies at 51ft. 6in. centres (see Plate 157). They were fitted with through pipes, screw handbrake and plate-back roller bearing bogies of 5ft. 6in. wheelbase. The position of the six bolsters could not be altered, but the stanchions could be fixed in ten different places along the side and in eight positions on the bolsters. These wagons continue in use and were TOPS-coded BRP, although they are now used by Taunton concrete works and are coded YNP.

Borail EB, EC and MB

There were two variants of the next design, both carried 50 tons, but they were of very distinctive appearance. Diagram No. 1/482, the BORAIL EC, did not have bolsters, the stanchions simply located into the floor at five positions along the wagon (see Plate 158). These wagons were for pre-stressed concrete beams. On Diagram No. 1/483, the BORAIL EB or MB, five high bolsters were fixed in place; these were constructed of steel channel topped with a baulk of wood (see Plate 159). These were for rail. In all other respects the two diagrams were the same, and both are illustrated by **Figure 39**. They were 62ft. over headstocks with 8ft. wheelbase plate-back bogies at 47ft. centres. There were no sides, so the plank floor showed, and instead of channel solebars, there were fabricated sides which were narrow over the bogies and swept to a deep fish-belly between. A small flap across the end of the wagon could be folded out over the buffers. Vacuum brakes and a screw handbrake were fitted. These wagons, TOPS code BRV, were mostly withdrawn during 1982 for conversion to air-braking.

Air Brake Borail

During 1981/2, most of the fish-belly wagons were converted to air brake. Unlike most other air brake conversions, the body design was altered. Allocated Diagram No. BR006A, the new wagons had six bolsters of similar design to the earlier vacuum-braked wagons (a few of these wagons had been converted to have six bolsters earlier). They also had a low side and end, of 8in. depth, and this was cut into at six places where taughteners for the webbing straps were located. The lashing rings for chaining down, which were positioned along the side frames, were removed. The planking of the floor, which no longer showed from the side, was replaced. Y25C bogies with a hand wheel brake were used (see Plate 160). The wagons were painted in the new livery; the sides, ends and bolsters were in 'Railfreight' red and the underframe was black. Originally TOPS-coded BRA, in early 1983 they were transferred to the Engineer's Department becoming TOPS-coded YLA, with numbers prefixed DC, and the code name MULLET painted on the side, usually on a yellow panel.

Plate 156   The Borail WE, Diagram 1/480, has affinities to the Bogie Bolster C, and many were so coded during their career, although the lack of stanchion pockets on the curb rail readily identified them. No. B946032 (Swindon 1949, 2098), by now numbered as internal user 090620 in Grangemouth Docks, has such a code, although it had obviously seen better days. In this view, taken on 16th September 1981, the arrangements of the bolsters may be seen.

R. A. Silsbury

Plate 157   No. B946054 (L&Y Wagon Co. 1959, 3263) is one of the vacuum-piped Diagram 1/481 vehicles. In this photograph, taken at Queen-borough on 20th April 1980, the load of new rail has wooden spacers between the tiers, and the stanchions are located in the pockets adjacent to the bolster ends. The livery is bauxite.

R. A. Silsbury

Plates 158 & 159 The last design of vacuum-braked Borails were basically the same. **Plate 158** features No. B946213 (Derby 1961, 3334) to Diagram 1/482, which has no bolsters, whilst **Plate 159** illustrates No. B946151 (Derby 1961, 3333). Diagram 1/483, has five high bolsters. Both are in bauxite livery, the former at Toton on 17th September 1978, and the latter with a load of scrap rail at Queenborough on 20th April 1980.

R. A. Silsbury

Figure 39

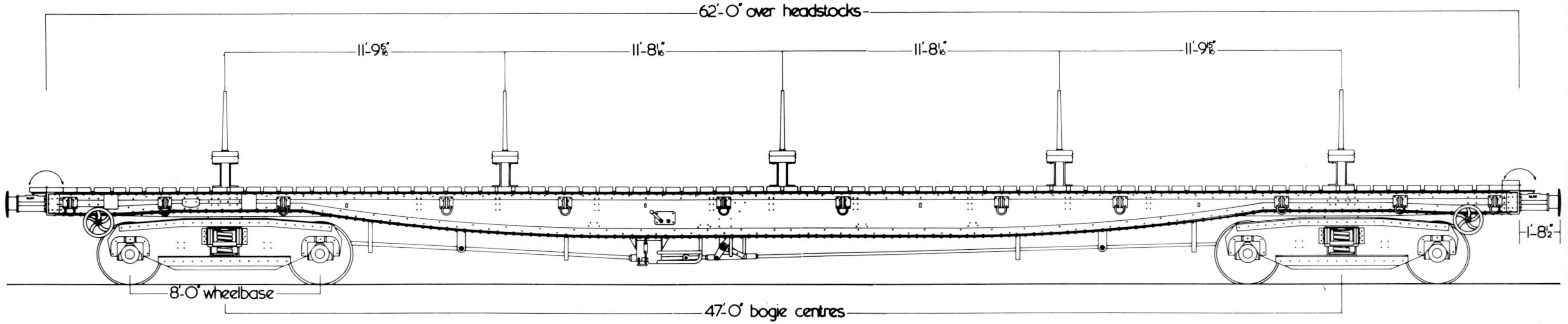

SIDE ELEVATION

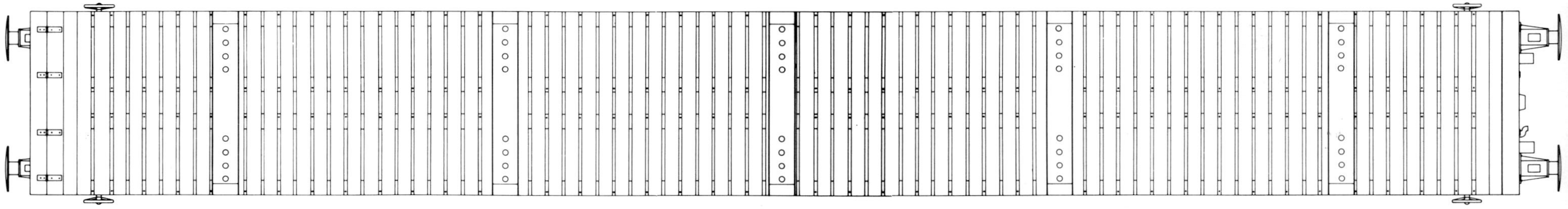

62'-0" over headstocks

47'-0" bogie centres

8'-0" wheelbase

1'-8⅛"

11'-9½"   11'-8⅝"   11'-8⅝"   11'-8⅝"   11'-9⅝"

PLAN

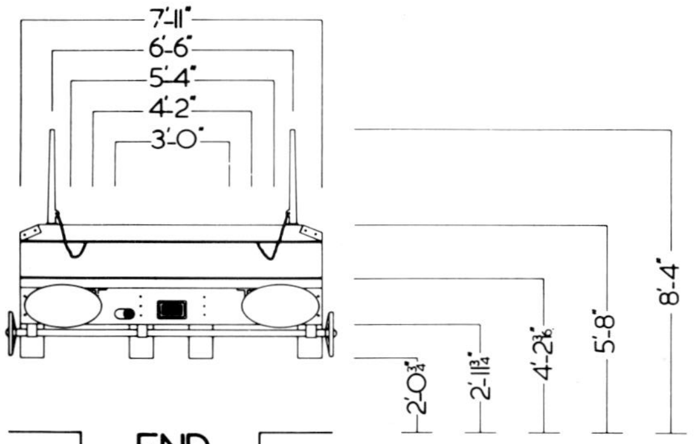

END ELEVATION

8'-4"
5'-8"
4'-2½"
2'-11½"
2'-0½"

7'-11"
6'-6"
5'-4"
4'-2"
3'-0"

BRHSG
British Railways 50 ton
"Borail EB/MB" and "Borail
EC".
Diagrams 1/482 and 1/483.
A.Ward & T.Mann © 1984
WD 1-482 AW/TM.

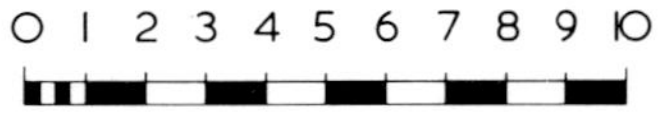

0 1 2 3 4 5 6 7 8 9 10

Scale in Feet

Main drawing represents "Borail MB" or
"Borail EB" diagram 1/482. For "Borail EC".
diagram 1/483, omit bolsters and replace
with steel sheet and fittings at identical
spacings. All other details as drawn.

Detail of Borail EC –

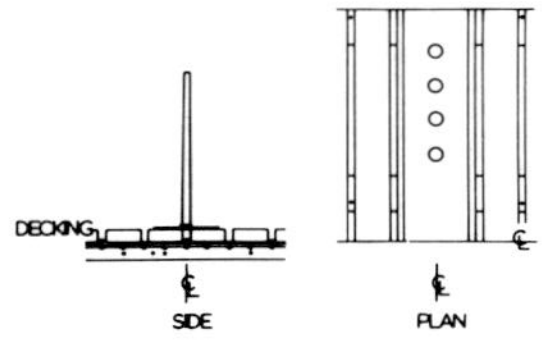

PLAN

SIDE

DECKING

Originally drawn by Andrew Ward using
British Railways General Arrangement
Drawing No. SW DE 1377. Redrawn and
traced Trevor Mann.

Borail EB/MB – diagram 1/483 – labeled –
"50 ton Bogie Bolster".

Borail EC – diagram 1/482 – labeled – "For
Conveyance of Pre-Stressed Concrete
Beams".

Lot 3267 – Borail EC   – diagram 1/482
Lot 3268 – Borail EB/MB – diagram 1/483
Lot 3333 – Borail EB/MB – diagram 1/483
Lot 3334 – Borail EC   – diagram 1/482

129

Plate 160 When air-braked, the Borails presented a different appearance, with low sides and Y25C bogies. No. 967526 (Shildon 1981, 4012) has a load of new flat-bottomed rail, held down by nylon straps, and painted in the, then, new Railfreight red livery when photographed at Eastleigh on 3rd November 1981.

R. A. Silsbury

Plates (Details of the 'Plates' are in Table 25)

Unfitted Designs

Both the LMS and LNER had built similar all steel wagons for the carriage of 22 tons of steel plate, which was laid flat in the wagon. BR continued this design, initially allocating Diagram No. 1/430 to LMS Diagram No. 2083 and No. 1/431 to LNER Diagram No. 123; the diagrams differed by No. 1/431 being 0 ¼ in. higher. They had fixed ends, which were variously of welded and riveted construction, and sides as a pair of drop

doors of welded construction **(see Plate 161)**. All were unfitted with a 15ft. wheelbase RCH long-link underframe which was 27ft. 1½ in. over headstocks. Reference should be made to **MRC Annual 1983, page 93** for drawing, and also to **Figure 34** of the 'Double Bolster' which is similar, apart from the bolsters. They were branded PLATE and later the TOPS code was SPO. By 1977, the remaining wagons were stored out of use and they were scrapped in 1980. Similar wagons, with their own number series, were built for the Engineer's Department.

TABLE 25

PLATES

Diag No.	Lot No.	Qnty	Builder	Date	Running numbers	Underframe type	Brake type
1/430	2037	250	Shildon	1949	B930000 - 930249	RCH long-link	Unfit
1/430	2132	300	Shildon	1950	B930250 - 930549	RCH long-link	Unfit
1/430	2151	500	Turner	1950/1	B930550 - 931049	RCH long-link	Unfit
1/431	2199	540	Shildon	1951	B931050 - 931589	RCH long-link	Unfit
1/431	2327	160	Shildon	1952	B931590 - 931749	RCH long-link	Unfit
1/431	2476	225	Shildon	1953	B931750 - 931974	RCH long-link	Unfit
1/431	2604	850	Shildon	1954	B931975 - 932824	RCH long-link	Unfit
1/432	2734	550	Shildon	1956-8	B932825 - 933374	LNER clasp	Vacuum
1/432	2862	500	Shildon	1957	B933375 - 933874	LNER clasp	Vacuum
1/432	3128	150	Shildon	1958	B933875 - 934024	LNER clasp	Vacuum
1/434	3223	1500	Shildon	1959/60	B934025 - 935524	BR clasp	Vacuum
1/434	3338	1000	Shildon	1960/1	B935525 - 936524	BR clasp	Vacuum
1/433pt	3362	2	Ashford	1961	B710251, B710252	BR clasp	Vacuum
SP019A	3914	2	Ashford	1977	460000 - 460001	–	Air
SP020A	3839	600	Shildon	1979	460002 - 460601	–	Air
SP020A	3962	500	Shildon	1980/1	460602 - 461101	–	Air
	Total	7629					

Vaccum Brake Designs

In 1956, vacuum-braking was introduced for 'Plates', and BR returned to LNER Diagram No. 196 which became Diagram No. 1/432. These had the characteristic LNER clasp vacuum brake. These are shown in **Figure 40 and Plate 162**. Diagram No. 1/434 was introduced in 1959 for wagons with a form of BR clasp brake. Bodies were similar to the earlier diagrams **(see Plate 163)**. Some of the earlier unfitted 'Plates' were converted to vacuum brake using the BR clasp brake. The vacuum-braked 'Plates' were usually branded 'PLATE VB' and SPV for TOPS. By May 1984, a total of 168 remained in the revenue fleet and others were in Engineer's use. Some others had been converted to 'Rod Coil' wagons, and 447 continued in use.

Prototypes

In 1961, No. B710252, a 'Plate', was included in the series of prototypes built to Lot 3362. It had the vacuum brake underframe design common to all of these, which was 35ft. over headstocks with a 20ft. 9in. wheelbase. It had a 14ft. 6¾in. wide drop door flanked on either side by doors of 9ft. 9⅜in. width. Possibly within a year it was joined by No. B710251 which was converted from the 'Prototype Quadruple Bolster' **(see page 111)** and Diagram No. 1/433 was issued, the only diagram for any of these related prototypes. All of these prototypes had all the special underframe fittings for each of the wagons in the series, so body exchange was easy. Nothing further came of the prototype design and no more 'Plates' were built until 1977.

Air Brake Plates

The pair of prototype air-braked 'Plates' of Diagram No. SP019A had steel ends and sides dropping as four doors. The underframe was 33ft. 6in. over headstocks with a 20ft. 9in. wheelbase. They were painted bauxite with 'Railfreight' lettering. Neither ever seems to have been used for plate traffic and they became barriers, RBA, in 1981. In 1982, No. RDC460000 was rebuilt as a structure-gauging car by the Research Division.

The production batch of air-braked 'Plates' of Diagram No. SP020A carried 31½ tonnes. They had the sides dropping as three doors and a fixed end supported by four 6in. 'U' channel stanchions **(see Plate 164)**. The latter arrangement was repeated with the later OCAs **(see page 51)** and the Engineer's TURBOT. They were the same length as the prototypes but the underframe was different, having a straight solebar. All of them had 'Railfreight' red bodies and 'Railfreight' lettering which changed position from being at the right-hand end to the left during production. Steel shortages affected the building of these wagons and many were stored without wheels and bearings for a period during 1980. Later, these were produced with Terrol rotating roller bearings and Bruninghaus suspension. Lot 3962 was incomplete as it had originally been for 900. The TOPS code was SPA.

Soon after introduction some were converted to 'Coils' with simple cradles, and later, during 1983, fifty were converted to 'Rod Coil' wagons; these were TOPS code KOA which was altered to SKA in early 1984. During 1983, the first 330 were transferred for Engineer's use and code-named PIKE, TOPS code ZAA.

Plate 161 No. B930287 (Shildon 1950, 2132) is a Diagram 1/430 unfitted Plate wagon. Comparison with the Double Bolster in **Plate 142** will reveal that the only differences are the lack of bolsters, and pockets on the solebars. When recorded on 13th July 1978 at Llandeilo Junction, No. B930287 was stored out of use. Its livery was light grey, and the sunlight shining on the axle reveals that some floor planks are missing.

R. A. Silsbury

Plate 162   Also appearing as **Figure 40**, the Diagram 1/432 'Plate' wagon is illustrated by No. B933554 (Shildon 1957, 2862). The bodywork is virtually identical to the earlier Plate wagons, although an extra hinge has been provided on each door. The LNER vacuum brakegear has only one 'V' hanger on the side with the brake cylinder. The livery, once bauxite, was nearly all bare rust when seen at Oxford on 17th June 1980.

R. A. Silsbury

Figure 40

Measured by Trevor Mann

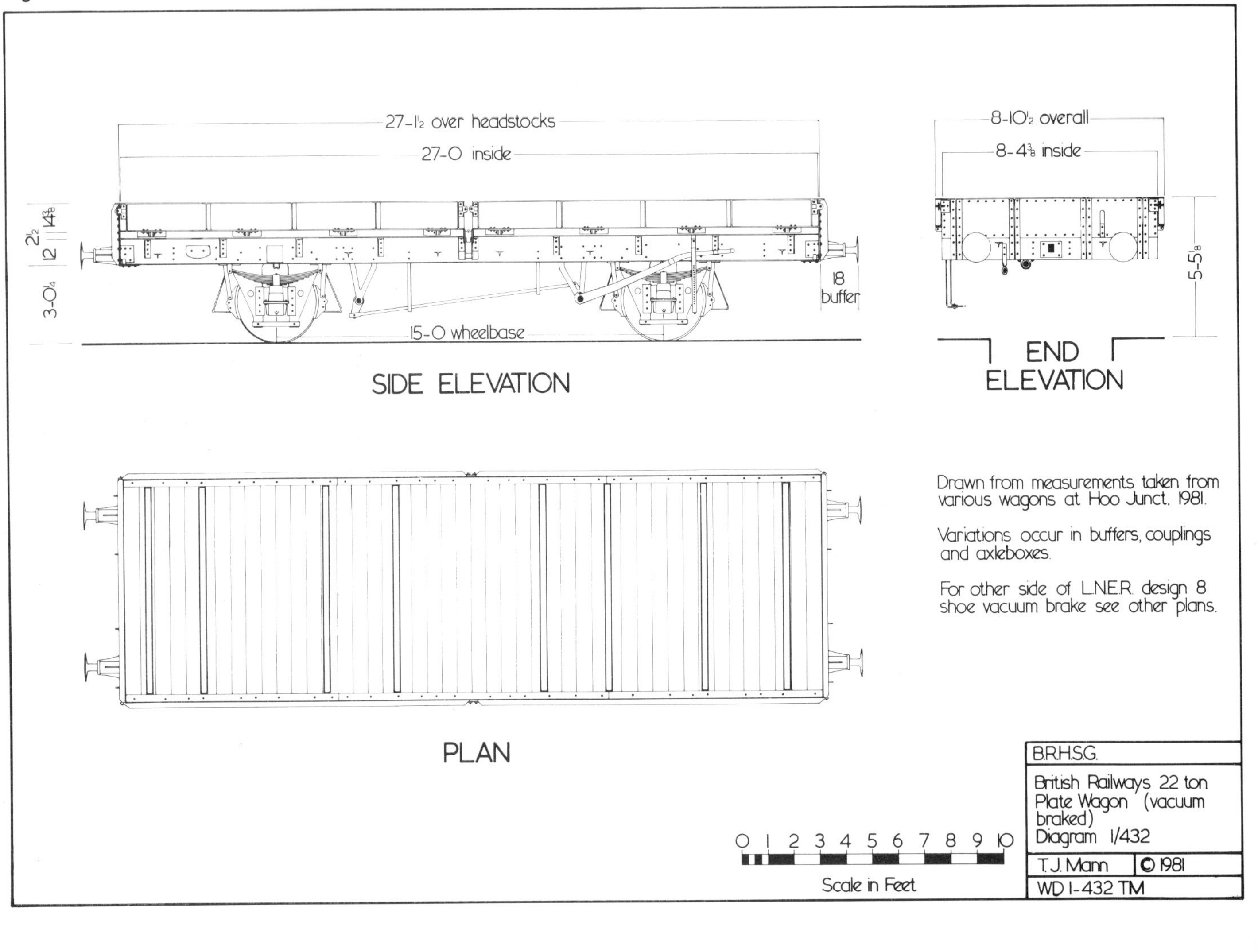

27-1½ over headstocks

27-0 inside

3-0¼ 2²⁄₁₂ 14⅛

15-0 wheelbase

18 buffer

SIDE ELEVATION

8-10½ overall

8-4⅜ inside

5-5⅝

END ELEVATION

PLAN

Drawn from measurements taken from various wagons at Hoo Junct. 1981.

Variations occur in buffers, couplings and axleboxes.

For other side of L.N.E.R. design 8 shoe vacuum brake see other plans.

0 1 2 3 4 5 6 7 8 9 10

Scale in Feet

B.R.H.S.G.	
British Railways 22 ton Plate Wagon (vacuum braked) Diagram 1/432	
T.J. Mann	© 1981
WD 1-432 TM	

Plate 163 No. B935511 (Shildon 1960, 3223) is to Diagram 1/434, which was issued to differentiate those vacuum-braked Plate wagons having BR clasp brakegear. It has also been fitted with roller bearing axleboxes, of two types, and Oleo pneumatic buffers, and was rather rusty when photographed at Oxford on 17th June 1980.

R. A. Silsbury

Plate 164 The production air-braked Plate wagons, TOPS code SPA, were a robust design. The ratchets, with nylon straps for securing the load, were located on the curb rails, the straps passing through the gap between the door and the floor. Displaying full flame red Railfreight livery, No. 460004 (Shildon 1979, 3839) was photographed at Port Talbot on 13th October 1981.

R. A. Silsbury

Bogie Plates

'Bogie Plates' were introduced by the LNER in 1930, and the LMS used a similar design. BR continued to build identical designs which only changed with the modernisation of the running gear. Details of these are given in **Table 26**. They all had a 42 ton capacity and were 52ft. over headstocks with bogies at 40ft. centres. The ends were fixed steel and the two plank sides dropped as two doors. Lot 2010 differed to the remainder of Diagram No. 1/490 by having LMS diamond bogies, one of which has Simplex brakes with the brake lever mounted on it; this was similar to LMS Diagram No. P18B **(see Plate 165)**. The wheels were of 2ft. 8½in. diameter, unlike all later wagons which had 3ft. 1½in. wheels. The other unfitted Diagram No. 1/490 'Boplates' had plate bogies, those of Lot 2185 having GWR features. They had a conventional hand lever brake on each side so that each braked one bogie. **Figure 41 and Plate 166** are of this type. Similar wagons, with their own number series, were built for the Engineer's Department. Lots 3235 and 3236 were vacuum-fitted and had plate-back bogies with roller bearings and a hand wheel brake.

Diagram No. 1/491 was an LNER design, LNER Diagram No. 68, with LNER diamond bogies and two hand lever brakes on each side **(see Plate 167)**. This diagram was a nominal 1in. narrower than the others.

Diagram No. 1/492 was also 1in. narrower than No. 1/490. Lot 3240 had similar running gear to Lots 3235/6 **(see Plate 168)**. Lot 3229 had cast Davis & Lloyd AAR 38BF bogies and hand wheel brake. This batch was popular for conversion and, by the late 1970s, none remained as 'Boplates', some were 'Boflats', and others were five different types of 'Conflat'.

Air Brake Boplates

In 1980 and 1981, unfitted 'Boplates' were converted to air brake. They had new Y25C bogies with hand wheel brakes mounted on them. Other accompanying running gear was also altered but the body remained the same **(see Plate 169)**. They carried 58½ tonnes. The bodies were painted in 'Railfreight' red.

'Boplates' were useful for large or long, but low, merchandise such as lorry trailers and large ingots of steel, as well as steel plate. The unfitted examples were withdrawn by 1981 and only 52 vacuum-braked examples remained in May 1984. The wagons were branded 'BOPLATE E' and 'BOPLATE E VB'; the TOPS codes were BPO, BPV and BPA respectively. The Engineer's Department used a few 'Boplates' and during 1984 some BPAs were transferred and given the TOPS code YNA.

TABLE 26

BOGIE PLATES

Diag No.	Lot No.	Qnty	Builder	Date	Running numbers	Bogie type	Brake type
1/490	2010	50	Derby	1949	B947000 – 947049	LMS Diamond	Unfit
1/490	2185	50	Derby	1951	B947125 – 947174	GWR Plate	Unfit
1/490	2344	20	Shildon	1952	B947175 – 947194	BR/GW Plate	Unfit
1/490	2455	40	Derby	1954	B947195 – 947234	BR/GW Plate	Unfit
1/490	2618	75	Cambrian	1954	B947235 – 947309	BR/GW Plate	Unfit
1/490	2722	40	Cambrian	1955	B947310 – 947349	BR/GW Plate	Unfit
1/490	2930	50	Cambrian	1957	B947350 – 947399	BR/GW Plate	Unfit
1/490	3046	160	Cambrian	1957/8	B947400 – 947559	BR/GW Plate	Unfit
1/490	3055	150	Hurst Nelson	1958	B947560 – 947709	BR/GW Plate	Unfit
1/490	3056	150	Pickering	1957/8	B947710 – 947859	BR/GW Plate	Unfit
1/490	3235	125	Derby	1958/9	B948010 – 948134	Plateback	Vacuum
1/490	3236	125	Derby	1960	B948135 – 948259	Plateback	Vacuum
1/491	2133	75	Shildon	1951	B947050 – 947124	LNER Diamond	Unfit
1/492	3229	150	Ashford	1960/1	B947860 – 948009	Davis & Lloyd	Vacuum
1/492	3240	150	Ashford	1959/60	B948260 – 948409	Plateback	Vacuum
BP004A	3985	50	Shildon	1980	965000 – 965049	Y25C	Air
BP004A	4011	30	Shildon	1981	965050 – 965079	Y25C	Air
Total		1490					

Plate 165 KDB No. 947017 (Derby 1949, 2010) is from the first batch of Diagram 1/490 'Boplates', and fitted with LMS diamond frame bogies, with the Simplex brake on the bogie (see **Plate 47** for detail). This low angle view, taken at Doncaster on 2nd July 1983, emphasises the small diameter wheels, and the more heavily-braced truss rods than later builds.

P. W. Bartlett

Plate 166 Other Diagram 1/490 vehicles had plate-back bogies, with a modified form of Simplex brake lever external to the bogie. Although nominally an LMS design, the buffers are of the fabricated open guide type favoured by the LNER. No. B947363 (Cambrian 1957, 2930) was photographed at Wrexham on 4th August 1980, and the livery was light grey, with chocolate brown underframe.

R. A. Silsbury

Plate 167 The LNER-originated Diagram 1/491 is represented here by No. B947074 (Shildon 1950, 2133) nearing the end of its days as internal user No. 090423 at Grangemouth Docks on 16th August 1981. This illustration was chosen as it shows the doors in the open position, although the nearest end has its planks missing. The main differences from Diagram 1/490 are the bogies and brakegear.

R. A. Silsbury

Plate 168 No. B948261 (Ashford 1959, 3240) to Diagram 1/492 displays more modern features, welded ends, oval-headed self-contained buffers, roller bearing axleboxes, and vacuum brake with wheel handbrake, and is painted in bauxite livery. Its load of two ingots are placed one over each bogie, and it is pictured at Margam on 13th October 1981.

R. A. Silsbury

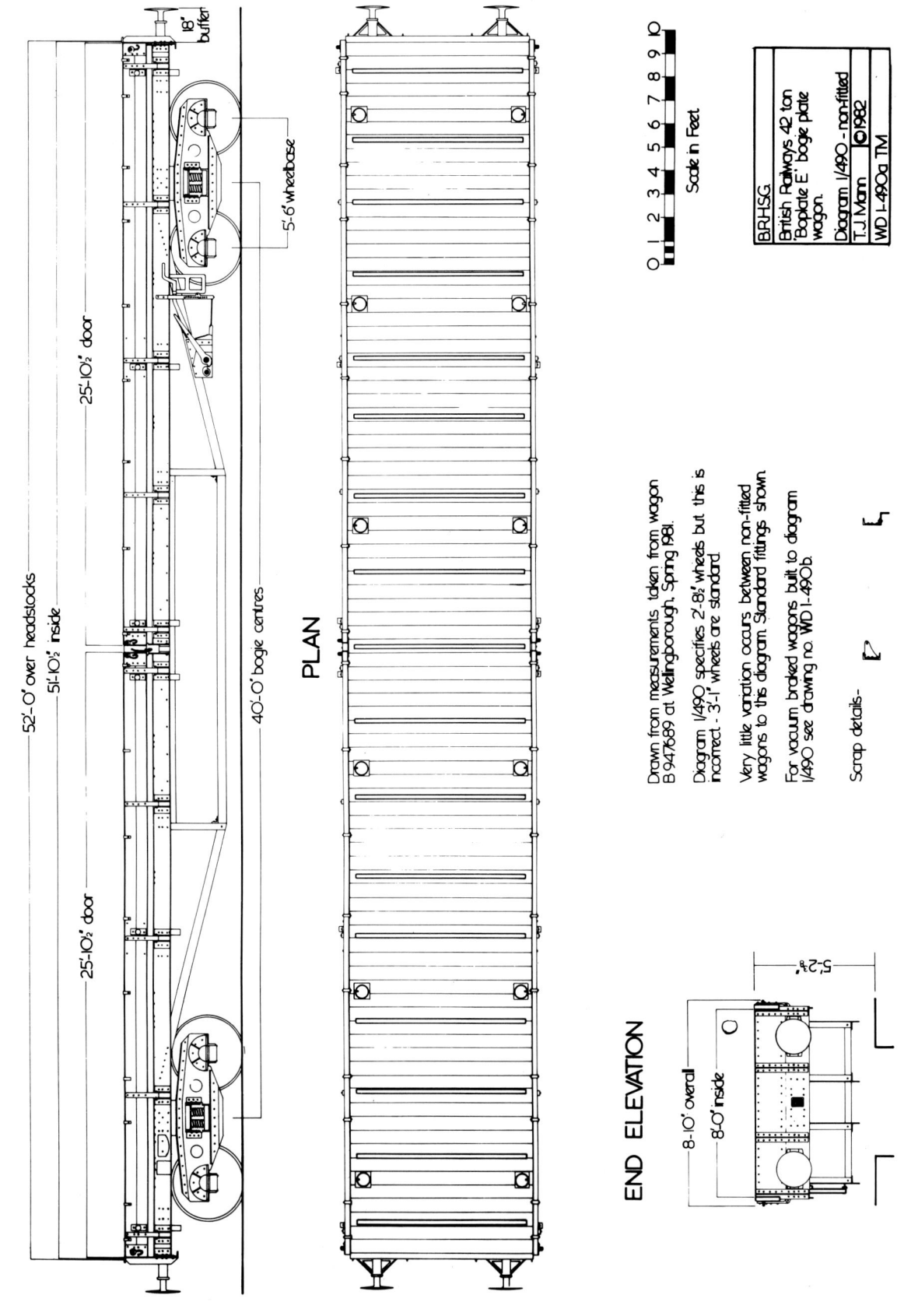

SIDE ELEVATION

52'-0" over headstocks

51'-10½" inside

25'-10½" door

25'-10½" door

5'-6" wheelbase

40'-0" bogie centres

18" buffer

PLAN

END ELEVATION

8'-10" overall

8'-0" inside

5'-2⅜"

Drawn from measurements taken from wagon
B 947689 at Wellingborough. Spring 1981.

Diagram 1/490 specifies 2-8½' wheels but this is
incorrect - 3'-1" wheels are standard.

Very little variation occurs between non-fitted
wagons to this diagram. Standard fittings shown

For vacuum braked wagons built to diagram
1/490 see drawing no. WD 1-490b.

Scrap details-

A Hinge   B Door Spring

Scale in Feet

0 1 2 3 4 5 6 7 8 9 10

BRHSG
British Railways 42 ton
'Boplate E' bogie plate
wagon.
Diagram 1/490 - non-fitted
T.J.Mann   © 1982
WD 1-490a TM

Measured by Paul Bartlett and Trevor Mann

Figure 41

136

Plate 169 The air-braked 'Boplates' had new bogies, brakes and buffers, whilst retaining the original bodywork. This view of No. 965039 (Shildon 1980, 3985) taken from the footbridge over Scunthorpe Yard on 2nd May 1981, shows the load of steel plates. Details to note include the inside of the doors, the lashing rings set into the floor, and the battens to raise the load; the Railfreight red livery does not have symbols.

R. A. Silsbury

TABLE 27

TRESTLES AND TRESTROLS

Diag No.	Lot No.	Qnty	Builder	Date	Running numbers	Bogie type	Brake type	Branding
2/491	2434	25	Tees-side SBE	1953/4	B903600 - 903624	LNER Diamond	Unfit	TRESTLE ED
2/491	3066	24	Tees-side SBE	1957	B903625 - 903648	BR/GW Plate	Unfit	TRESTLE ED
2/492	3124	16	Darlington	1958	B903649 - 903664	4-wh BR clasp	Vacuum	TRESTLE EA & AA
2/493	3231	19	Derby	1959	B903665 - 903683	Plateback	Vacuum	TRESTLE ED
2/495	3410	20	Chas Roberts	1961/2	B903684 - 903703	Gloucester	Vacuum	TRESTLE ED
2/680	2205	10	Head Wrightson	1951	B901500 - 901509	LMS Diamond	Unfit	TRESTROL AD
2/681	2175	4	Tees-side SBE	1950/1	B901600 - 901603	6-wh bogies	Unfit	TRESTROL EC
2/682	2355	10	Lancing	1953	B901510 - 901519	BR/GW plate	Unfit	TRESTROL AD & EO
2/682	3017	11	Lancing	1958/9	B901520 - 901530	–	Unfit	TRESTROL MO & EO
2/682	3112	11	Ashford	1958/9	B901531 - 901541	–	Unfit/pipe	TRESTROL AO & EO
2/682	3247	35	Ashford	1959	B901542 - 901576	Plateback	Vacpipe	TRESTROL EO
2/682	3309	50	Derby	1960	B901702 - 901751	Plateback	Vacpipe	TRESTROL EO
2/683	2575	1	Lancing	1955	B901650	4-wh well	Unfit	TRESTROL EJ
2/684	2576	2	Lancing	1956	B901700 - 901701	–	Unfit	TRESTROL EN
-	3911	1	Ashford	1977	990000	Y25C	Air brake	XVA
XV005A	3961	50	Shildon	1979	990001 - 990050	Y25C	Air brake	XVA

Total		289						

Trestles and Trestrols

The wagons in these two closely-related categories were included in the 'Special' diagram book 2 but, as they had only a single use, the carriage of large steel plates, they are more suitably included in this chapter. All of them had heavy wood or steel framing against which the plates were leant, and this allowed broader plates to be carried than was possible on the conventional 'Plate' wagons. The wagons were of various designs; some were 4-wheeled, most were bogied. The 'Trestles' all had a straight bed above the bogies, the 'Trestrols' had a well between the wheels or bogies in which the plate rested; this allowed for the maximum use of the space available. **Table 27** describes these wagons.

Trestles

The first diagram for new wagons was No. 2/491. This was for the 'Trestle ED' which was 52ft. over headstocks with bogies at 40ft. centres and a low side of 9in. The trestle was a long continuous steel frame of 50ft. 9in. in length. The bogies differed according to lot and Lot 3066 had roller bearings although all were unfitted. Diagram No. 2/493 was for Lot 3231, which had an identical body type but was vacuum-braked with an SAB regulator **(Plate 170)**. Another diagram, No. 2/495 for Lot 3410, had a similar body design but at 10ft. 3¾in. was ¾in. higher than the earlier designs. These wagons were also vacuum-braked with SAB regulator, and had roller bearing Gloucester cast bogies. All of these similar wagons carried 42 tons.

Diagram No. 2/492 was for the vacuum-braked 21 ton 'Trestle EA and AAs'. These were 4-wheeled wagons which had a 15ft. wheelbase, and were 27ft. 1½in. over headstocks **(see Plate 171)**. These dimensions were similar to the 'Plates' and the design was based on LNER Diagram No. 96 and BR Diagram No. 2/490 which was for a batch of 'Double Bolsters' converted to 'Trestle EA'.

The trestle of this design was made from heavy wood baulks and was 27ft. 1½in. long, the body was 10ft. 0½in. high. They had the later BR clasp underframe as used on the later 'Plates' with Athermos roller bearings.

Air Brake Trestles

Fifty one wagons were converted to air brake from 'Trestle EDs' during 1979/80. They carried 43 tonnes. These had Y25C bogies with a hand wheel brake on the bogie. The body was slightly altered with extra strengthening ribs vertically welded to the side and taughteners for webbing straps **(see Plate 172)**. These wagons were painted in the new freight red for the trestle and side, and black for the underframe. The TOPS code was XVA which changed to BXA during 1984. The other 'Trestles' went out of use during 1980 or 1981.

Trestrols

The 'Trestrols' were less numerous but more varied. The first design was Diagram No. 2/680 which was very similar to LMS Diagram No. 122A. They were described as 'Trestrol MO' on the diagram but were reclassified to 'AD' between 1959 and 1964. They carried 40 tons and were 61ft. 9in. over headstocks with LMS diamond bogies, fitted with Simplex brake and 2ft. 8½in. diameter wheels, at 52ft. 3in. centres. There were three separate steel trestles, each 6ft. 6in. wide. The usable length of well was 40ft. 3in. **(see Plate 173)**. The deck of the wagons was like a 'Weltrol' with the plate being carried slotted between the main girders of the floor. These wagons were TOPS code XTO and went out of use during 1980.

Diagram No. 2/681 was for the largest design, the 'Trestrol EC', which was the same as LNER Diagram No. 102 and LMS Diagram No. 134A. These unfitted wagons, which carried 55 tons, were mounted on 6-wheel bogies which had a 5ft. 6in. by 5ft. 6in. wheelbase. Each bogie had a screw hand wheel brake. The length was 68ft. over headstocks with the bogies at 53ft. centres. The trestle was 30ft. 6½in. long and made of steel, the usable length of well was 36ft. 8in. long and the wagon was 10ft. 4½in. high. Later in their lives three of the wagons were acquired by the Research Department at Derby who converted them substantially.

The next design, Diagram No. 2/682, was the standard 'Trestrol', variously coded AO, EO and MO according to the region operating the wagon. These carried 40 tons and were 61ft. 9in. over headstocks with the bogies at 52ft. 3in. centres. There were three steel trestles, 6ft. 6in. wide and 9ft. 6in. high. The usable well length was 40ft. 3in. **(see Figure 42)**. Early wagons had GW/BR plate bogies without holes and later wagons had roller bearing plate-back bogies **(see Plate 174)**. Early wagons were unfitted and later ones vacuum-piped, including Nos. B901538-41. They all had a hand wheel brake on the side of the wagon. The TOPS codes were XTO and XTP. All were withdrawn by about the end of 1980, except for the occasional wagons converted to 'Weltrol' for use by the Engineer's Department.

The single 'Trestrol EJ' of Diagram No. 2/683 was 4-wheeled with a 23ft. wheelbase and 29ft. over headstocks. It carried 20 tons on a single steel trestle of 14ft. 3in. length. The usable well length was 19ft. 2in. and the overall height was 9ft. 2¾in. It was the only 'Trestrol' fitted with special chocks so that circular plates could be carried, but other 'Trestrols' were used for these. The wagon was unfitted with screw hand brake. The fate of the wagon is not known to us.

The final 'Trestrol' was the EN. This was Diagram No. 2/684 and carried 30 tons. Only two were built and, as we have not seen them, we are unsure of the details. They had 5ft. 6in. wheelbase bogies at 50ft. centres and were 60ft. over headstocks. The wheels were 2ft. 9in. in diameter. The steel trestle was 34ft. 3¾in. long and the usable length of well was 40ft. The wagons were 10ft. 6in. high. From the diagram the design appears to have departed from using a wagon which was very similar to a 'Weltrol' by having the lower part of the trestle integral with the floor. This diagram was cancelled during 1971 so the wagons will have been withdrawn then, or earlier.

No 'Trestrols' were converted to air brake, and we believe that all had been withdrawn by 1983; the wagon in **Figure 42** had been stored out of use.

Plate 170 Photographed at Derby on 18th August 1959 when new, Diagram 2/493 Trestle-ED, No. B903665 (Derby 1959, 3231) displays the main features of the Trestle wagons. The curb rail was only required along one side, to butt the foot of the load to, and is fitted with shackles for lashing chains. No floor was needed.

BR/OPC

Plate 171 Although this print is not as clear as we should have liked, it does show a Diagram 2/492 Trestle-AA in service carrying four steel plates. Compared to the bogie type, it has curb rails on both sides, and the trestle itself is constructed of wood. No. B903663 (Darlington 1958, 3124) is in bauxite livery, with post-1964 style boxed lettering, and was photographed at Queenborough in May 1974.

D. Larkin

Plate 172 As with Boplates, unfitted vehicles were rebuilt with modern bogies and fittings, and air brakes. This view of No. 990017 (Shildon 1979, 3961) at Scunthorpe Yard on 2nd May 1981, loaded with several short wide plates, shows the lack of decking, the additional side strengtheners, nylon straps, and, just visible, the almost full length step at the back of the trestle to assist in loading and lashing. Another Trestle wagon appears in the background, loaded only with two small plates, and 990014 features on the front cover of the dust jacket and shows the back of the trestle.

R. A. Silsbury

Plate 173 The LMS Simplex-braked diamond frame bogie appears again under Trestrol-AD, No. B901506 (Head, Wrightson 1951, 2205) built to Diagram 2/680. The livery is light grey, and the photograph was taken at Hartlepool during August 1969. Compared to the Trestle wagons, Trestrols featured three separate fabrications to support the load.

D. Larkin

Figure 42

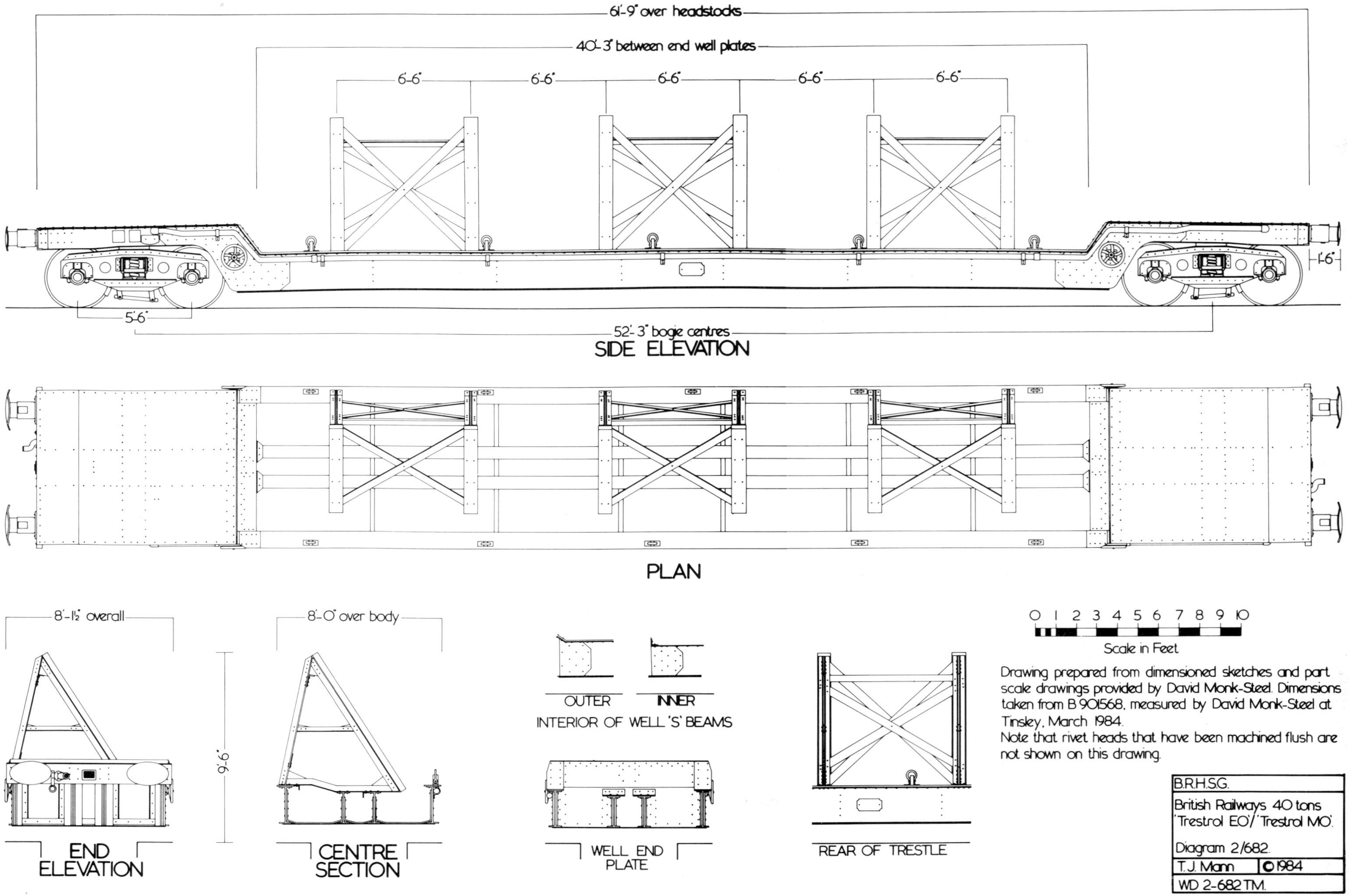

6'-9" over headstocks

40'-3" between end well plates

6'-6"   6'-6"   6'-6"   6'-6"   6'-6"   6'-6"

1'-6"

5'-6"

52'-3" bogie centres

SIDE ELEVATION

PLAN

Scale in Feet

0 1 2 3 4 5 6 7 8 9 10

Drawing prepared from dimensioned sketches and part scale drawings provided by David Monk-Steel. Dimensions taken from B 901568, measured by David Monk-Steel at Tinsley, March 1984.
Note that rivet heads that have been machined flush are not shown on this drawing.

B.R.H.S.G.

British Railways 40 tons
'Trestrol EO'/'Trestrol MO'

Diagram 2/682

T.J. Mann   © 1984

WD 2-682 T.M.

REAR OF TRESTLE

OUTER   INNER

INTERIOR OF WELL'S BEAMS

WELL END PLATE

8'-0" over body

9'-6"

CENTRE SECTION

8'-1½" overall

END ELEVATION

141

Plate 174 Basically similar to the Diagram 2/680, later batches of vehicles, to Diagram 2/682, had roller bearing axleboxes and vacuum through pipes. No. B901702 (Derby 1960, 3309) was the first of the final batch, and posed new at Derby on 1st July 1960, painted in bauxite livery; the 'Trestrol' code has no regional allocation. The cast plate centrally reads 'Load in Well/40 tons overall/30 tons over 10 feet'. The trestles themselves could be removed, permitting use as a Weltrol, and the two tare weights are quoted at the right-hand end of the frame. **Figure 42** is of this type.

BR/OPC

Coils, Stripcoils and Slabs

A considerable fleet of very varied 'Coil' wagons has been developed by BR but, as many of these are conversions of other wagons which retained their original numbers, they are outside the scope of this book. The term 'Coil' is used for several different types of steel products, the name having derived from the long thin plates of steel which are coiled up for despatch. Another different type is thin rods of steel which are coiled up, known as rod-coil. Finally, some of these wagons also carry huge slabs of steel which have been only rolled once. Most of these products are very heavy and thus the wagons are strongly constructed. As will be seen, although there are early wagons in the fleet, most date from the 1960s. This is because of the increase in the manufacture of consumer durables, in particular road vehicles and kitchen equipment, and the rationalisation of the steel manufacturing plants requiring semi-finished products to be moved between them. Most of the designs had hoods to prevent the cold steel rusting before it was tin-plated, but no hood was necessary for coils which were loaded hot.

Before discussing the diagram in detail, it is worth pointing out that they are mixed in with the 'Single' and 'Double Bolsters', although there is no obvious reason for this.

Bogie Coils (see Table 28)

Strip Coils

The first diagram, No. 1/401, was for carrying 42 tons of Strip Coil from Abbey Works at Port Talbot. It pre-dates the other 'Coils' by many years. Built in 1950, until 1952 it was given both GWR/BR Diagram No. O46 and BR Diagram No. 1/080. The body had all steel fixed sides and ends of 2ft. internal depth. Diagram No. O46 shows that they were lined with wooden planks, but these were absent when the measurements for **Figure 43** were taken, and the BR diagrams do not show this detail (see comments about Diagram No. 1/407). Initially, however, the floor had cross-wise planks, later all had 'I' beams, some of which had strips of holes through them into which bars could locate to hold the coil. These short wagons were mounted on a heavy duty underframe of 30ft. over headstocks with GWR plate bogie (without holes) at 18ft. centres. They were unfitted with a short brake lever and the 'V' hanger offset towards one end. **FWLGW Figure 45** shows a wagon in this condition; interestingly all of the lettering, in white, is painted directly on to the grey of the body side without a black ground.

Figure 46 in that book shows the conversion to vacuum brake which was carried out in 1958. They had two vacuum cylinders diagonally opposite to the brake lever and also an additional 'V' hanger. The wagons continued in the Abbey Works traffic until 1982 when most were condemned. The TOPS code was JAV, but several have been noted as JWV and JYV without being rated as 62 tons.

No. B949004 was given Diagram No. 1/406 when it was converted to having a coil cradle for Abbey Works traffic, in 1955. The cradle was 20ft. 1in. over bedplate, which was shorter than Diagram No. 1/404, but may have been a prototype. It was unfitted when converted **(see Plate 176)**.

No. B949021 became Diagram No. 1/407 when it was converted to a 'Hot Coil' in 1955. It had a raised floor which was described as steel-faced asbestos. All the other wagons were converted to this condition; the lack of wood-lined sides and

TABLE 28

BOGIE COIL CARRIERS

Diag No.	Lot No.	Qnty	Builder	Date	Running numbers	Bogie type	Brake type	Branding
1/401	2209	35	Swindon	1950	B949000 - 949034	GWR Plate	Unfit	STRIPCOIL
1/403	3014	15	Head Wrightson	1957	B949035 - 949049	BR/GW Plate	Vacuum	STRIPCOIL
1/404	3015	40	Head Wrightson	1957	B949050 - 949089	BR/GW Plate	Vacuum	STRIPCOIL
1/408	3359	50	Swindon	1961/2	B949501 - 949550	Plateback	Vacuum	SLAB
1/411	3424	58	Swindon	1962	B949551 - 949608	Plateback	Vacuum	SLAB/COIL
1/413	3399	40	Swindon	1961/2	B949090 - 949129	Plateback	Vacuum	STRIP/COIL
1/468	3813	24	Simonside C & W	1975	B960000 - 960023	GWR Plate	Unfit	COIL X

	Total	262						

ends and the floor described above and drawn in **Figure 43** are probably this conversion (**see OPC photograph list P4 OW135**).

Diagram No. 1/403 wagons were very similar to No. 1/401. They had vacuum brakes from new, which was of the same arrangement as the earlier wagons, after they were converted. The bodies and floor were similar to the Diagram No. 1/407 conversion, except that the floor was described as being of steel and the in clear length was ½in. longer at 29ft.8¼in. They had GW/BR plate bogies. These wagons also worked to Abbey Works (**see Plate 175**).

The forty wagons of Diagram No. 1/413 were very similar to No. 1/403, except that plate-back bogies with roller bearings and hydraulic buffers, instead of self-contained, were fitted from new. The body differed by having diagonal strapping on the two panels at each end of the side. They were also capable of carrying a greater load of 60 tons. They worked in Scotland from Ravenscraig to Gartcosh, and were TOPS code JWV.

At first, the forty wagons of Diagram No. 1/404 had a large steel open coil cradle, which was 26ft. 2in. over bedplate. Four adjustable beams crossed the top of the cradle to hold the coils in place. They were vacuum-braked and rated at 56 tons (**see Plate 177**).

From 1963, these wagons were fitted with large nylon hoods which were supported by a new end and three tarpaulin bars. Similar supports were located slightly off the centre of the wagons, so the hood could fold sideways in two differing length parts. A step was positioned near the centre of the wagon. A new diagram, No. 1/404, was issued for these.

Later, many of the wagons had a row of cleats on the solebar to tie the hood down. These wagons continue in use, in particular in Abbey Works traffic, and 25 of the remaining 32 had been fitted with an air pipe from 1983; the TOPS code of these was JVW which changed to BVW in 1984 and the others were TOPS code JVV, which changed to BVV (**see Plate 178**).

Slab and Strip Coil

The history of the next type is also complex. Initially the fifty wagons of Diagram No. 1/408 were for the carriage of 57 tons of slab steel. They had a high open framework between which the slabs were loaded. The underframe had an unusual appearance because the solebars were flush-faced, instead of the usual channel, and heavily riveted. Handwheel brakes were fitted at both ends, they were vacuum-braked, and the plate-back bogies had roller bearings. They also worked from Abbey Works. It is not known to us how long they remained in this condition, as they were soon converted to three different designs.

Diagram No. 1/408 was reissued as a 60 ton Strip Coil K for twenty wagons, Nos. B949503/06/08/09/11/12/17/19/25/27/ 35-37/39/41/42/45/48-50. We are not sure when this was done, but it may have been during 1966. It was new works Order No. NWO 7867/58000. These had two coil-carrying cradles, one was 7ft. 3¼in. long and the other 14ft. 1¼in. Each was covered with its own sideways-folding hood, which was supported by

three tarpaulin bars. The underframe was modified by the addition of an air brake and, as well as a large air cylinder beneath the underframe, there was an additional 'V' hanger. These wagons were branded 'COIL K' and TOPS-coded JKX. At a later date, possibly after 1977, ten of these wagons were redesignated, unmodified for ferry use (Continental Diagram No. E490). These wagons were numbered in the series 20 70 4641 000-8 to 20 70 4641 009-9 with TOPS code JIX (**see Plate 180**). In 1984, nineteen of these wagons remained, and all were TOPS code BNX.

The other two designs were very similar; the underframes of both remained the same and they carried 57 tons. Diagram No. 1/417 was for seventeen wagons, Nos. B949504/10/13/14/20-24/29/31-34/38/40/44, which became 'Slab B'. They had a new open framework which remained at 20ft. 6in. in clear, but the space between the frames increased to 13ft. 6in. These were for single tier loading of six slabs. Diagram No. 1/419 had a new framework of similar dimensions but its height was increased from 4ft. 9⅜in. to 6ft. 0⅜in. There were thirteen of these, branded 'SLAB C', Nos. B949501/02/05/07/15/16/18/26/28/ 30/43/46/47.

Both of these latter designs were subsequently converted to 60 ton Coil T wagons and given Diagram No. 1/458 (**see Plate 181**). The diagram describes twenty nine as being converted; one 'Slab' was condemned in 1966 which accounts for the loss. These 'Coils' had a single coil cradle of 20ft. 11¼in. internal length, which was covered by a single nylon hood and lined with wood planks. The underframe was unmodified. These were TOPS code JTV and given the new code BYV in 1984. They were omitted from **Table 1** because they were stored out of use, but they had returned to traffic at Immingham by July 1984.

Slabcoil

The final newly-built bogie design, Diagram No. 1/411, was for fifty eight wagons, which could be used for either slabs or coils, thus they were branded SLABCOIL; the TOPS code was JZV. These 45 ton payload wagons had a well and a high framework which gave a slab loading length of 20ft. 6in. The slabs sat on wooden baulks. The platform over the bogies was surrounded by a low railing of 'T' angle, and a similar short railing protected the well. All of the flat surfaces of the floor consisted of 'I' beams and were similar to Diagram No. 1/403 which meant coils could be loaded in the well and over the bogies. The underframe had a lever vacuum brake and roller bearing plate-back bogies. These wagons worked from the Abbey Works, Port Talbot, and were out of use or condemned during 1982. **Figure 44 and Plates 182 & 183** are of these wagons.

The final bogie design to be considered is the 'Coil X'. These were converted 'Borail WE' but, as they received new numbers, we have included them. The main structure of the wagon remained unchanged; the bolsters were replaced by wooden baulks which held the coils in place (**see Plate 184**). As they remained unfitted, they were short-lived, all being condemned during 1981.

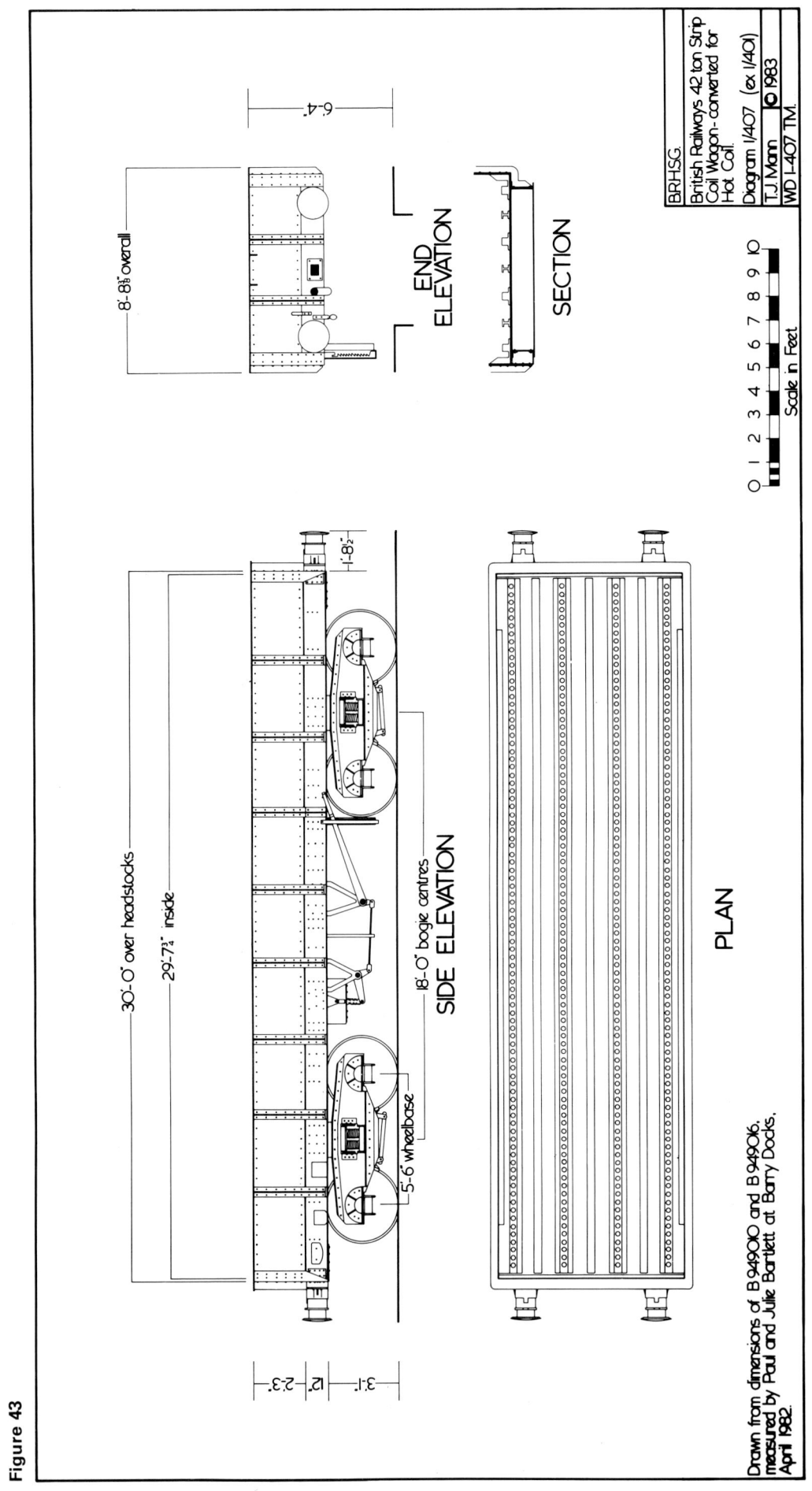

Figure 43

144

END ELEVATION

SECTION

SIDE ELEVATION

PLAN

8'-8⅝" overall

6'-4".

30'-0" over headstocks

29'-7¼" inside

18'-0" bogie centres

5'-6" wheelbase

1'-8½"

3'-1". 1'-2¼". 2'-3".

0 1 2 3 4 5 6 7 8 9 10

Scale in Feet

BRHSG

British Railways 42 ton Strip
Coil Wagon-converted for
Hot Coil.

Diagram 1/407 (ex 1/401)

T J Mann   © 1983

WD 1-407 T.M.

Drawn from dimensions of B 949010 and B 949016,
measured by Paul and Julie Bartlett at Barry Docks,
April 1982.

Plate 175 No. B949042 (Head, Wrightson 1957, 3014) is a Diagram 1/403 vehicle, and is identical to the Diagram 1/401 type as rebuilt with vacuum brakes. It carries TOPS code JYV, and was in rusty, bauxite livery at Margam on 21st October 1980. The remains of two brandings, both of which read 'Return Empty to Abbey works, Port Talbot' can just be discerned on the second panel from the left.

R. A. Silsbury

Plate 176 As discussed in the text, No. B949004 (Swindon 1950, 2209) was rebuilt in 1955 and allocated to Diagram 1/406. It was photographed at Swindon on 1st July 1955 after conversion. The coil cradle was divided into two unequal sections, and the adjustable baulks, which located into the top framing, had screw tighteners, permitting up to three coils, of maximum width 4ft. 2¼ in. to be carried. The livery is light grey, the unfitted underframe being unaltered.

BR/OPC

Plate 177 Comparison with **Plate 176** will reveal that the coil cradle of the Diagram 1/404 vehicle, as built, is an extended version of that on No. B949004. It was divided internally into three unequal sections, and the adjustable baulks could be arranged to carry up to four coils, those at each end of a maximum width of 4ft. 0⅝ in., and the centre pair, maximum 3ft. 11½ in. The small door in the end of the cradle permitted lifting gear to be inserted through the coil. No. B949050 was built at Head, Wrightson during February 1957, to Lot 3015, and formally photographed at Swindon on 6th March. Being vacuum-braked, the livery is bauxite. No hood is fitted.

BR/OPC

Plate 178 No. B949050 again features, this time in rebuilt form. The cradle was divided centrally, still accommodating the same size coils, but now fitted with three sheet support rails. Unusually, for vehicles with permanent hoods, snap hooks are not fitted; instead a series of rope hooks are provided along the solebars and headstocks, the hood being lashed down. In this view, taken at Severn Tunnel Junction on 2nd September 1980, the vehicle has a pair of replacement spoked wheels fitted at the far end.

R. A. Silsbury

Plate 179 As built, Diagram 1/408 vehicles carried slab steel vertically between the frameworks over each bogie. In common with many other coil types, these too were branded 'Return Empty to Abbey Works, Port Talbot, W. R.'. They were very short for a bogie vehicle, only 27ft. 6in. over headstocks, and vacuum-braked, with roller bearing axleboxes. No. B949502 (Swindon 1961, 3359) carries bauxite livery in original condition.

D. Larkin Collection

Plate 180 The reissued Diagram 1/408 is illustrated by internationally numbered 20 70 464-1 005-7, (BR number B949535), and is seen at Immingham Docks on 18th April 1982. The air cylinders can be seen to the left of the right-hand bogie.

P. W. Bartlett

Plate 181 The final version of the other 30 Slab Coil wagons was as 'Coil T', to Diagram 1/458. This had a single coil cradle and one overall hood. No. B949540 was recorded at Mossend on 16th August 1981 and, in common with all hooded coil wagons, the hood is kept closed even when unloaded.

R. A. Silsbury

Plates 182 & 183 In **Figure 44**, it shows just how complicated the 45 ton 'Slabcoil' wagons to Diagram 1/411 are. No. B949595 in **Plate 182** is loaded with two large steel slabs, at Margam on 13th October 1981. **Plate 183 (Overleaf)** is a view along the deck of No. B949580, at Margam on 21st October 1980, and shows plenty of detail. The holes in the 'I' beams could accommodate stanchions if required, and there are wood baulks between the vertical slab frame.

R. A. Silsbury

Figure 44

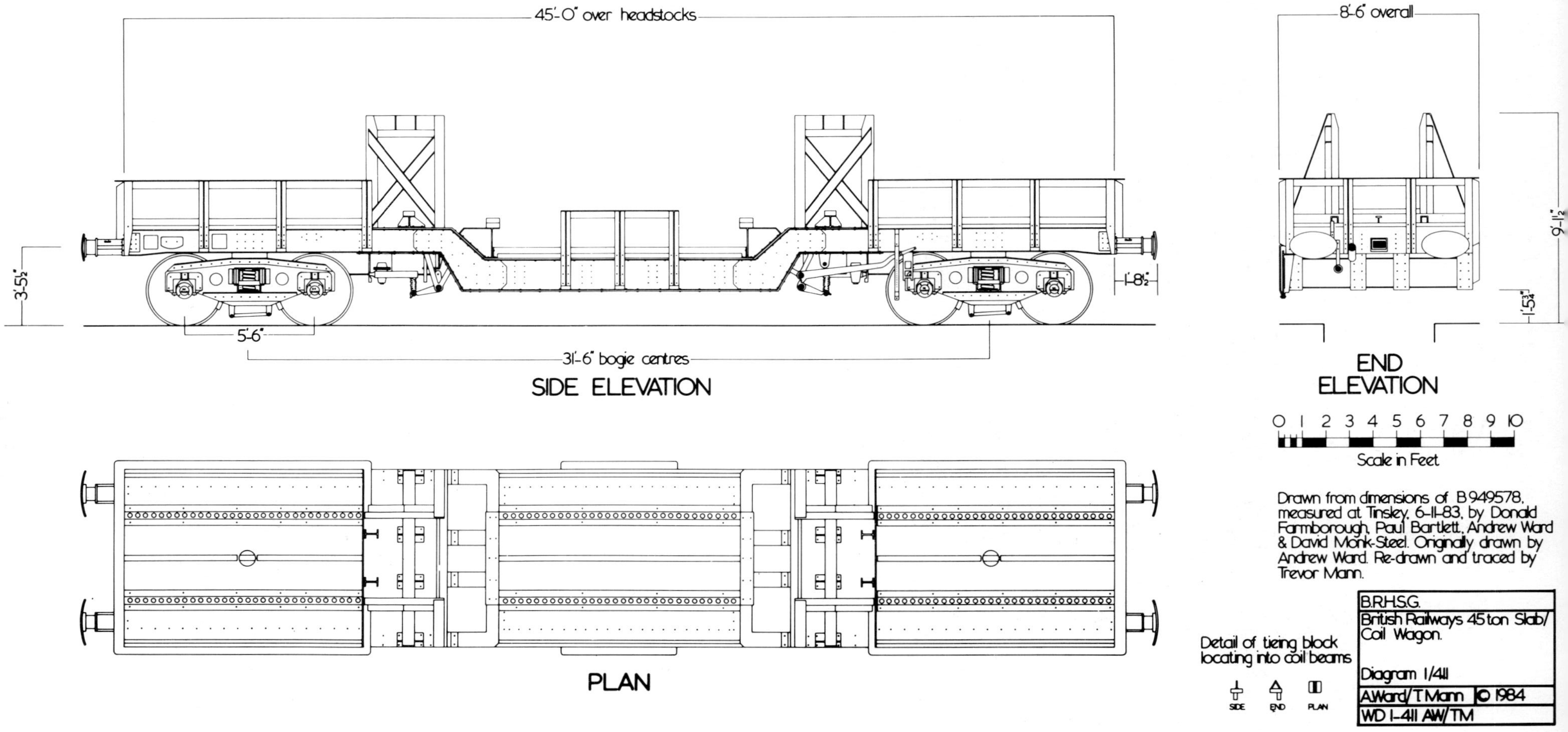

8'-6 overall

9'-1½"

1'-5¾"

END
ELEVATION

Scale in Feet

0 1 2 3 4 5 6 7 8 9 10

Drawn from dimensions of B949578,
measured at Tinsley, 6-11-83, by Donald
Farnborough, Paul Bartlett, Andrew Ward
& David Monk-Steel. Originally drawn by
Andrew Ward. Re-drawn and traced by
Trevor Mann.

BRHSG.
British Railways 45 ton Slab/
Coil Wagon.

Diagram 1/411

A Ward/T Mann © 1984
WD 1-411 AW/TM

Detail of tieing block
locating into coil beams

SIDE   END   PLAN

45'-0" over headstocks

1'-8½"

31'-6' bogie centres

SIDE ELEVATION

5'-6'

3'-5½"

PLAN

149

Plate 184 Although vehicles rebuilt to a new use are generally outside the scope of this book, an exception has been made for the Diagram 1/468 'Coil X', as they were renumbered into a new series. Twenty four Borail WE, dating from 1949 **(see Table 24 and Plate 156)** were given two coil cradles, one over each bogie, the work being carried out by Simonside C&W Works to Lot 3813 during 1975. No. B960014, still plated Swindon 1949, 2098, was recorded at Longport on 7th August 1980, in plain black livery.

R. A. Silsbury

4-Wheel Coils

Table 29 describes the two designs of 4-wheel coil carriers. These were all similar in appearance. Both Diagrams Nos. 1/412 and 1/414 had 12ft. wheelbase BR clasp brake underframes, and were 21ft. 6in. over headstocks. Diagram No. 1/412 was branded COIL A, TOPS code KAV, and SFV from 1984, had self-adjusting brakes, and carried 21 tons **(see Figure 45 and Plate 185)**. The underframes were diverted from Lot 3390 '21 ton Mineral Wagons'. These wagons were initially allocated to J. Summers Engineering, (WR) use. Diagram No. 1/414 was 'Coil B', TOPS code KBV, and SGV from 1984, and carried 24 tons **(see Plate 186)**. Both of the coil cradles were 18ft. in the well and

lined with narrow wood planks. However, the 'Coil B' had a shallower cradle although the height to the top of the nylon hood was greater, 10ft. 8⅞in. instead of 10ft. 1½in. Adjustable beams crossed the cradle to hold the coils in place. Lots 3478, 3484 and 3514 were allotted to the Scottish Region and Lot 3513 was allotted to Margam (WR). In 1984, the twenty nine remaining 'Coil As' continued to work in South Wales and had been joined by twenty seven 'Coil Bs'.

As we have described, most of the specialist 'Slab' and 'Coil' wagons were redundant by 1983. Air-braked 'Bogie bolsters' carried much of the traffic, sometimes having a cradle, but often they were unmodified. If a coil of steel needed protection, it was individually wrapped in polythene.

TABLE 29

FOUR WHEEL COILS

Diag No.	Lot No.	Qnty	Build -er	Date	Running numbers	Underframe type	Brake type	Brand -ing
1/412	3450	50	Derby	1963	B949130 - 949179	Late BR clasp with SAB	Vacuum	COIL A
1/414	3464	6	Derby	1962	B949180 - 949185	Late BR clasp with SAB	Vacuum	COIL B
1/414	3478	6	Derby	1963/4	B949186 - 949191	Late BR clasp with SAB	Vacuum	COIL B
1/414	3484	6	Derby	1963/4	B949192 - 949197	Late BR clasp with SAB	Vacuum	COIL B
1/414	3513	12	Derby	1964	B949198 - 949209	Late BR clasp with SAB	Vacuum	COIL B
1/414	3514	10	Derby	1964	B949210 - 949219	Late BR clasp with SAB	Vacuum	COIL B
Total		90						

Plate 185 The four-wheeled Coil wagons, A and B, were very similar, the 'Bs' having a shallower wider cradle to enable larger coils of steel to be carried. An interior view of Coil A No. B949147 (Derby 1961, 3450) amplifies the details in **Figure 45**; the adjustable beams are kept in position by pins through holes in the side members. It is pictured at Goole on 4th May 1981.

R. A. Silsbury

Figure 45

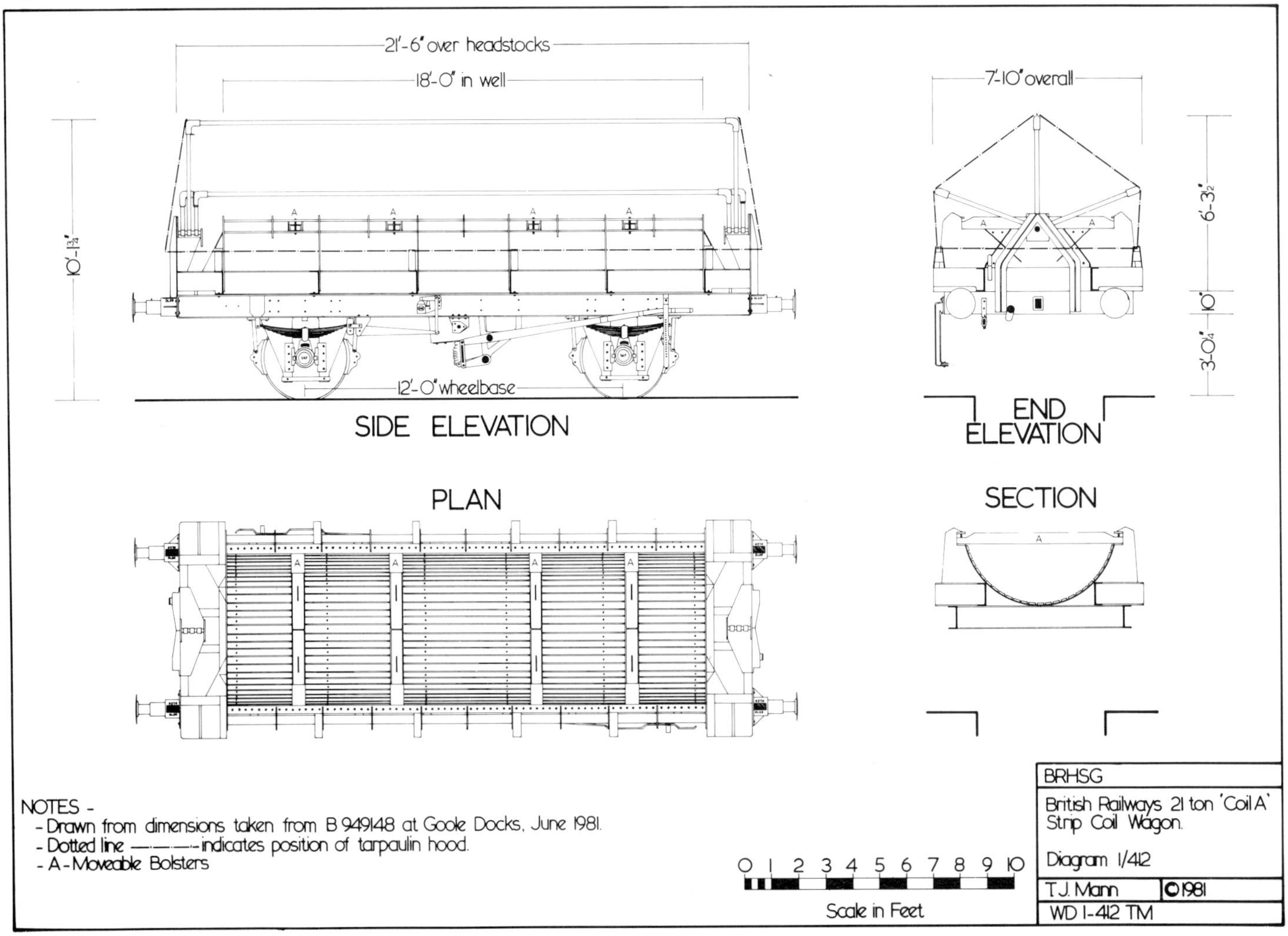

21'-6" over headstocks

18'-0" in well

10'-1¾"

12'-0" wheelbase

SIDE ELEVATION

7'-10" overall

6'-3"

3'-0¾"

10'

END ELEVATION

PLAN

SECTION

NOTES -
- Drawn from dimensions taken from B 949148 at Goole Docks, June 1981.
- Dotted line ———— indicates position of tarpaulin hood.
- A - Moveable Bolsters

0 1 2 3 4 5 6 7 8 9 10

Scale in Feet

BRHSG

British Railways 21 ton 'Coil A' Strip Coil Wagon.

Diagram 1/412

T. J. Mann   © 1981

WD 1-412 TM

152

Plate 186 Apart from the hood being 7in. higher, the main visible difference between the Coil wagons A & B lies in the shape of the wing brackets supporting the cradle. Underframes are identical. Here No. B949199 (Derby 1964, 3513) a 'Coil B' stands in the autumn sunshine at Port Talbot on 13th October 1981. The livery was originally bauxite — now mainly rusty.
R. A. Silsbury

Pig Irons

These wagons were for the carriage of freshly produced iron from the blast furnaces to the rolling mills, and other places where these were used. The iron was crudely cast in moulds called 'Pigs', because of their shape, which gave the wagons their name. Simple strong wagons were needed for this traffic and their details are given in **Table 30**.

Diagram No. 1/003 was for a wagon with fixed steel sides and ends of 8½ in. height which carried 13 tons. These wagons had conventional unfitted underframes, 17ft. 6in. over headstocks, a 10ft. wheelbase and a Morton brake. Internally, there were shackles for holding the load in place **(see Plate 187)**. Their low payload was a disadvantage and these wagons appear to have been scrapped during the early 1970s, or possibly even earlier.

The next design, Diagram No. 1/004, was the most numerous type. These had a greater payload of 20 tons, but they were a smaller wagon of only 16ft. 6in. over headstocks with a 9ft. wheelbase. They were unfitted with an independent double brake **(see Plate 188)**. The body was 1ft. 5¼ in. high internally. The welded fixed steel sides had vertical strengthening webs which divided it into nine panels; the ends were riveted and the floor was planked.

The body of Diagram No. 1/007 was identical to No. 1/004 but this design differed in the underframe. The wheelbase was increased to 10ft. and the BR clasp brake was used; most unusually the vacuum brake was not fitted even though items such as the triangular casting, which normally holds the vacuum cylinder in place, was carried. The reason for not completing the underframe is not known **(see Figure 46 and Plate 189)**. These wagons were sometimes branded simply PIG; on TOPS they were UPO.

Some of these designs were converted to 'Coil C' in the mid-

1960s and by 1984, thirty of these remained as SCO, which meant they were amongst the last unfitted wagons left. The remaining 'Pig Irons' went out of use by 1980, although many had gone much earlier.

The final diagram, No. 1/005, was strikingly different. These wagons were built to carry 30 tons of hot pig iron from Scunthorpe, so they were designed to withstand the 'hot pigs' being dropped into the wagon and then doused with water **(see Plate 190)**. The wagons were 17ft. 6in. over headstocks with a wheelbase of 10ft. The unfitted underframe was of the RCH type except that, instead of a dog clutch on one side, the lever went past the 'V' and then dropped down to the brake rod by linkages.

The body, including the floor, was of all welded construction. The floor was angled in towards the centre, and a gap was left down the centre line so that water could drain away. In addition, the floor sloped up to meet the ends at about 45 degrees. The floor was supported on seven 'I' beams, which were higher than the top of the solebar, so could be seen. Externally, the end showed the slope of the floor because the 'I' beam was exposed above the headstocks. The end had four 'T' stanchions, two vertical and two which angled in from the base of the vertical ones and met on the centre line. This feature was not shown on the diagram. The sides also had a pair of upright 'T' stanchions, and around the top of the entire body was heavy channel capping **(see Plate 191)**.

Another unusual feature was that they had a cast-steel plate bolted to the solebar at the left-hand end. It read PIG IRON TRAFFIC, EMPTY TO AES Co, SCUNTHORPE. These wagons were TOPS-coded URO, and the last went out of pig iron use in 1980. A number were converted to two designs of coil carrier, some as early as 1964.

TABLE 30

PIG IRONS

Diag No.	Lot No.	Qnty	Builder	Date	Running numbers	Underframe type	Brake type
1/003	2313	100	Derby	1953	B451400 - 451499	Morton	Unfit
1/003	2413	200	Derby	1954	B451500 - 451699	Morton	Unfit
1/004	2446	100	Derby	1954	B744000 - 744099	Double	Unfit
1/004	2586	500	Derby	1954-5	B744100 - 744599	Double	Unfit
1/005	2835	1	Shildon	1955	B744620	RCH link	Unfit
1/005	2857	139	Shildon	1956	B744621 - 744759	RCH link	Unfit
1/007	3085	100	Derby	1958	B744780 - 744879	BR clasp	Unfit
Total		1140					

Plate 187 The smallest of the Pig Iron wagons was the Diagram 1/003, rated at 13 tons. No. B451587 (Derby 1954, 2413) poses, when new, during March, in light grey livery, with black patches for all lettering.

BR/OPC

Plate 188 No. B744083 (Derby 1954, 2446) is a 20 ton vehicle to Diagram 1/004, photographed new at Derby in May. The independent brakes unusually have linkage to the brake lever, and a tiebar is fitted; most received roller bearing axleboxes and instanter couplings later in life. Note that no tare weight has been painted on, indicating that the wagon had yet to be weighed.

BR/OPC

20T
B744789
UPO
POOL
3703
BT

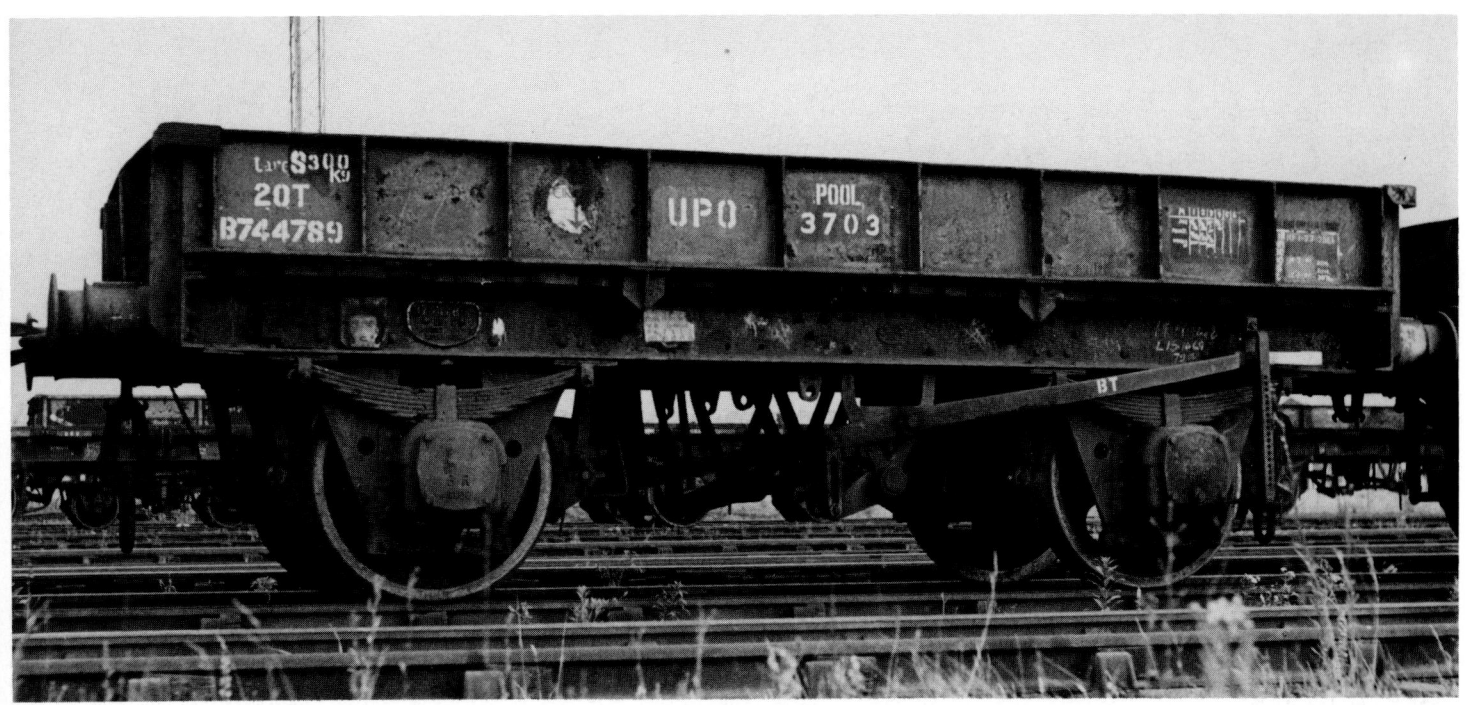

Plate 189 The Diagram 1/007 vehicles employed identical bodywork to Diagram 1/004. The solebar was increased in depth by 1in., to 10in., the wheelbase increased to 10ft., and self-contained buffers were fitted from new. The brackets which would normally carry the vacuum cylinders can clearly be seen in this view of No. B744789 (Derby 1958, 3085) taken at Workington on 5th August 1980, but they were never fitted. The diagram sheet records the brake as 'Hand clasp type'. The livery was, unusually for an unfitted vehicle, bauxite.

R. A. Silsbury

Figure 46

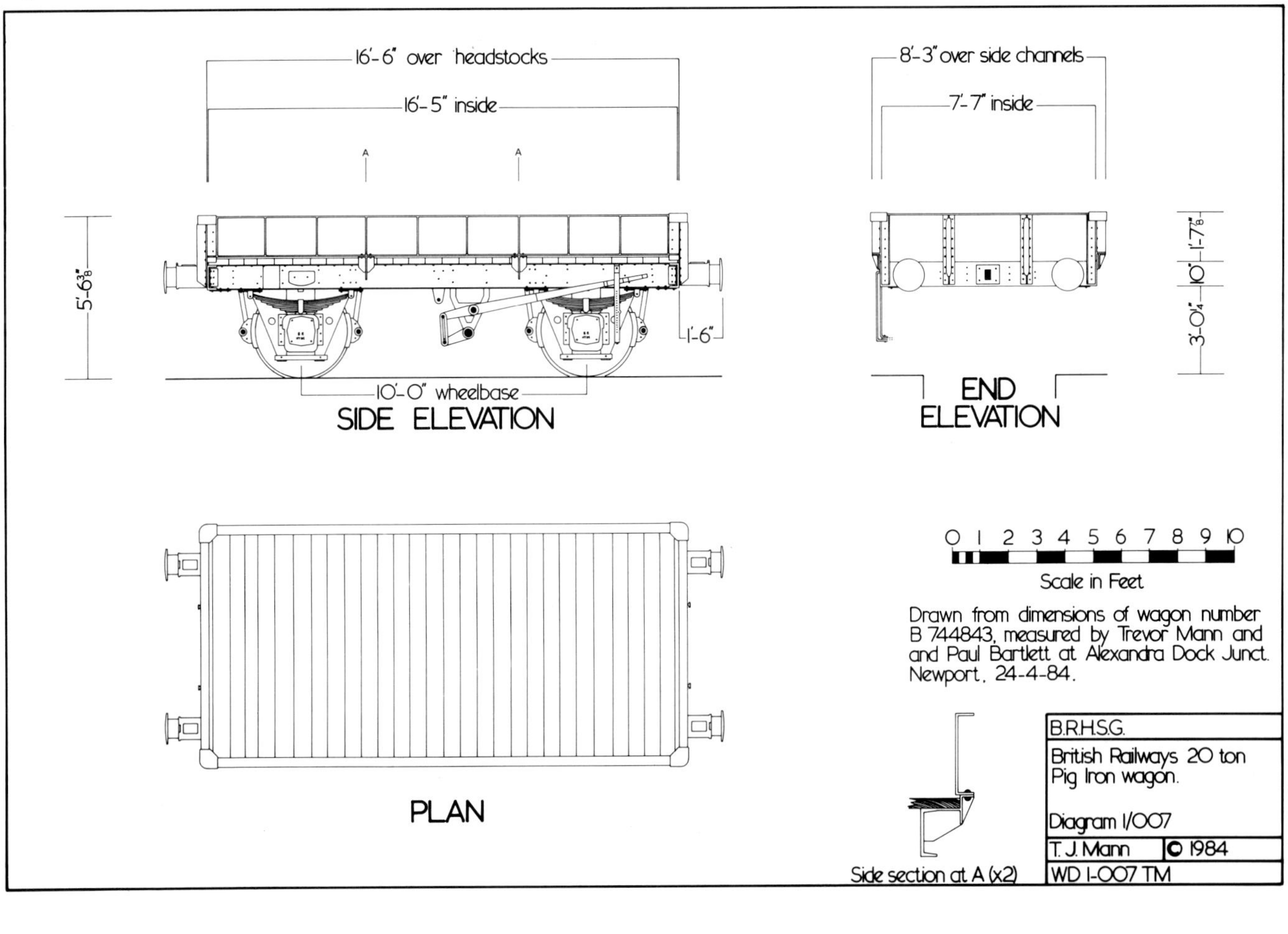
16'-6" over headstocks
16'-5" inside
A
A
5'-6⅜"
1'-6"
10'-0" wheelbase
SIDE ELEVATION
8'-3" over side channels
7'-7" inside
1'-7⅞"
10"
3'-0¼"
END
ELEVATION
PLAN
0 1 2 3 4 5 6 7 8 9 10
Scale in Feet
Drawn from dimensions of wagon number
B 744843, measured by Trevor Mann and
and Paul Bartlett at Alexandra Dock Junct.
Newport, 24-4-84.
Side section at A (x2)
B.R.H.S.G.
British Railways 20 ton
Pig Iron wagon.
Diagram 1/007
T. J. Mann
© 1984
WD 1-007 TM

Plates 190 & 191   These two photographs show No. B744647 (Shildon 1956, 2857) one of the Diagram 1/005 'Hot Pig Iron' wagons, rated at 30 tons. Special features to note are the shape of the interior, with drainage holes along the centre line, the transverse 'I' girders supporting the body, and the cast instruction plate at the left-hand end of the solebar. The side panels are bulged from damage when loading, and almost devoid of paint. It is pictured at Northfleet on 12th March 1978 when out of use.

R. A. Silsbury

Chapter 7
Non-hoppered Mineral Wagons

Numerically the 'Non-Hopper Mineral Wagons' were the most important component of the post-nationalisation wagon fleet, numbering hundreds of thousands of wagons. Most were normally reserved for carrying coal, although one important class was used for iron ore. They could also be used for other mineral and bulk commodities, such as alumina and sugar beet. Some other minerals, such as sand, were carried by specialist open wagons (see Chapter 4) although the wagons discussed in this chapter could be used instead.

The numerical dominance of this class on BR is different to the situation pre-nationalisation. Then, each of the companies had some 'Non-Hopper Mineral Wagons', in particular for the càrriage of locomotive coal, a well as some for general traffic, but most domestic and industrial coal had been transported in privately-owned wagons. At the beginning of World War II, the Government requisitioned these privately-owned wagons and they were never returned, although they continued to carry their private owner livery, and when this was worn, the owner's name and address was painted on a small black panel on the wagon side. At nationalisation, these ex-private owner wagons were numbered in a separate series, and each number was prefixed 'P' (see Model Trains (1982) 3 (6) pages 262 to 271). The war also complicates the story of the BR 'Mineral Wagon' fleet, and we must start by considering a series of wagon types that were built during wartime and the immediate post-war period.

16 ton Mineral Wagons with 9ft. wheelbase

Many wagons were built during and immediately after the war, and thus pre-date BR but, as they were subsequently numbered into the 'B series', we have included them. The early wagons of those to be described were built for the Ministry of War Transport. After victory, the new Labour Government was obviously considering the imminent nationalisation of the companies, and allowed the earlier orders to be continued, adding to them many placed by the Ministry of Transport. Some of these orders were used to ease the rundown in the production at the many Royal Ordnance Factories. All the 20,000 wagons built by ROF were of welded construction.

All of these early 'Mineral Wagons' were considered to be privately-owned, thus they were registered by the Railway Clearing House and had registration plates. Those built to MoWT orders continued the series used by the GWR, LMS or LNER according to the location of the factory. The MOT-ordered wagons started a new series from No. 1, and the LMS registered all these wagons. After nationalisation, registration was to cease from spring 1948. The London Midland Region continued to record the deliveries for a while and the job then passed to the Eastern Region who recorded the final deliveries in 1949.

Table 31 details the wagons built before the formation of BR which remained in Britain, and Table 32 details wagons built at the same time, purposely for use by the SNCF in France. Their design was unacceptably small for European use, and they returned in 1950. (see Page 165).

TABLE 31

PRE B R BUILT 16 TON MINERALS WITH 9 FT. WHEELBASE, PREFIXXED B

Diag No.	Qnty	Builder	Year	Running numbers			Brake type	Body type	Top flap & bottom doors?	Side shape	Reg auth
1/100	839*	Metro Cammell	1944-6	B3002	–	4100	Double,	Rivet,	no top, bottom,	slope	LMS
1/100	250*	D G Hall	1945-7	B4101	–	4250	Double,	Rivet,	no top, bottom,	slope	GWR
1/100	797*	Birmingham RCW	1944-6	B4251	–	5665	Double,	Rivet,	no top, bottom,	slope	GWR
1/100	750*	Gloucester RCW	1946/7	B5666	–	6415	Double,	Rivet,	no top, bottom,	slope	LMS
1/100	1779*	Chas. Roberts	1944-7	B6431	–	8715	Double,	Rivet,	no top, bottom,	slope	LMS
1/100	500*	Birmingham RCW	1946/7	B8816	–	9315	Double,	Rivet,	no top, bottom,	slope	GWR
1/100	131*	Pickering	1945	B9316	–	9565	Double,	Rivet,	no top, bottom,	slope	LMS
1/100	62*	Cravens	1944-7	B9566	–	9930	Double,	Rivet,	no top, bottom,	slope	LNER
1/100	146*	Head Wrightsom	1944/5	B9931	–	10460	Double,	Rivet,	no top, bottom,	slope	LNER
1/100	212*	R & Y Pickering	1944/5	B10465	–	10860	Double,	Rivet,	no top, bottom,	slope	LMS
1/100	375*	G R Turner	1944/5	B10861	–	11520	Double,	Rivet,	no top, bottom,	slope	LMS
1/100	220*	P & W Mclellan	1944/5	B11521	–	11850	Double,	Rivet,	no top, bottom,	slope	LMS

See others of diagram 1/100 in Table 32.

| 1/101 | 591* | Hurst Nelson | 1944/5 | B11863 | – | 12750 | Double, | Rivet, | no top, bottom, | straight | LMS |

* – There are gaps in these number series which cannot be shown, the qnty's are believed accurate.

1/102	4000	R O F Woolwich	1946/7	B13001	–	17000	Double,	Weld,	no top, bottom,	straight	LMS
1/102	500	R O F Dalmuir	1946/7	B17001	–	17500	Double,	Weld,	no top, bottom,	straight	LMS
1/102	51	R O F Hayes	1946	B17501	–	17551	Double,	Weld,	no top, bottom,	straight	LMS
1/102	3449	R O F Dalmuir	1947/8	B17552	–	21000	Double,	Weld,	no top, bottom,	straight	LMS
1/102	2000	R O F Patricroft	1946/7	B21001	–	23000	Double,	Weld,	no top, bottom,	straight	LMS
1/102	1000	Birmingham RCW	1946-8	B24001	–	25000	Double,	Weld,	no top, bottom,	straight	GWR
1/102	500	Fairfield S & E	1946/7	B25001	–	25500	Double,	Weld,	no top, bottom,	straight	GWR
1/102	500	Butterley	1947/8	B27001	–	27500	Double,	Weld,	no top, bottom,	straight	LMS
1/102	1000	Chas. Roberts	1947/8	B27751	–	28750	Double,	Weld,	no top, bottom,	straight	LMS
1/102	1400	Tees-side SBE	1947/8	B30251	–	31650	Double,	Weld,	no top, bottom,	straight	LNER
1/102	250	Derbyshire C & W	1947/8	B31651	–	31900	Double,	Weld,	no top, bottom,	straight	LMS
1/102	650	Fairfield S & E	1947-9	B31901	–	32550	Double,	Weld,	no top, bottom,	straight	GWR
1/102	300	G R Turner	1947/8	B32701	–	33000	Double,	Weld,	no top, bottom,	straight	LMS
1/102	500	R O F Dalmuir	1948	B33501	–	34000	Double,	Weld,	no top, bottom,	straight	LMS
1/102	2500	R O F Woolwich	1947/8	B34001	–	36500	Double,	Weld,	no top, bottom,	straight	LMS
1/102	1000	R O F Dalmuir	1948	B36501	–	37500	Double,	Weld,	no top, bottom,	straight	LMS
1/102	1000	R O F Woolwich	1948	B37501	–	38500	Double,	Weld,	no top, bottom,	straight	LMS
1/102	80	R O F Patricroft	1947/8	B38501	–	38580	Double,	Weld,	no top, bottom,	straight	LMS
1/102	920	R O F Dalmuir	1948	B38581	–	39500	Double,	Weld,	no top, bottom,	straight	LMS

TABLE 31 Continued

Diag No.	Qnty	Builder	Year	Running numbers			Brake type	Body type	Top flap & bottom doors?	Side shape	Reg auth
1/103	500	G R Turner	1946/7	B23001	-	23500	Double,	Rivet,	no top, bottom,	straight	LMS
1/103	250	Head Wrightson	1946/7	B23501	-	23750	Double,	Rivet,	no top, bottom,	straight	LNER
1/103	250	R & Y Pickering	1946/7	B23751	-	24000	Double,	Rivet,	no top, bottom,	straight	LMS
1/103	500	Cambrian	1946/7	B25501	-	26000	Double,	Rivet,	no top, bottom,	straight	GWR
1/103	499	- Tees-side S B E	1946	B26001	-	26499	Double,	Rivet,	no top, bottom,	straight	LNER
1/103	501#	P & W McLellan	1947	B26501	-	27000	Double,	Rivet,	no top, bottom,	straight	LMS
1/103	750	Hurst Nelson	1947/8	B27501	-	27750	Double,	Rivet,	no top, bottom,	straight	LMS
1/103	850	P & W McLellan	1947/8	B28751	-	29600	Double,	Rivet,	no top, bottom,	straight	LMS
1/103	650	Cambrian	1947/8	B29601	-	30250	Double,	Rivet,	no top, bottom,	straight	GWR
1/103	150	Metro Cammell	1947/8	B32551	-	32700	Double,	Rivet,	no top, bottom,	straight	LMS
1/103	1572	Metro Cammell	1948	B39501	-	41072	Double,	Rivet,	no top, bottom,	straight	LMS
1/103	1300	Tees-side S B E	1948/9	B61701	-	63000	Double,	Rivet,	no top, bottom,	straight	LNER
1/104	500	Birmingham R C W	1948	B33001	-	33500	Double,	Weld,	top & bottom,	straight	GWR
1/104	3000	Birmingham R C W	1948/9	B41351	-	44350	Double,	Weld,	top & bottom,	straight	GWR
1/104	1250	Butterley	1948/9	B44351	-	45600	Double,	Weld,	top & bottom,	straight	LMS
1/104	750	Derbyshire C & W	1948/9	B45601	-	46350	Double,	Weld,	top & bottom,	straight	LMS
1/104	1200	Fairfield S & E	1948/9	B46351	-	47550	Double,	Weld,	top & bottom,	straight	GWR
1/104	100	Cambrian	1948	B47551	-	47650	Double,	Weld,	top & bottom,	straight	GWR
1/104	1200	Cambrian	1948/9	B47851	-	49050	Double,	Weld,	top & bottom,	straight	GWR
1/104	1000	Chas. Roberts	1948/9	B51801	-	52800	Double,	Weld,	top & bottom,	straight	LMS
1/104	400	G R Turner	1948/9	B52801	-	53200	Double,	Weld,	top & bottom,	straight	LMS
1/104	500	Gloucester RCW	1949	B54700	-	55200	Double,	Weld,	top & bottom,	straight	-
1/104	450	R O F Dalmuir	1948/9	B55201	-	57650	Double,	Weld,	top & bottom,	straight	LMS
1/104	3550	R O F Woolwich	1948/9	B57651	-	61200	Double,	Weld,	top & bottom,	straight	LMS
1/104	500	Cravens	1949	B61201	-	61700	Double,	Weld,	top & bottom,	straight	-

See others of diagram 1/104 in Table 33.

1/105	278	Metro Cammell	1949	B41073	-	41350	Double,	Rivet,	top & bottom,	straight	-
1/105	200	Cambrian	1948	B47651	-	47850	Double,	Rivet,	top & bottom,	straight	GWR
1/105	750	Hurst Nelson	1949	B49051	-	49800	Double,	Rivet,	top & bottom,	straight	-
1/105	2000	P & W McLellan	1948/9	B49801	-	51800	Double,	Rivet,	top & bottom,	straight	LMS
1/105	500	G R Turner	1949	B53200	-	53700	Double,	Rivet,	top & bottom,	straight	-
1/105	999	Gloucester R C W	1948/9	B53701	-	54699	Double,	Rivet,	top & bottom,	straight	LMS

Total 55151

\# - two wagons were numbered B26501.

Plate 192a   An end view of No. B9774, now internal user No. 070475, at Teesport on 2nd June 1983.

P. W. Bartlett

The 'MoWT Slope-Sided Mineral'

Diagram No. 1/100 appears in **both Tables** and was a distinctive design of riveted construction which had a vertical upper part and sloped-in lower sides. Fabricated end doors appear to have been usual but the drop-down side door was of either riveted or pressed construction. The double design of handbrake was fitted because, like the contemporary private owner wagons, they had a pair of trap doors in the floor. These doors would foul the cross-shaft of any alternative brake; the capacity was 637cu. ft. They were all withdrawn by about 1966. Reference should be made to **Plates 192 & 193, and Figure 47.**

Plate 192b The choice of a photograph taken at St. Albans on 4th August 1946, some 17 months before nationalisation, may seem strange for a book about BR wagons. However, as explained in the text, the 16 ton Minerals built for the MoWT and MoT were subsequently numbered in the 'B' series, and it is certain that many of these vehicles ran in the early bauxite livery well into the BR period, before being repainted into unfitted light grey livery, and given the 'B' prefix. MoWT No. 9512 was built by Pickering in 1945, and registered by the LMS, No. 177338, later being classed in BR Diagram 1/100. The two diagonal white lines on the side door indicate that the vehicle has bottom drop doors, actuated by the pin below the solebar to the left of the 'V' hangers. The plates affixed to the solebar are, at the left-hand end, the registration plate, to the right of the label clip, the elliptical owner's plate, and at the far right, the builder's plate.

E. Bruton

Plate 193 No. B197525 was another Diagram 1/100 vehicle, built in 1945 by Roberts, and sent to France. It returned during 1950, and after refurbishment under Lot 2287 at New Cross Gate, entered BR service during 1951. It is seen here at Connah's Quay in February 1965.

E. Gent

Figure 47

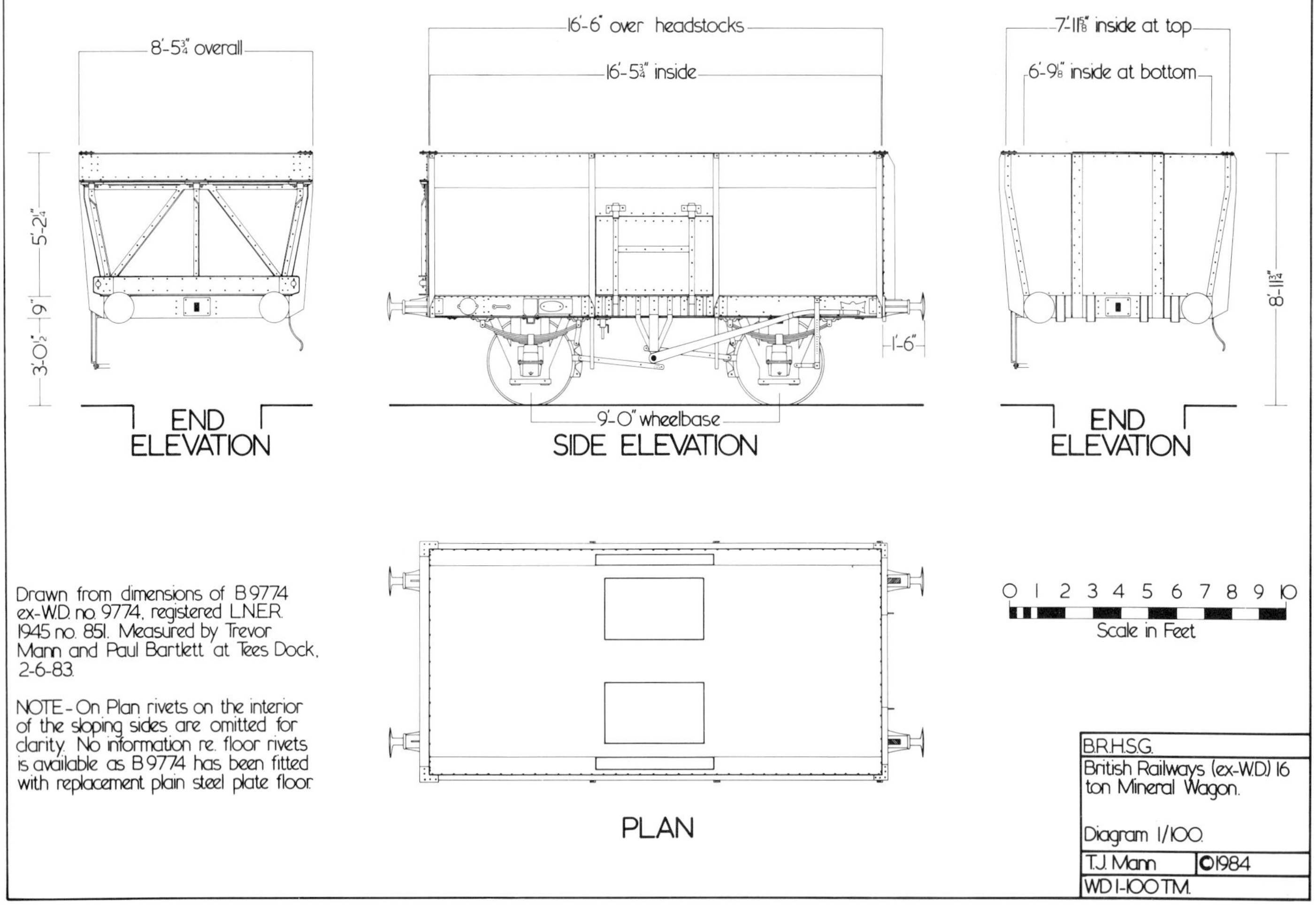

8'-5¾" overall

16'-6" over headstocks

16'-5¾" inside

7'-11⅞" inside at top

6'-9⅜" inside at bottom

5'-2¼"

3'-0½" | 9"

END
ELEVATION

1'-6"

9'-0" wheelbase

SIDE ELEVATION

8'-11¼"

END
ELEVATION

Drawn from dimensions of B.9774
ex-W.D. no. 9774, registered L.N.E.R.
1945 no. 851. Measured by Trevor
Mann and Paul Bartlett at Tees Dock,
2-6-83.

NOTE - On Plan rivets on the interior
of the sloping sides are omitted for
clarity. No information re. floor rivets
is available as B.9774 has been fitted
with replacement plain steel plate floor

PLAN

0 1 2 3 4 5 6 7 8 9 10
Scale in Feet

B.R.H.S.G.
British Railways (ex-W.D.) 16
ton Mineral Wagon.

Diagram 1/100.

T.J. Mann   ©1984
WD 1-100 TM.

Plate 194 The Diagram 1/101 and 1/113 vehicles were less numerous than the other MoWT types. Although generally withdrawn during the mid-1960s, some found further use in industry. NCB No. 78293 is one such; it is a Diagram 1/113 vehicle built by Hurst Nelson, but positive identification was impossible because of replating and a broken number plate. Note the pressed end door, and the minimum number of stiffening webs in the girder over it. The livery, when photographed at Bargoed on 15th September 1981, was plain black.   *R. A. Silsbury*

The 'MoWT Straight-Sided Minerals'

At the same time, Hurst Nelson built batches of wagons which were later allocated either Diagram No. 1/101 or No. 1/113 depending on whether or not they had seen service in France. These wagons were of distinctive appearance, being riveted with 'U' channel side stanchions. Both the side and end doors were of pressed construction but, unlike other designs, the pressings were narrow, partially imitating the construction of fabricated doors. They had a capacity of 630cu. ft. Their underframes and withdrawal dates were similar to Diagram No. 1/100 wagons **(see Plate 194)**.

Four diagrams were used to describe the remainder of the 'Mineral Wagons' which stayed in Britain after the war. Most of them had a capacity of 648cu. ft. They all had underframes which were similar to the earlier diagrams with bottom trap doors. The bodies were all of steel, but the construction details varied. Wagons built to Diagram No. 1/102 were welded with no top door, and the side and end doors were of pressed construc-

tion. **Figure 48 and Plate 195** is of this diagram. There may have been some differences between batches as different presses were used, and fabricated doors may have been used initially or substituted later.

Wagons to Diagram No. 1/103 were similar but of riveted construction with either pressed or fabricated doors. They also lacked top doors **(see Plate 196)**. Diagram No. 1/104 was used for wagons of welded construction **(see Plate 197)** and Diagram No. 1/105 for ones of riveted construction which were of only 646cu. ft. capacity **(see Plate 198)**. Both of these designs had a drop-down top door over the side door. Both of the diagrams show fabricated doors, but examples of both construction types are known to have been equipped with pressed end doors. This alternative is stated on Diagram No. 1/105. These designs, without the bottom door feature, were developed into the BR standard types as Diagrams Nos. 1/108 and 1/109 respectively.

Plate 195 No. B34085 is a Diagram 1/102 vehicle, built by the RoF Woolwich in 1947, and registered by the LMS, No. 14325, and was photographed at Hoo Junction in May 1968. Features to note include the extra strengthening webs over the end door, which is of pressed construction, and the deep channel stiffener to the top of the bodyside. On the diagram, pressed side doors are shown, but as side and end doors might be changed during repairs, like did not always replace like.

D. Larkin

Plate 196 The dimensionally similar Diagram 1/103 riveted vehicles are represented by No. B26248, built by Tees-side S&E in 1946, and registered by the LNER, No. 2038. Being of riveted construction, no deep top channel was used, and it is virtually identical to contemporary vehicles built for the LNER by the same builder. It was photographed at Connah's Quay in February 1965.

E. Gent

Figure 48

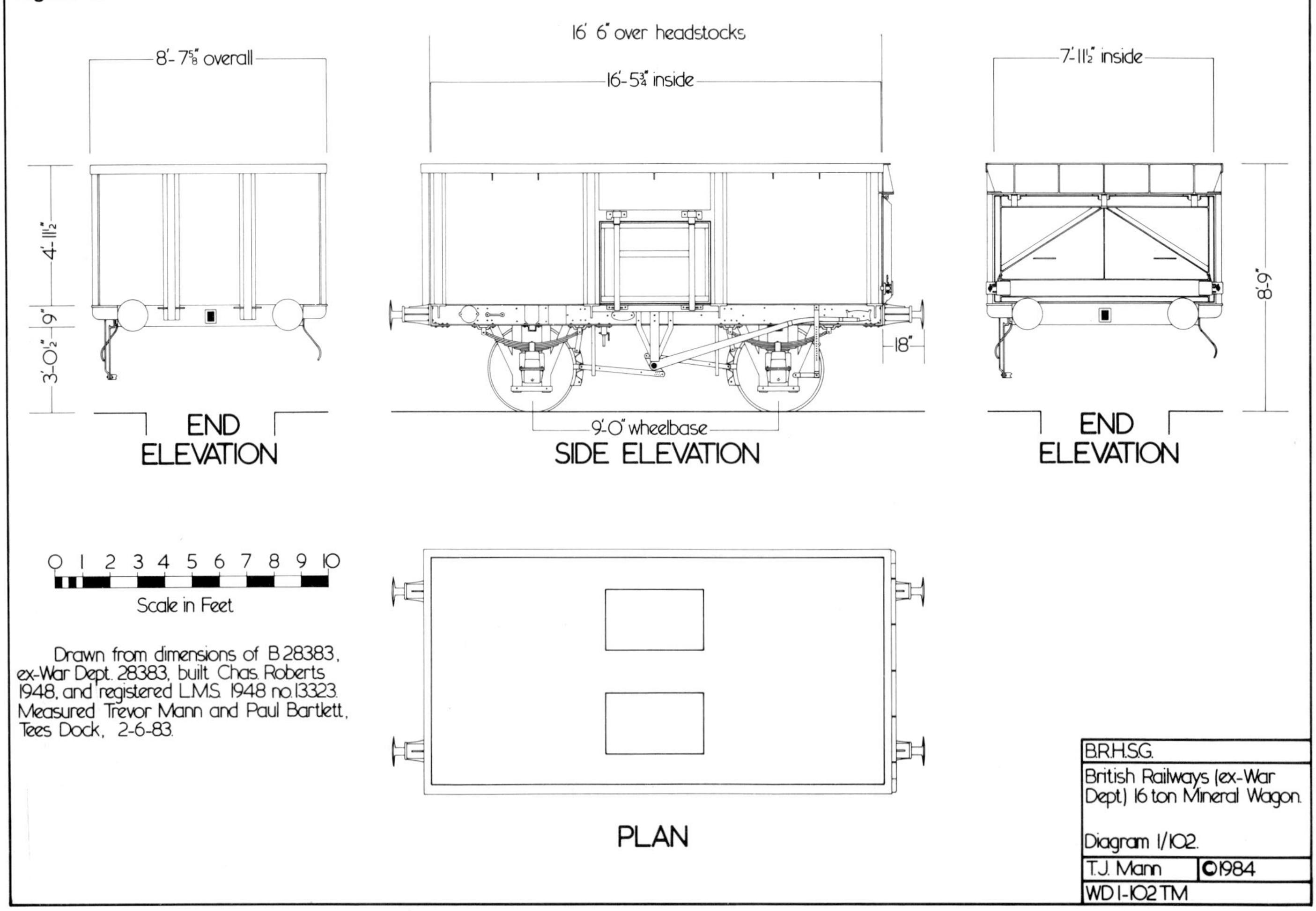

8'-7⅝" overall

16' 6" over headstocks

16'-5¾" inside

7'-11½" inside

4'-11½"

3'-0½" 1'-9"

END ELEVATION

18"

9'-0" wheelbase

SIDE ELEVATION

8'-9"

END ELEVATION

0 1 2 3 4 5 6 7 8 9 10

Scale in Feet

Drawn from dimensions of B 28383, ex-War Dept. 28383, built. Chas. Roberts 1948, and registered L.M.S. 1948 no.13323. Measured Trevor Mann and Paul Bartlett, Tees Dock, 2-6-83.

PLAN

B.R.H.S.G.

British Railways (ex-War Dept) 16 ton Mineral Wagon.

Diagram 1/102.

T.J. Mann   ©1984

WD 1-102 TM

162

Plate 197 Diagrams 1/104 and 1/105 introduced the small drop flap door over the main side door. Diagram 1/104 was for welded vehicles but, as shown, at least one was of riveted construction. MoT No. 47600 was built by the Cambrian Wagon Works in 1948, and registered by the GWR, No. 3060. It is believed that the diagram book is in error for the Cambrian built batches, as that particular works built exclusively riveted 16 ton Minerals. MoT No. 47600 was photographed at Teignmouth on 29th May 1949, and was in bauxite livery.

E. Bruton

Plate 198 No. B53990 is correct, being Diagram 1/105, and built by Gloucester RC&W in January 1949. Registration of this particular batch ceased after No. 53960, and these later vehicles entered traffic with the 'B' prefix from new; livery was still bauxite, however. Note the cast number plate, devoid of course of a lot number.

BR/OPC

'MoS Cupboard Door Minerals'

One wartime design remains to be described and this was unique. Early in 1945, the Ministry of Supply, the SNCF and Metropolitan Carriage and Wagon Co. Ltd. met to discuss the provision of wagons for the SNCF. The MoS had decided to provide 10,000 wagons, 3,000 to the designs later allocated Diagram Nos. 1/100 and 1/113, and 7,000 to a new design, later allocated Diagram No. 1/112. This had the standard RCH underframe but the body was typically French with 'bulb-T' stanchions and full height cupboard doors. Continental fittings such as lashing rings, through pipes, towing irons, screw couplings, ticket holders, signal brackets and commode handles were provided.

The wagon bodies and underframes were shipped to France as prefabricated sub-assemblies early in 1946, and were assembled in Bordeaux at the rate of thirty per day. Initially, they were numbered 6.562001-6.569000 but, in 1949, they became Nos. 7.733000-7.739999. Because the Ministry of Supply had been unable to supply spares, the SNCF had to fit whatever it could find. Thus German axleboxes and wheel sets, and buffer stocks from the Etat and Paris-Orleans Railways were used.

By 1950, the design had been superseded by larger and superior SNCF-built wagons, so the British-built wagons were purchased for BR use. They were all reconditioned by the beginning of 1953, losing their through pipe, signal bracket and ticket holders. The reconditioning does not seem to have been thorough as wagons were photographed in BR service retaining both SNCF numbers and Continental running gear.

The wagons were not a success on BR because they lacked end doors, and had a low capacity of 595cu. ft. A serious accident was caused by the cupboard doors, which fouled the loading gauge when open, and this resulted in the entire class being branded 'Not to be used for PW ballast or other Engineer's materials'. A number were used in chemical traffic before being replaced by the 'Covhops', but by October 1965 only 110 remained in capital stock, and these were all gone soon afterwards. No. CDB191191, which continued in use into the late 1970s, had been cut down in height and fitted with the standard drop-down fabricated 'Mineral Wagon' door. On withdrawal from the BR fleet, some were sold for private use and others went into internal usage, that measured for **Figure 49** being in such use at a sugar refinery. **Table 32** gives details of these wagons and reference should be made to **Plate 199**.

Plate 199 No. B192158 is to Diagram 1/112, and was built by Metropolitan Cammell in 1946 for service in France. Upon return in 1950, it was refurbished at Earlestown under Lot 2286. When photographed at Connah's Quay in May 1963, it still retained a Continental style buffer at the left-hand end, several lashing rings, and screw couplings.

E. Gent

Figure 49   Measured by Trevor Mann at Wissington in 1980

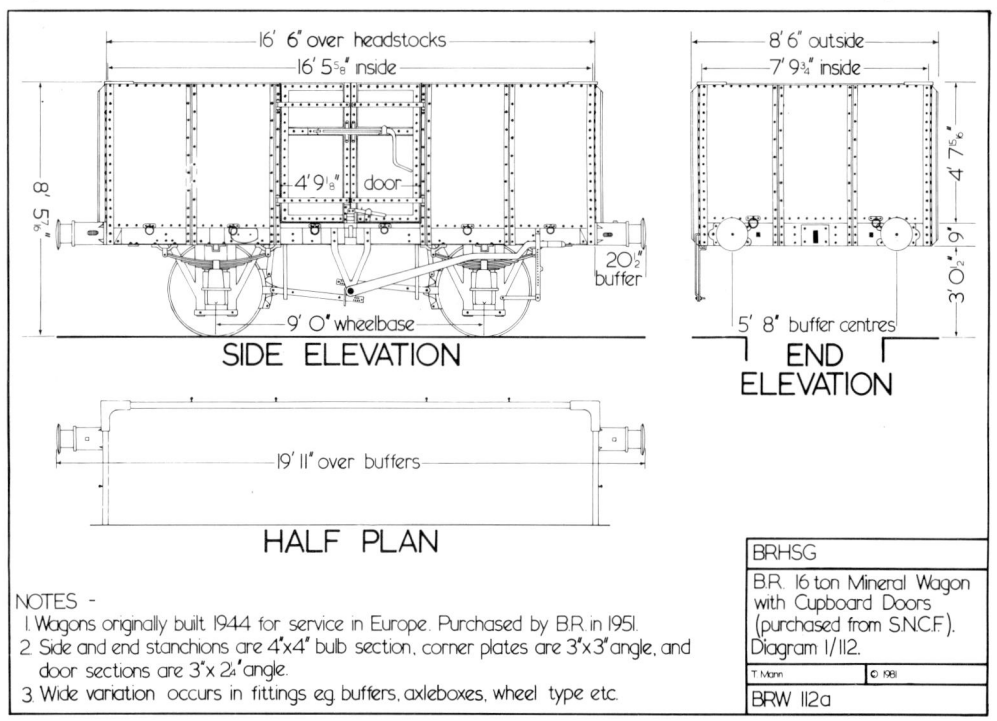

SIDE ELEVATION

END ELEVATION

HALF PLAN

NOTES -
1. Wagons originally built 1944 for service in Europe. Purchased by B.R. in 1951.
2. Side and end stanchions are 4"x4" bulb section, corner plates are 3"x3" angle, and door sections are 3"x 2¼"angle.
3. Wide variation occurs in fittings eg. buffers, axleboxes, wheel type etc.

BRHSG

B.R. 16 ton Mineral Wagon with Cupboard Doors (purchased from S.N.C.F.). Diagram 1/112.

T. Mann   © 1981

BRW 112a

TABLE 32

16 TON MINERAL WAGONS BUILT FOR, USE BY THE SNCF AS USED BY BR

Diag No.	Lot No.	Qnty	Builder	Year	Recondi- -tioner	Running numbers	Brake type	Body type	Type of doors (see below)
1/112	2286	1000	Metro Cammell	1945/6	Earlestown	B190000 - 190999	Double,	Rivet,	c., no b. or end
1/112	2286	300	Metro Cammell	1945/6	New X Gate	B191000 - 191299	Double,	Rivet,	c., no b. or end
1/112	2286	1000	Metro Cammell	1945/6	Earlestown	B191300 - 192299	Double,	Rivet,	c., no b. or end
1/112	2286	300	Metro Cammell	1945/6	New X Gate	B192300 - 192599	Double,	Rivet,	c., no b. or end
1/112	2286	2200	Metro Cammell	1945/6	Earlestown	B192600 - 194799	Double,	Rivet,	c., no b. or end
1/112	2286	2200	Metro Cammell	1945/6	New X Gate	B194800 - 196999	Double,	Rivet,	c., no b. or end
		(18 wagons never entered BR service)							
1/100	2287	250	Chas. Roberts	1945/6	Earlestown	B197000 - 197249	Double,	Rivet,	b. & end, no top
1/100	2287	75	Chas. Roberts	1945/6	Earlestown	B197250 - 197324	Double,	Rivet,	b. & end, no top
1/100	2287	425	Chas. Roberts	1945/6	New X Gate	B197325 - 197749	Double,	Rivet,	b. & end, no top
1/100	2287	100	Chas. Roberts	1945/6	New X Gate	B197750 - 197849	Double,	Rivet,	b. & end, no top
1/100	2287	250	Chas. Roberts	1945/6	Earlestown	B197850 - 198099	Double,	Rivet,	b. & end, no top
1/100	2287	500	Chas. Roberts	1945/6	Earlestown	B198100 - 198599	Double,	Rivet,	b. & end, no top
1/100	2287	150	Chas. Roberts	1945/6	New X Gate	B198600 - 198749	Double,	Rivet,	b. & end, no top
1/100	2287	142	Chas. Roberts	1945/6	Earlestown	B198750 - 198891	Double,	Rivet,	b. & end, no top
		(25 wagons never entered BR service)							
1/113	2288	60	Hurst Nelson	1945/6	Earlestown	B199000 - 199059	Double,	Rivet,	b. & end, no top
1/113	2288	40	Hurst Nelson	1945/6	New X Gate	B199060 - 199099	Double,	Rivet,	b. & end, no top
1/113	2288	60	Hurst Nelson	1945/6	New X Gate	B199100 - 199159	Double,	Rivet,	b. & end, no top
1/113	2288	60	Hurst Nelson	1945/6	Earlestown	B199160 - 199219	Double,	Rivet,	b. & end, no top
1/113	2288	60	Hurst Nelson	1945/6	Earlestown	B199220 - 199279	Double,	Rivet,	b. & end, no top
1/113	2288	28	Hurst Nelson	1945/6	New X Gate	B199280 - 199307	Double,	Rivet,	b. & end, no top
		(3 wagons never entered BR service)							
Total		9154							

(Key to door types - c = cupboard; b.= bottom in floor; top = flap over side; end = top hinged)

Early BR-period 'Minerals'

The remaining wagons to be considered were all built for BR, many by private manufacturers, as can be seen in **Table 33**. Diagram No. 1/104 has already been discussed, and the 1950-built wagons were identical. Diagram No. 1/106 illustrated very similar wagons of all welded construction, the diagram showing only the most nominal differences of an increase in inside length by $^1/_{16}$in. to 16ft. $5^{13}/_{16}$in. and in width by ⅛in. to 7ft. 11⅝in. The top door was increased in depth by ⅛in. to $10^{11}/_{16}$in. All of these wagons were built by Derby **(see Plate 200 and Page 173)**.

The Standard 'Minerals'

What must be considered as the standard 'Mineral Wagons' follow. Those of welded construction were to Diagram 1/108 **(see Plates 201, 202 & 203)** and those of riveted construction were to Diagram No. 1/109 **(see Plate 204)**. None of these had bottom doors and this was the reason for the issuing of new diagrams as dimensionally they were identical to Diagrams Nos. 1/104 and 1/105 respectively. As before, the riveted wagons were nominally smaller with a capacity of 646cu. ft. and a side which was 4ft. 10⅞in. in internal height; the internal length was 16ft. 7¼in. and the internal width was 7ft. 11½in. The welded wagons were the same width but the internal length was 16ft. 5¾in. and the internal height of the sides was 4ft. 11¼in. Their capacity was 648cu. ft.

Complete details of these wagons are not known to us. BR records do not make it clear which lots were of welded or riveted construction, or if a lot had both types. The type of construction used for doors is not always known, but few pressed-end doors have been seen on Diagram No. 1/108 wagons, whilst many of Diagram No. 1/109 had them. Riveted doors have occasionally been seen on welded wagons but, as our observations and records mostly relate to the late 1960s onwards, it is impossible to know how much of this variance has been introduced by swapping during repairs. Diagram No. 1/109 actually shows fabricated doors, but we believe this was unusual.

Another early change was that from independent double brake to Morton brake with one brake per wheel on one side only. In **Table 33**, we have assumed that the Morton brake was fitted unless a wagon with the double brake has been observed; if examples of both have been seen fitted to a single lot this is stated. Thus our table is as accurate as we have been able to make it from observations and records. It seems likely that the first lot built by each of the manufacturers had some wagons with the double brake (Lots 2221-2232 and 2250); as there were no bottom trap doors the double brake was unnecessary.

There then followed a long series of very consistent wagons when construction was on a scale more usually associated with the car manufacturing industry. In particular, the size of orders given to and rate of production by Pressed Steel can have been rarely equalled or surpassed on railways in Britain; 70,000 wagons in about seven years or 200 per week allowing for some holidays! **Figure 50** is of Diagram No. 1/108.

Some numerically much smaller diagrams remain to be described. Diagram No. 1/111 wagons were all built by BR workshops and appear to be identical to those designated Diagram No. 1/106, except that they did not have bottom trap doors. As with Diagram Nos. 1/108 and 1/109, the earliest lot was built with the double brake and the later lots had Morton type.

Diagram No. 1/114 was issued to cover the first vacuum-braked 'Minerals'. Body dimensions were identical to Diagram No. 1/111. It would seem that the concept of vacuum braking all 300 was dropped as the diagram has a written-in annotation, '100 vehicles to lot 2331 AVB and 200 unfitted' dated August 1953. From photographic evidence, the first one hundred had the RCH vacuum brake from new, **(see the background of Plate 204 and Railway Modeller (1980) 31 (360) page 376)**. The authors' observations of the latter two hundred wagons show them all to have had the clasp vacuum brake, but this must have been fitted later than 1956.

The one hundred wagons of Diagram No. 1/116 were interesting because they were of aluminium riveted construction. Although they had some small dimensional differences to the other 'Minerals', they did share all major design features with fabricated end, top and side doors and Morton handbrake. The most

notable difference was in the nominal tare with reduction from 7 tons 14cwt. of Diagram No. 1/108 to 6 tons 6cwt. We know little about the success of these wagons, but as no more aluminium 'Mineral Wagons' were attempted, it seems likely that they were unable to withstand the buffeting of daily use.

The final diagram, No. 1/117, was introduced in 1955. These wagons were of the, by then, conventional welded construction with fabricated side, top and end doors. Most of the body dimensions were identical to Diagram No. 1/111 but, unlike all the earlier welded diagrams, the inside height was increased by ¹/₁₆in. to 4ft. 11⁵/₁₆in. and this allowed for an increase in the cubic capacity by 1cu. ft. to 649.

Vacuum Brake 'Minerals'

Table 33 shows the later complicating feature of these wagons; vacuum braking. Once again records seem inadequate. Some wagons with the clasp brake, two vacuum cylinders and a change-over lever seem to have been built in many of the later lots, while others were converted to this design. **The Frontispiece** shows No. B88672, newly converted in 1956. Some wagons were built with the inner 'V' hanger to support a vacuum cylinder which was never fitted, while others were built with the full clasp brake, again without cylinder. It would be easy to exaggerate how many wagons were vacuum-braked from new. In October 1965 there were only 11,104 so many which we have seen with this brake gear must have been converted in more recent years. We know of no way to distinguish conversions from wagons built new with the vacuum brake. In the 1970s, more previously unfitted wagons were given a simpler RCH-type vacuum brake with only a single vacuum cylinder and one brake shoe acting on each wheel **(Plate 205)**.

Repairs and Rebuilds

Unfitted and vacuum-braked wagons were the subject of heavy body repairs, which usually meant extensive replating or, from about 1971 onwards, rebodying. Wagons selected to receive new bodies had been examined to ensure that their underframes were fit to last a further ten years. Different styles of new bodies were built, the most common being all welded with a noticeable curve at the bottom of the wagon side as it tucked under **(see Plates 206 to 210)**. This was to alleviate the corrosion problems of the square-bodied designs. Diagram No. 1/099 (second issue) was allocated to the rebuilds, but not issued. The new bodies all lacked the top drop-down door, and many of the heavy body repairs often included plating over or welding up this door. **Figure 51 and Plate 207** are of vacuum-braked rebuilt wagons.

Use, Branding and Condemnation

Condemnation of 16 ton steel 'Minerals' began in the early 1960s with the wartime production and, by the late 1960s, many of the earlier BR wagons had gone. Some of these wagons were transferred to the Engineer's Department and others were used in internal user fleets at docks and collieries. The huge fleet was reduced year after year. In 1982, the South Wales coalfields were freed from unfitted examples and only a few remained in use in Yorkshire. In 1983, some vacuum-braked examples remained, but their use was nearly at an end and a large number were transferred to the Engineer's Department. Until 1963, no special coding was carried; post-1963 the official code was COAL 16 for unfitted vehicles and COAL-16-VB for vacuum-braked examples, although unofficial variants were MIN and MINFIT. Later, the TOPS codes became MCO and MCV respectively. In 1982, the TOPS code MXV was introduced to differentiate those vehicles fitted with RCH vacuum brakegear.

Plate 200 Diagram 1/106 was issued to cover vehicles built to the former LMS Diagram D2134. Although no bottom doors were fitted, most had double brakes, except for part of the last batch. No. B68837 (Derby 1951, 2210) is one of those with the Morton brake, and has had some replating to the bodysides. The livery is the rusty remains of light grey, with 'dashed box' lettering, and this view was taken at Burry Port on 13th July 1978. *R. A. Silsbury*

Plate 201 The ubiquitous Diagram 1/108 16 ton Mineral appeared in several guises, and reference to **Figure 1**, and the ensuing plates, will make obvious the limitations of the drawn diagram. No. B84198 (Pressed Steel 1952, 2253) is in original condition, with Morton brake, and shows the top flap door opened. Note the three-link coupling, and the mixture of split spoke and disc wheels. The location is not known, and from the chalked marks on the underframe the date would be 1960. *A. Foulner*

Plate 202 No. B216227 (Metropolitan Cammell 1955, 2702) depicts an identical vehicle at a later period, at Newbury on 3rd December 1979, and shows the side door open. Much of the bodyside has been replated, and the lettering includes the 'MIN' code. However, the stencilled number must have been incorrectly applied, and subsequently corrected to accord with the plate. The livery is light grey. *R. A. Silsbury*

Plate 203 No. DB254270 (Metropolitan Cammell 1956, 2799) was in Engineering Department use when photographed at Northwich on 13th August 1981, and shows a variation on Diagram 1/108; the bodyside is supported by inverted 'U' channel brackets. This example has all four such brackets; others have been observed with only the centre pair so made. A vast amount of body plating has been renewed, and the top drop flap door replaced with a piece of blank plate. The livery is the very rusty remains of light grey. *R. A. Silsbury*

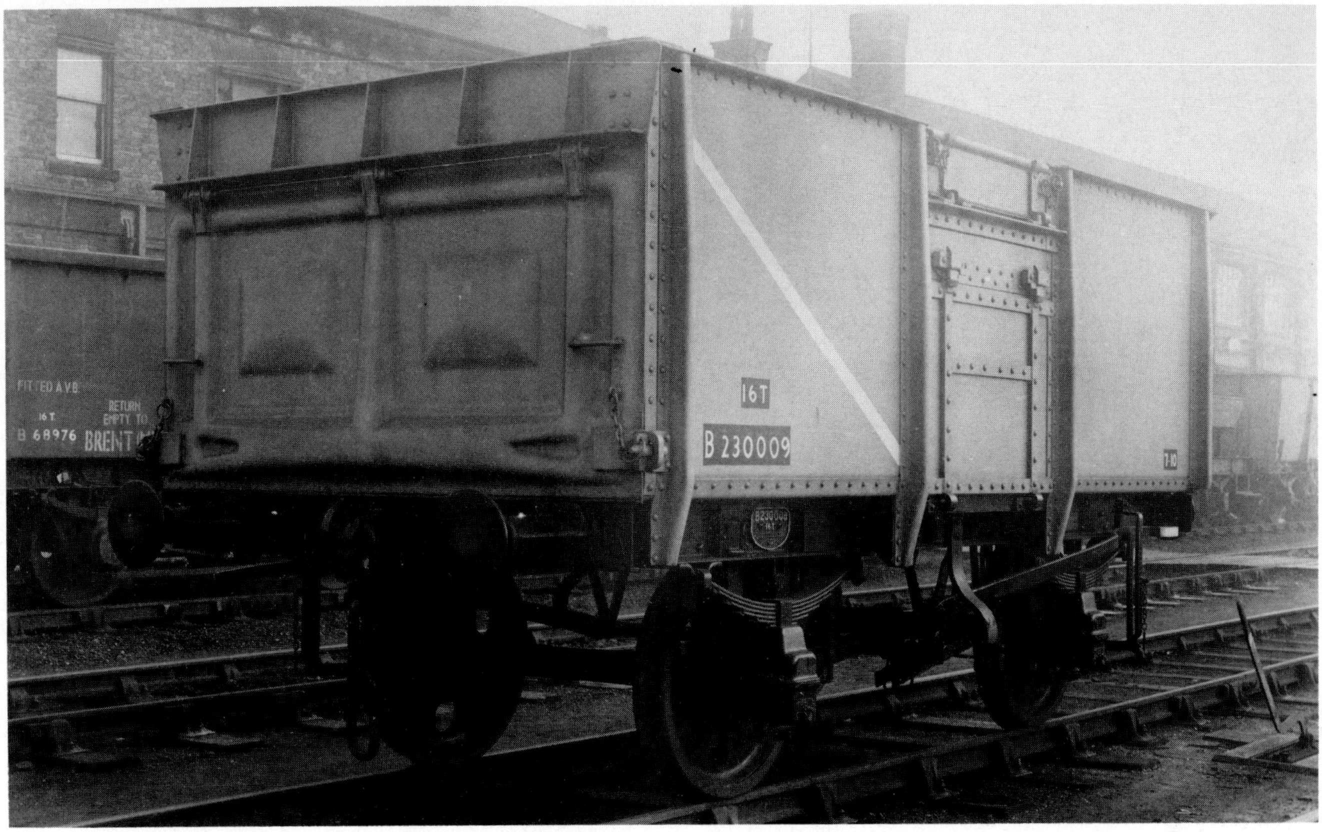

Plate 204 Diagram 1/109 is depicted by No. B230009 (Hurst, Nelson 1955, 2746) pictured when new (exact date and location unknown) and shows to advantage the pressed end door and riveted side door. Also of particular interest in the background is part of a Diagram 1/114 vacuum-braked 16 ton Mineral, No. B68976 (Derby 1951, 2331) one of those involved in the brake trials, **(see Chapter 1)**) As can be seen, it has 'Hyde' pattern axleboxes, RCH vacuum brake with tiebar between the 'W' irons, and is branded 'Fitted A.V.B.' and 'Return Empty to Brent (Mid)'. BR/OPC

Figure 50

Measured by Trevor Mann

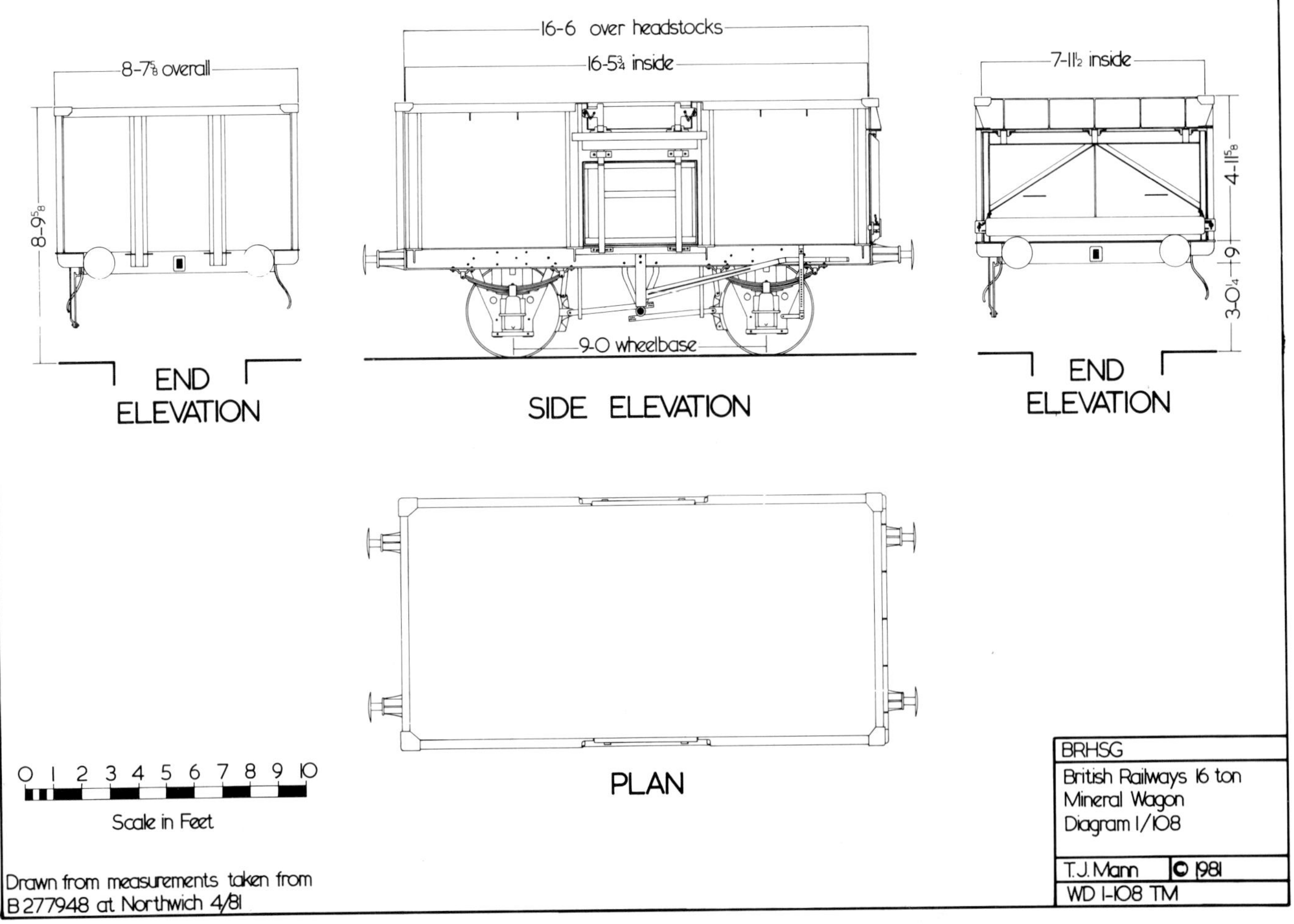

8-7⅞ overall

8-9⅝

END ELEVATION

16-6 over headstocks

16-5¾ inside

9-0 wheelbase

SIDE ELEVATION

7-11½ inside

4-11⅝

3-0¼ 9

END ELEVATION

PLAN

0 1 2 3 4 5 6 7 8 9 10
Scale in Feet

Drawn from measurements taken from B 277948 at Northwich 4/81

BRHSG

British Railways 16 ton Mineral Wagon Diagram 1/108

T.J.Mann © 1981

WD 1-108 TM

Plate 205 No. B569425 (Pressed Steel 1956, 2921) was originally built as an unfitted Diagram 1/108 vehicle. By the time it was recorded at Wellingborough on 11th June 1978, it had been vacuum-braked, with the RCH 4-shoe type, and tie-bar between the 'W' irons. The livery was bauxite. Note the star painted on the side door to indicate the position of the vacuum release cord.   *R. A. Silsbury*

Plate 206 The wagon pictured at Goole, on 2nd May 1981, depicts the standard type of rebody, with curved bottom to the bodysides. However, the underframe is of especial interest, as it has BR clasp brakegear, but without ever receiving the vacuum cylinder and pipes. No doubt this helped to fool the painter who, although the body is painted light grey, has applied the wrong TOPS code, MCV instead of MCO, and he even put the number on wrongly. At least it was correct on the other side of the wagon, and the cast number plate confirms this vehicle to be No. B592093 (Derby 1958, 2993) to Diagram 1/117 before rebodying.   *R. A. Silsbury*

Plate 207 Another standard rebody is fitted to No. B564872 (Pressed Steel 1956, 2920) and was carried out at Horwich during 1976. Originally unfitted, to Diagram 1/108, this vehicle subsequently received RCH vacuum brakes, when the brake cylinder would be positioned furthest from the end door. When rebodied, it depended on which way round a vehicle entered the workshop whether the end door remained at the original end or, as in this case, was reversed. Standard bauxite livery has 'dash boxed' lettering with a 'Coal 16 VB' code, and is unusually on black patches. It was photographed at Eastleigh on 27th February 1978.   *R. A. Silsbury*

Figure 51   Measured by Trevor Mann

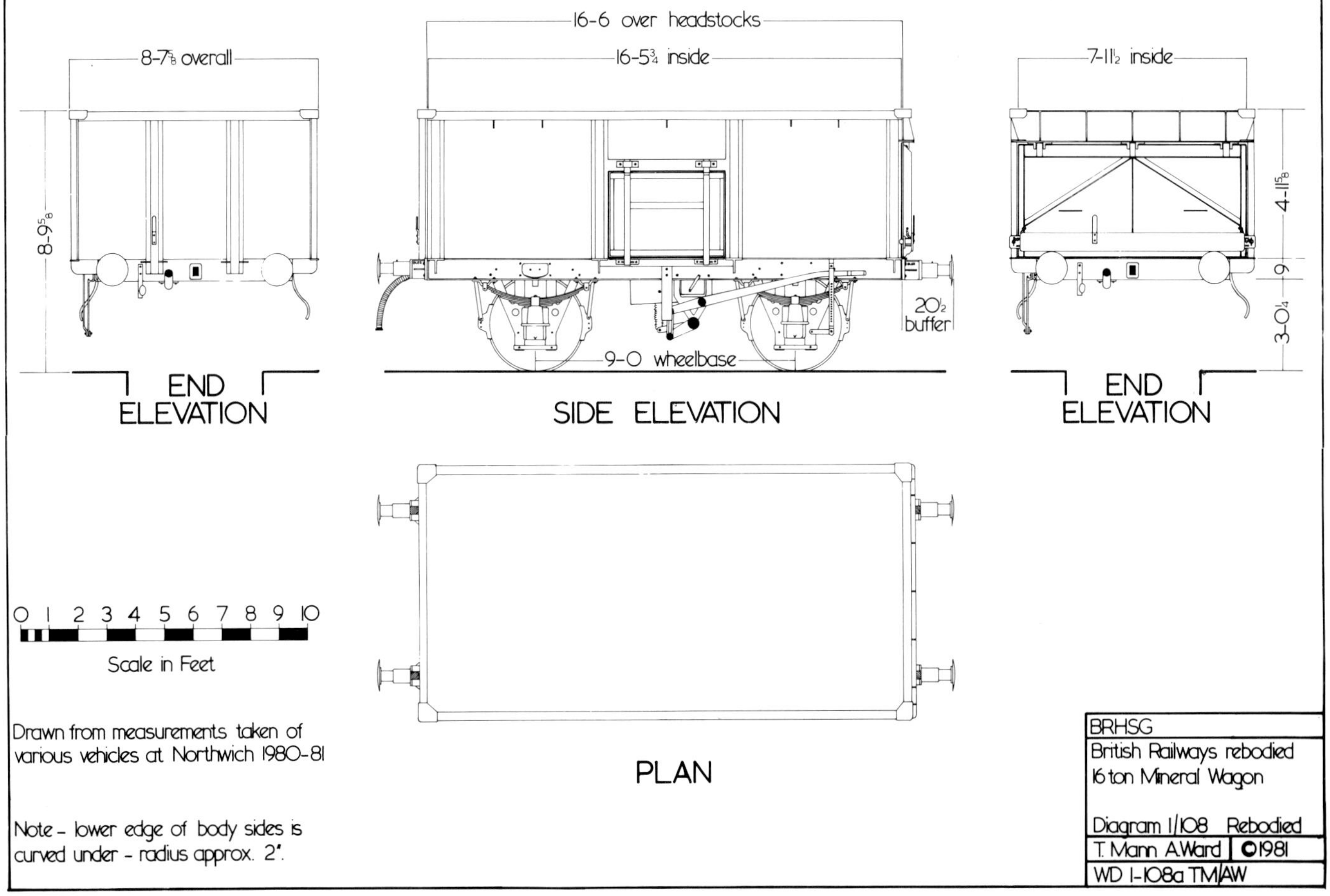

8-7⅞ overall

16-6 over headstocks

16-5¾ inside

7-11½ inside

8-9⅝

4-11⅝

3-0¼

9

20½ buffer

9-0 wheelbase

END ELEVATION

SIDE ELEVATION

END ELEVATION

PLAN

0 1 2 3 4 5 6 7 8 9 10
Scale in Feet

Drawn from measurements taken of various vehicles at Northwich 1980-81

Note - lower edge of body sides is curved under - radius approx. 2".

BRHSG
British Railways rebodied 16 ton Mineral Wagon

Diagram 1/108   Rebodied
T. Mann A. Ward   ©1981
WD 1-108a TM/AW

171

Plate 208   No. B210895 (Pressed Steel 1955, 2686), originally to Diagram 1/108, has a variation on the rebodying, where double channel section has been used for the uprights. Note the cutaways to clear the side doors, and the end door locking pins. Again the new body has been positioned the wrong way; original unfitted vehicles have the end door to the right on the non-brake shoe side. The original number plate has been replaced by one crudely manufactured with a welder's torch. The livery is rusting light grey, and the headstocks and solebars are in the main body colour. It was recorded at Margam on 13th October 1981.

R. A. Silsbury

Plate 209   Early rebodies perpetuated the use of the square bottom to the bodyside, which had been such a source of corrosion. No. B225908 (Tees-side S&E 1955, 2742) was given its new body at Derby in 1970, and is the same way round as the original one. Note the code 'COAL' when photographed in Swansea Docks on 10th July 1978.

R. A. Silsbury

Plate 210 Within a week of being released to traffic, former Diagram 1/108 Mineral wagon No. B555332 (Tees-side S&E 1958, 3144) lies resplendent in pristine bauxite livery at Stewarts Lane on 12th March 1978. It is fitted with 8-shoe clasp vacuum brakegear, employing two cylinders and change-over lever, indicated by the 'drop' mark on the side door, and has 2ft. 0½ in. Oleo pneumatic buffers. Once again, the body is reversed from that originally fitted.

R. A. Silsbury

TABLE 33

B R BUILT 16 TON MINERALS WITH 9 FT. WHEELBASE

Diag No.	Lot No.	Qnty	Builder	Year	Running numbers		Brake type	Body type	Top & bottom doors fitted?
1/104	2160	100	Fairfield S & E	1950	B67000	– 67099	Double unfit,	Weld,	top & bottom
1/104	2161	400	Derbyshire C & W	1950	B67100	– 67499	Double unfit,	Weld,	top & bottom
1/104	2162	100	Cambrian	1950	B67500	– 67599	Double unfit,	Weld,	top & bottom
1/104	2242	100	G R Turner	1950	B74450	– 74549	Double unfit,	Weld,	top & bottom
1/104	2243	650	Fairfield S & E	1950	B74550	– 75199	Double unfit,	Weld,	top & bottom
See others of diagram 1/104 in Table 31									
1/106	2104	1500	Derby	1950	B64000	– 65499	Double unfit,	Weld,	top & bottom
1/106	2184	500	Derby	1950	B67600	– 68099	Double unfit,	Weld,	top & bottom
1/106	2210	800	Derby	1951	B68100	– 68899	Double & Morton,	Weld,	top & bottom
1/108	2223	500	Birmingham	1951	B70400	– 70899	Double unfit,	Weld,	top, #
1/108	2224	700	P & W McLellan	1951	B70900	– 71599	Morton unfit,	Weld,	top,
1/108	2225	600	Tees-side S B E	1950	B71600	– 72199	Morton unfit,	Weld,	top,
1/108	2226	400	Butterley	1950	B72200	– 72599	Double unfit,	Weld,	top,
1/108	2227	500	Head Wrightson	1951	B72600	– 73099	Double & Morton,	Weld,	top,
1/108	2229	150	G R Turner	1951	B73600	– 73749	Morton unfit,	Weld,	top,
1/108	2230	400	Derbyshire C & W	1950/1	B73750	– 74149	Double unfit,	Weld,	top,
1/108	2231	200	Fairfield S & E	1950/1	B74150	– 74349	Morton unfit,	Weld,	top,
1/108	2232	100	Cravens	1950	B74350	– 74449	Morton unfit,	Weld,	top,
1/108	2250	2500	Pressed Steel	1951	B75200	– 77699	Double & Morton,	Weld,	top,
1/108	2251	2500	Pressed Steel	1951	B77700	– 80199	Morton unfit,	Weld,	top,
1/108	2252	2500	Pressed Steel	1951/2	B80200	– 82699	Morton unfit,	Weld,	top,
1/108	2253	2500	Pressed Steel	1952	B82700	– 85199	Morton unfit,	Weld,	top,
1/108	2254	2500	Pressed Steel	1952/3	B85200	– 87699	Morton unfit,	Weld,	top, *@
1/108	2255	2500	Pressed Steel	1953	B87700	– 90199	Morton unfit,	Weld,	top,
1/108	2256	2500	Pressed Steel	1953	B90200	– 92699	Morton unfit,	Weld,	top,
1/108	2257	2500	Pressed Steel	1953	B92700	– 95199	Morton unfit,	Weld,	top,
1/108	2258	2500	Pressed Steel	1953/4	B95200	– 97699	Morton unfit,	Weld,	top,
1/108	2259	2500	Pressed Steel	1954	B97700	– 100199	Morton unfit,	Weld,	top,
1/108	2290	1500	Birmingham R C W	1952	B100200	– 101699	Morton unfit,	Weld,	top,
1/108	2291	600	Butterley	1952	B101700	– 102299	Morton unfit,	Weld,	top,
1/108	2293	600	Cravens	1951	B103650	– 104249	Morton unfit,	Weld,	top,
1/108	2294	711	Derbyshire C & W	1951	B104250	– 104960	Morton unfit,	Weld,	top,
1/108	2295	700	Fairfield S & E	1951	B104961	– 105660	Morton unfit,	Weld,	top,
1/108	2296	500	Gloucester R C W	1951	B105661	– 106160	Morton unfit,	Weld,	top,

TABLE 33 Continued

Diag No.	Lot No.	Qnty	Builder	Year	Running numbers	Brake type	Body type	Top & bottom doors fitted?
1/108	2298	1400	P & W McLellan	1951/2	B106961 - 108360	Morton unfit,	Weld,	top,
1/108	2300	2150	Chas. Roberts	1951/2	B110361 - 112510	Morton unfit,	Weld,	top,
1/108	2301	1400	Tees-side S B E	1951	B112511 - 113910	Morton unfit,	Weld,	top,
1/108	2302	450	G R Turner	1951/2	B113911 - 114360	Morton unfit,	Weld,	top,
1/108	2377	1250	Chas. Roberts	1952/3	B114361 - 115610	Morton unfit,	Weld,	top,
1/108	2378	1000	Cravens	1954	B115611 - 116610	Morton unfit,	Weld,	top,
1/108	2379	1600	Head Wrightson	1952-4	B116611 - 118210	Morton unfit,	Weld,	top,
1/108	2380	1850	Gloucester R C W	1952-4	B118211 - 120060	Morton unfit,	Weld,	top,
1/108	2381	1200	Butterley	1952/3	B120061 - 121260	Morton unfit,	Weld,	top,
1/108	2382	1700	Fairfield S & E	1953/4	B121261 - 122960	Morton unfit,	Weld,	top,
1/108	2383	1850	Tees-side S B E	1952	B122961 - 124810	Morton unfit,	Weld,	top,
1/108	2385	1250	Derbyshire C & W	1952/3	B125611 - 126860	Morton unfit,	Weld,	top, %@
1/108	2387	1800	P & W McLellan	1952/3	B129361 - 131160	Morton unfit,	Weld,	top,
1/108	2388	1350	Metro-Cammell	1953	B131161 - 132510	Morton unfit,	Weld,	top,
1/108	2389	350	G R Turner	1955	B132511 - 132860	Morton unfit,	Weld,	top,
1/108	2390	1500	Birmingham R C W	1953	B132861 - 134360	Morton unfit,	Weld,	top, #
1/108	2391	500	R & Y Pickering	1954	B134361 - 134860	Morton unfit,	Weld,	top,
1/108	2463	1800	Derby	1954	B134861 - 136660	Morton unfit,	Weld,	top,
1/108	2464	1700	Derby	1954/5	B136661 - 138360	Morton unfit,	Weld,	top, #
1/108	2508	500	Birmingham R C W	1953/4	B143361 - 143860	Morton unfit,	Weld,	top,
1/108	2509	400	Butterley	1953	B143861 - 144260	Morton unfit,	Weld,	top,
1/108	2510	500	Butterley	1953	B144261 - 144760	Morton unfit,	Weld,	top,
1/108	2514	400	Derbyshire C & W	1953/4	B146094 - 146493	Morton unfit,	Weld,	top,
1/108	2515	500	Derbyshire C & W	1954	B146494 - 146993	Morton unfit,	Weld,	top,
1/108	2516	500	Gloucester R C W	1954	B146994 - 147493	Morton unfit,	Weld,	top,
1/108	2519	367	P & W McLellan	1954	B148461 - 148827	Morton unfit,	Weld,	top,
1/108	2520	500	P & W McLellan	1953/4	B148828 - 149327	Morton unfit,	Weld,	top,
1/108	2521	667	Metro Cammell	1953	B149328 - 149994	Morton unfit,	Weld,	top,
1/108	2522	500	Metro Cammell	1953/4	B149995 - 150494	Morton unfit,	Weld,	top,
1/108	2523	500	Metro Cammell	1954	B150495 - 150994	Morton unfit,	Weld,	top,
1/108	2524	500	Chas. Roberts	1953	B150995 - 151494	Morton unfit,	Weld,	top,
1/108	2525	500	Chas. Roberts	1954	B151495 - 151994	Morton unfit,	Weld,	top,
1/108	2526	500	Chas. Roberts	1954	B151995 - 152494	Morton unfit,	Weld,	top,
1/108	2527	500	Chas. Roberts	1954	B152495 - 152994	Morton unfit,	Weld,	top,
1/108	2528	627	Tees-side	1953	B152995 - 153621	Morton unfit,	Weld,	top,
1/108	2529	600	Tees-side	1953	B153622 - 154221	Morton unfit,	Weld,	top,
1/108	2530	500	Tees-side	1953	B154222 - 154721	Morton unfit,	Weld,	top,
1/108	2531	500	Tees-side	1954	B154722 - 155221	Morton unfit,	Weld,	top,
1/108	2547	500	Metro Cammell	1954	B155222 - 155721	Morton unfit,	Weld,	top,
1/108	2548	500	Metro Cammell	1954	B155722 - 156221	Morton unfit,	Weld,	top,
1/108	2549	500	Metro Cammell	1954	B156222 - 156721	Morton unfit,	Weld,	top,
1/108	2550	500	Metro Cammell	1954	B156722 - 157221	Morton unfit,	Weld,	top,
1/108	2611	947	Tees-side	1954	B160572 - 161518	Morton unfit,	Weld,	top, *@
1/108	2612	666	Tees-side	1954	B161519 - 162184	Morton unfit,	Weld,	top,
1/108	2626	500	Derbyshire C & W	1954	B162185 - 162684	Morton unfit,	Weld,	top,
1/108	2627	500	Derbyshire C & W	1954/5	B162685 - 163184	Morton unfit,	Weld,	top,
1/108	2630	500	P & W McLellan	1954	B164852 - 165351	Morton unfit,	Weld,	top,
1/108	2631	500	P & W McLellan	1953/4	B165352 - 165851	Morton unfit,	Weld,	top,
1/108	2633	2500	Pressed Steel	1954	B165852 - 168351	Morton unfit,	Weld,	top,
1/108	2634	2500	Pressed Steel	1954-6	B168352 - 170851	Morton unfit,	Weld,	top,
1/108	2635	2500	Pressed Steel	1954/5	B170852 - 173351	Morton unfit,	Weld,	top, *@
1/108	2636	2500	Pressed Steel	1955	B173352 - 175851	Morton unfit,	Weld,	top,
1/108	2637	2500	Pressed Steel	1955	B175852 - 178351	Morton unfit,	Weld,	top, *@
1/108	2639	700	Butterley	1955	B178352 - 179051	Morton unfit,	Weld,	top,
1/108	2640	400	Butterley	1954/5	B179052 - 179451	Morton unfit,	Weld,	top,
1/108	2653	1250	Derby	1955	B179452 - 180701	Morton unfit,	Weld,	top,
1/108	2654	1250	Derby	1956	B180702 - 181951	Morton unfit,	Weld,	top,
1/108	2663	1500	Metro Cammell	1954/5	B181952 - 183451	Morton unfit,	Weld,	top,
1/108	2664	1500	Metro Cammell	1955	B183452 - 184951	Morton unfit,	Weld,	top,
1/108	2670	500	Derby	1956	B187367 - 187866	Morton unfit,	Weld,	top,
1/108	2674	1000	Gloucester	1954/5	B187867 - 188866	Morton unfit,	Weld,	top,
1/108	2675	1000	Chas. Roberts	1954/	B188867 - 189866	Morton unfit,	Weld,	top,
1/108	2676	909	Birmingham R C W	1954	B203000 - 203908	Morton unfit,	Weld,	top,
1/108	2677	1091	Birmingham R C W	1954	B203909 - 204999	Morton unfit,	Weld,	top,
1/108	2678	1000	Birmingham R C W	1955	B205000 - 205999	Morton unfit,	Weld,	top, #
1/108	2685	2500	Pressed Steel	1955	B206000 - 208499	Morton unfit,	Weld,	top,
1/108	2686	2500	Pressed Steel	1955	B208500 - 210999	Morton unfit,	Weld,	top,
1/108	2687	1000	Pressed Steel	1955	B211000 - 211999	Morton unfit,	Weld,	top,
1/108	2698	1000	Birmingham R C W	1954	B212000 - 212999	Morton unfit,	Weld,	top,
1/108pt	2699	198	Cambrian	1955	B213000 - 213197	Morton unfit,	Weld,	top,
1/108	2701	933	P & W McLellan	1955	B214833 - 215765	Morton unfit,	Weld,	top, #
1/108	2702	1543	Metro Cammell	1955/6	B215766 - 217308	Morton unfit,	Weld,	top,
1/108	2703	1000	Tees-side S B E	1954/5	B217309 - 218308	Morton unfit,	Weld,	top,
1/108	2711	1000	Derby	1956	B218309 - 219308	Morton unfit,	Weld,	top,
1/108	2715	1500	Birmingham R C W	1955	B219309 - 220808	Morton unfit,	Weld,	top,
1/108	2716	1500	Birmingham R C W	1955/6	B220809 - 222308	Morton unfit,	Weld,	top, #
1/108	2717	750	Gloucester R C W	1955	B222309 - 223058	Morton unfit,	Weld,	top,
1/108	2718	750	Gloucester R C W	1955	B223059 - 223808	Morton unfit,	Weld,	top,
1/108	2719	1000	Chas. Roberts	1955	B223809 - 224808	Morton unfit,	Weld,	top,
1/108	2720	1000	Chas. Roberts	1955/6	B224809 - 225808	Morton unfit,	Weld,	top,

TABLE 33 Continued

Diag No.	Lot No.	Qnty	Builder	Year	Running numbers	Brake type	Body type	Top & bottom doors fitted?
1/108	2742	1500	Tees-side S B E	1955	B225809 - 227308	Morton unfit,	Weld,	top,
1/108	2743	800	Butterley	1955/6	B227309 - 228108	Morton unfit,	Weld,	top,
1/108	2745	700	Derbyshire C & W	1955	B229309 - 230008	Morton unfit,	Weld,	top,
1/108	2747	1000	P & W McLellan	1955/6	B230709 - 231708	Morton unfit,	Weld,	top,
1/108	2748	1540	Metro Cammell	1955/6	B231709 - 233248	Morton unfit,	Weld,	top,
1/108	2749	700	R & Y Pickering	1954	B233249 - 233948	Morton unfit,	Weld,	top,
1/108	2750	1000	Cravens	1954/5	B233949 - 234948	Morton unfit,	Weld,	top,
1/108	2751	1400	Fairfield S & E	1955/6	B234949 - 236348	Morton unfit,	Weld,	top,
1/108	2752	1500	R & Y Pickering	1955	B236349 - 237848	Morton unfit,	Weld,	top,
1/108	2756	250	G R Turner	1955/6	B237849 - 238098	Morton unfit,	Weld,	top,
1/108	2757	910	Central	1955/6	B238099 - 239008	Morton unfit,	Weld,	top,
1/108	2788	2000	Birmingham R C W	1956	B239009 - 241008	Morton unfit,	Weld,	top,
1/108	2789	2000	Birmingham R C W	1956/7	B241009 - 243008	Morton unfit,	Weld,	top,
1/108	2790	1100	Butterley	1956	B243009 - 244108	Morton unfit,	Weld,	top,
1/108	2793	1000	Derbyshire C & W	1956/7	B246609 - 247608	Morton unfit,	Weld,	top, #
1/108	2794	1000	Gloucester R C W	1956/7	B247609 - 248608	Morton unfit,	Weld,	top,
1/108	2796	1000	P & W McLellan	1956	B249609 - 250608	Morton unfit,	Weld,	top,
1/108	2797	1000	P & W McLellan	1956/7	B250609 - 251608	Morton unfit,	Weld,	Top, #
1/108	2798	2000	Metro Cammell	1956	B251609 - 253608	Morton unfit,	Weld,	top,
1/108	2799	2000	Metro Cammell	1956/7	B253609 - 255608	Morton unfit,	Weld,	top,
1/108	2800	1000	Chas. Roberts	1956	B255609 - 256608	Morton unfit,	Weld,	top,
1/108	2801	1000	Chas. Roberts	1956	B256609 - 257608	Morton unfit,	Weld,	top,
1/108	2802	1000	Tees-side S B E	1955/6	B257609 - 258608	Morton unfit,	Weld,	top,
1/108	2803	1000	Tees-side S B E	1956	B258609 - 259608	Morton unfit,	Weld,	top,
1/108	2804	700	Birmingham	1957/8	B259609 - 260308	Morton unfit,	Weld,	top, *@^
1/108	2805	700	Butterley	1957	B260609 - 261308	Morton unfit,	Weld,	top,
1/108	2808	950	Derbyshire C & W	1957	B264209 - 265158	Morton unfit,	Weld,	top,
1/108	2809	500	Gloucester R C W	1957	B265209 - 265708	Morton unfit,	Weld,	top,
1/108	2810	800	Gloucester R C W	1957/8	[B266209 - 266808	Clasp VB]	Weld,	top,
					[B266809 - 267008	Morton unfit]		
1/108	2813	1000	Metro Cammell	1957	B267709 - 268708	Morton unfit,	Weld,	top,
1/108	2814	1000	Chas. Roberts	1957	B271209 - 272208	Morton unfit,	Weld,	top,
1/108	2816	1000	Tees-side SBE	1956/7	B273209 - 274208	Morton unfit,	Weld,	top,
1/108	2817	1000	Tees-side SBE	1957	B274209 - 275208	Morton unfit,	Weld,	top,
1/108	2896	500	Central	1956	B275209 - 275708	Morton unfit,	Weld,	top,
1/108	2897	500	Central	1956	B275709 - 276208	Morton unfit,	Weld,	top,
1/108	2898	500	Cravens	1956	B276209 - 276708	Morton unfit,	Weld,	top,
1/108	2899	500	Cravens	1956/7	B276709 - 277208	Morton unfit,	Weld,	top,
1/108	2900	600	Fairfield S & E	1956	B277209 - 277808	Morton unfit,	Weld,	top,
1/108	2901	600	Fairfield S & E	1956/7	B277809 - 278408	Morton unfit,	Weld,	top,
1/108	2902	1000	R & Y Pickering	1955/6/7	B278409 - 279408	Morton unfit,	Weld,	top,
1/108	2903	200	G R Turner	1956	B279409 - 279608	Morton unfit,	Weld,	top,
1/108	2904	50	G R Turner	1957	B279609 - 279658	Morton unfit,	Weld,	top,
1/108	2906	720	P & W McLellan	1957	B159072 - 159791	Morton unfit,	Weld,	top,
1/108	2907	1450	Birmingham R C W	1958/9	[B550000 - 550499	Clasp VB]	Weld,	top,
					[B550500 - 551449	Morton unfit]		
1/108	2909	500	Central	1957	B553000 - 553499	Morton unfit,	Weld,	top,
1/108	2910	500	Central	1957	B553500 - 553999	Morton unfit,	Weld,	top,
1/108	2911	430	Cravens	1957	B554000 - 554429	Morton unfit,	Weld,	top,
1/108	2912	570	Cravens	1957/8	[B554430 - 554899	Clasp VB]	Weld,	top,
					[B554900 - 554999	Morton unfit]		
1/108	2913	250	Cravens	1957	B555000 - 555249	Morton unfit,	Weld,	top,
1/108	2915	1550	Metro Cammell	1957/8	[B556050 - 557049	Clasp VB]	Weld,	top,
					[B557050 - 557599	Morton unfit]		
1/108	2917	1000	R & Y Pickering	1956	B560200 - 561199	Morton unfit,	Weld,	top, *@
1/108	2918	1000	R & Y Pickering	1956	B561200 - 562199	Morton unfit,	Weld,	top, *@
1/108	2919	600	Tees-side S B E	1956/7	B562200 - 562799	Morton unfit,	Weld,	top, *@
1/108	2920	6500	Pressed Steel	1955/6	B562800 - 569299	Morton unfit,	Weld,	top, *@
1/108	2921	7000	Pressed Steel	1956	B569300 - 576299	Morton unfit,	Weld,	top, *@
1/108	2922	7000	Pressed Steel	1957	B576300 - 583299	Morton unfit,	Weld,	top, *@
1/108	2923	7000	Pressed Steel	1957/8	[B583300 - 587299	Morton unfit]	Weld,	top, ^
					[B587300 - 590299	Clasp VB]		
1/103	3053	100	Cambrian	1956	B228709 - 228808	Morton unfit,	Weld,	top,
1/103	3054	500	Cambrian	1956/7	[B228809 - 229208	Morton unfit]	Weld,	top,
					[B229209 - 229252	Clasp VB]		
					[B229253 - 229308	Morton unfit]		
1/108	3058	500	Tees-side S B E	1957	B593700 - 594199	Morton unfit,	Weld,	top, *@
1/108	3062	150	Butterley	1958	B594200 - 594349	Morton unfit,	Weld,	top, *
1/108	3063	550	Derbyshire C & W	1958	[B595150 - 595499	Clasp VB]	Weld,	top,
					[B595500 - 595699	Morton unfit]		
1/108	3143	780	P & W McLellan	1957/8	[B159792 - 159891	Morton unfit]	Weld,	top,
					[B159892 - 160571	Clasp VB]		
1/108	3144	500	Tees-side S B E	1958	B555250 - 555749	Morton unfit,	Weld,	top, *
1/108	3178	200	Butterley	1958	B261309 - 261508	Clasp VB,	Weld,	top,
1/108	3219	400	Butterley	1959	B594350 - 594749	Morton unfit,	Weld,	top,
1/109	2221	500	Hurst Nelson	1950	B69600 - 70099	Morton unfit,	Rivet,	top,
1/109	2222	300	Gloucester RCW	1950	B70100 - 70399	Morton unfit,	Rivet,	top,
1/109	2228	500	Cambrian	1951	B73100 - 73599	Double unfit,	Rivet,	top,
1/109	2292	1350	Cambrian	1951	B102300 - 103649	Morton unfit,	Rivet,	top,
1/109	2297	800	Hurst Nelson	1951	B106161 - 106960	Morton unfit,	Rivet,	top,

TABLE 33 Continued

Diag No.	Lot No.	Qnty	Builder	Year	Running numbers	Brake type	Body type	Top & bottom doors fitted?
1/109	2299	2000	Metro Cammell	1951	B108361 - 110360	Morton unfit,	Rivet,	top,
1/109	2384	800	Hurst Nelson	1952/3	B124811 - 125610	Morton unfit,	Rivet,	top,
1/109	2386	2500	Cambrian	1952/3	B126861 - 129360	Morton unfit,	Rivet,	top,
1/109	2485	1000	Ashford	1953	B141361 - 142360	Morton unfit,	Rivet,	top,
1/109	2486	1000	Ashford	1954/5	B142361 - 143360	Morton unfit,	Rivet,	top,
1/109	2511	333	Cambrian	1953/4	B144761 - 145093	Morton unfit,	Rivet,	top,
1/109	2512	500	Cambrian	1954	B145094 - 145593	Morton unfit,	Rivet,	top,
1/109	2513	500	Cambrian	1954	B145594 - 146093	Morton unfit,	Rivet,	top,
1/109	2517	467	Hurst Nelson	1953	B147494 - 147960	Morton unfit,	Rivet,	top,
1/109	2518	500	Hurst Nelson	1954	B147961 - 148460	Morton unfit,	Rivet,	top,
1/109	2567	350	Ashford	1954/5	B157222 - 157571	Morton unfit,	Rivet,	top,
1/109	2628	667	Cambrian	1954	B163185 - 163851	Morton unfit,	Rivet,	top,
1/109	2629	1000	Cambrian	1955	B163852 - 164851	Morton unfit,	Rivet,	top,
1/109	2666	500	Hurst Nelson	1954	B184952 - 185451	Morton unfit,	Rivet,	top,
1/109	2667	1000	Hurst Nelson	1954/5	B185452 - 186451	Morton unfit,	Rivet,	top,
1/109	2669	915	Ashford	1955	B186452 - 187366	Morton unfit,	Rivet,	top,
1/109	pt2699	1099	Cambrian	1955/6	B213201 - 214299	Morton unfit,	Rivet,	top, #
1/109	2700	533	Hurst Nelson	1955	B214300 - 214832	Morton unfit,	Rivet,	top,
1/109	2744	600	Cambrian	1956	B228109 - 228708	Morton unfit,	Rivet,	top,
1/109	2746	700	Hurst Nelson	1955/6	B230009 - 230708	Morton unfit,	Rivet,	top,
1/109	2791	1250	Cambrian	1956/7	B244109 - 245358	Morton unfit,	Rivet,	top,
1/109	2792	500	Cambrian	1957	B245359 - 245858	Morton unfit,	Rivet,	top,
1/109	2795	1000	Hurst Nelson	1956	B248609 - 249608	Morton unfit,	Rivet,	top,
1/109	2806	1100	Cambrian	1958/9	[B261509 - 261714	Clasp VB]	Rivet,	top,
					[B261715 - 262608	Morton unfit]		
1/109	2811	500	Hurst Nelson	1956	B267209 - 267708	Morton unfit,	Rivet,	top,
1/109	3152	250	Cambrian	1957	B262909 - 263159	Morton unfit,	Rivet,	top, *@
1/111	2105	1000	Derby	1950	B65500 - 66499	Double unfit,	Weld,	top & bottom
1/111	2123	500	Derby	1951	B66500 - 66999	Double unfit,	Weld,	top
1/111	2473	760	Shildon	1953	B138361 - 139120	Morton unfit,	Weld,	top
1/111	2480	1000	Shildon	1953/4	B139121 - 140120	Morton unfit,	Weld,	top
1/111	2502	1140	Shildon	1954	B140121 - 141260	Morton unfit,	Weld,	top
1/114	2331	300	Derby	1951	B68900 - 69199	100 VB & 200 Morton,	Weld,	top,
1/116	2761	100	Shildon	1954	B141261 - 141360	Morton unfit,	Rivet Al.top,	
1/117	2599	1500	Shildon	1955/6	B157572 - 159071	Morton unfit,	Weld,	top, #
1/117	2992	1200	Derby	1957	B590300 - 591499	Morton unfit,	Weld,	top,
1/117	2993	700	Derby	1957/8	B591500 - 592199	Morton unfit,	Weld,	top, *@^
1/117	3042	500	Central	1956-8	B592700 - 593199	Morton unfit,	Weld,	top, *@^
1/117	3043	500	Central	1958	B593200 - 593699	Morton unfit,	Weld,	top, *@
1/117	3076	500	Derby	1958	B592200 - 592699	Morton unfit,	Weld,	top, *
1/117	3145	1350	Pressed Steel	1958	B551600 - 552949	Morton unfit,	Weld,	top, *
1/117	3146	2000	Pressed Steel	1958	[B557750 - 558749	Clasp VB]	Weld,	top, *@
					[B558750 - 559749	Morton unfit]		

```
        ------
Total   239673
```

- indicates one at least of this Lot has been seen fitted with a pressed end door.
* - indicates that we believe some of this Lot were built new with clasp vacuum brake or were converted early.
@ - indicates that unfitted examples of this Lot have been seen.
^ - indicates that some were built with additional V hangers for vacuum brake, which was not fitted.
% - indicates that part of this lot were built new with self-adjusting clasp vacuum brake.

The number series from B279700 was used for rebodied wagons whose previous identity was untraceable.

16 ton Minerals with 10ft. wheelbase

In 1975 a new design of 'Mineral Wagon' was introduced as Diagram No. 1/194 **(see Table 34 and Plate 211)**. This took the rebuilding of wagons a logical step further by using redundant vacuum brake underframes of 17ft. 6in. over headstocks and 10ft. wheelbase to form the base for newly constructed steel welded bodies. These had fabricated side and end doors of similar dimension to the earlier 'Minerals', but like other rebuilds there was no top door. The underframes were from 'Palbricks' and so are of different designs. Most are RCH type, others are BR clasp, and a few are LMS clasp (from 'Medfits' which had been converted to 'Palbrick'). One at least of these had lost its rubber auxiliary suspension. A few of these wagons had roller bearings. Early examples were branded COAL 16 VB. The TOPS code was MCV.

TABLE 34

B R BUILT 16 TON MINERALS WITH 10 FT. WHEELBASE

Diag No.	Lot No.	Qnty	Builder	Year	Running numbers	Brake type	Body type	Top flap, end & bottom doors fitted?
1/194	3863	394	Horwich	1975-8	B596000 - 596393	Mixed Vacuum	Weld,	end, no top or bottom

Plate 211 To conclude the illustrations depicting 16 ton 'Minerals' is this view, taken at Southampton on 2nd April 1979, of No. B596333 (Horwich 1978, 3863) which had started life as a Diagram 1/024 Palbrick B, No. B462021 (Ashford 1958, 2724). In 1970, it was rebuilt as a Coil P, in 1973 further rebuilt as a Coil V, and finally to a 16 ton Mineral in February 1978. To fit the 17ft. 6in. underframe, the standard mineral rebody was extended by one foot. The main features distinguishing these Lot 3863 vehicles, apart from the 'W.B. 10' -0"' legend are the underframe and buffer variations, particularly roller bearing axleboxes which were very rarely fitted to standard 16 ton Minerals.

R. A. Silsbury

21 ton Minerals with 12ft. wheelbase (see Table 35)

Unfitted designs

Although the pre-nationalisation companies and some private owners had had some 20 or 21 ton steel 'Mineral Wagons', none were built by the MoWT or MoS during the wartime period. Thus the first we have to consider were those built in 1950. Like the 16 ton wagons, two diagrams were issued initially; Diagram No. 1/107 was for wagons of welded construction **(see Plate 212)** and Diagram No. 1/110 was for those of riveted construction

(see Plate 213). Both were on RCH long-linked unfitted underframes which were 21ft. 6in. long over headstocks and had 12ft. wheelbases. The welded version had 21ft. 5¾in. inside length, an interior height of 5ft. 2¾in. and a capacity of 893cu. ft. The riveted version had a 21ft. 7¼in. inside length, an interior height of 5ft. 2⅜in. and a capacity of 892cu. ft. Both had a 7ft. 11½in. inside width, a pair of fabricated doors in each side,

TABLE 35

BR BUILT 21 TON MINERALS WITH 12 FT. WHEELBASE

Diag No.	Lot No.	Qnty	Builder	Year	Running numbers	Brake type	Body type	Top, end & bottom doors fitted?
1/110	2190	1000	Metro Cammell	1950/1	B200000 - 200999	RCH L-1 unfit,	Rivet,	end, no top or b.
1/107	2191	500	P W McLellan	1950	B201000 - 201499	RCH L-1 unfit,	Weld,	end, no top or b.
1/107	2192	500	Chas. Roberts	1950	B201500 - 201999	RCH L-1 unfit,	Weld,	end, no top or b.
1/107	2193	500	Birmingham	1950/1	B202000 - 202499	RCH L-1 unfit,	Weld,	end, no top or b.
1/119	3387	1000	Shildon	1961/2	B310000 - 310999	BR clasp Man VB,	Weld,	end & top, no b.
1/120	3390	950	Derby	1961/2	B311000 - 311949	BR clasp SAB VB,	Weld,	end & top, no b.
1/120	3430	1500	Derby	1962/3	B312000 - 313499	BR clasp SAB VB,	Weld,	end & top, no b.
1/120	3438	1000	Shildon	1962/3	B313500 - 314499	BR clasp SAB VB,	Weld,	end & top, no b.
1/120	3439	500	Derby	1963	B314500 - 314999	BR clasp SAB VB,	Weld,	end & top, no b.
-	-	2600	Shildon	1971-2	B315000 - 317599	Mixed, unfit,	Weld,	end, no top or b.
Total		10050						

(Key to door types - b.= bottom in floor; top = flap over side; end = top hinged)
(Key to brake type - SAB = Self adjusting brake; Man = Manual; L-1 = Long-link)

and a fabricated end door, although some of the riveted wagons had pressed doors. Surprisingly, no top-flap doors were fitted, because this would weaken the body; a contrast to the '16 ton Minerals' of this period. **Figure 52** shows one of the riveted wagons.

Vacuum Brake Design

In 1951, the Ideal Stocks Committee decided that no more '16 or 21 ton Minerals' would be built, the larger '24½ ton Mineral' was to be the new standard. However, in 1961, a new diagram, No. 1/119 was issued, which was quickly followed by Diagram No. 1/120 **(Plate 214 and Figure 53)**. These all had the same body drawing number, SW/DN29184. This was of welded construction of 21ft. 5¾in. inside length, 7ft. 11½in. inside width and 5ft. 2in. inside height. The capacity was 885cu. ft. Like the earlier wagons they had two fabricated side doors and an end door, but in addition they had top-flap doors. Dimensionally, the underframe was as the earlier wagons but all were vacuum-fitted with a BR clasp brake arrangement. The difference between the diagrams was that Diagram No. 1/119 had an empty/loaded changeover lever, which was replaced by self-adjusting brake (SAB) on Diagram No. 1/120. One interesting item was that fifty of the underframes, originally allocated to Lot 3390, which should have been for 1,000 wagons, were used for 'Coil A' wagons.

Rebuilds; First Design

Rebuilt wagons constitute the remainder of this type of wagon. During 1971/2, 2,600 wagons were built by placing newly constructed welded bodies on to redundant underframes. The bodies which were all of welded construction, had a pair of fabricated side doors and an end door. There were no top-flap doors. The underframes were from '21 and 24½ ton Hopper Wagons' fitted with several brake variants. A total of 2,441 of the rebuilt wagons had the RCH long-link brake, 145 had the LNER-type underframe with a clasp brake on both wheels of one side only, 11 had the special type of 8-shoe clasp brake fitted to the earlier '24½ ton Hoppers' and 3 had the long-lever push rod brake of later '24½ ton Hoppers'. Diagram No. 1/098 (second issue) was allocated, but not issued, for this design but no lot number was issued **(see Plate 215)**.

Rebuilds; Second Design

Further rebuilding followed with 296 unfitted wagons receiving a new body design which lacked end doors, and had a single drop door in each side, arranged near the left-hand end of the wagon. Once again, no lot number or diagram was issued. In addition, five of the 1961-3 vacuum-braked wagons were rebodied with a similar design of body. **Figure 54 and Plate 216** are of these wagons.

Use, Branding and Condemnation

The '21 ton Minerals' were originally coded MIN XX but this was not carried on the body. A few were branded LOCO in large letters on the central body panel. From 1963, they were coded COAL 21 and COAL-21-VB. A 'K' suffix after the number also identified the wagon as being of 21 tons. Many of the '21 ton VB' wagons were branded 'To work in S. Wales and Monmouthshire only'. Under TOPS, they were coded MDO and MDV. These wagons often worked in block trains and, although built in comparatively small numbers, they were successful. Many unrebuilt unfitted wagons continued in use until 1983 but then they, and many of the rebuilds, were stored out of use, although some remained in traffic in South Wales because Swansea Docks could not end-tip vacuum-braked wagons. The vacuum-braked wagons continue in use although many were condemned during 1984. Further details of the '21 ton Minerals' can be found in **MRC (1983) 51 Nos. 595 & 596**.

Plate 212 Three batches of Diagram 1/107 21 ton 'Minerals' were built concurrently. No. B202065 is by Birmingham RC&W 1951, 2193. As can be seen in this photograph, taken at Margam on 13th October 1981, the bodywork closely resembles the style of rebodied 16 ton 'Minerals'. Extensive replating has been carried out, and much of the livery is obscured by rust.

R. A. Silsbury

Figure 52

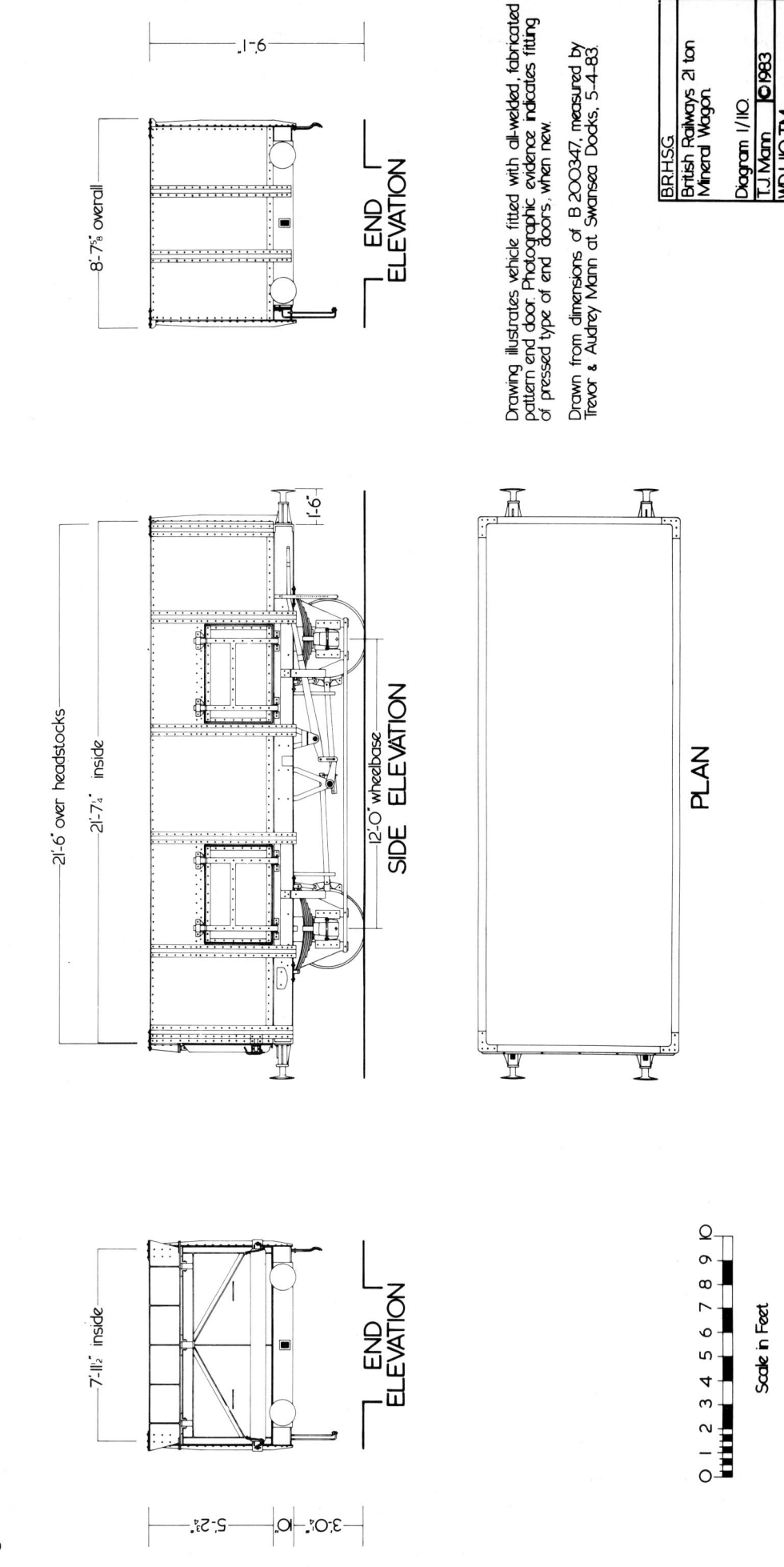

9'-1"

8'-7⅞" overall

END
ELEVATION

Drawing illustrates vehicle fitted with all-welded, fabricated
pattern end door. Photographic evidence indicates fitting
of pressed type of end doors, when new.

Drawn from dimensions of B 200347, measured by
Trevor & Audrey Mann at Swansea Docks, 5-4-83.

B.R.H.S.G.
British Railways 21 ton
Mineral Wagon

Diagram 1/110.

T.J.Mann.   ©1983

WD 1-110 T.M.

21'-6" over headstocks

21'-7¼" inside

1'-6"

SIDE ELEVATION

12'-0" wheelbase

PLAN

7'-11½" inside

END
ELEVATION

5'-2¼"   0'-10"   3'-0"

0 1 2 3 4 5 6 7 8 9 10

Scale in Feet

Plate 213 No. B200364 (Metropolitan Cammell 1950, 2190) depicts the Diagram 1/110 riveted body version of the 21 ton 'Mineral' wagon, and is also drawn in **Figure 52**. As with the 16 tonners, repairs found fabricated doors fitted to riveted vehicles, and vice-versa, as all the doors were interchangeable between 16 and 21 ton Minerals. No. B200364 was recorded at Tyseley on 3rd April 1977.

R. A. Silsbury

Plate 214 Many of the vacuum-braked 21 ton 'Mineral' wagons received brandings, the most common carried by 3,850 of the total of 4,950 built being 'To work within South Wales and Monmouthshire only'. Most others were in circuit work feeding a specific power-station, and No. B314533 (Derby 1963, 3439) to Diagram 1/120 carried 'Load only to Castle Donnington Power Station, CEGB', although by the time it was photographed, on 25th April 1984, it was with many of its colleagues in South Wales, at Ebbw Junction.

P. W. Bartlett

Figure 53

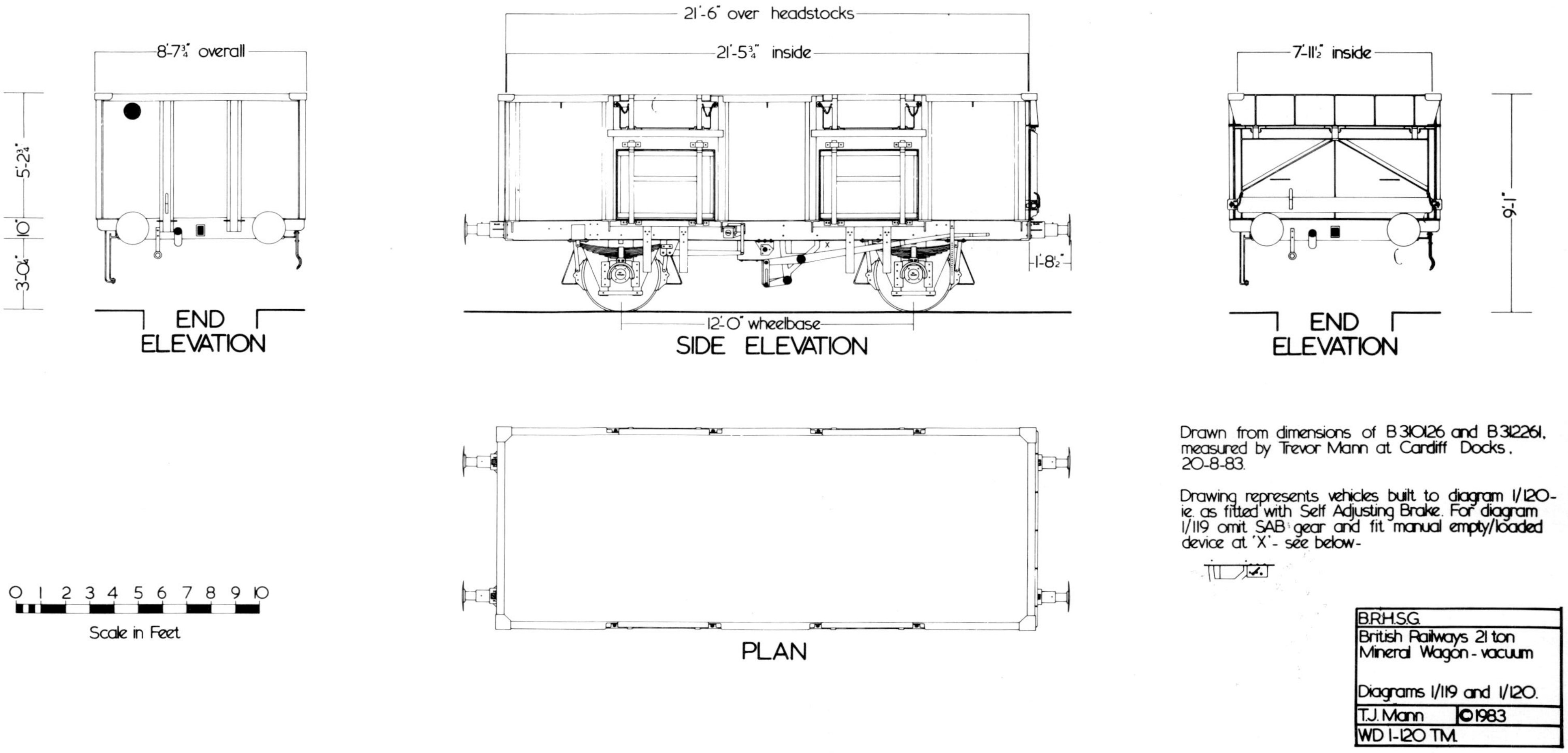

7'-11½" inside

END ELEVATION

9'-1."

BRHSG.
British Railways 21 ton
Mineral Wagon – vacuum

Diagrams 1/119 and 1/120.

T.J.Mann ©1983

WD 1-120 TM

Drawn from dimensions of B 310126 and B 312261,
measured by Trevor Mann at Cardiff Docks.
20-8-83

Drawing represents vehicles built to diagram 1/120-
le as fitted with Self Adjusting Brake. For diagram
1/119 omit SAB gear and fit manual empty/loaded
device at 'X' – see below –

21'-6" over headstocks

21'-5¾" inside

1'-8½"

12'-0" wheelbase

SIDE ELEVATION

PLAN

8'-7¾" overall

END ELEVATION

5'-2½"

3'-0." 1'-0."

0 1 2 3 4 5 6 7 8 9 10

Scale in Feet

181

Plate 215 At Llandeilo Junction, on 13th July 1978, No. B315232K (Rebodied at Shildon, 1972) — no original building details — displays the first design of 21 ton Mineral rebuild. The top channel stiffener is narrower than on 16 ton Mineral rebuilds. The light grey livery has black patches for the lettering. Note the code 'COAL 21' and the 'K' suffix to the number, used to assist clerks in determining a wagon's capacity from a list of vehicle numbers.

R. A. Silsbury

Plate 216 The second design rebuild dispensed with the end door, and had only one door at each side, offset to the left. Although unfitted, the bodies were painted bauxite, and the original numbers were retained. No. B200915 was originally by Metropolitan Cammell in 1951 to Lot 2190, and rebodied at Shildon during 1978. It is pictured at Hams Hall Power-Station on 2nd September 1982.

R. A. Silsbury

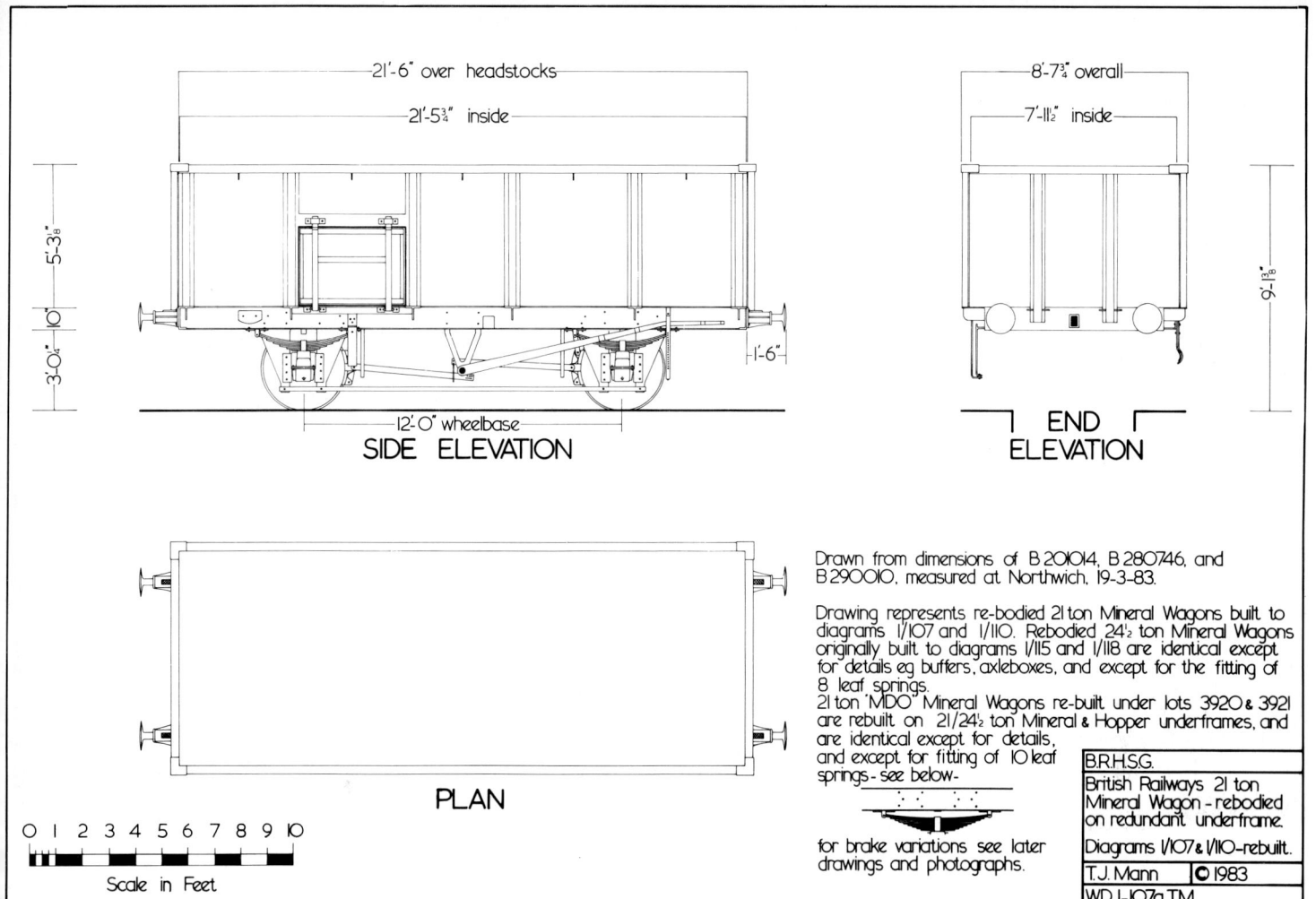

Side Elevation

21'-6" over headstocks
21'-5¾" inside
5'-3⅛"
3'-0¼"
10"
12'-0" wheelbase
1'-6"

SIDE ELEVATION

End Elevation

8'-7¾" overall
7'-11½" inside
9'-1⅜"

END ELEVATION

PLAN

Drawn from dimensions of B 201014, B 280746, and B 290010, measured at Northwich, 19-3-83.

Drawing represents re-bodied 21 ton Mineral Wagons built to diagrams 1/107 and 1/110. Rebodied 24½ ton Mineral Wagons originally built to diagrams 1/115 and 1/118 are identical except for details eg buffers, axleboxes, and except for the fitting of 8 leaf springs.
21 ton 'MDO' Mineral Wagons re-built under lots 3920 & 3921 are rebuilt on 21/24½ ton Mineral & Hopper underframes, and are identical except for details, and except for fitting of 10 leaf springs - see below-

for brake variations see later drawings and photographs.

B.R.H.S.G.
British Railways 21 ton Mineral Wagon - rebodied on redundant underframe.
Diagrams 1/107 & 1/110-rebuilt.
T.J.Mann © 1983
WD 1-107a TM

0 1 2 3 4 5 6 7 8 9 10
Scale in Feet

Figure 54

24½ ton Minerals with 12ft. wheelbase (see Table 36)

After the complexity of the history of the earlier 'Minerals', that of these wagons, which were rated at 24½ tons, was simple. Two diagrams were issued but the wagons were all very similar. They had RCH long-link unfitted underframes which were 21ft. 6in. over headstocks with a 12ft. wheelbase. The bodies were all-steel and of welded construction with an end door and two side doors which had a deep top-flap over them. Usually of fabricated construction, some of the early wagons had pressed side doors.

Diagram No. 1/115 had an inside length of 21ft. 5³/₁₆in. and an inside width of 7ft. 1⅝in. The bearings were plain. Diagram No. 1/118 had an inside length of 21ft. 5¾in. and an inside width of 7ft. 11½in. Roller bearing axleboxes were fitted. Both diagrams had an inside height of 6ft. 0⅛in. and a capacity of 1,028cu. ft. **Figure 55 and Plate 217** illustrates these wagons.

TABLE 36

BR BUILT 24½ TON MINERALS WITH 12 FT. WHEELBASE

Diag No.	Lot No.	Qnty No.	Builder	Year	Running numbers	Brake type	Body type	Top, end & bottom doors fitted?
1/115	2460	650	Shildon	1953	B280000 - 280649	BR Long-link unfit,	Weld,	end & top, no bottom
1/115	2600	1000	Shildon	1955/6	B281150 - 282149	BR Long-link unfit,	Weld,	end & top, no bottom
1/115	2602	500	Shildon	1954	B280650 - 281149	BR Long-link unfit,	Weld,	end & top, no bottom
1/118	3244	620	Ashford	1959	B282150 - 282769	BR Long-link unfit,	Weld,	end & top, no bottom
1/118	3302	225	Ashford	1960	B282770 - 282994	BR Long-link unfit,	Weld,	end & top, no bottom
1/118	3388	135	Shildon	1961	B282995 - 283129	BR Long-link unfit,	Weld,	end & top, no bottom
1/118	3427	265	Shildon	1962	B283130 - 283394	BR Long-link unfit,	Weld,	end & top, no bottom
-	3920	459*	Shildon/ Ashford	1977/8	[B290000 - 290199] [B290220 - 290485]	Mixed, unfit,	Weld,	no end, top or bottom
-	3921	3*	Shildon/ Ashford	1977	B290200 - 290219	BR clasp Vacuum,	Weld,	no end, top or bottom
Total	3857							

* - There are gaps in number series which cannot be shown here, the quantities are believed accurate

Use, Branding and Condemnation

These wagons were usually branded for a particular working, often from a colliery to a power-station. As well as the code 'COAL 24½' they had a large solid yellow triangle between the doors to distinguish them from '21 ton Minerals'. A 'N' suffix after the number also identified the wagon as being 24½ tons. They were TOPS-coded MEO. Although a high capacity wagon designed to serve more modern facilities, by 1982 they had been superseded by 'Air-Braked Hoppers', and were all withdrawn.

Rebuilding to produce '24½ ton Minerals'

The rebuilding of these wagons is complex as it also included the use of some more of the '21 ton Minerals'. Early on, sometime before 1965, some of the '24½ ton Minerals' had their side doors removed and the doorway plated over. They were branded 'NO DOORS' in large lettering; this was inappropriate as the end door remained (see Plate 218).

From about 1977, a total of 651 was rebodied just as the '21 ton' wagons had been, with a body which lacked end doors and had only a single door offset to the left-hand side. These retained their original numbers. No lot number or diagram was issued. **Figure 54** shows details of these wagons.

The final batches were Lots 3920 and 3921. Underframes from '21 tons' wagons were uprated by being fitted with new 10-leaf springs and newly constructed bodies of the design described above. In addition, underframes from '24½ ton Hoppers' and 'Non-Hopper Minerals' were used, which meant that they varied in appearance, just as described for the '21 ton' rebuilds. All of these wagons were mixed into the new number series beginning at B290000 and were branded to carry 25 metric tonnes. **Figure 54 and Plate 219** also shows this variant.

Use, Branding and Condemnation of Rebuilds

All of these rebuilt wagons were painted bauxite which was unusual for unfitted wagons. Although they should have been TOPS-coded MEO, they were given either MDO or MDV and most were soon downrated to 21½ tons. Wagons of this type continue in use, in particular in the Midlands and South Wales, although many have been stored or condemned.

Plate 217 The two diagrams for 24½ ton 'Minerals' were very similar, and essentially a taller version of the 21 ton type. The side and end doors were dimensionally identical with the 16 and 21 ton 'Minerals'. No. B282904 (Ashford 1960, 3302) is to Diagram 1/118, and was recorded at Connah's Quay in May 1963. The livery was light grey, with black patches for all lettering. The yellow triangle between the side doors was a visual aid to differentiate the 24½ tonner from the 21 ton type. A wide variety of either 'Empty to . . . ' or 'Load only to . . . ' brandings were carried, No. B282904 being one of a batch of sixty with the instruction 'Load only to / John Summers & Sons Ltd. / Hawarden Bridge / Shotwick Sidings LMR (GC).'

E. Gent

Figure 55

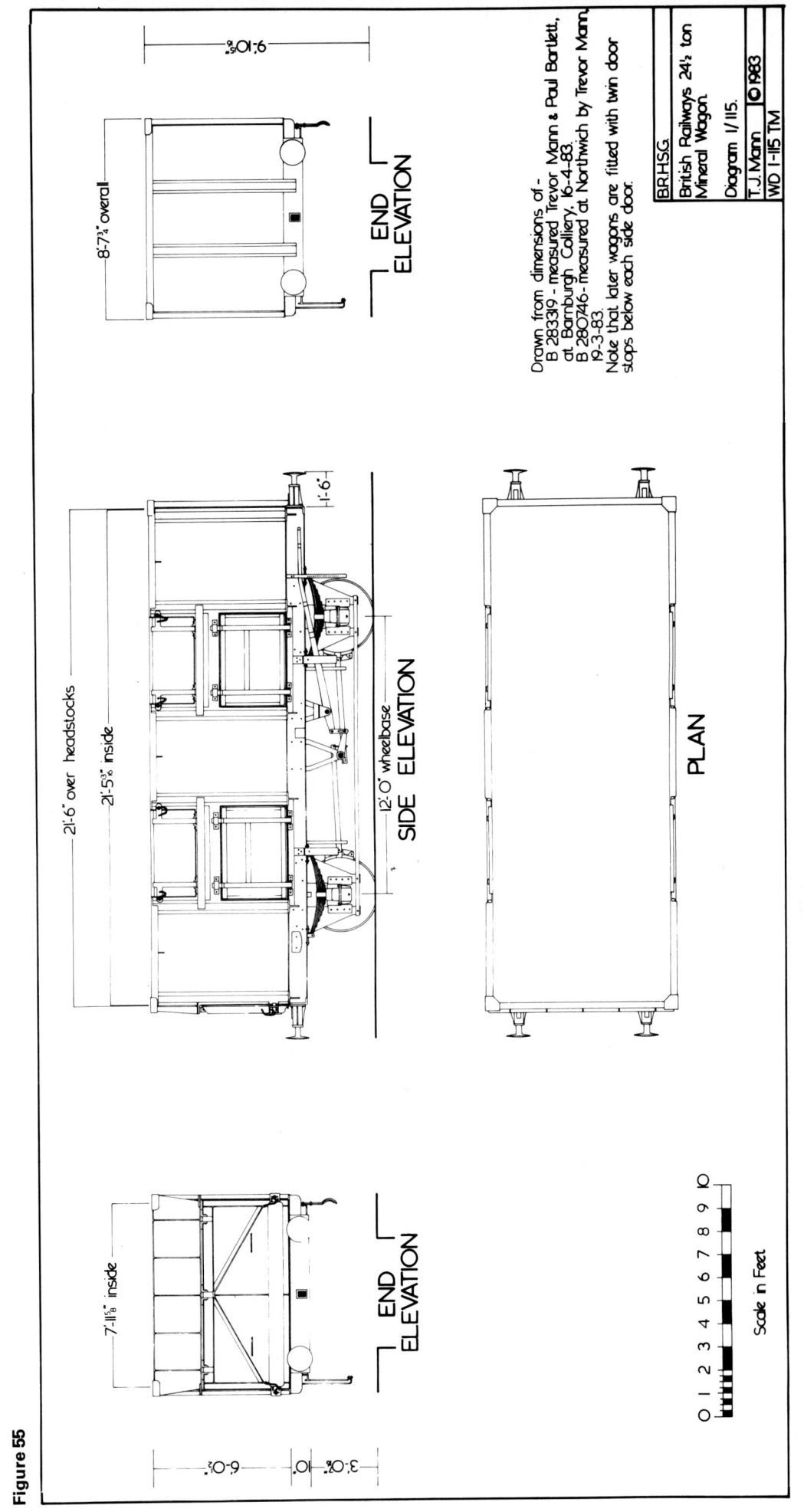

9:10⅝"

8'-7¾" overall

END
ELEVATION

1'-6"

21'-6" over headstocks

21'-5⅜" inside

12'-0" wheelbase

SIDE ELEVATION

PLAN

7'-11⅝" inside

END
ELEVATION

6'-0⅜"

3'-0⅜" 1'-0⅜"

B.R.H.S.G.
British Railways 24½ ton
Mineral Wagon.
Diagram 1/115.
T.J. Mann   © 1983
WD 1-115 TM

Drawn from dimensions of -
B 28339 - measured Trevor Mann & Paul Bartlett,
at Barnburgh Colliery, 16-4-83.
B 280746 - measured at Northwich by Trevor Mann
19-3-83.
Note that later wagons are fitted with twin door
stops below each side door.

0 1 2 3 4 5 6 7 8 9 10
Scale in Feet

Plate 218   As described in the text, some 24½ ton 'Minerals' had all the side doors sealed with plain plate, and the topside strengthening angle joined across the gap where the top doors had been. No. B280070 (Shildon 1953, 2460) was a Diagram 1/115 vehicle from the original batch, with plain axleboxes, and bears the prominent legend 'No doors', although the end door remains, as can be seen in this view taken at Toton on 17th September 1978.

R. A. Silsbury

Plate 219   Those vehicles rebodied circa 1978 received identical bodies to the 21 ton types, and some ex-21 ton underframes were upgraded by fitting ten leaf springs to compensate for the additional load; oil axleboxes, if fitted, were retained. The TOPS code MDO was carried rather than MEO, and some vehicles have since been downrated to 21 tons. No. B290365 was plated Shildon 1978, Lot 3920, and the bauxite livery was carried down to include the headstocks and sole-bars. It is pictured at Hams Hall Power-Station on 2nd September 1982.

R. A. Silsbury

Iron Ore, Chalk, Sand and Stone Tipplers (see Table 37)

These wagons are normally simply referred to as 'Iron Ore Tipplers'. The LMS had rated some of their conventional steel 'Mineral Wagons' at 27 tons to carry this dense ore, although most of it had been carried in 'Hoppers' before nationalisation. BR introduced a new design of ore carrier in 1951 which was of simple but rugged construction. Subsequently, all of the 'Tipplers' continued the basic features of a welded steel open body, which lacked any doors, carried on a 2-axle underframe.

Diagram Nos. 1/180 and 1/181 were 16ft. 6in. long over headstocks with a 9ft. wheelbase. Both had an inside height of 4ft. 11¼in., a capacity of 648cu. ft. and carried 27 tons. Diagram No. 1/180 **(see Plate 220)** had an inside length of 16ft. 5½in. and an inside width of 7ft. 11½in. Diagram No. 1/181 had an inside length of 16ft. 5⅝in. and an inside width of 7ft. 11⅝in. The double brake allowed the use of unloading mechanisms which held the wagon in place by putting locking bars over the axle. A brake cross-shaft might have been fouled by these. **Figure 56** illustrates these wagons.

Diagram No. 1/183 **(see Plate 221)** had the same underframe as the earlier 'Tipplers', and the main body dimensions were the same as Diagram No. 1/180, except that the interior height was reduced to 4ft. 7¼in. Although this meant that the capacity was reduced to 603cu. ft., they continued to be rated at 27 tons. The reduction in height was probably due to experience of excessive loading of the earlier wagons. The final lot of this design had a 10ft. wheelbase, which means that it was similar to Diagram No. 1/184.

This diagram had the 10ft. wheelbase, but all body dimensions remained as per Diagram No. 1/183 except that the thickness of the end plate was decreased to ³/₁₆in. **(Plate 222)**. In the 1970s, many of this diagram were converted to clasp vacuum brake which had a pair of vacuum cylinders and a changeover lever.

Diagram No. 1/185 wagons were built new with a BR clasp vacuum brake **(see Plate 223)**. All basic dimensions of the body and underframe were the same as Diagram No. 1/184 but, because of the increased tare weight, they were rated to carry only 26 tons.

Use, Branding and Condemnation

The specialist design of these wagons restricted the places where they could be loaded to, and they usually worked in block trains. Most 'Tipplers' were branded IRON ORE TIPPLER in large letters on a central panel. By 1965, ninety four wagons were branded for CHALK and ninety one for SAND. 'Tipplers' continued in sand traffic in the Stoke area until the early 1980s. By that time most continued to be branded SAND but, unusually, very few were TOPS-coded. Occassionally USO was used.

In the early 1970s, there was a huge increase in the transport of aggregates and many of the 'Tipplers' were transferred to this traffic and branded STONE. When converted to vacuum brake, they often had a large Pool number and a special 'stone' symbol which was designed to have the appearance of a railway wagon. Under TOPS, the wagons in ore or aggregates traffic were coded MSO or MSV as suitable.

From the mid-1970s, some 'Tipplers' were used for 'Ingot Mould' traffic, the floor being lined with ballast. After an accident, large holes were cut in the sides so that staff could position the load while standing outside the wagon. They were distinctively lettered on a large yellow panel and they were TOPS-coded SMO. The Engineer's Department also used many of these wagons during the 1980s; these were TOPS-coded ZKO.

TABLE 37

IRON ORE AND CHALK TIPPLERS

Diag No.	Lot No.	Qnty	Builder	Year	Running numbers	Brake type	Wheel-base
1/180	2274	700	Cravens	1953	B380000 – 380699	Double unfit	9 ft.
1/180	2275	800	Head Wrightson	1951	B380700 – 381499	Double unfit	9 ft.
1/181	2310	400	Derby	1951	B381500 – 381899	Double unfit	9 ft.
1/181	2601	500	Shildon	1954	B383140 – 383639	Double unfit	9 ft.
1/183	2498	1240	Shildon	1953	B381900 – 383139	Double unfit	9 ft.
1/183	2730	1500	Shildon	1955	B383640 – 385139	Double unfit	9 ft.
1/183	2844	500	Derby	1957	B385140 – 385639	Double unfit	9 ft.
1/183	2988	476	Derby	1957	B747500 – 747975	Double unfit	9 ft.
1/183	3075	24	Derby	1957	B747976 – 747999	Double unfit	9 ft.
1/183	3324	1000	Derby	1960	B387090 – 388089	Double unfit	10 ft.
1/184	3091	1450	Derby	1958	B385640 – 387089	Double unfit	10 ft.
1/185	3363	1000	Derby	1960/1	B388090 – 389089	BR clasp VB	10 ft.
	Total	9590					

Plate 220   No. B381123 (Head, Wrightson 1951, 2275) is to Diagram 1/180. Although only 9ft. wheelbase, the weight when loaded required the use of a tiebar between the 'W' irons to ensure efficient action of the independent brakes. Two different pattern roller bearing axleboxes are fitted. Besides use for Iron Ore, No. B381123 carries the brand 'Stone' on the centre body panel, and its current use, when photographed at Warrington on 7th August 1980, was for carrying Ingot Moulds; large steel pieces which required a bed of gravel in the wagon. The brand panel and top angle of the body are painted yellow, otherwise the livery is rather rusty, formerly light grey.

R. A. Silsbury

Plate 221   In contrast to **Plate 220**, No. B382833 (Shildon 1953, 2498) was less than one month old when photographed at Gloucester on 9th May 1953. It is a Diagram 1/183 vehicle, has oil axleboxes, and displays the original light grey livery and lettering, without blemish.

E. Bruton

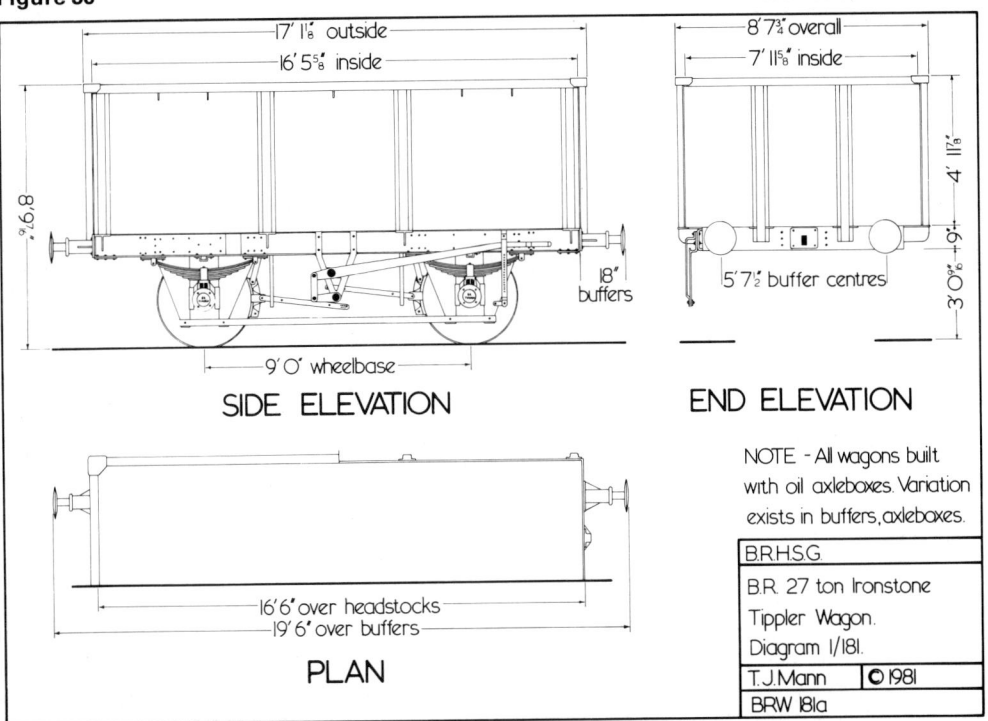

Figure 56

Measured by Trevor Mann

17′1⅛″ outside
16′5⅝″ inside

9′6″

9′0″ wheelbase

18″ buffers

SIDE ELEVATION

8′7¾″ overall
7′11⅝″ inside

4′11⅛″

3′0⅜″ 9′4″

5′7½″ buffer centres

END ELEVATION

NOTE - All wagons built with oil axleboxes. Variation exists in buffers, axleboxes.

B.R.H.S.G	
B.R. 27 ton Ironstone Tippler Wagon. Diagram 1/181.	
T.J.Mann	© 1981
BRW 181a	

16′6″ over headstocks
19′6″ over buffers

PLAN

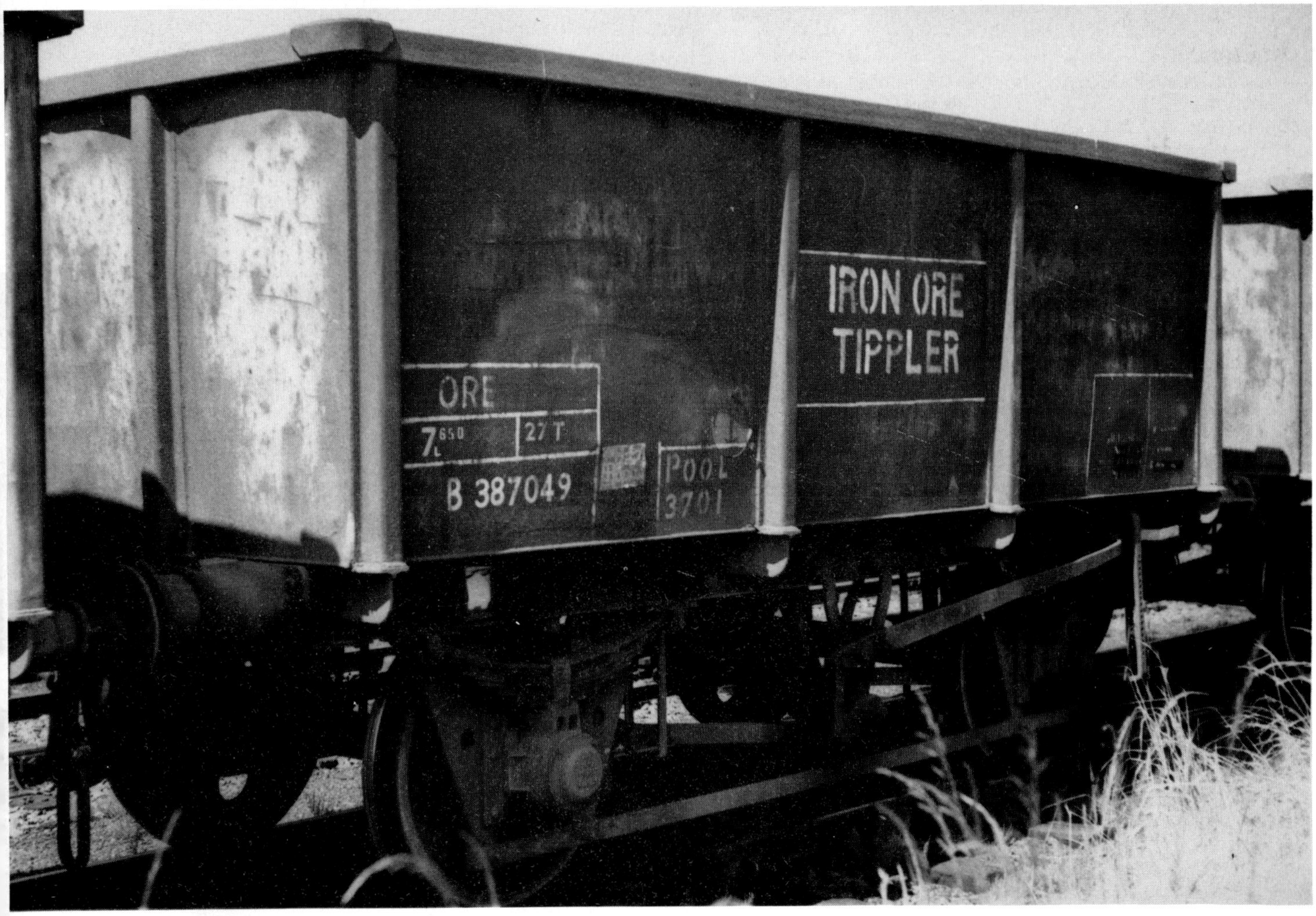

Plate 222 No. B387049 (Derby 1958, 3091) is to Diagram 1/184, has the 10ft. wheelbase, and is seen at Wellingborough on 11th June 1978. The light grey livery is somewhat rusty, but the boxed lettering and code 'Ore' are noteworthy, also the transposed positions of the load and tare weights.

R. A. Silsbury

Plate 223 The final 'Tippler' design, to Diagram 1/185, photographed at Fratton on 8th May 1979, is illustrated by No. B388404 (Derby 1961, 3363). It has BR clasp vacuum brake, change-over lever, Dowty hydraulic buffers and roller bearing axleboxes as originally built, although the bauxite livery has been amended for its use in aggregate traffic, witness the 'Stone' symbol. The Pool number is 7681, and because of the intensive use, the Preventive Maintenance date is included in the number panel.

R. A. Silsbury

Index